To the One who made the Alaskan skies,

to John Manning,

to my brother, Gregory Benedict Irvin, a native Alaskan,

and in memory of Helen Irwin LeVision (Levinson).

'We live our lives as a tale that is told...'

Psalm 90:9b

Alias: Georgina Jane O'Shaughnessy

'Who is she that looks forth as the morning, fair as the moon, clear as the sun, and terrible as an army with banners?'

Song of Solomon 6:10

Shawn Irvin Manning

WHEN FAIRIES DANCED

AUSTIN MACAULEY PUBLISHERS™

LONDON * CAMBRIDGE * NEW YORK * SHARJAH

A CIP catalogue record for this title is available from the British Library.

ISBN 9781528988261 (Paperback)
ISBN 9781528988278 (Hardback)
ISBN 9781528988285 (ePub e-book)

www.austinmacauley.com

First Published (2021)
Austin Macauley Publishers Ltd
25 Canada Square
Canary Wharf
London
E14 5LQ

Table of Contents

Cast of Characters   9

Prologue   10

Chapter One: Leavin' the South Behind   13

Chapter Two: Bags Full of Surprises   51

Chapter Three: North to Alaska   90

Chapter Four: Deep Waters Turn to Soaring   133

Chapter Five: Flight of Fairies: An Interlude   188

Chapter Six: Food for Thought   219

Chapter Seven: Native Realities   260

Chapter Eight: Green Biscuits   283

Chapter Nine: Under Cold Alaskan Skies   304

Chapter Ten: In and Out of Hot Water   327

Chapter Eleven: Saying Her Good-Byes   348

Cast of Characters

Georgina Jane O'Shaughnessy (aged six to nine)
Eugene O'Shaughnessy (nicknamed, 'Genio', father to Georgina Jane) Claudia Jane O'Shaughnessy (mother to Georgina Jane)
Twin sisters: Katrina Josephina O'Shaughnessy and Gretchen Gabriella O'Shaughnessy
Three brothers: Roger Eugenio, Peter Martin and Roraigh Arthur O'Shaughnessy Myrtle, the black maid in Kentucky (also known as 'Myrtle the turtle')
Juanita Gomez (best friend to Georgina Jane O'Shaughnessy)
Mrs. Gomez, Carmelita, Hortenzia, Ninacita and their good old brother, Pepe Jose (family of Juanita Gomez)
Dwyann MacDermott; army buddy of Georgina Jane's father, who crashes into the mountain on that foggy night
Parental Grandparents: Eugenio Sr and Mrs. Olivia Gonzalez O'Shaughnessy Maternal Grandmother, called 'Manga' (also known as Helen or by her nickname, (Nellie)
Ship's captain
Ten-year-old boy, Henry, and his mother, Uncle Bufford (nicknamed Uncle 'Bubba')
Aunt Adie (wife of Uncle Bubba and sister to Claudia) Ethel May (mother of Uncle Bubba)
Bridgetta, Leah, Rachel, Suzanna and Carolina and their two nameless brothers (cousins of Georgina Jane)
Friends of Georgina Jane in Alaska: Afton, the Eskimo girl in Fairbanks and Claire, the white girl in Fort Wainwright, army guys in Fort Wainwright, Eskimos in Fairbanks.

Prologue

Families often scatter to the four winds and beyond, leaving behind the crumbs of memories. Memories of togetherness. Fragments of those memories remain in the mind. In the heart. In the soul. Untouched for years. Crumbs not swept away. Crumbs still lurking in the shadows. Swept under carpets of hearts. Laying there untouched. Lying there, like the ungathered, mislaid eggs of my chickens. Chickens that run wild. Run free. Chickens that sleep up in trees. Chickens that leave their eggs where no one can ever find them.

Eggs laid. Eggs, like memories, laying (no lie) in the tall grass of the fields within the mind fields of vision. Visions hitherto unexplained. Eggs laying where the chickens have been. Eggs, laying there unseen. Lying there unused. Lying there unknown. Laying like silently lying stones, not the living things they are. Feeding no one. Birthing nothing.

Chickens and eggs that play a children's game of hide and seek. Hide and seek like my memories played. My memories that beckoned to me. Beckoned to me to find them. Find them and tell their story. Their story of childhood. A childhood long over and done with. But a childhood waiting to be remembered. Remembered as myth. Remembered as legend. Remembered as fantasy. Remembered as a journey. Remembered as a legacy. A legacy for, to and about family. A legacy told for my family and for families everywhere. And told for those, like me, lonely for their mislaid family. This telling is for them. This telling is for myself. My mislaid self.

This story, this scouting expedition, goes looking for something. Something big. Something real. Combining fact with fiction, past with present, people known, with figments of my imagination, remnants of truth with utter fantasy, the tale evolved. My idea was to regroup. To gather together parts of myself. Parts lost in the tall grass of chaos and abandonment. Parts that I couldn't find. Wanted to find. Find like those eggs laying there. Lying there unknown even to my conscious self. By looking back at the journey of my life, maybe I'd understand better who I am. May be then, I could fill in the empty places time and experience had left behind. Maybe then, I would understand. Understand myself. Maybe I'd be whole again. Had I ever been whole? I had to remember in order to discover the answer.

So, almost accidentally, the journey began. A journey of words. A journey of times long past. A journey into the deep unknown of my subconscious heart; where feelings lay buried. No lie. Feelings too deep to realize without feeling back into those long-ago places of my mind. Happy places. Bleak places. Private places. Places hidden to my conscious stream of reality in the here. In the now.

Abrupt changes in geographic spaces can cause a new person to emerge in a way that being static cannot. Moving away from the familiar creates insecurity. Creates tension. This is not a value judgement on the often-moveable domicile of peoples. Would we all be better off to never move from place to place? Would life be more enriching without such changes? Would life seem safer that way? More secure? Perhaps, yes. Perhaps, no. Perhaps we'll never know.

Way back when I was young, at the tender age of six and a half or so, my family left behind what was familiar. But then, I was (or should have been) used to that. It seemed we'd always been on the move. We were like a nomadic people. We were a tribe of vagabonds, traversing many parts of the globe. Parts of the globe which were unyearned for. Nether regions and parts not sought after. But places we resided in for brief intervals nevertheless. Like gypsies, we left behind used-up campsites. Military outposts scattered over the earth. Fortifications of power. Gatherings of personnel from every corner of the country, who became as one because of their association with the Armed Services. People who made life feel safe. Made children feel patriot and protected. Even if you moved away from one group, in one fort, others, whose lives were of a similar purpose, awaited you, ready to greet you, in new locations. Greet you in new faraway localities.

So, my journey began one balmy summer's day, so long ago now. So many years in the past. The distant past of my life. Come now. Let us reason together. Let us journey together. Come now. We better go now. Let us leave together. Let us explore the vast unknowns of time and place. The place of family. The place of friends long gone, but never forgotten. Gaze with me upon the peaks of high mountaintops. Smell the fields of wildflowers. Where rambling girls traversed in search of new adventures and discoveries, in a time when the world, this aging planet, was recovering from the unhappiness of war. Recovering from angry retaliations. Recovering from fear and not-so-surgical strikes of a mighty one nation under God on another beautiful people living on islands faraway. A time when Hitler's reign of terror in Europe was thankfully over. Peace of a sort had come at last. It was a time of childhood for many. It was a time. A time and a half. A time when the singing of the birds had come. A time when little girls pretended to be fairies who danced together.

Come to my supper. Taste and see what I have spread before you. Spread before you a family's feast. Spread before you a walk through a cool Alaskan forest next to flowing icy rivers. Come with me. I will be your guide. Come with me back in time. Back in time when fairies danced. Follow me through the thicket. I am the child hiding behind a chair. Now you see me. Now you don't. I am the child speaking to you from behind the chair of words. I have stopped you with my words. I have fixed you with my eye. My glittering eye. I have fixed you by the eye. Stopped you with my words. My eye, to see and to show you. My eye. My bright eye, to take you through the eye of the storm. The storm of a life. I've stopped you like the very, very old, even the Ancient Mariner, stopped others. But I am not ancient. I am young. I am what you might call a 'young mariner'. I want to gather you up like a tribe of doodle bugs in the telling of my story. I want to take you with me on my journey.

Come with me. I will be your guide. I will show you the way. Come with me on a journey. A magical mystery tour. A magical mystery tour of duty. A tour of changes. A tour of my country. The old country, yet so new compared to older places. Come with me. I will guide you on our journey together. And for the duration, for the duration of our journey together, just call me... Georgina Jane O'Shaughnessy.

Chapter One
Leavin' the South Behind

Fort Campbell, Kentucky summer 1958

Doodlebugs All Together

She put the tiny doodlebugs, as she called them, into her small, black, velvet purse with its short brass chain handle. The diminutive girl had spent hours watching these minuscule organisms, scratching the dirt to find more and more of them. They seemed to her to be almost prehistoric, like miniature creatures from another time, from the long-ago age when the dinosaurs used to live in her neighbourhood. These wood lice were almost like her family, she knew them so well. Georgina Jane O'Shaughnessy even felt that they kept her company if she was feeling lonely. She knew that these special little bugs had their own families. And, so carefully, the child picked up more and more of these roly-poly insects and gently inserted them into her soft, little handbag. There she knew that they'd be safe and sound, and she could keep a close eye on them while they all travelled together. She hoped that all of the brother and sister bugs were now together, snuggled up close, oh, so close, oh so very, very close to their mommy bug.

Once she had seen a mother doodlebug giving birth to lots of baby doodlebugs. That grey mother, like a flexible stone, had rolled over on to her back, and Georgina had watched as what had seemed like hundreds of baby doodlebugs came out of the mother doodlebug's tummy. The grey bug's babies were white. Specks so small that she could hardly see them with her squinting hazel eyes. But she had looked closely. What the child saw amazed her more than almost anything she knew about. The tiny baby doodlebugs had extraordinary infinitesimal hinges on their little bodies, just like their mother had! She saw that these minute white babies could even roll up in a ball, exactly the same way their mommy could roll so tightly. Like a beetle's bowling ball! After they were carefully selected, the girl packed them into her black, velvet bag. Georgina worried about the bugs she was leaving behind, and hoped that she had gotten all of the mother's babies together as a family of tiny doodlers.

Those cute, little bugs that tickled your arm when they crawled up it with all of those jiggling little feet of theirs would have a long trip together, travelling all the way up to the North Star's state. What was happening to the child and to the doodlebugs, you might ask. Why did they have to move away? They lived in Ft. Campbell, Kentucky. That was their home. They liked it there. Georgina sat on the curb and sighed. Her heart felt heavy. Hanging her little feet over the curb's edge, she thought about her life and what her feelings were about moving. It felt strange to her. She didn't like strange feelings. They made her stomach feel all jittery and fluttery. Moving made her feel insecure, like the world that she knew was ending. Like her world was coming to an end.

"Look, Mother, see my doodlebugs! See how many I got? Do you think that they'll like Alaska?" The girl opened her purse wide and proudly showed her mother her special collection of gathered wood lice.

"That's very nice, dear, now hurry up and get your dolls ready. We have to leave for the trip any minute now. As soon as your father drives into the driveway, we will have to leave immediately."

Moving past the little girl who stood there with her purse held wide open containing her treasure, her special doodlebugs, Mother wiped down the green kitchen counter with a clean dishrag, which her colored maid, Myrtle, had made from the girl's daddy's old white t-shirt. Myrtle had torn that undershirt into strips for just such a job. Mother was wiping down that kitchen counter for the third time since her children had had their breakfast. Her nerves were killing her. Pretty soon, she'd wear that countertop down to practically nothing.

"There are still so many things to do. I just hope that we'll be ready in time to miss all of the traffic. It gets so busy in downtown Louisville at rush hour. I wish that your father would hurry up and get back."

Looking out the kitchen window, "What on earth could he be doing? We've got to leave soon. The baby will wake up any minute and it will be so hard to get him back to sleep."

Katrina Josephina, one of Georgina's four-year-old twin sisters stood in the kitchen doorway, impatiently tapping her foot on the squares of black and white linoleum. "Mammie. Mother," correcting herself. (Katrina knew that her mother absolutely hated that affected Southern accent she sometimes slipped into.) "I get first turn sitting in the front seat, okay?"

"Katrina Josephine, that's fine with me. But could you please scoot out of my way, dear. Mother has so many things left to do to get ready for the trip. Have you gotten your room clean yet? Do you have your dolls all packed up and ready for the trip?"

Adeptly steering clear of her determined daughter, Mother moved into the living room, bare of all furnishings, ever since the movers had come yesterday and taken all of her precious treasures away. Every single stick of the furniture that they had left in the house was loaned junk that the Army had brought over for their last night in the now forlorn place.

"I hope that those movers don't break anything. The last time we moved, when we came here from San Marcos, they broke so many pieces of my delicate oriental tea set. I hope that they remembered to mark those boxes with FRAGILE. I hope that none of my things gets broken on this move. I feel just dreadful. I feel so worried about my fragile things. My collection of ceramic pots is probably worth a fortune, but movers are so careless. They are never careful enough not to worry about breakables. I wonder if all of my treasures will make it safely to Alaska?"

The woman was talking to herself now, successfully ignoring Georgina's inaneness and her silly pride in her purse full of doodlebugs. Katrina Josephina had gone back upstairs to the girls' room to argue and to inform her twin sister, Gretchen Gabriella, that she got to have the first turn in the front seat with Mommy and Daddy. And how did the stupid girl like that? She'd had the sense to ask their mother first, and so she would get the prize favour of being the first one to ride in the front bench seat of their new automobile.

Back in the kitchen, and looking out the window nervously again for a sighting of her husband back from the gas station, back from saying good-bye to his fellow soldiers on the base, she said to herself, "Where on earth is that man? Where on earth can he be? I wish he'd hurry up! We'll never get on our way at this rate!" She was like the girl who sang that song about her lost puppy. *Oh where, oh where has my little dog gone? Oh where, oh where can he be?* Georgina worried about her father too. She remembered the last time that Daddy disappeared. She remembered her anxiety about him not being there. Not being there for Mommy. Not being there for the new baby. Not being there for his whole family. Not being there for her. His not being there made her feel anxious.

15

But today, they were leaving. But today, she was wearing Mother's new dress whether she liked it or not. She thought about her daddy and his family. She thought about the doodlebugs, and decided to go back outside and find more of them to take to Alaska. That would cheer her up. She'd been out there, sitting in the dirt by the side of their house, searching for her travelling companions when Mother called to the girl from the back porch. Georgina was out there in the dirt again! Digging around for the third time that morning! She'd be filthy dirty before they even left Ft. Campbell! What on earth did she think that she was doing? What was the point of dressing her up so nicely in new clothes? She might as well have just worn old blue jeans like her friend, that simple Juanita did. A feeling of fury started to well up inside the woman as she watched her daughter out there in that dirt. What on earth did she think that she was doing now? So, her mother called out and told her, "Hurry up, Georgina Jane!"

Today they were leaving. And though they didn't have to dress up because it wasn't a school day and it wasn't Sunday, so they weren't going to church, Mother laid out a big surprise for them. It was like a special going-away ceremony. The girls would all be so thrilled by the matching green and white dresses with bright red watermelons on the fabric. All three girls got to wear these identical dresses. And wasn't that just fine and dandy? Wasn't that just great? Mother was so proud of those dresses, because she thought they looked 'summery'. She'd even made a sleeveless dress for herself out of the same fabric, with a scooped neckline, minus the girls' puffy sleeves edged with white cotton eyelet lace trim. Mother/daughter dresses were the *in* thing in the 1950s.

And although she had had a million and one things to do, and was feeling overwhelmed and a bit frantic, she had found the time to sew the three girls and herself all new matching dresses for the trip, on her well-used electric sewing machine before the movers came to pack it and take it up to Alaska with the rest of their furniture, books, toys, clothes, fragile breakables and whatnots. All of their family heirlooms were on the move – going north to Alaska. It would be almost like a race to see who would get there first!

Georgina liked it when she could wear shorts or pedal pushers, but she'd rather wear blue jeans like her friend, Juanita. Mother said that blue jeans were not *'lady-like'*, and so she wasn't allowed to wear blue jeans, even though her best friend, Juanita, was allowed by her mother to wear blue jeans.

"Blue jeans are what poor people from the country wear, Georgina Jane. Blue jeans are not lady-like. Well-bred, young ladies do not wear blue jeans. Only poorly bred little girls wear blue jeans. Farmers wear blue jeans and denim overalls. And in our family, we don't wear blue jeans or overalls! They're not lady-like. No, you cannot wear blue jeans. If Juanita's mother lets her daughter wear blue jeans, like farmers and cowboys wear, that's her business. But for the last time, no, you may not wear blue jeans! Period. So, stopping asking me about it," her mother had told her.

That meant that the subject was closed forever. There was no point in arguing with the woman, or expressing another opinion. Georgina knew that she didn't have the ready cash, or the ability to purchase blue jeans, no matter how much she wanted to wear them. Mother insisted that she wear *'ladies'* clothes, blue jeans were out of the question. Mother had firmly told her,

"Now please put your new dress on like Gretchen Gabriella and Katrina Josephina have put theirs on. I've told you that I've gone to a lot of trouble making that new dress for you. And you don't even appreciate what I've done for you. I would never have treated my mother the way you are treating me. Now get a move on. I've told you that we're in a bit of a hurry today and Mother doesn't have time to argue with you."

But in dresses, the boys could see her underwear if she climbed up too high on the monkey bars at the playground. If she climbed up high enough on that jungle gym, she could touch the sky. But when she was up high, touching the sky, she couldn't understand why the boys liked to stand under her. When she climbed up higher and higher, the little naughty boys would gather together and stand underneath her and giggle and point. She heard them laughing at her underwear with its lacy white eyelet trim, and she hated that. So, the girl would rather not wear dresses. Sometimes she got cold knees with those *'lady-like'* dresses on, and she didn't like to get cold knees either.

Mother did not understand about blue jeans one little bit. She also didn't understand that little girls of six have to be very careful to select just the right doodlebugs for the new place where they were going. The girl was double-checking, making sure that her selection of bugs was really and truly complete. To her mother, it seemed that Georgina was dawdling, but to the child it was serious business picking out just the right wood lice to take with them on the trip to an army base near Fairbanks, Alaska. They were moving to Fort Something or other up in the Yukon. She had been told that they would not be coming back to Kentucky. This place that had been her home for several years. She felt sad to leave, even though her parents had told her that the trip would be very, very exciting. Besides, Manga, her mother's mother was going with them to live in Alaska. They were picking up the *'old battle axe'*, as her father called his mother-in-law, in San Antonio, Texas, and she would be driving with them to their new home way up North.

Georgina didn't realize how far away Alaska was. How could she know? To a child, geographical distance is not an easily calculated and comprehendible measurement. Even understanding the difference between the morning and the afternoon sometimes gets confusing. Up and down, North and South, were they about the same? Could the long trip ahead of them be calculated in time, like hours and minutes and seconds? Or was it better to think of the journey's distance in terms of days of the week? Would it last say from Monday to Thursday? Or could she grasp it by thinking in terms of how many diapers her baby brother needed changing? How many times her father might pick his nose? Or the number of times he would roll down the new car's window and spit again? Would the number of times her usually gentle mother thumbed Katrina Josephina on the head with her middle finger for saying *darnitall* after she had told the girl, "Do not say that word again, young lady." Would that be a good measurement of time? That had to happen at least a couple of times every day, so maybe that was a good way of counting off the states that would soon recede behind her.

All she knew was that she was about to leave her friends, and everything she knew in her neighbourhood in Ft. Campbell's army base, her family's home. And soon, she'd leave lots of other things there that she loved and knew. Somehow, without being told, Georgina knew that she would never ever see all of those familiar things again. Even food might taste differently in Alaska. Once they got all loaded up in the car and drove away for good, everything she knew of would soon vanish forever.

Pretty soon now, Georgina Jane would have to say good-bye to Kentucky. She was leaving the South behind. The family's station wagon was already loaded with all of the things that they would need for the trip. The baby buggy and the twin's old stroller for Roger Eugenio and Peter Martin had been tightly tied to the luggage rack on top of the car, along with all of their luggage. The back section of the station wagon was made into a bed of soft pillows and blankets. Four little kids and a squirmy baby could get awful tired stuck in the car for such a very, very long time. Those children would need plenty of treats to keep them quiet and still for such a long time, for what would seem like forever in that car. It was going to be a long, long trip all of the way up to Alaska where Georgina Jane, her family and the doodlebugs were moving to.

The Baby, the Belly Button and the Dolls

Kentucky had been the state she would always remember as the place where she had almost lost both of her parents. Her mother and the baby, Peter Martin, nearly didn't make it through a long and painful labour and delivery. That baby got all tangled up with a kind of rope or something or other before he was even born. Georgina didn't understand everything, or even much at all about these things. In fact, she knew practically nothing about babies and where they even came from. It was still a mystery to her young mind and she wasn't sure how to try to imagine about it.

No one discussed these things with children in those days. All the girl knew was that the new baby had a funny, brown pungent piece of smelly stuff coming out of his belly where that mean old cord used to be before he was born. Her mother told her that the doctor had to cut that rope off of the new baby just to make him happier. That cry baby couldn't even have a bath until that ugly, rotting turd-like thing finally fell off of him. You had to keep his tummy very dry or that brown piece of grung would get all soggy and gooey. Pretty soon, that brown old ugly thing would fall off of his tummy and then her Mom's new baby would probably be as glad as Georgina Jane was to see the last of the rotten old lump. No one talked about the value of stem cell research, nor discussed the merits of DNA back then in 1958; at least not publicly nor to their children.

Georgina Jane had overheard a conversation about that very thing. Her little sister, Gretchen, was a very curious child, who was already, within hours of the new baby being brought home from the hospital, examining each and every part of her new brother's anatomy.

"What is that smelly piece of goo on Peter Martin's tummy, Mommy?"

Gretchen wanted to know. She'd been observing her mother change the new baby's diapers. She knew all about it. She hadn't noticed before that moment, the remains of his naval cord, tied off with a strip of sterile cloth at the hospital. "That's his navel, dear. It will fall off soon. Don't worry," Mother assured her.

"Well, that baby sure is stinky! Why does he smell so bad on his tummy button? I hate that smell! Is he gonna smell like that forever? It smells like something died on his tummy. It looks like ka! He needs a better bath! Do you want me to help you with his bath? I could wash his tummy better for you? You aren't doing a very good job."

"No, he is not going to smell like this forever. All babies have to wait a week to lose it. I know that it smells funny."

He had slept so soundly, even for a baby, for the first few days, that he blended right in. Now he was beginning to really come to life, and his liveliness and his personality got everybody in the house's attention.

Gretchen envisioned the new baby as an addition to her doll collection, all clean, sweet-smelling and well-dressed. She took great pride in her dollies' appearance, unlike Katrina Josephina who was just the opposite. Katrina cut the dollies' lovely long hair too short and crooked with Mother's pinking shears. She took them out to the sand box and buried them up to their necks in the sand. That bratty girl deliberately tore their doll clothes, so that they looked like they were wearing rags. Mother told her that such dolls were a disgrace to their family, but Katrina just laughed, never caring about the appearance of such inanimate objects. And she didn't seem to mind about the new baby's navel cord, smelly or not. But to Gretchen, baby dolls that could drink bottles and wet their diapers were real little friends. Those dolls were alive. And Gretch treated her living dolls like they were the crown jewels.

Baby dolls had come out on the market, mass-produced for the baby boomers. Children who had practically everything. Their parents might have had less in the way of toys growing up in the 1930s and 1940s. Their grandparents might have had deprived childhoods by comparison, but those brats were spoiled rotten with oodles and oodles of toys of every size and description! Grandmother O'Shaughnessy had complained about it when she visited them when the new baby arrived. She said that her grandchildren were *'spoiled rotten'* and derided their absent mother for *'ruining'* them with so many dolls and such a large collection of expensive toys. Granny said that their Daddy didn't have enough money to waste on such a vast collection of expensive dolls.

The Invasion of the Spanish Grandmother and Papa's Plane Crash

It was a terrible, scary time not to have her parents at home with her. The child felt that the weight of the whole wide world was placed on her shoulders during that time when both of her parents vanished without telling her where on earth they were going. They hadn't consulted her. And then, suddenly, without warning, without telling her, an over-powering, domineering old lady whom Georgina vaguely knew from another place and another time, was staying at their house. Granny was sleeping on their couch in the living room. The woman said that she *'didn't want to get the clean sheets dirty'*. As soon as she had arrived, Granny had stripped Georgina's parents' bed, ironed some fresh sheets (Mother didn't iron sheets), and then closed the door, forbidding her granddaughters to enter it. Georgina felt that the world had closed in on her when Granny shut Mommy and Daddy's bedroom door, barring her entrance to what in her child's mind was a place of safety, comfort and solace in her parent's absence.

Everything got pretty lonely and sad at her house because her Mommy and Daddy weren't home. All that the child knew was that her paternal grandmother had come to stay with *'Georgie-Jane'*, as Granny called her, and with the other children; because their mother was trying and trying to get that new baby out of her tummy. Her father wasn't home either. So, he couldn't watch his children. That's why Granny had to come to Georgina Jane's house, to iron sheets, and to check on how spoiled the grandkids were. And to babysit on them. Grandmother (or *'Granny'* as Georgina called her) was Spanish. She was Daddy's mother.

It was bad enough for Mother to be away from home. But the part that really worried Georgina Jane the most was that her daddy was gone too. Not only had her mother gone away, and the girl was told that, "There are problems…" with all of the dread that statement brought to her, but now her father, flying home from a training mission with an inexperienced pilot, had gone missing too. No one knew where her daddy was. No one knew that her daddy and his army buddy had flown into a mountain in the wilderness. Their instruments had failed when they were flying through a dense fog of all things. No one knew that her daddy was walking down the side of that mountain, lost in the woods, carrying his army buddy over his shoulders. No one knew that her daddy was bleeding. He and the other pilot were lost. Gone missing. Just vanished as far as the military could tell. That's what the Army had told her mother. The girl had thought about what the big shots in the Army had told her mother.

She wondered, *How could that happen? How could the Army lose my daddy?*

For a day and a night, they couldn't find him. The child remembered Granny anxiously pacing the floor and saying her *'Hail Marys'*. Why was she saying the rosary over and over again? Clicking those black beads together like that? Round and round in circle after round circle? Georgina watched. Faster and faster, her grandmother's hands, with their clean, rapid, slender, smooth fingers that always smelled of Avon skin cream, moved over the worn rosary beads, never even missing a Glory Bee. Granny's trimmed, unpolished fingernails encompassed those pebble-like beads, all strung together in sets of tens. She was speaking so fast that it sounded like chickens clucking. It might have been another language from another planet altogether. It was foreign to the child. The woman could speak it so quickly. Her grandmother's words just blended together like the rapid sounding of the firing toy tommy guns Georgina had heard those rascals, their neighbourhood boys fire at each other as they snuck up on other members of their gang from around bushes or the corners of houses.

Rat-a-tat-tat Rat-a-tat-tat Rat-a-tat-tat! Hail Mary full of grace, the Lord is with thee became something else entirely. It began to sound more like, HaMerifulagrasaLoeswithe said over and over. It was like an incantation or a Tibetan Buddhist's chanting sound to the girl. She followed Grandmother around the house while the distraught old lady looked for her snoot rag to blow her dripping nose and wipe her weeping eyes.

Her Granny was staying with them because Mother was in the hospital trying to have another new baby. Someone had to look after Georgina Jane and her two sisters and her little brother, Roger Eugenio. So, their funny old Spanish granny came all the way from San Antonio, Texas, to their army house in Kentucky. She cooked flour tortillas for Georgina and for her little sisters and for the old baby, Roger Eugenio. Even though Roger was just thirteen months old now, he would be pretty big compared to the brand-new baby. That kid still wore diapers and he sucked on bottles of milk and on his thumb too (even though nothing came out of that shrivelled old-looking brown thumb of his). So, the girls knew that Roger Eugenio was still technically a baby too because of all of that wetting and sucking that he did. That kid definitely could chew Granny's special homemade flour tortillas! Grandmother had lifted his squirmy little body up in the air and plopped him in his high chair, moving his tiny fingers out of the way, to keep the metal tray from pinching them. Rodger sat up nice and straight in his high chair, beating on the metal tray with his breakable glass bottle, waiting for the moment that Grandmother would give him his own little plastic dish filled with cut up pieces of piping hot flour tortilla!

Roger Eugenio had teeth that could bite through shoe leather! They were sharp as anything! If Katrina Josephina teased him, took away his bottle or pulled his thumb out of that kid's mouth, look out! Down on her arm would come

Roger's sharp little white teeth, leaving what seemed like indelible marks. His inborn fury was evident then! But that girl was so stubborn, she wouldn't even cry. She would just thump her hard head against Roger's little brown head with a clunk. Then they'd be even.

Georgina observed the matronly Spaniard, who had taken over their household with her robust presence. The serious aproned lady used a rolling pin, or even an empty jam jar; whatever was handy. She made those 'tias', as Gretchen called them, almost as thin as a piece of construction paper; except Grandmother's dough was white, not red or green or blue or yellow.

Because she was a big girl now, and had lots of responsibilities to prove it, Georgina got to help roll out and flatten those flour tortillas, making them nice and thin, like Grandmother said to. The kids' granny put the round circles of dough on a very hot flat grill to cook them on both sides. When those soft doughy circles had brown spots on the front and back of them and puffed up a little bit, they were ready to eat. Granny piled them up in a basket with a towel in it to keep the tortillas warm. As soon as the pile was big enough, the kids could pick them up, moving the hot tortillas from hand to hand. They put them one by one onto their plates. Then they gobbled those tortillas up as fast as they could eat them. Butter spread on the tops of the chewy tortillas. Butter wound up on their hands and smeared all over little faces, all looking up from the breakfast table with looks of great satisfaction. It was always a race between Gretchen and Katrina Josephina to see which one could eat the most of Granny's flour tortillas. Those girls couldn't get enough of them. Such good flour tortillas could almost make Georgina Jane forget about her loneliness without Mommy and her daddy, who had been gone for what seemed like such a long, long time.

The girls gathered around their grandmother in the kitchen. Katrina Josephina piped up, "Do ya want me to help you make those tillas, Grandmother? I know how to stir things." Katrina Josephina was their family's authority on stirring Betty Crocker cake mixes, pancake batter, any kind of semi liquid cooking recipe that needed stirring. That girl would hold the bowls tightly with one chubby clenched hand, and half stick her tongue out of her mouth. Then she'd stir and bite. Stir and bite. If she wasn't half biting that tongue of hers off, she wouldn't be able to stir so well. Katrina did the same thing when she was coloring in those coloring books of hers. One day that poor sore tongue was gonna fall right out of her mouth. Then she wouldn't be able to give her sisters such a hard time with that fiery little pink tongue of hers.

"Okay, *mi hita,* but move out of my way and let me pour the boiling water in first. You could get burned if this hot water spills on you. Let Grandmother pour the water in by herself. Then you can stir."

Pancakes didn't need boiling water, flour tortillas did. But Granny seemed to know what she was doing, so Katrina Josephina for once, actually listened to someone and did as she was told.

Grandmother stayed at their house for weeks and weeks. Mommy came home with the brand-new baby and she was exhausted and depressed. But Grandmother wasn't leaving anytime soon. She wasn't going anywhere until her son got out of the hospital. Grandmother was Mommy's mother-in-law. Grandmother annoyed her mother, Georgina could tell. Because Mother clipped her words when she spoke to Daddy's mother and was overly polite to her. Only rolling her tired blue eyes when Granny left the room.

Weeks later, Georgina's father reappeared, having nearly lost his life. He was very pale and withdrawn, not at all himself. Granny said that he had almost bled his life away. And with all of those broken ribs and an arm that was badly cut in a lot of places, he would be in bed for a long, long time. His face was bruised too, with a few gouged cuts on it as well. That gave her daddy a deeper complexion than he usually had. He had an almost tarnished look about him. After the terrible plane crash, she remembered him seeming smaller when he came home from the army hospital.

She thought, *My daddy was bigger before he went to the hospital.*

And in between the tarnished bits of skin on his face, he looked like all of the dark-reddish skin he used to have, must have gotten washed off, up there in the mountains when he crashed the army's airplane in the fog that night. Now he had marks and cuts in lots of places. His face looked worn and tired. That must be where all of his fat and color came out of him, up high in that mountain, walking through the fog and the rain for so long. When the Army finally found their lost soldiers again, they stuck them in the base hospital to rest for a while. But at least they knew where her daddy was then. Georgina wanted him to hurry up and come home to her. But in the hospital, Daddy could rest and get well. That was how they explained it. The army could keep an eye on her daddy in the base hospital.

She colored a picture of the new baby for Daddy while he was away. Granny could take it to him at the hospital where the old lady went religiously every day, taking her homemade flour tortillas to her son, because she said that the hospital food wasn't to Daddy's liking and it *'looked just like mush'!* Lieutenant O'Shaughnessy wasn't hungry. Even Granny's tortillas couldn't tempt him. He was laying low. He was resting and shrinking. So, when Georgina finally saw him again, Daddy was so much smaller than he used to be. It made sense. She realized that when her mother came back from the hospital, after that new baby came out of her tummy, she was smaller too. The girl thought that was what happened to you if you went into the hospital, you shrank.

In conversations overheard between the child's mother and grandmother, she learned that there had also been problems with something called her father's 'vital organs'. But this didn't make sense, because all her father could play was the accordion. He didn't even have an organ. They didn't even have a piano back then. It didn't really make any sense to her, and a lack of understanding made it all the more troubling. For years later, when she would see his scars, she'd wonder about this man who was her whole security. It made her sad to think that her daddy could be hurt and bleed. No one seemed to notice that the child was worried. Everyone was too busy with the new baby. Everyone was worried about her father.

Her mother seemed very tired too. Did having a new baby make someone tired? That brand new baby wasn't tired. He cried a lot and needed his diaper changed all the time. That was because he drank too many bottles. Roger Eugenio still drank a bottle, but he was big enough to hold it himself. Georgina's thoughts made her worry about things. She knew that crashing the army's airplane and having a baby made people very tired. That's why families had grandmothers to take care of them if they went crashing into mountains or if a new baby came to live at their house. It was a good idea to have a grandmother around when you needed one.

From her memory, she remembered that when her father had left for work on the morning of the plane crash, he seemed all right and was in a happy mood. He had given her mother a hug and a kiss goodbye. He had patted all of his little kids on their heads as they sat eating bowls of breakfast cereal, slurping their milk. He had told them to be good for their mother. Who would have thought that her daddy would be so silly as to slam the army's airplane into the side of an invisible mountain on his way home in the dark on that cloudy, lonely night?

Once he was home again, Georgina tried to ask her father what happened to him on that terrible, mean old, dark mountain. It became obvious that he didn't want to talk about it. Whenever she asked him, he just turned away from her and looked at the wall next to his bed. He was having to spend so much time in bed. It wasn't like him, he was usually so busy all of the time, working for the army. Mother said that Daddy had to rest a lot, after his airplane crashed into the side of that mountain. During the day, George could play on the floor next to where her daddy rested in the bed he shared with Mother. The girl could stay there, as long as she was quiet.

She could be very quiet when she made her dollies speak in hushed whispers in her parent's room, where her daddy was resting. But it's hard to be quiet when you are only six years old and you have so many questions to ask. When she asked her father what had happened on that foggy, foggy night up there in the Appalachian Mountains, he wouldn't even look at his daughter's face. Daddy would just wince and look away. He would never really discuss this experience with her. For the rest of his life, he blamed his plane-crash scars on the Indians.

"Papa, how did you get so many hurts on you? Did you fall down and hurt yourself when you were a little kid?"

Georgina was worried. All of these scars made her father look like a prize-fighter. He had been a golden glove boxer in his flyweight youth, but not anymore. Now he was in the Army Aviation. Now he was a pilot soldier.

"Honey, the Indians cut me with their knives and bows and arrows and spears. Now stop talking. Daddy needs his sleep. Daddy needs to rest now, so be quiet, okay? That's a good girl. Sit quietly, or leave the room, please."

After her father's near fatal airplane crash, the family needed a new beginning. The Army had given him a promotion from being a Lieutenant to being a captain. Georgina knew that her daddy was a very important person. He got a prize from the army, like one of those gold stick-on stars some kids got at school for being so smart. Daddy got shiny new pins from the Army for being so tough and so brave. That was because he had saved his army buddy's life by carrying him to the single-track dirt road way out there in the sticks when their plane came down. Now, the Army was rewarding him by stationing Daddy on another one of their bases, in a place way up in the frozen tundra. Georgina Jane had noticed her father shiver at just the mention of the place, in discussions she overheard between her parents after bedtime when all of the children were supposed to be asleep, not up, hiding behind chairs, or stair railings eavesdropping on adult conversations. And the girl could tell that this was not going to be easy, because they would be leaving behind her grandparents and her aunts and uncles and cousins in the South.

"You have more cousins up north in Alaska."

Her mother had told her that, so it must be true. But her tone of voice was dubious. Who was she reassuring? The girl, or herself? It was all highly suspect. Granddaddy had a used car lot, a gas station and a hamburger stand to run. Grandmother had her Stanley Home Products to sell. Granny was an Avon lady and worked as a dinner lady in a school cafeteria. It was a good thing that they had their jobs to keep them busy. That way they wouldn't miss Georgie-Jane and her little sisters and baby brothers. Now that his flight training had been finished after he learned to fly by crashing into that mountain, Georgina Jane's father would be flying those enormous airplanes and cargo helicopters out into the boondocks in Alaska's far northern territories.

The Army told him that he and his family would have to move to a place where they had never been before. A place they knew so little about. Not a place like Kentucky where they knew practically everybody. Not a place where they knew their way around so well. Not a place where they had so many neighbourhood friends. Not a place where people drank sugary iced tea with lemon and mint. Alaska was too different. Alaska was too far away. Alaska was too unknown. Alaska was too cold. She had heard that Alaska had polar bears that could bite little children with their sharp pointy teeth. She had heard that the snow fell so deeply in Alaska that it turned into avalanches that could bury kids alive. Bury kids so that nobody could ever find them again. She had heard that the only houses that they even had in Alaska were made from blocks of ice. She had heard that people in Alaska got frostbite and their toes turned black and fell right off of their bodies! She wasn't sure that she really even wanted to go there at all. She wasn't sure that it was such a good idea to move to Alaska.

Georgina had gotten to know Grandmother better since she'd spent time with her. Granddaddy came to her house in Ft. Campbell too. Granddaddy was Grandmother's husband. He was a Mexican Irishman with hazel eyes and dark skin that made his teeth look very white. He had wavy brown Irish hair, not straight black hair like his Indian mother, Lola had hair growing on her head. Granddaddy drove all the way to Kentucky to pick his wife up, see his injured son and greet the new baby grandson, Peter Martin. Granddaddy came all the way to Kentucky to bounce Roger Eugenio on his knee. Granddaddy came to Kentucky to bring special bags of tooth-rotting candy and special colorful Mexican sweet rolls to his granddaughters. Granddaddy came to Kentucky to surprise Georgina's daddy, and to cheer him up. Granddaddy gave her daddy a great big black and white surprise.

Soon he would leave with Grandmother. Granddaddy and Grandmother were taking the big Greyhound bus all the way back to San Antonio, Texas, leaving the surprise behind. Granny had made flour tortillas for their journey back to *Tejas*, as Granddaddy called his home State. Tortillas all wrapped up in Granny's clean hankies and waxed paper. Granny cried, and said, "Sure. I'm going to miss you, *mi hita.*" Georgina knew that Granny and Granddaddy would miss the new baby, Peter Martin, too, because her grandmother kept speaking rapidly and excitedly in Spanish and saying, "*Mi hito! Mi hito!*" and kissing the new baby a lot, squeezing the wiggling mass as she did so. Georgina Jane was afraid that her grandmother would squeeze the new baby too hard. Her grandmother kissed and hugged all of her grandchildren. Granny squeezed her and gave the girl hugs so tight, that the child thought she had stopped breathing until her grandmother let go and she could gasp for air again. And Granny kissed Georgina all over her face, laughing when she did it and saying, "*Mi Hita! Mi hita! Yo te amo*! I love you! I love you! I love you!*"

Granny had funny ways. Georgie-Jane's mother didn't hug her so tightly that she nearly stopped breathing. Her mother didn't kiss her either. Her mother thought that Granny was *'peculiar'*. So, Granny must be *'peculiar'*. What did *'peculiar'* mean anyway? The way Mother said it, made it sound uncomplimentary. But life was meant to be lived, not through her child's eyes, but seen through her mother's eyes. She knew that by now.

Her grandfather gave them a car from his used car lot. After the birth of Georgina Jane's brother, Peter Martin, and all the trouble that they had when he was born, and her father being in the hospital; her grandparents were just glad to know that their son's family was all right.

"You'll need a bigger car now, son."

Granddaddy told her father, as he handed his son the set of shiny jingling car keys.

She could see what he meant. They had to start using the twin's stroller again. Roger Eugenio was only thirteen months old when Peter Martin was born. Now *'Gi Gi'*, as Roger called her, had a new job, folding the endless loads of cloth diapers for those two babies.

28

Diapers, Boxer Shorts and the Black and White Car

Long strips of white cloth had to be folded four times. When the twins were babies, and their family had lived in Okinawa, Mother had an Okinawan lady who came to the house and ironed all of those blond twin girl babies' diapers. But they moved from Okinawa, before Georgina Jane's brothers were born, and now folding diapers was the girl's job. Baby diapers were like her daddy's boxer shorts. They covered the new baby and Roger Eugenio's bottoms so that all of that ka ka didn't fall out everywhere they went. Crawling babies who were clad in diapers and weren't wearing plastic pants were a household menace. They left trails of ka ka balls everywhere they went. Georgina Jane knew that folding diapers was a pretty important job.

Her mother told her that the laundry lady in Okinawa loved to iron.

"She ironed everything, sheets, diapers, hankies, all of the clothes, even your father's boxer shorts!"

Georgina thought that was a pretty funny story. Sometimes, when he was feeling better, she saw her daddy in his boxer shorts and tee shirt before he put on his stiff green army uniform, more like khaki green cardboard than cotton fabric, due to the heavy starch put on by the base's laundry. With its gleaming sharp pinned on insignias, he looked very handsome. Her daddy loved his boxer shorts. He would dance around, singing in Spanish, twittering like a happy bird who had caught lots of worms in its beak that very morning. Swinging and twirling her mother around the room wearing his boxer shorts, a t-shirt and his socks, which made his shoeless feet more slippery and thus faster moving. Her daddy was a sight to behold. Boxer shorts were his favourite dancing outfit. Maybe ironing those boxer shorts helped the way he could dance when he was wearing them. Ironed boxer shorts became magic. Ironed boxer shorts could turn Daddy into a funny, happy, comical dancing man; dancing and singing to his own Latin rhythm, that he remembered from his childhood in San Antonio, Texas. Putting on his stiff army uniform made him much more serious than just wearing his glad old boxer shorts and dancing did. She loved to watch her daddy dancing and being so silly and happy again. It made her feel happy too.

The new car from her granddaddy was a 1957 black and white Pontiac station wagon. "It's almost new and big enough for the whole family," her grandfather had said. Those were the days of bench seats in the front. Bucket seats were unheard of in family cars back then. Seat belts hadn't come into vogue either.

Three people could all sit together in the front seat. Georgina thought that she would rather sit in the back seat or lie down on the bed in the back of the car and look at books as they began their trip to San Antonio to say good-bye to their relatives there and pick up Manga before heading up to the frosty northwest.

Now they were leaving Kentucky. It was almost *'time to go'*. Daddy finally pulled the car back into the driveway. It had been packed earlier that morning by Mother, and was all ready for their trip. Stuffed to the gills with all of the family's gear stashed into every crevice, it looked almost comical. All of the nooks and crannies were jam-packed with every conceivable kind of children's toys, books, diapers, maps, a cooler with crushed ice from the gas station poured over soda pop in bottles that you had to use a bottle cap opener to prise the lid off. Mother had done most of the packing, and she knew from all of her travelling experiences just how to slot everything into place like it was supposed to be. Luggage was already tied to the rack on top of the car. So was the baby buggy and the twin's old stroller.

The Twins Say Good-Bye and Georgina Gets Cookies

For the twins, Katrina Josephina and Gretchen Gabriela, now four, the excitement of sitting in the front seat between their father and mother on the first leg of their exhilarating journey was too much for them to handle quietly. It was time to leave Ft. Campbell. The moment of their departure was finally, after months of preparations, there. Georgina could feel the tension and anticipation in their household. The twins were overly excited. Those two rambucous girls both wanted to sit in the front seat, and they began shrieking at each other and getting very overly excited and hot underneath their pert little white eyelet collars. There was only enough room for one of them to sit between Mommy and Daddy at a time. Who was gonna get that privilege first? It became a contest. It became a battle of their individual, but twin wills.

Georgina watched them. Like two cats. Their fight began with a firm pat against a cheek. She knew that they were getting into a huff. Georgina knew what was coming next. And she hated this. Her sisters were going to cause a scene and there was nothing that she could do to stop them. Their squabble was quickly gaining momentum and snowballing with increasingly vehement cattiness and almost venomous intent.

Arguments and name-calling ensued between them, building a pace with anger and mounting fury. "I want to sit in the front seat first!" This was said by Gretchen with a pouting tone to her agitated exclamation. She had her heart set on being close to baby Peter Martin while he sat on his mother's lap. Rubbing his little head helped him to fall asleep, and Gretchen felt that she was just the one to do the job.

"No, me first," retorted Katrina Josephina, shoving her twin sister out of the way.

"Daddy said that I get to have the first turn, you meany, meany Trina," was Gretchen's response.

Georgina could see what was coming next. She had been in the kitchen when Katrina Josephina asked their mother if she could have the first turn in the front seat. Georgina knew that the twins would have their own special way of saying goodbye to Fort Campbell, Kentucky. A way of saying good-bye that nobody would ever forget.

"You ka ka baby! Mommy said me first!" yelled Katrina Josephina, as she insulted her sister and pulled Gretchen Gabriela's stubby little blond braids, making her cry like the sudden gush of water from a faucet.

That got the better of her twin. And the usually placid and sweet-tempered Gretchen was so angry that she pinched Katrina Josephina on the bare skin of her soft white bicep next to where her cute little green and white sleeve gave a sweet little puff. At that, Katrina Josephina started hollering at the top of her lungs as though she had been savagely gored. That kid could scream bloody murder better than anyone Georgina Jane knew.

A whole tribe of army brats by then had gathered outside of the O'Shaughnessys' apartment. Some had come to say good-bye to their departing friends. Moving from base to base was such a commonplace occurrence to all of them, that it was almost always met with a bittersweet sadness and a sort of soul-rending internal ripping and emotional tearing for people too aware of being at the mercy of the needs, and to the children, the seeming whims of the big-shots in the military. Favourite departing compatriots or flustered new arrivals were usually celebrated by a sad send-off or greeted by a warm and friendly welcoming of some kind. The crowd of bemused on-lookers was swelling by the minute, as the temperamental display of Georgina's sisters, the identical O'Shaughnessy twins, with a reputation for such performances, was getting into full swing. No wonder Daddy called them his *'blond bombers'*! They had often explosive friction between them. Just underneath their pretty feminine daintiness and fragile exteriors they were real tough, brash broads with wills of steely determination.

Others, among the by now swollen and ever-growing crowd of assorted neighbourhood kids, some with their mothers in tow, had simply heard the ruckus and had decided that it was great early morning entertainment; too good a show to miss in the days when not everyone had the relatively new must-have invention, a television set, to create insularity as they watched their favourite shows. Georgina's best friend, Juanita, had come to give her chum a sad forlorn farewell. She and Georgina stood there together, watching the twins fight it out, with their mouths open.

Juanita Gomez had come to see her friend for the very last time. She had come to say goodbye to Georgina, and was carrying a round metal box of tollhouse cookies with either chocolate chips and chopped pecan nuts in the wonderful recipe that her mother had just finished baking that very morning. The cookies were the same color Juanita's skin was, a warm toasty brown color. The warmth of those freshly home-baked cookies acted like a mini oven to the round metal box that held them, warm like the friendship of the two girls had been. The faded *'Merry Christmas'* painted on the top of the metal box revealed its former usage. It had once contained Christmas candy and had been constantly in use as a household cookie jar of sorts, to keep fresh the ever-flowing plethora of home-baked tollhouse cookies made for Juanita, her brother and her sisters, Hortensia, Carmelita and the baby, Ninacita, on a regular basis. Their quiet domesticated mother, Mrs. Gomez, a Latino version of Betty Crocker herself, was kindly donating this family heirloom containing her fresh, warm, homemade cookies to the O'Shaughnessys for their trip.

The disturbance between Gretchen Gabriela and Katrina Josephina was by now building in tempo. It had become a massive display of strong and gutsy female wills, and girlish strengths of cat-ish intensity. Neither twin was willing to give an inch or concede defeat. Neither had the slightest shred of dignity. Causing a scene like that didn't phase them or cause them even the slightest tinge of embarrassment. Both wanted to win too badly. They didn't care how they looked to other people. They didn't care if they embarrassed Georgina. They were oblivious to outside distractions. They were shameless in their efforts to succeed.

This was becoming a source of great embarrassment to Georgina Jane, who, having completed her important job of gathering her tribe of well-behaved doodlebugs, was now carrying a small pink patent leather suitcase containing her few remaining unpacked dolls and their miniature wardrobe full of tiny doll clothes to the back of the black and white station wagon; where she planned to set up camp. Many of the dolls' clothes had been made by her mother's mother, her Irish granny, who loved to sew, and was very good at it. They were too special to entrust to the potentially careless movers. She would take them to Alaska herself.

Scratching! Hair pulling! Pinching! Loud shrieking! And then, the final unlady-like act of socking their opponent in each other's faces, tummies and arms, eventually lead to the further undignified tactic of kicking the opposing twin in the shin. Gretchen by then was hysterical with sobbing, being the more sissy-ish of the two. Her face was now stained with her ever-increasing tears. Her intense fury was obvious by the fact that she could no longer catch her runaway breath. But that sign of frailty deterred the, by now scruffy, Katrina Josephina, not one iota. She had no pride, except the pride that came from winning. Being the victor was everything to that girl.

Out of sheer frustration and anger, Gretchen took the initiative and lunged at her twin, grabbing a tight hold of the identical head of blond hair. She used that grip as a device to get a firm hold on her sister with no intention whatsoever of letting her go. It was hard to get away from anyone who had a hold of your thick blond mane of hair and would not let go of it no matter what. Grasping Katrina's locks as a last resort, it looked for a moment that Gretchen might be bringing the fight to an end. But, Katrina Josephina, sore head or no sore head, pulled back, and like an angry charging bull, began head-butting her twin in the chest and the belly. Both girls then tumbled, like a charade out of Jack and Jill, onto the steep patch of lawn next to the driveway, where grass stains tarnished their new summery dresses Mother had sewn especially for the occasion.

From out of seemingly nowhere, Daddy appeared. "Cut that out, kids! That's enough! Behave yourselves, young ladies!" Taking them both by their arms and pushing them apart, her father intervened and tried to calm them down. He wasn't even embarrassed that they had utterly disgraced him and the rest of his family in front of the whole entire neighbourhood. They'd acted as though their furious fight was nothing more than a final departing curtain call before they made their departure with their notorious family tribe. They were leaving the neighbourhood in stunned amazement and they could not have cared less.

Didn't the army expect better discipline from the residents of its bases? The unruliness of her twin sisters left Georgina feeling a vague sense of uneasiness and a churning stomach. Everything would go back to normal for those two by lunchtime; they were used to fighting constantly with each other. But she would be left with that agitated sentiment for a much longer duration. Living with her siblings was a challenge which she didn't always feel up to. They would not soon be forgotten in Ft. Campbell's army base camp.

She knew that terrible embarrassment would be the last feeling that she would feel as they pulled out of that old familiar driveway for the last time. Leaving for Alaska, as soon as they drove away from the home that the Army had loaned to their family during her father's flight training years, she would look behind them and feel her heart like a stone inside of her chest. Her churned-up tummy would collide inside of her, with that small, but heavy, heart. She would feel like Lot's wife, whose whole body turned to a hard, standing pillar of salt. The girl would look behind as her father drove away from their home in Ft. Campbell, as their old home vanished forever from her sight. Part of her would always be there.

What a great relief it had been to see her father walking forcefully towards the twins. *He is so smart*, thought Georgina, *he knows how to handle everything.*

"Young ladies, stop your fighting! One of you can sit in the front seat for the first part of the trip, and the other one can sit there after lunch," he patiently explained to the twins, consoling the sobbing Gretchen. How he could tell them apart or decide which one got the first turn, she didn't know. It didn't matter. The fight was over. Tears would soon dry, though the swollen face of Gretchen would stay red and throbbing, with puffy eyelids for a long time, judging from the looks of the girl. Their father took note and had pity on his crying daughter.

"Gretchen gets to have the first turn. And Katrina Josephina, I expect you to behave and be a good girl for Daddy. No more fighting. Not today, and not tomorrow either. Do you hear me, *mi hita*?"

Katrina stood there stone-faced, tapping her right foot on the ground. She was growing very impatient with the man. Now he was even giving her orders. Even though, in her mind, she'd won the fight for the front seat fair and square, he had the unmitigated gall to treat her victory with utter derision. She hated that bossiness of his more than almost anything. She stood there impatiently, folded her arms across her small chest, let out a giant angry huff and an indignant sigh and just scowled angrily at her father, not willing to concede the slightest defeat, not now, not ever. She'd have her revenge later, in her own good time, in her own sly way. *Wait and see who has the last word.* Those were her final thoughts on the matter.

Her face spoke volumes and seemed to say this, with that frowning, disapproving look, and that solemn uppity way of hers. Her grey-green eyes glinted. They were full to the brim with animosity for his authority over her.

Mother always dressed those twins alike and fixed their hair the same way, with matching ribbons and barrettes. Their mother spoiled those cute little identical twin girls. It was obvious to everyone that Katrina Josephina got away with anything and everything, and was sometimes badly behaved. Her mother never got cross with her. Even if she screamed to get her own way, or if Katrina Josephina hit sweet little Gretchen, their mother was so calm and gentle. Too calm and gentle for Georgina's liking.

"Why don't you make those two be good girls?" she would ask her mother.

"Oh, they are so adorable that I just can't get mad at them," Mother would respond with her funny lisping voice. "And sometimes, even I can't tell them apart and I might get mad at the wrong one!"

"Then why don't you put different clothes on them?" Georgina would ask.

That question was never really answered. The twins could do as they pleased. Her mother thought that they were too cute and too funny and too adorable to discipline properly.

Her father wasn't taken in by their cuteness. His military firmness would always rule the day. Katrina Josephina couldn't hoodwink Daddy the way she could with Mother. Much as her father loved his children, he would put up with no nonsense from those little twin girls, who seemed to be always fighting. Georgina could see that he would handle the situation. She didn't worry that her father needed her help in these circumstances. She understood that her daddy always knew how to keep his family in order, like he did at his other job, with the soldiers.

Juanita stood in front of her friend, eyes down. Eyes that were brimming with tears she was trying desperately to control. Her big friendly how-now-brown-cow eyes filled with sad, unwanted liquid, and soon the salty tears began to stain the front of her checked boys' shirt, a hand-me-down from her good old brother, Pepe Jose.

"I wish you weren't movin'. Can I come to 'laska too? We could ask my mom. Do you think your mother would let me come too?"

Georgina hated this. Her friend couldn't bear the thought of her leaving, and that only compounded her own fractured heart and tired mind. The stress was beginning to wear her down and to really and truly get to her. She knew that it wasn't quite like asking her mother if Juanita, her best friend in the whole wide world, could come over to their crowded house and just spend the night. Didn't she understand that no, of course she couldn't come with them to Alaska? Didn't she even know how far away Alaska was from Kentucky? It was like that chubby, cookie-eating Mexican girl had never even heard of the North and the South before. She sure didn't get it that they were pretty far, far apart. What was the matter with her anyway? Boy, she sure was dumb. And having dumb friends was a really, really hard job to have. How on earth could Georgina respond without adding further insult to injury and devastating her dear little friend, who stood there sucking her bottom lip, in the way she always did if she got upset by something?

"I don't know, Juanita. I could ask her, but I doubt it. We've got too many kids in our family already. The car will be pretty full."

Driving Lessons

But why Granddaddy kept giving more cars to his son, she didn't understand. Didn't her grandfather worry about their safety? Couldn't he even count yet? She had heard all about when her daddy was younger. He apparently hadn't been a much better driver than her mother was. Hadn't she overheard her grandparents talking about their son's *'bad driving record'*? Didn't they say that her daddy had *'wrecked five cars'*? Or was it fifteen? Maybe it was twenty-five. She knew it had a five in the number somewhere. She couldn't quite remember, but she did know that it was a lot of smashed up cars. Her mother was a scary driver too. She couldn't really even drive yet, even though she was nearly twenty-seven years old.

Georgina's memory reached back to a time when her father had tried to teach her mother to drive. Why had her mother let him teach her to drive when she obviously had such trouble with her hands and with her feet? Didn't you have to use your feet to drive? Didn't you have to steer the car in the right direction with your hands? And if her mother knew about Daddy's *'driving record'*, wasn't she worried that he would teach her the wrong things? Couldn't her mother see from his *'driving record'* that he was not a very good person to learn from? Didn't she understand that he was not a competent person to teach her how to drive?

Her father's driving sometimes made her mother nervous. Georgina Jane could tell that by the expression on her mother's face. It was like her mother's face was sometimes frozen solid when she was in the car with Daddy driving them around the army base. It was like her mother's neck was stiff as a board, and her head was immoveable, too afraid to look to the left or to the right. Georgina's father's driving set her mother's nerves on end. Her mother would never admit that his driving made her nervous, but the child knew that it was true.

The girl remembered her father teaching her mother to drive. Georgina could see it in her mind. There was her mother sitting behind the wheel of their car. It was a grey car; she remembered that. She was two and a half then. She was standing up between her parents in the front seat. There they were, the three of them in the car. Her father guided her mother through the preliminary steps of using the car.

"Put in the key to the mission. Press your feet on the munch. Be careful with the fast pebble."

She heard her father say all of these things. Only then can you make the car go. The girl remembered all of his words to her mother. He had tried to be careful when he explained it to her how to drive the car. But her mother didn't always understand what people meant when they talked to her. Maybe she had grown up speaking another language too, like Georgina Jane's father. He could speak in Spanish like the girl's grandparents could. Maybe that had been the problem, Georgina's mother did not understand what Daddy's words had meant. Like the girl, maybe her mother didn't even know what a *'fast pebble'* was.

The two younger children, her twin sisters, had been left behind with Grandmother. They were just babies and had to stay at home. They weren't allowed to go out for special driving lessons. But she was a big girl. She was two years old. So, her parents took their big girl with them. Off they went, her mother sat behind the wheel of the 1949 Dodge Coronet. Slowly at first, her mother drove around the block. She seemed to be doing rather well. "Just fine," Georgina's father had said. "Just fine, dear." Just fine that is, until she missed the brake pebble, panicked and took her hands off of the steering wheel, hit the curb and crashed headlong into a stop sign. That was what Georgina could remember about it. Except for Mother bending over her little girl as Daddy carried his child out of the hospital and back to their grey car with its crumpled-up front end.

The memory of being in the hospital emergency room was virtually blanked out. The girl remembered seeing the anxious look on her mother's face. The fractured child knew from her mother's face that something was very wrong. It was at that moment that she felt the physical sensation of the plaster cast on her tiny chest. What had they done to her? It was a heavy itchy thing encasing her. That heavy cast was squeezing her chest and nearly suffocating her. It was filling her with feelings of claustrophobia that would probably last a lifetime. It was miserable to have that awful cast on in the summer's hot Texas sun. She didn't remember the doctors putting this terrible constricting thing on her shattered shoulders. She thought that her parents had done this to her.

That was a long time ago. But the girl remembered that feeling of lightness at the moment when her mother crashed into that stop sign. That sensation of flying through the air from a standing up position on the front seat of the car, where she had been one minute; to her flight to the dashboard of the car the next second, stayed with her all of her life. She still remembered that brief, split second of flight. That *'flight'* had ended with her collision into the dashboard of their big grey car, where the girl's small clavicle was broken, like the clipped and broken wing of a tiny bird.

Now they wanted her to drive across the country with them? Travel all of the way to Alaska, which they said was a very long way to go? She wasn't sure if she could trust them. And leaving behind her friends in the by now dispersing crowd was not going to be easy. But at least she could take some doodlebugs with her, her mother had told her that she could take as many bugs as she wanted to take. So now that their neighbourhood friends had said goodbye, the twins had been washed-up and were again presentable and the doodlebugs were safely in her favourite, sweet, little, black, velvet purse, they could leave Kentucky.

Leaving Juanita, Myrtle and Kentucky

Georgina's mother had told them that she had some special surprises when they got into the car *'like good girls'*. Her dad called them *'my girls'*. But her mother called the twins *'the little girls'*. She guessed it depended on how *'well behaved'* they were. Sometimes her dad's girls became *'young ladies'* if they were very naughty. Georgina wondered if there was a difference between being a lady or being a girl. And she didn't like it when her father raised his voice and called them *'young ladies'*. She'd just rather be his girl.

Juanita had sadly walked back to her family's house with her sisters and her mother. Her head had hung down as she looked down at the sidewalk. Empty-handed and crying, her small brown feet clumping one foot in front of the other one in heavy lumbering motions, wearing her blue jeans. That was the day her best friend left Ft. Campbell. It felt like the world was coming to an end. Juanita felt that she couldn't breathe or think beyond this painful moment in her young life. Her very best friend in the whole wide world was departing for good. It was not all talk. It was really happening. She was losing a big part of herself. And to make matters worse, Georgina was taking the tin of homemade cookies with her, both never to be seen again.

Now they were leaving Kentucky. They were all in the car together. Usually, they weren't all in the car together, except on Sundays when everyone in their family got dressed up and went to church. But her daddy had to drive the new car and take them all up to Alaska. He was on *'leave'* for a month from his duties in the Army. He had changed out of his stiff army fatigues and was wearing civilian clothes. *Civies* they called those other non-army outfits. For a month, Daddy could pretend to be just like other men. He could pretend that he didn't belong to the Army. He could just wear civilian clothes for one whole month, instead of his fatigues.

Leaving Louisville, her father drove to a filling station. He'd forgotten to double check the oil, and though she knew nothing about automobiles, his wife was nagging him about it, saying that it was probably too low. She was getting on his nerves. He didn't want to stop again once they got out on the open highway. He thought that it might shut her up to check and see, so he pulled over and opened the hood of the car. With the dipstick in one hand, and an old diaper rag in the other, he dipped and re-dipped the oil dip stick. His wife was right. The car did need oil and now he'd have to admit that he had forgotten to do it earlier.

His mind had been on other things. It had been so hard to say good-bye to all of his army buddies. They'd been through so much together during Flight School. Hugging his buddy, Dwayne MacDermet was the worst. And he had simply forgotten about the oil after that good-bye. But even though he felt sad saying good-bye, at least he and Dwayne had lived through that plane crash. Thank God for that.

Georgina Jane had been staring out the car window. Driving past city block after city block of dilapidated clapboard houses, some with peeling paint and partially rusting metal lawn chairs that burned your bottom in the summer if you sat on them after they were left out in the sun and got too hot, she noticed that all of the houses had colored people, or Negroes as they called them, sitting on their front porches or steps. Almost all of these dark people were sitting in rocking chairs or gently swinging in porch swings on their small verandas. They all seemed to be talking to each other. They sure were friendly with each other. The girl wondered what they talked about. They must have had a lot of fun together. Nobody seemed to be at work. They all had time to talk to each other and not be at work all of the time like her daddy had to be.

Sweet Chocolate People

The girl knew all about colored people. They were the color of chocolate candy bars, which Georgina Jane and the twins got to have for a treat if they were good girls. Colored people had skin like the yummy creamy delicious dark chocolate candy bars that the girls loved. *Hershey's* chocolate was Gretchen's favourite kind of candy bar. It came in a brown wrapper with the name *'Hershey's'* on it. Those candy bars were wrapped in a thin sheet of tin foil underneath the brown logo paper wrapper. Katrina Josephina liked *Hershey's* *'Kisses'* the very best. Mother liked *Hershey's* chocolate with almonds mixed into the candy bar, called *'Almond Joy'*. Little girls weren't big enough for chocolate candy bars with almonds in them, because the almonds might choke them.

"When you are older, maybe when you are seven or eight years old, then you can have candy bars with almonds in them," her mother had told her. "Nuts can choke little children."

Georgina thought that her mother probably just didn't want to share her *Almond Joy* candy bars, anymore than Katrina Josephina wanted to share her chocolate *Kisses*. When her mother wasn't in her and Daddy's bedroom, Georgina Jane had been like an Indian scout, and she'd found her mother's giant hidden candy bar with its almonds in it. That big secret *Hershey's* chocolate candy bar with the almonds in it was hidden away, wrapped up in her mother's fancy underwear and silky nightgowns in the back of her bedside nightstand, so no one would find it. Her mother would never miss just one tiny piece of it. So, the girl had sneaked a chunk of her mother's candy bar with almonds mixed into it, and it hadn't choked her at all. It was obvious to her why her mother wouldn't share her huge *Almond Joy* chocolate bars. They were too delicious to share, even with your own daughter. Those potentially choking almonds made all of the difference. She knew all about candy bars with almonds in them, even though her mother thought that she was too young for them.

So, when her father drove past all of those people with skin like chocolate candy bars, who were sitting in their front yards, it reminded the girl of getting treats, even if she had to sneak them from her mother's hiding place. Her mother had a maid named Myrtle who had skin like creamy-brown chocolate candy bars. Now, they were leaving Myrtle behind in Kentucky. That colored maid was a good worker. She helped Mother to wash the clothes, sweep the house and do the dishes or whatever Mother needed help with. Myrtle came to their house every Wednesday mornin'. She stayed all day long. She was carried to their house on the bus from a long way away from the army base. Katrina Josephina called her *'Myrtle the turtle'*, and followed the colored woman around the house, sweepin' the floor behind the brown woman's ample bottom with her child's miniature broom in gleeful imitation. Katrina Josephina knew about rhyming words from learning about another large lady with an ample posterior named Mother Goose.

Sweepin' With Myrtle

"I can sweep better 'en you can, Gretchen. Watch me sweep, Myrtle. Ain't I doin' a good job helpin' ya?" Trina wanted to know.

Mother hated it when the twins picked up their colored maid's accent. That Southern drawl, leaving out whole letters, dropping off complete syllables was so annoying. It grated on her nerves. She could overhear their conversation, and as soon as Myrtle left for the day, she would correct them. But she didn't want to make her black-like-the-night maid feel stupid; even though her diction and annunciation were, according to Georgina's mother: appalling and dreadful. She was too tired today to correct them. She was too tired to argue. She was too tired today to give her twin daughters elocution lessons at the moment. Those girls took such delight in following their mother's maid around and imitating her every word, duplicating her every action. It was as though that colored maid hung the very moon itself. What in the world they saw in the cleaning lady was beyond the comprehension of their proud and well-educated, poised mother. Those girls followed Myrtle around like moon-sick puppy dogs. They hung on her every word, mispronounced or not.

"Ya're doin jest fine, honey. You keep it up, someday you'll be the best floor sweeper in Kentucky!" their maid said with laughter in her voice.

"I can do it better than you can, Trina. Watch me. See! I cleaned so much better than you did, you dopey girl."

"You did not. You're an idiot, Gretchen. Myrtle says I'm the best sweeper in Kentucky. Didn't you say that, Myrtle the turtle? I sweep so much better than Gretchen Gabriella, don't I?"

"Do not!" was Gretchen's response.

"Do so!" Katrina Josephina, who was a last word addict, told her twin sister.

"Granny says you're just plain feo feo feo! You ugly ugly rotten girl!"

"I can't stand you."

"You make me sick!"

"Laud have mercy! Why don't you gals go en get the mop for me, now, and stop all of that fussin'? All righty? Ya hears me? Now ya'll be good little gals for Myrtle. Okay, honey child?"

Myrtle was so tactful and tried her darnedest to keep those twins from flyin' at each other like prissy little kitty cats did out in barnyards.

"I'll do it!"

The proud Katrina Josephina raced to the broom cupboard door.

"No! I'll do it! She meant me! Not you, Trina!"

Gretchen-the-not-so-meek was screaming, in a state of complete panic and near hysterics by then, trying to outdo her identical twin, but losing in the race to the closet.

"One of you git out the mop, and the other gits to carry the pail. Now stop that fussin', ya hear me?"

Pushin', shovin', that me-first-attitude ever present, those twins were up to no good again. She'd better fetch that mop and pail herself. Even good ole Myrtle's patience was wearing thin, and that hardly ever happened. But she hoped that by delegating odd jobs for those twins, things might just run more smoothly. She was very diplomatic, always a move ahead of those O'Shaughnessy twins. Ya had ta be. Ta stop the fightin'. She took the pail and powdered cleanin' soap out of the broom closet with her own two dark brown hands, chocolatey hands.

Gretchen stopped her whining long enough to look up at their maid and ask Myrtle about her songs.

"Oh, Honey Bun, does ya really want ta hear me sing taday? You and yer sister don't seem ta want ta do nothin' but argue with one 'nother."

"We'll be good! We'll be good. Sing for us, Myrtle! Sing for us, okay? We really will be good girls for ya."

"Okay, Suga, but ya have to promise now, ya hear?"

"We will. We do, don't we, Katrina? We will try to be better girls for ya, won't we?"

Katrina Josephina thought about it for a minute, and only promised with her fingers crossed behind her back as she proceeded to tell Myrtle off in no uncertain terms for letting her roosters and chickens out of the broom cupboard. Sometimes Katrina Josephina pretended to be Farmer McGregor who wore blue jean overalls like in the Peter Rabbit story. That storage cupboard was her barn where she locked those critters up at night before she went to bed and sometimes even said her prayers. Didn't their mother's maid know that the closet was where her baby chickens lived in there with the broom, the mop, the ironing board, the iron, the Hoover vacuum cleaner and cleaning products? She was the one who was supposed to get that pail out herself. And she was still mad about it too.

'Myrtle the turtle' was a big fat colored woman like the syrup woman named Aunt Jemima. She had big, dark-black limpid eyes like liquid pools or shadowy watering holes where wild animals could come to drink and refresh themselves.

Aunt Jemima gave the girls all of that runny brown syrup for pancakes on Saturday mornin'. Pancake syrup came in brown glass bottles shaped like the real Aunt Jemima, who was probably related to good old 'Myrtle the turtle'. Those two colored ladies looked very similar.

Aunt Jemima wore an apron over her long floor length skirt and she had a scarf on her head. She smiled at all of those children, who loved to eat stacks and stacks of pancakes smothered with her sticky brown syrup that came from maple trees in places like Vermont; where the trees dripped drop by drop into buckets that caught the gooey elixir. Sometimes the girls ate their pancakes with 'Log Cabin' syrup that came in a bottle the shape of a real log cabin like the pioneers used to live in, out in the American frontier when the Indians were still wild and the colored people were still slaves a long time ago.

'Myrtle the turtle' wore an apron like Aunt Jemima, the syrup lady did. She wore a turban that partially covered most of her wiry black and grey hair made from a red and white bandana too. Sometimes Myrtle made buttermilk pancakes for the girls and little Roger Eugenio, once he got some teeth in his baby mouth. That baby used to squeeze those pancakes with his little brown hands until the pancakes oozed through his fingers. Then he'd stuff great handfuls of the smashed-up pancakes into his happy gurgling mouth. Myrtle let the girls take turns stirring her creamy pancake batter, that was the color of Georgina Jane and her family's skin.

Everybody in their family had creamy skin except for baby Roger Eugenio and his daddy. Their skin was brownish red like Granddaddy's skin. Granddaddy was half of an Indian, so his skin was not too creamy like Myrtle's pancake batter was. His skin was like already cooked pancakes were. Roger Eugenio looked like he was from another family, except for his blue eyes. His beautiful, blue eyes that glowed. His blue eyes that matched Mother's eyes. That toddler was half like his daddy and half like his mommy, or 'Mammie' like Katrina Josephina teasingly called their mother. That's what happened if you married a man whose dad was half of an Indian and you had a colored maid. Your children might be born with brown skin or would easily pick up another dialect, whether you liked it or not.

'Myrtle the turtle' was different from the girl's family in ways other than skin color. She was not a Catholic like the Semitic-Irish-Mexican-Indian-Spaniards she cleaned for. Hers was a deep Southern Baptist background, a Holy Roller version of the sect. Hers was a place of worship where they sang loudly and swayed in time and clapped to those good ole Gospel tunes, sung with soulful voices and such persuasive intensity. Not like the solemn Latin requiem, Masses of Georgina's family with bells and incense and genuflecting. Nobody rolled down their family's aisles, holy or not. But at Myrtle's church, they all rolled in happy adulation! It was not a stand-up-sit-down-kneel-bow-your-head-stand-up-again-sit-down-again-kneel-again kind of place. Those overly emotional coloreds fell all over the place like spontaneous combustion was settin' their place of worship on fire!

Loud, *"Amen! Yes Laud! Praise you Laud Jesus! Great God Almighty!"* rang out in response to some passage of scripture or in answer to the minister's message at Myrtle's church.

So, as she swept, the woman sang. Over and over, inadvertently perhaps. No one could really say that that darkie was deliberately evangelical in her intentions. No one would give her that much credit. She was just full of soul, which flooded into her and then spilled out of her like a cup overflowing. She was full of joy, and the words and melodies just had to ooze out of her somehow, sometime, anytime, anywhere. Those Gospel songs with rhythm and melody rang out in the O'Shaughnessy household, a place where a small white plastic glow-in-the-dark holy water fountain was attached to the wall inside the front door. The children were taught to dip their hands into it from an early age. Their priest, Father Delgado, had blessed the water, so they knew it was pretty holy. It was nailed low enough for them to be able to reach it. The holy water was a reminder to be good children, and the sign of the Cross was to teach them about the crucifixion.

'What a friend we have in Jesus! All our sins and griefs to bear!
What a privilege to carry, everything to God in prayer!'

Week after week, their maid's joyous singin' sounded through every room. It seemed that the chocolate-colored woman couldn't sweep, mop or clean one dish, without all of that melodic singin'. Sweepin' floors was just another chance for their maid to move her large brown body to her own favourite Gospel hit list, sung with her very own deep melodious voice. She was a walkin', sweepin', laughin', dustin', singin', cleanin' choir, complete with high notes and lower (very low) notes too.

Poor Nell

Singing like that got on Mother's nerves, though she was too polite to say so to her maid's face. When Myrtle wasn't there, Mother would pretend that her skin was black too and that she could sing just like their colored maid did! In an over-exaggerated off-key singin' voice, she'd sweep and pretend that she was Myrtle the turtle. But she couldn't always remember all of the words to those songs. She sang out of tune. And she sang with a lisp, just like she talked with one. Her impersonations were meant to amuse her children, not to hurt Myrtle's feelings. She would never ever do that sort of joke in front of the person she was pretending to be. That would be rude.

Mother could pretend to be all sorts of characters. One of her favourite one-woman-plays used a hankie gathered up in the middle. Then she could pretend to be a villain, a hero and even little Nell. If Mother was impersonating the villain, she used the hankie as a moustache. Villains had to have hair growing

45

underneath their noses for some reason. She'd pretend to be mean old Simon McGree and demand the rent from poor helpless Nell.

She'd say, "You must pay the rent! You must pay the rent! You must pay the rent right now!"

The she would be poor penniless Nell with the hankie on her head like a hair ribbon. And in a weak, high-pitched different voice she would say,

"I can't pay the rent! I can't pay the rent! I can't pay the rent right now!"

Suddenly, the villain would reappear by moving the hankie back underneath Mother's nose. He would threaten to tie poor Nell on the railroad tracks or do something even worse. When out of the blue, the hero would appear. Moving the hankie to his neck like a bow tie he'd say in a loud, self-confident heroic voice, "I'll pay the rent!"

And Nell would say, (You knew it was Nell because the hankie was now a ribbon back in her hair.) "My hero!"

Mother was very believable as every single character. Her impersonations of Myrtle had props too. She would wrap her head with a triangular scarf tied over her hair for effect, and shuffle as she swept and partially sing some Gospel tune, which she, like her children, had picked up from good old Myrtle. But the lisping singing gave her away. She couldn't sing like a black person, scarf or no scarf. Mother liked to pretend she was Myrtle or some other make-believe character. Mother could pretend to be almost anyone. Myrtle, on the other hand, didn't pretend to be anybody else. She was just herself.

Myrtle the Turtle

Knowin' *'Myrtle the turtle'* gave Georgina a good feelin' about all of those colored people rockin' on their porches. If those dark people were even half as nice as her mother's maid, they must be some of the best people in Kentucky. Those dark people must be like Georgina Jane's pet doodlebugs, who were movin' to Alaska with her. They must be related to each other, like one big happy family. All of those dark-skinned people sure did look an awful lot alike. It was hard to tell them apart. To the girl, it was like all of the colored people in the whole wide world were related to good old *'Myrtle the turtle'*. Myrtle, who sang so many nice songs. Myrtle, who cooked such yummy, appetising food for them.

Good old, nappy-headed Myrtle, who loved the girl and her family. Good old *'Myrtle the turtle'*. Myrtle, who cried the last day she came to their house in Fort Campbell, Kentucky. Good old Myrtle. Myrtle, who came over to sweep the floor with Katrina Josephina, one last time. Good old *'Myrtle the turtle'*. Good old Myrtle, their sweet-chocolate-colored maid, who cried because of them *'movin' ta 'laska'*.

Mother's maid loved their family so much that she would even rinse Roger Eugenio and the new baby, Peter Martin's stinky ka ka diapers out in the toilet. Dunking, dunking, dunking, dunking those diapers over and over again into the potty to get all of that stuck on ka ka off of them. You had to love someone an awful lot to wash that smelly ka ka off of their stinky cloth diapers. Knowin' good old *'Myrtle the turtle'* had been one of the best things about Kentucky. Leavin' her behind, and leavin' behind the flavour she gave to livin' in the South, was a very, very hard thing to do. The girl would never ever forget Myrtle. Myrtle. Myrtle, the very best maid in all of Kentucky. Myrtle, the very best maid in the whole wide world. Myrtle, the best maid ever.

Sambo's Past Times

Less than a hundred years before the child's memory was conceived, her country had been in the midst of a Civil War. Just about everybody in the country had been fightin' over what kind of a place in their society the forefathers of Myrtle and of all of those other colored people, would have. President Abraham Lincoln had been the president way back then. Honest Abe was born in Kentucky, like her baby brother, Peter Martin, had been born there.

Tryin' to ease the tensions of the North/South divide, as he began his first term in office, President Lincoln wanted to heal wounds between the people who wanted the colored people to stay slaves, and the ones who'd been willin' to fight and die to set them free. In his first inaugural address of 1861, alludin' to the unity of the patriotic colonists during the Revolutionary War, he had said, tryin' to make peace between his people:

"We must not be enemies, but friends.
We must not be enemies.
Though passion may have strained,
It must not break our bonds of affection,
The mystic cords of memory,
Stretching from every battlefield and patriot grave,
To every living heart and hearthstone
All over this broad land

Will yet swell the chorus of the Union,
When again touched,
As surely as they will be by the
Better angels of our nature."

When he, Abraham Lincoln, the lawyer with a dirt poor and mainly self-educated background, became President Lincoln, the abolition of the slavery of the blacks had not yet been achieved. It had taken a lot of arguments, like Katrina Josephina and Gretchen Gabriela had. It had taken a lot of fights between people who were countrymen. People who should have been family. People who should of been friends. To change things. Arguments had turned into more than pinchin', hair-pullin'-fist fights by angry, funny-to-watch tumblin' little twin girls, both wantin' to sit in the front seat at the same time. Hostilities had flared for years on the soil of her countrymen. Countrymen who wanted the blacks to be freed men. Countrymen who wanted them to remain in slavery.

Battles. Fights. And finally, smoke and burnin' and a lot of dead soldiers from both sides of the arguments. With their sad, dead, broken-up bodies all piled up in misty killin' fields. Fields soakin' with the blood of mothers' sons. That made things change. Those dead bodies finally made things change. Time had moved on since then. But less than a hundred years later, the ashes from the blazes of those fightin' people still remained in hearts. It remained there. It remained there just under the surface. And those inner voices still spoke out in their differing opinions.

Georgina Jane saw the Negroes sittin' on their porches, or stoops as they used to call them. She thought that the blacks were just havin' fun or enjoyin' *'leisure'* time. She did not understand about prejudice. She did not understand about unemployment. She did not understand about a lack of trade skills or opportunities for advancement of the coloreds. She did not understand about discriminatory lack of opportunities. She did not understand about educational deprivation. She didn't understand about families torn apart by greed and cruelty. She didn't understand about the resultin' War Between the States. The terrible Civil War.

Neither the poverty, nor the issue of the color of their skin, was within the child's grasp of comprehension. These were not topics of discussion which her parents would have thought necessary to explain to her. These things were not ever discussed by those who chose to turn away from the unpleasantness of the sufferings of other, different people. People of polite society did not speak of such things. They did not speak of such things. They did not speak of such things. They did not speak of such things; especially in front of their children.

The emotional roots of slavery were still buried deep in the psyche of the girl's society. Some lay right under the surface. But to her young mind, these were just chocolate people. They were people like *'Myrtle the turtle'* was. The girl was unaware of Chief Justice Earl Warren from the Supreme Court. She didn't know, nor had she met President Ike Eisenhower who lived in The White House back then in 1958. They might have passed court judgments. Or they might have said noble words about the plight of the coloreds in the United States of Georgina's America at that time. But the girl could see it for herself. These darker, sweet, chocolatey people still had their own side of town.

She wondered, *Why do all of these people have dark skin?*

She didn't understand yet about segregation of the blacks from the whites. She knew nothin' at all of the implications of laws. What the sentiments of adults who judged others by their skin color meant, was a complete mystery to the child. She didn't realize that the color of your skin was such an important issue. Why was being chocolate such a big deal anyway? She had never even heard of the Poll Tax. Who was Jim Crow? Or what were his laws? Laws which disenfranchised those of another, darker skin color? Laws makin' votin' nigh impossible for the poorer blacks? Laws makin' it too hard for them to be able to pay to vote? Laws makin' it too hard for them to vote for their rights?

Laws makin' segregation a legality? Laws effectively ghettoizin' those thought inferior to the other residents of her country? Laws that made them less than really and truly American citizens? Those laws would have made no sense to her tender young mind. Even if someone had told her about those laws, she would not have understood their implications.

Why did these black people have to ride in the back of the bus? Why did they have to sit upstairs in theaters? Why did they have to live in a certain part of town? Who made them do all of these things? And why? All of these things were still a mystery to her naïve, young mind. Property values based on the color of the people livin' on a particular street, meant nothin' to her.

She had never heard of brave Harriet Tubman, who worked a long, long time ago on the Underground Railroad, secretly followin' the North Star in the dead of night. That gal, Rosa Parks, and her defiant ride on that city bus in Montgomery, Alabama might have been a serious news item. But the little girl had never heard of her. At any rate, the significance of these events to the colored people she saw that day, sittin' and rockin' on their porches, would have been a mystery to the child. Their relation to *'Myrtle the turtle'*, and to those strong black women, who risked their own safety and freedom, held no relevance to the child. The way those colored gals had lived their lives, as they courageously lead their people out of slavery and the mentality of bondage and cruel subjugation, pointin' the way to liberty and change; were not even as real to the girl, as the storybook characters she read about in her favourite books. Martin Luther King Jr. hadn't even talked about his 'dream' yet. Desegregation was still in the future.

The South Side of Town

So, when she saw all of those dark faces. When her family drove through the South side of town. She didn't understand about the implications. A little girl, Georgina Jane O'Shaughnessy, wondered about those darker people, who, unlike her daddy, had time to sit on their front porches and talk to one another.

So, as she and her family drove out of town, Georgina asked her father,

"Why do all of these people have skin that's so dark, Daddy?"

"This is the poor side of town, honey. This is where they all live," said her father.

She wasn't sure what being *'poor'* meant.

"Do the poor people like it better if they live close together?" she asked her daddy.

"I don't know, sweetheart," he said.

Georgina Jane O'Shaughnessy didn't know either.

Chapter Two
Bags Full of Surprises

Goodie Bags

This time, they were really off on their trip. The whole tribe was all together.

Mother counted heads: one (Daddy), two (Mother), three (Georgina Jane), four (Katrina Josephina, the twin who was born first), five (the twin who was born second), six (Roger Eugenio who sat there in the back seat nestled up against his pillow, holding tightly to his old yellow blanket, sucking his thumb), seven (Peter Martin, the six-month-old baby, the latest addition to their family). Now they could leave Kentucky. Everyone was present and accounted for. All of their little clan was gathered together and they were off.

Mother had packed *'goodie bags'*, full of new surprises for the trip. And it felt just like a small and happy Christmas in the back seat of the car. Daddy was singing a song in Spanish to Georgina Jane's mother. He told Georgina, when she asked him about the meaning of the words he was singing, that the song was about a naughty little girl, (like Katrina). The girl in the song was named *'Maria Christina'*. That girl, like somebody her father knew, didn't want to be dictated to about her behaviour and would not be governed, even though the guy singing to her wanted to rule her. Daddy winked at Georgina when he said the word *'somebody'*. Georgina Jane knew what he meant.

The baby, Peter Martin, was asleep across Mommy's lap up in the front seat. Gretchen was rubbing the baby's head and humming softly to herself, staring contentedly at the scenery, whizzing past their automobile. Katrina Josephina was ecstatic about her bag of surprises, prizes she called them. She actually squealed aloud when she opened up her bag and looked inside. All three of the girls had some of the same things. But Georgina Jane, because she was older, had some grown-up things, because she was able to read a little bit and the twins, 'the babies', she still called them, could not read. Her little brothers, Roger Eugenio and Peter Martin were too little to understand, but they each had a bag of new rattles and baby books, which they shook, jingled, chewed on and threw down.

That's the game babies love the very best. It is called *I-throw-it-down-you-pick-it-up*. They love that game more than anything in the whole wide world, except for their bottles. Those babies played that game over and over again. Their other favourite pastime was *peek-a-boo-I-see-you*, which Gretchen played with Peter Martin over the top of the front seat when she wasn't sitting next to the new baby and he wasn't asleep on Mommy's lap. That was the happiest baby. He gurgled and giggled almost all the way to San Antonio. He loved his big sisters and laughed for his big brother (who was, after all thirteen months older than he was). Roger Eugenio would stick that baby's tiny thumb in his brother's mouth and then pull it out again with a pop! He was trying to teach that baby to suck his thumb. But all Peter Martin wanted to do was laugh, laugh, laugh!

That game wore him out though, and so he slept a lot. The game of *Ithrowitdownyoupickitup* exhausted Mother, but she wouldn't admit it, and she smiled sweetly at her baby son and humoured him with good grace when, for the hundredth time, he threw his new book about baby duckies down on the floorboard of the car again. Mostly Georgina's brothers had bottles, jars of Gerber's baby food and bags and bags of soft white diapers. Mother said it would be hard to stop to wash out the diapers; so that's why they had to take so many with them on the trip.

The thrill of the whole family being together in their black and white station wagon, and the lure of the bags of surprises overcame Georgina's reluctance to leave Kentucky and say goodbye to her best friend, Juanita. After her father had filled their Pontiac up with gas, they were on their way – out on the open road. The children sat as quietly as any little child possibly could sit, as their father drove to the highway. Finally, when they had been good enough and quiet enough, the bags of surprises were handed out. They were heading southwest to Texas, through the Southern states of: Tennessee, Mississippi, Arkansas and the north-western corner of Louisiana.

Even though she knew that these bags of surprises were really bribes by her mother to keep those twin sisters of hers quiet, Georgina thought that it was a wonderful idea to get presents when it wasn't even your birthday. These things would keep those twins busy and happy, so that her daddy could concentrate and drive the car safely. Georgina Jane loved getting presents. New little things were precious, the smaller the better, so that you could fit them into your pockets. Or, if you were a big girl, like Georgina, you could put these tiny treasures into your purse and the doodlebugs could play with them.

For several hours, the children entertained themselves with their bags of surprises. It seemed like only minutes passed. Into Georgina Jane's bag, her mother had put a card game of 'Old Maid', a tiny baby doll with her own bottle and a little straw basket for the baby doll to sleep in. Mother had made miniature nightgowns for the girls' baby dolls, which matched the ones she had made for her daughters for the trip to Alaska. The nightgowns were beautiful, with white cotton seersucker fabric covered with tiny pink rosebuds. Mother had put a magnifying glass for Georgie to be able to see her doodlebugs even better, so that those special little bugs would look bigger. She said that she hoped that seeing giant grey creatures wouldn't scare the life out of Georgina! That was pretty funny. When they got to the Pacific Ocean, Mother told her that if she looked at the whales in the ocean with her magnifying glass, it might really scare her. The magnifying glass was only for small creatures like the doodlebugs were. Pretty soon, she would see giant whales and wasn't that exciting?

In her bag, there were coloring books and a brand-new pack of sixty-four new colors with a pencil sharpener in the back of the box, so that Georgina Jane could sharpen her crayons if they got blunt. The twins had smaller boxes of crayons with less colors, which made Katrina Josephina jealous. There were two connect the dots 'Dot-to-Dot' books, because Georgina had learned her numbers and could count to a hundred now. There were three new sharpened pencils with their own erasers to write in the connect the dots 'Dot-to-Dot' books and to keep a record of the trip in the diary that her mother had bought for her to write about her trip to Alaska. There were brand new blunt-ended children's scissors. There were books of paper dolls, who came alive when the girls cut them out and dressed them up in their paper doll clothes. And one of her bestest things was a kaleidoscope that had magic patterns of fabulous colors hidden inside of it.

All of the girls got brightly colored children's sunglasses with little animals on them. Gretchen's sunglasses were pink with sweet little bunny rabbits on them. Katrina's were green with cute little kitty-cats on them. And Georgina's were blue, a boy's color, with blue birds perched on the plastic rims. The three girls put the shaded eyewear on. It was a sunny summer's day. Georgina Jane starred out the car window, feeling like a real, live movie star with her big black hat and her sunglasses shading her eyes from the sun's glare. Her mother was right, the scenery was very interesting and fun to look at. It was summertime, so the car windows were rolled down a little bit. And there was a gentle breeze blowing right over them as Daddy drove the car down the Interstate Highway.

All of the girls got candy treats in their goodie bags. *Tootsie Rolls*, jelly beans, and lolly pops and liquorice gum drops that turned your tongue black-like-the-night. Soda pop was a treat saved for later when they stopped for a picnic. Today was a special day because they were hardly ever allowed to have so many sugary candies. Soda pop was only for special occasions too. White milk was all a kid usually got to drink at mealtimes. That was because Mother knew that sugar could rot your baby teeth right out of your mouth. No decent mother would let her children have too many sweets, because that was bad for you. But to start the trip to Alaska, because it was such a special occasion, the girls could have junk food just that once.

For fun in the evenings, to help the kids wind down and make the trip a special event, Mother had bought new games of *Tiddly-Winks*, jacks, Chinese Checkers and *Pick-up-Sticks*. Nights spent at motels dotted along the two-lane highways that seemed to stretch on forever in front of them, were unlike being back in their old living room in Kentucky with all of their furniture around them. Furniture collected from all of their family's travels. Furniture that Mother was so proud of. Furniture surrounding them made them feel safe. But on the trip, they didn't have their furniture with them. Games were always played sitting on the floor, so the motels floors were turned into a playing space, a place that was made to seem familiar by old comfortable quilts laid down for them to sit on the floor and play their new games on. New games brought along to entertain them, kept them busy till Daddy said, "Lights out! Everybody, time to go to sleep!"

More History, School Days a Typhoon and a Turtle

Later the second day, after they left Kentucky and after several potty stops, they arrived in Nashville, Tennessee, a famous place where battles in the Civil War were fought a long, long time ago. That was the town that started off on the Confederate side, and ended up on the Union side of the War Between the States. Lots of dead soldiers' bones were still there, buried underneath the ground. Those guys had lost so much of their blood, because the people in the North, and the folks in the South just couldn't get along in the same country. That's why they had used guns, like in the movies, to shoot holes into each other. That's how their blood came oozing out of them until they died. They were left to practically rot away to skeletons left in fields far away from their worried mommies and daddies who probably loved them very much. The girl's father had told her all about how the soldiers in the Army were, back in the olden days. So, she knew that it must be true. Her daddy liked to talk about people's blood and guts. He thought that the idea of blood and guts was pretty interesting.

Those guys' bones lying in those fields must have been a very sad sight, was what the girl was thinking. That was when her father interrupted her day dream and said, "Pretty soon we'll be in Memphis, kids. Why don't you settle down and take a nap until we get there?"

"What will we see in Memphis, Daddy?" she asked her father.

"Memphis is where the Mississippi River is. You'll see some boats with big wheels on the back of them, called river boats, when we get there, Georgie. Can you spell Mississippi? No? Well, why don't you take a nap or read your book to Katrina and Roger? I'll tell you when we get there, okay?"

Eventually, the girl started to doze off; faintly hearing her daddy listening to the car radio and singing some song to her mother about *'hound dogs'* and teasing her little sister, Gretchen Gabriella about *'crying all the time'*!

What a crazy song, thought Georgina, *why would anyone want to sing a song like that,* as the Tennessee scenery whizzed by her window in their new car. History was in the making, but to the girl, it was just a long day, driving in the station wagon with her family, on their way to see her grandparents again. That night they would stay in a highway motel with a swimming pool just outside of Tupelo, Mississippi, where Elvis, the man who had long sideburns growing on his cheeks and who gyrated those hips of his, when he sang that song about hound dogs and crying, was born.

Daddy had told them all a big important story, as he drove.

"This is the Deep South. Lots of history was made here. Tomorrow we will go to Vicksburg, Mississippi. I'll show you where some famous soldiers in the army used to fight. That was where an important battle took place a long time ago."

But the next day, that forty-seven-day stand-off between the North and the South had little meaning for his kids, as their father showed them around the town of Vicksburg and they looked at all of the historical markers saying about what had happened there. Mother liked to read every single historical marker out loud. Even though she had a lisp, it didn't embarrass her at all. She had to teach her children about the history of their famous country. Practically, the whole town, and everyone standing around them could hear her lisping words about the battles and historical events too, with Mother reading like that.

The girl knew all about American history. It seemed like everywhere she went, there was something to learn about her country's history and all of the things that had happened there in the olden days. Her daddy had taken her whole family to Fredericksburg, Virginia or maybe it was Williamsburg? She wasn't quite sure, only remembering that it was named after some famous man from the olden days. Anyway, that was so that they could see all of the men in their funny wigs and all of those old painted houses that the colonials built a long time ago. And they got to ride in an old-fashioned horse trot wagon all through the town. It was almost like showing off, because there were so many cute little kids belonging to her daddy in the wagon. She remembered Fredericksburg, or maybe it was Williamsburg, because her daddy let his girls play in a park with swings, which he knew they loved. Swinging was the best ride of all. The girl could still see all of the brightly colored leaves piled up underneath her feet as she had swung high up into the clear blue sky that day.

Her memories were like her very own storybooks. They were like the Injuns' trail-markers, like mind-markers in her head that she could follow and then reread sometimes if she wanted to. They were like films at the movie theater that could be played over and over again rerunning inside of the girl's conscious mind. That was long before day-dreaming became labelled and so well-known as visualisation, the deliberate rethinking of events just to make yourself feel good, or maybe even remember sad or bad things too.

Conscious remembering was something that the girl liked to do, even if it made her seem a bit scatter-brained to her teacher at the old school in Kentucky, when she stared out the classroom window to do it. No amount of scolding could make Georgina not look out of the schoolroom window when the weather was so sunny and nice, and she just plain felt like doing it. When the teacher's back was turned because the tired old lady was writing something nearly incomprehensible on the blackboard with chalk that made a terrible fingernails-against-slate sound, George'd take a quick glance outside.

Outside where the sky was so big – bigger than any classroom in the whole wide world – the big blue sky let her feel like she could breath, like she had room to move. The big, blue sky with its clouds and rainbows and flying birds and butterflies didn't make her feel stuffy, like the stale classroom did. So she'd look out the window rather than listening to ideas that she felt were confining. Being outside in the sunshine, even just by looking, was much better than being stuck inside of, by comparison, a relatively dark schoolroom classroom trying to listen to subjects that might or might not interest her.

She'd be sure to get into trouble again for being such a bad girl if she were caught. Mrs. Dwyer would be just plain furious with the stupid, quiet, little dark-headed girl who sat staring out the window every day in that over-crowded classroom so far away from home. That teacher had even threatened to take Georgina by the hand to the principal's office if that rotten, absent-minded child 'didn't pay more attention' to what the boring, over-anxious teacher was saying. How could she ever possibly hope to learn a single thing with such a bad 'absent-minded' attitude?

But learning some other way must be better than facing straight ahead, not talking, not looking out of the window. Not even moving one single solitary muscle. School was pretty boring. Every day, it was the same things repeated over and over again, like the constant dripping of water on a rainy day. The child felt that she had to tune the woman out, or she'd go crazy, stark raving mad. But that unruly, bad, disrespectful-of-authority attitude didn't win her any popularity contest in that classroom environment. School bored her, it wasn't exciting. But travelling was different, it didn't bore her one little bit.

As they travelled, she thought about the past in her short little life. She'd been to a lot of places already, and knew about the other ways people lived and even how they thought differently, and did things in other ways than she was used to. When she was small, her family had lived in Okinawa, over by Japan, for a while. That's where the twins were born – in between two typhoons! No wonder that Katrina Josephina could be so uncontrollable in her behaviour! The stormy tempestuous weather must have really affected that girl's personality! Those wild and woolly oriental storms collided that day when Katrina Josephina and Gretchen were born. George had vivid memories of her worried father that day. She was nearly two years old, after all. And she could think and feel about a lot of things that happened in the world around her, even if she couldn't accurately verbally express her feelings.

The winds seemed to want to blow their house down, like in the story of the Three Little Pigs and the big bad wolf. Blowing! Blowing! Blowing! Would it never stop making so much racket? Would it just please be quiet? Pretty soon, that huffing, puffing wind would blow the house down! That wind was a very big, very bad wolf. Daddy was trying not to act like a nervous wreck, but even before the age of two, she was able to see through the man. She knew what he was thinking. George was able to read his face like one of the books he and Mommy read aloud to her. She knew just by looking at him, that he missed her Mommy and was wondering how she was getting on in her delivery of those two new blondies of his, before he even knew that he had twins with soft fluffy yellow fuzz, like duck's downy feathers poking off of the tops of their tiny new-born heads.

The phone lines were blown down, and he couldn't even call the quansit hut army base hospital and check on his wife's progress. His nerves were not made of steel, you know. But showing fear or worry to his nearly twenty-one-month-old daughter, whom he loved like his life, was something that he just wasn't about to do. So, with the wind blowing, and the gales flashing and great stinging torrents of water descending down on, and into, their little flat, Daddy did the sensible things any man might think of doing in his situation. He piled straw tattomies high up in the middle of the room.

Water was pouring in, right underneath the door of the dwelling he inhabited with his wife and their little daughter. What was the use of having a door anyway, if water during two typhoons could come in great gushes and flow like a river right through your house, making life so difficult? What if Georgina Jane fell off of the tatommies stacked up so high? What if she fell and drowned in the foot and a half high river that was now flowing through their house?

He could sit up there on those tattomies with her for much of the time, reading picture books to his quiet child, trying to make her laugh by tickling her, playing peek-a-boo, or trying to get her to nap amidst the blankets and pillows he had placed her on and surrounded her with. But with the battery-operated radio on, telling him, as well as informing his daughter, who did, after all, understand the English language, her native tongue, that the weather showed no signs of improving until tomorrow – perhaps; concern was a constant thing.

The girl remembered back to that time, and she remembered the feelings she had back then. Sitting high up in the air, hoping that she wouldn't fall off, she looked over the edge of the towering high tatommies. The rain was pouring, not just underneath the door, but had begun to come through the keyhole! What a frightening sight! Floods were scary things. And floods in your very own house were really, really bad.

Daddy was in the kitchen popping popcorn for them to celebrate the day of the birth of her new sister or brother. Even if their house was flooding, and the radio was predicting more and more stormy weather, he was trying his best to ease their tension. He was trying to pretend that their house wasn't a flooding house. He was trying to pretend that he and his daughter were just nonchalantly sitting together at the movie theater eating their big bowl of homemade buttered popcorn, instead of panicking over their flooded house.

Georgina had been watching him carefully. Looking for any signs of panic in his demeanour. He had stopped bailing the water out a long time ago. It was useless. He couldn't keep up with the flooding waterways in their house. So he gave up trying, telling Georgina Jane that he would wait until after the rain stopped, to mop up the mess that the flood was making. She knew that he thought that she didn't understand his words, but she knew what he meant. Mommy liked for her house to be spotless, or she got nervous. Daddy knew that by now too. He was popping popcorn so that they could sit together on those tatommies and eat their popcorn and pretend that they were really at the movies watching an exciting Hollywood film. He was trying so hard to make it a special day.

She could hear the sound, of not just the rain pelting their metal roof, but the very similar sounds coming from the kitchen. Popping corn kernels hitting the sides and lid of the metal pan were like the sheets of rain falling that day. Where was her daddy? Why had he left her there, instead of carrying her away from all of this? She could smell the aroma of the salted popcorn and butter coming from the kitchen where he was hiding from her. This was not fun. She didn't like it one little bit when he went away. Perhaps he would never come back to her and she might spend the rest of her childhood right there, all by herself on top of six straw tatommies stacked one on top of the other, surrounded by rain that was not outside, where it belonged, but had invaded their safe haven. That flood was ruining everything Mommy kept so orderly. Ruining everything that Mommy loved.

But Georgina knew somehow, that the man in the kitchen was her friend, not just a daddy. He would take care of her. He wouldn't let her drown in that indoor watercourse, even if she did fall off from that great height; where she sat perched, like a tiny sparrow in a treetop. He'd hear her splash and then he would come back and get her. He would keep her safe.

Daddy had been like a stranger to her when she was a baby, because the Army stationed him in Okinawa way ahead of her and Mommy going there. They had to stay in San Antonio, Texas with Manga a long time without him. He didn't see her and Mommy for nine months, from the time his baby girl was six weeks old, until she was ten and a half months old. She had learned to walk without him holding her hand. On the boat over to where her daddy was stationed, reeling and walking all at the same time, she had found her gait. The ocean's rolling, tempestuous waves had been her teacher then. When they got off the ship, disembarking in the Orient, Papa had scooped her up, out of her mother's familiar arms. He was so delighted to see his baby girl again, and began to smother her with big playful, scratchy, slobbery kisses. She remembered the look on his face at that first moment when he saw her again, knowing her only from photographs and her mother's letters for month after long month.

His face when he finally had his family back was inscribed on her mind's eyes. She would never forget how he looked at her that day. He had kept repeating 'Chula, Chula, Chula' over and over again. And he'd hugged her so tightly that it had frightened her, even as a toddler baby. And when he put her down to see her walk, like Mommy had said so proudly his baby girl had learned to do on the journey to rejoin him, Georgina just fell flat on her face. There was no ship's frothy undulation to help steady her steps. She had stood there for a moment, waiting for the swaying of the ship's hull to move with her and help to steady her tentative steps. The seaworthy vessel's motion was something which she had gotten used to on their passage. That boat was her schoolmaster, making motion, of many kinds, a reality, and propelling her into an unknown future, wherever her growing feet would carry her.

But they were on dry land now, and the boat's movement never came to help her. So, she collapsed and had to relearn to walk again. This time it was on unmoving ground, not on a rolling big boat. In a few weeks, they'd board another big passenger ship, headed for Seward's harbour in Southern Alaska. The twins would celebrate their fifth birthdays on board that next ship. Mommy and Daddy had told them all about what that might be like for them, encouraging what would remain a lifelong sense of wanderlust and longing for adventure in their children.

They had told her about her first birthday, celebrated on the Okinowan beach. But she had her own vivid memories of that day too. That was the day she climbed on the back of a giant sea turtle. Climbing on it and riding it like it was a horsey at the old Five and Dime store back in San Antonio, Texas. Mommy could make that old horsey go real fast by putting in some kind of coin, so that her baby daughter could make the horsey go. She could make that pony go real fast. She learned to ride a mechanical horse before her feet learned to take steps on land or on sea. Children had to learn how to hold on to the reins of mechanical horses all over the country, like those kids were still part of the Old Wild West. It was an integral part of growing up amidst a culture of myths and the Old West legends of the place. Every child could become an instant cowboy or cowgirl or a wild Indian just by putting a nickel in a mechanical dime store horsey complete with saddle and stir-ups, and leather reins to get hold of. Riding. Riding. Riding those wild jolting horseys.

The huge terrapin she saw on her first birthday wasn't moving too quickly though. He had such a big belly that he could just dig with his feet, not seeming to be going anywhere at all, despite all the motion of his clawed appendages. The Okinawan sea turtle was beautiful, with its big yellow eyes looking at her, and its wonderful multi-hued shell that was both rough and smooth all at the same time. She had patted him on the back and loved that sea turtle just by looking at him, as she stroked his sweet smooth nose. It was the most magnificently wonderful creature she had ever seen before in all of her born days.

Being one-year-old, she could walk and even talk a little bit, telling her mother to put her 'Down, please', if she'd rather walk on her own. Or if she was trying to pick some real pretty flowers for her Mommy, she'd pull and pull and pull, finally feeling frustrated and realizing that she was too small, and that her hands weren't strong enough to pick flowers like her Mommy did. So she'd shrug her little shoulders with a sigh of despair that she couldn't pick flowers because they were too stuck. Mommy loved flowers. They were so pretty sitting in the blue glassy vase on her kitchen table. But the toddler-girl couldn't pull flowers out of the ground like a grown-up. So, she gave up and just let out a little sigh of resignation as she shrugged and said aloud to herself, "Too tight."

She knew about little and big. That sea turtle was big. She was little. She patted that big turtle, and talked to him through her interpreter, her mother.

Did he know her Mommy? Had he ever met her daddy? Did he like swimming in the great big blue ocean? Did he know any other little girls in Okinanowa? What had he eaten for his breakfast? Did he know that it was Georgina Jane's first birthday?

Mother talked on and on to the aquatic being, as though, like Georgina, he hung on and almost understood her every word. Mommy thought that she was helping to make a new friend for her daughter, a special first birthday friend. But that sea turtle didn't like Georgina, even if it was her first birthday. And he bit her tiny hand, not wanting to release it. The mark was still there. As her father drove them on the long trip up to Alaska, she looked down at the top of her left hand and remembered that day on that faraway beach where that sea turtle probably still lived.

Even as a small girl, she remembered that feeling of worry that perhaps the large sea tortoise might continue to grasp her hand in his sharp beak. He didn't seem to want to let go of her. He would not release her. Might he even drag her with him into the sea for a little swim? Perhaps that had just been his way of making friends, and he didn't realize how much the tight grasp of his sharp beak was really, really hurting her. He was making her cry in shock and disbelief that their conversation was so unimportant to him. He didn't care that her friendship of him should be treated in such a mean way. He had made her hand bleed and bleed. She remembered her very own red blood dripping from her hand that day.

Georgina's daydreaming went on and on, covering a vast terrain. She remembered lots of other past days as they were driving down the Interstate highway. How bright the sunshine was, on the Okinawan beach, and that day in Fredericksburg. She thought back to the time when they rode horses and the carriage around the town in. One of the horseys even wore a straw hat with flowers on it. Someone had cut two holes in the straw brim to make room for the horsey's ears to fit through. Tied underneath the horsey's chin was a green ribbon which matched the twin's eyes. The man driving the carriage was real nice, and he let the three girls stroke the horsey's nose with their fingers. They had been somewhat hesitant at first, but the nice man said it was okay, that the horse liked to be stroked.

That was a day when she remembered her parents seeming happy. Nobody in their family was in a bad mood on that day, so Georgina deliberately tried to recapture in her mind's eye, all of the things that had happened that day and on lots of other days. Yesterday, they'd eaten at a drive-in restaurant that had a children's playground in the middle of it. They had scoffed down their lunch of chilli-dogs, hamburgers and French fries and tiny mugs of root beer. The carhops had brought their food to them on metal trays that attached to the car's windows. Daddy had to roll the windows down halfway, so that the metal tray had something to hang onto. Those trays looked like they were floating on thin air with that clear glass window holding them up so well.

Fried Chicken Really, Really Gets to Ya

Today they'd have fried chicken. Soon they would stop at a nice place to have lunch at a restaurant that served fried chicken, smashed potatoes with gravy, black eyed peas, and corn bread with lots and lots of butter on it. Everyone in her family just loved fried chicken. Her mother made the bestest fried chicken in the whole wide world. Sometimes Georgina helped her mother dip the dead chicken around in egg and milk and then into flour mixed with smashed-up Saltine cracker crumbs and a pinch of salt and a dash of pepper on top. It made a big, gooey mess that stuck to her fingers when she helped Mommy dip the drumsticks into the egg and milk and then roll those body parts from the dead chickens in smashed up crackers. Chicken sure tasted good after her mother fried it in that hot popping Crisco oil.

Once inside the 'Chicken Shack', the family was seated around a big, circular, booth-like table with benches encircling it. Georgina sat there, thinking about what a fashionable young lady she was. She sat there confidently and serenely, at the age of six; wearing a ladies' big black hat that her mother had given to her; though she had taken off her sunglasses by then. It was a hat that used to belong to Mother, but she said that George could have the handmedown hat for the trip to Alaska because she was so grown up now. It would match her black velvet purse with the doodlebugs inside of it. How were they doing? She'd better check. Did wood lice like smashed potatoes?

Turning her menu upside down, in order to read it better, and feeling very grown-up, special and important, the girl decided what she would eat for lunch. She opened her velvet purse and checked on her pet doodlebugs. Her doodlebugs were still happy. They were all curled up together, sleeping in her purse. She and the doodlebugs had come a long way from their old army base home in Kentucky. She and the doodlebugs had been in the station wagon for nearly two days. Now they were headed for Texas and then on to a new home in Alaska, the land of the midnight's sun. Wasn't it just great?

A young fair-haired, freckled waitress carried a large tray billowing with steaming food to their table. Everyone except for the baby, Peter Martin, had their own plates. He sat in a high chair and Mother spooned Gerber's baby food into his open mouth. Usually at home, the kids had plastic plates made out of shiny colored plastic. Breakable plates could easily wind up on the floor in a broken heap of sharp shard pieces if the little kids got the chance to cause some extra excitement. But the restaurant lady was giving them each a breakable plate of food. Even Roger Eugenio got one. She must not know that little brown boy and the twins very well.

The Southern fried chicken smelled absolutely delicious. It sure was good. It was scrumptious! The taste of the South's recipes was so delicious. Georgina was starving. She was really, really hungry. Her sisters, Katrina Josephina and Gretchen Gabriela started singing a song that they had learned at nursery school, even though singing at the table during mealtimes was strictly forbidden, and they knew it. When kids are out in public, they think that they can get away with anything, even if they know it's a naughty thing to do.

On and on they sang,

"Old MacDonald had a farm.
Eee Iii Eee Iii Oh!
And on his farm he had a chicken.
Eee Iii Eee Iii Oh!
With a cluck cluck here,
A cluck there,
Here a cluck,
There a cluck
Everywhere a cluck cluck!"

Concentrating on that song, which had a lot of verses and farm animals in it, and wondering just how long her father was going to tolerate that kind of rambunctious behaviour before he told those identical look-a-like girls to 'Knock it off!' or he'd 'Knock their block off!', Georgina momentarily took her mind off of chewing her food. She was trying to savour the yummy taste of that chicken. She and that drumstick were happy together. When she took a giant bite out of that yummy piece of chicken, something was wrong with that piece of chicken. It left her mouth too fast, because it was in a hurry to get to her tummy. Something was making it very hard for the girl to breathe. She sat there amidst all of her family's conversations and that loud singing, feeling invisible. Did any of the rest of the family even see her? She had a problem, but who took notice or seemed to care? No words could escape her lips. She sat there burbling underneath her hat with what breath she had left. And that's what happened when she started to choke on a bone from that piece of chicken.

Suddenly, without saying a word to her, her daddy was holding Georgina upside down by one of her legs and shaking her up and down. Her special big black hat with its wide brim fell to the floor. Someone might step on it. Her daddy was sticking his finger down her throat. That was no place for a finger to be, down someone's throat. The mortified six-year-old was so mad at her daddy. She felt just plain furious. She had worn her favourite pair of red underwear with its appliqued hearts, especially for the trip to Alaska. Her daddy was making her new blue and white checked dress fall down over her head. All of the people in the restaurant were staring at Georgina Jane's red underwear!

If my mother would let me wear blue jeans, like my friend, Juanita's mother lets her wear them, these people wouldn't be seeing my red underwear! thought Georgina, while she was suspended upside down getting that chicken bone taken out of her throat. It seemed to be taking her daddy forever to prise that bone loose. So, she'd had lots of time to think about how she felt while she was hanging upside down. Now she knew what the word *'choking'* really meant. She didn't think that she would ever want to eat fried chicken ever again. Finally, after what seemed to her like several eternities, her father set her back down on her seat. He stood high above her, proudly holding his souvenir in his hand. Her chicken bone!

Georgina was crying and her throat hurt. She was still so mad at her daddy for embarrassing her, that her face turned red, redder than even her red-like-a-raspberry underwear. But there he was, relieved as he could be. There he was. There he was, smiling at her! He was so proud of himself! There he was, holding up that stupid chicken's bone. That sharp chicken bone – for all the world to see. She didn't even want to look at that ugly grey bone ever again.

She felt faint, hardly hearing him say, "Here, Georgie, would you like to have this? Put it in your purse with the doodlebugs."

Had he taken leave of his senses? What kind of a stupid idiot was he anyway? After she'd indignantly picked up her fallen black ladies' hat, Georgina sat back down in a huff and stared at her breakable plate of food on the Formica table in front of her. She wanted to shrink away into nothing. She wanted to vanish into nothingness. She wanted to crawl into her black velvet purse with its short brass handle, and become one of the doodle bugs' family members. Being part of her own family felt like too hard a thing to be. Feelings began to well up inside of her that she had never really known before. So, this is what it feels like to be plain furious like Katrina Josephina got when she threw a whooper of a fit?

Looking across at her breakable plate an idea came over her. She just wanted to pick it up and throw the whole darn thing straight onto the floor and break every single bit of that ceramic plate into sharp little broken pieces. She wasn't hungry anymore. She wanted to scatter that stupid chicken dinner everywhere she possibly could. And she even wanted to smear the smashed buttery potatoes all over the diner's dumb old ugly avocado green walls. Sitting there beneath her giant black hat, she wished that she could just disappear forever.

How do you regain your shattered and splintered dignity in a situation like that? An unusual silence pervaded everywhere around her. Her mind was spinning. The twins weren't singing anymore. They stared at their big sister in dazed amazement. Even that little squirt, Roger Eugenio had stopped sucking his thumb in between bites of smashed potatoes, and his bright, blue eyes were watching her with a worried sideways glance.

Then Katrina started chattering again about something inane, but which was of paramount importance to the four-year-old. Everyone in the restaurant resumed their conversations again. Georgina's feelings were bruised and nobody really seemed to care. She realized that brushes with certain death, like her daddy had up on that dark misty mountain after his plane got caught in fog, and like she'd just had with that nasty old sharp stuck-in-her-throat chicken bone, meant nothing to them. George sat there, partly hidden beneath her huge dark hat, trying to compose herself and recapture her fragile dignity. Though she didn't look up, she just knew that everyone in the restaurant was still staring at her, and her alone; probably thinking about her red underwear and laughing to themselves like the boys standing underneath her on the playground had laughed.

Then Gretchen Gabriella started to pat Georgina on her back, very very softly, saying, "Are you all right, Georgie?" in that endearing little voice of hers. Tears welled up in Georgina's eyes, in a way that sometimes only kindness can release them. Her little sister's concern had touched her heart. But Georgina Jane stubbornly refused to let the tears fall. The situation was embarrassing enough without causing a further scene by crying like a baby about it.

When they had all finished their lunch, carefully chewing every single bite, like Mommy said to, her father went up to the cashier to pay for their fried chicken dinners. Holding out a quarter in-between his thumb and pointer finger, he said to the young lady behind the counter, "I'll flip you, double or nothing."

The lady shyly smiled at Daddy, not knowing how to answer him. With her Southern drawl, she said, "Ah bedda not, Suh."

Everyone was still in shock from the scene with the girl who had the chicken bone stuck in her throat. It was like they had never even seen cherry red underwear in their whole lives! Why didn't they take those bones out of children's chicken? Why was the world so crazy? Why was eating lunch, so unsafe? So dangerous? Why did people have to stare at a little girl's red underwear? Red underwear blazing like a red cherry? Red panties as crimson as a little girl's face?

The twins by then had forgotten her ordeal and were noisily attacking a glass gumball machine over by the cash register. Repeatedly opening up and slamming shut the metal slot where the gumballs came out, fighting to see who got the first piece of gum. Their elbows were poking straight out and they were poking each other in the ribs, each one more emphatic than the other about getting the first gumball in their favourite color. Getting the wrong color gumball from the penny machines was a disaster and could mean even louder arguments between them were sure to ensue.

"I get first turn!"

"No, me!"

"No, me first!"

"I want the green one!"

"I want the pink one!"

"If the green one comes out and it's your turn, you have to give it to me, Gretchen! Green's my very best color in the whole wide world!"

"No, I don't, either, Trina! Pink is **my** very best color in the whole wide world, and you never ever give it to me! So, I'm not sharing mine with you! You have to take the one you get! Not mine! I'm not sharing my very own gum ball with you no matter what color it is."

The idea of loud noises and other peoples' nerves being jangled, had never occurred to those twin sisters of hers. The term 'post-traumatic stress' wouldn't be popularly coined for decades. And if it had been used way back then, those twins wouldn't have given a darn. Colored gum balls were one of the most important things in the whole wide world to them.

"Can we have a penny, Daddy? Can we have some pennies? Give us some pennies, please!" This was said as though her very life depended upon it. As though the world would end tomorrow if Gretchen didn't get Daddy's pennies and get the first turn at the colorful and enticing glass gum ball machine. Those twin girls said the same dumb things over and over again. They jammed their chubby little covetous fists down deep into Daddy's pants pockets, trying to rob him blind. He was wearing civilian clothes on the trip, not the army's stiff ones in their pea-green-soup color.

He was happy. He was free. He was trying to act like he was a man all on his own in the world. He seemed oblivious to their gestures of over-possessiveness of what was his spare change, which he kept in his pockets. Nothing could ruffle his feathers. Even if his eldest child had nearly choked to death on that chicken bone, and those two female brats were invading his private space, he pretended that he didn't even notice, was not at all concerned. He was trying to act as though he had no dependants.

He was trying to act as though he had no wife either. He winked flirtatiously at the female cashier. He found pretty women much more preferable to his motley crew of over-tired youngsters at that moment. So he did what he always did in such situations. He flirted. He winked. He batted his eyelids enticingly. The woman behind the counter was blushing.

Ignoring his daughters, he said to the bashful young blond cashier, as casually as if he were asking for the time of day, "Want to buy some little kids cheap?"

The lady looked at Daddy and laughed out loud. But she didn't say a word or wink back at him. Her face was turning as red as Georgina's underwear. Usually, people around that part of the country said, "Howdy, ma'am," to Mother and, "Ya'll come back now, ya hear," to their customers. But that lady was just glad that choking Georgina and her noisy family were all finally leaving. The waitress just stuffed her hands into the pockets of her white cotton apron and stared at the O'Shaughnessy clan as they left. Speechless.

The Next Leg of the Journey

When they were all back in the car, with that charm of his still going strong, Daddy put his arm around his wife and said to Mother, "It's a bit out of the way, but let's spend the night in Hot Springs, okay, sweetheart? We've all had a hard day, and it will be good to take a break before we get to Texas. What do you say, kids, want to go to Hot Springs, Arkansas and play in the warm water?"

"Yeah!" came the unanimous response. And so, their next destination was decided. Making their way up through the south-eastern side of the state of Arkansas, they headed for Hot Springs National Park.

Lunch had tired Georgina out, and her throat still hurt. It was very sore from where that chicken bone had been stuck. She decided to sleep in the cozy bed made up in the back of the station wagon. And so, with little Roger settled down next to her, patting her on the back while he sucked his slippery brown thumb, she began to doze off as she sucked her own thumb. In times of stress, thumbs could be pretty useful things to have.

Katrina Josephina and Gretchen Gabriela sat in the middle seat and sang songs about the *'Farmer in the Dell'*, *'Round and Round the Mulberry Bush the Monkey Chased the Weasel'* and *'The Yellow Rose of Texas'*, along with a few Mitch Miller songs that their daddy had taught them. *'Tra-la la Boom de Aye'* and *'Roll out the Barrel, We'll have a Barrel of Fun'* were their very favourites.

Georgina vaguely remembered counting to nearly a hundred before she fell asleep listening to that barrel song. She dreamt that she was in a deep valley and that barrels, barrels, barrels were tumbling down on her from every side. Everywhere she looked in her dream, those wooden barrels just kept rolling, rolling, rolling towards her like waves. Barrels just kept coming and coming and coming – down on top of her. There was no escape in her dream from those barrels surrounding her like mounted armies of invading hordes about to descend upon her inside of her sleeping mind's eye.

She awoke in a strange bed. Daddy had carried her in from the back of the station wagon at about 7.00 the evening before. She couldn't remember him lifting her, his carrying her. Mother said to just let her sleep in her blue and white checked seersucker dress. So that's what she woke up in, not exactly remembering how she had gotten into a bed in a place before unknown to her. It was a cabin in a shady, leafy cul-du-sac, separated from the other identical huts in the same compound. A tiny veranda skirted the front of it, where Gretchen Gabriella and Katrina Josephina were already sitting outside, straddling the veranda's wooden railings, their bare feet dangling off the porch's containment. They were proudly wearing their brand new, never-been-worn swimming suits. Both girls' costumes were aqua colored with tiny pink rosebuds appliquéd to their low-cut necklines.

Georgina's new suit was laid out on the bed beside her. She knew that meant that she was supposed to put it on. An over-skirt was next to the swimming costume. Mother had made it, a complicated pleated pattern in lavender and baby blue fabric –her two favourite colors in the whole wide world. Her swimming suit was a different color to the twin's suits. Hers was deep lavender with paler lavender appliquéd rosebuds on her neckline. Mother had made the skirts to modestly cover her daughters' thighs to and from the pool. The twins hadn't put their skirts on yet. Modesty wasn't as important to four-year-olds as it was to their six-year-old sister.

So that next morning of their trip, after a breakfast of milk and cereal eaten in new-fangled miniature individual cereal boxes from the assortment which Daddy had bought from the corner grocery, and which he proudly displayed for them; time was spent in hot swimming holes next to their motel, having water fights with her daddy and twin sisters. And after a few hours of fun, splashing each other to let out any frustration, her father loaded them all back into the car, for one last leg of the journey.

Georgina felt happy because Mother had let her wear her new purple seersucker pedal pushers and a crisp white sleeveless cotton blouse that she buttoned all by herself, instead of a summer dress.

"We'll stop at the next town and have lunch, okay kids?" said her father.

A chorus of cheers went up from the back seat. It's hard to sit still when you are small. For some reason, it's easier for big people to sit still longer, maybe because they weigh more and that holds them still. But when you are a little person, you just want to jiggle about all of the time, especially at bedtime, that's when you want to wiggle the most. Holding still for a child, is like being put into a straightjacket to an adult.

After an active, tiring morning in the pools, and now in the car, the twins were beginning to get restless and crabby, bickering about any little thing. Mother told them, "Behave yourselves. Please be good, girls. Daddy's trying to drive. If you keep fighting like that, you might make him crash the car. And that wouldn't be nice, would it?"

But the twins didn't care. They had never even been in a car wreck. They didn't know anything at all about broken bones from car crashes. So they just kept bickering in the back seat of the car. Mother told Katrina Josephina she was acting like a 'crabapple', but that girl didn't even care one bit. She kept her tormenting of Gretchen up because she was frustrated, and knew that that was the only way she could annoy her parents enough to get what it was she wanted – freedom from the confines of the car's back seat. She took her frustration out on Gretchen, who was seated next to her, tapping her twin lightly on the shoulder just to annoy her and to get a rise out of her.

"Keep your hands to yourself, Trina Josephina!"

"You stay on your side of the car, Gretchen Gabbiella!"

"I **am** on my side of the car, you dough-dough!"

"You are not!"

"I am so!"

"Are not!"

"I am so, but you're bugging me on purpose, you ugly muchacha-girl!"

"You smell."

"You're ugly!"

"You're the ugly one, poo-poo-head!"

"Fea! Fea! Fea!"

"Cut it out, girls! Daddy's trying to drive the car. Silencio! Quiete sus bocas, muchachas! Immediatamente! Do you hear me?" roared their extremely angry father.

"We better stop for a potty stop," said Mother, "and get some gasoline. It looks like we're almost out of gas."

It annoyed Daddy that Mother acted like she was in charge and bossed him around, like he didn't know the needs of his own family or automobile. Mommy had to be in control. Mommy needed to be in charge in their family. Mommy had to be humoured. If Mommy didn't get her way, Daddy would never hear the end of it. So, he looked for the closest place to fill up with gasoline and to let the kids go to the bathroom. Georgina had been happily occupied, playing with her new surprises for the trip. After the potty stop, she now sat in the middle of Roger Eugenio and Katrina Josephina in order to keep the peace for Daddy. Sweet little Gretchen had moved to the middle of the front seat with their mother and father after her argument with her twin. Peter Martin, the baby, now six months old, sat on Mother's lap, perky as ever. Gretchen started to rub the baby's head ever so gently. And the wee baby boy started to fall asleep, nodding off so slowly that it was almost imperceptible. Until he reached the land of Nod itself, he fought against his own weariness. Travelling was exhausting. His long eyelashes fluttered against the tide of dreamland, but to no avail. Gretchen had a calming effect on everyone in their family, with the exception of Katrina Josephina, who was her nemesis and other half, both at the same time. All of that head-rubbing of hers was having its desired effect.

Georgina had to *'keep the little children happy'* for her father, so that he could *'concentrate on his driving'*. Her parents were always giving her a job to do. They thought it would be good for her. Although she tried to be patient with those *'little children'*, they wouldn't do one single little thing she said. They wouldn't mind her one little bit. Even though Daddy said that she was *'in charge'* of those little kids, it still didn't matter. What she really wanted, was to be an only child. Georgina knew about the concept of *'only'* children. Sometimes it seemed like a very good idea to her.

Some of the kids in her first-grade class had been *'only'* children. They didn't seem to mind it. At least Georgina never got the impression that it bothered them. She thought that *'only'* children must have an easy life. They could read whenever they wanted to. Their minds could go exploring and make-believing to their hearts content, and no one would interrupt them. No one would say, "Tag! You're it!" and go running off. Katrina Josephina always said, "Nanny, nanny, boo boo! You can't catch me!" in her most exaggerated whining tone of voice. That annoyed Georgina immensely. Katrina Josephina was always interrupting her train of thought. Only children could play with their dolls whenever they wanted to, and no one would pester them. It must be easier being an only child than to have all of this responsibility keeping so many *'little children happy and quiet'*.

It wasn't easy to keep them *'happy'* either. And it was impossible to keep them quiet. Katrina Josephina kept asking when it was going to be her turn to sit in the front seat and that was annoying Georgina's father. That sister of hers must not understand what *'after lunch'* meant! And Katrina Josephina had a bad habit of asking the same questions over and over again in such a grumbling and annoying tone of voice. No wonder her dad was starting to sound fed up. Pretty soon he would probably be mad at all of them. Georgina hated that. But that bratty girl, Katrina Josephina, just didn't care if she got on his nerves or not. Didn't she even know about plane crashes and all of his cuts and things? That girl was turning Daddy into a nervous wreck! She might even make him crash the family's new black and white station wagon if she didn't stop that snivelling of hers.

Finally, after what seemed like an eternity to the children, her father pulled up at another roadside filling station for gas. The car was beginning to stink. Someone had farted and everyone in their car could smell it. All of the children had to have potty stops, except for Roger Eugenio who was still wearing diapers. He and Peter Martin got their diapers changed. The girls thought their baby brothers' *'ka ka'* was disgusting and said so in groans and other revolted sounds while they held their noses, but stared anyway. How could her mother stand changing those smelly pungent diapers? She must love those baby brothers of Georgina Jane's a lot. Whenever Daddy changed smelly diapers, he always tied a clean one over his face, like he was a masked bandit. Daddy hated the smell of ka ka diapers. They made him gag. So usually, Mother had the job of changing smelly diapers. She didn't gag as much.

After paying the attendant, Daddy came back to the car. "There's a park just around the corner, so we can go and have a picnic, okay kids? Would you like to get out of the car and run around for a little while? I think that they even have a playground there."

"Yeah! Yeah!" said her excited sisters and her little brother Roger. Roger Eugenio just mimicked his sisters. He didn't even know what 'yeah!' meant yet. But because his big sisters said 'yeah!', that little kid said 'yeah!' too, whether he knew what the word meant or not.

They were only five hours away from her grandparents' house, but her dad thought that it would be a good idea for the children to have the lunch Mother had packed in their family's woven wicker picnic basket, which they took everywhere they went. It seemed like that wicker basket came along for every trip – short or long. Mother always filled it with such good things to eat. It was like the woman's sort of portable kitchen. They needed to eat, but did they have to go to a playground? Georgina thought that it was a bad idea. She didn't say so, but what she really wanted to do was to just get to her grandparents' house as soon as possible. But those little kids, they needed to get tired out, so that they would take a nap in the back of the car and leave Daddy in peace. They could sleep comfortably in the nest of pillows and blankets. Her father thought that it would be a good idea if the *'little children'* had a nap after lunch in the back of the car. He was probably right.

At least that Katrina Josephina would stop bugging him, and asking if she could sit in the front seat for the millionth time. He probably didn't want that kid in the front seat with all of that whining that she did. And when her dad said the *'little kids'* needed a nap, Georgina knew that he didn't mean a nap for her. She was too big for naps. She could have the whole back seat to herself and read her new book about Curious George, the monkey from Africa, where lots of dark people still lived. All of the children in Africa had mostly dark skin and ate lots of bananas like Curious George did. With the little kids asleep, nobody would disturb her train of thought. And that was something to look forward to.

Up High in a Swing

The car pulled into the gravel parking lot adjoining the park and the children scrambled out of the car as fast as their legs would carry them. Could they go on the swings? Who would get the first turn on the tetter-totter? They ran to the playground equipment full speed ahead. Katrina Josephina and Gretchen Gabriela tried to sit on both sides of the teeter-totter at once. Some stranger, who was watching his own kids swing at the park, lifted Katrina Josephina, who had yelled her head off because Gretchen Gabriela had straddled the teeter-totter first. Georgina always thought that they made teeter-totters too high for little children. That man had to lift her sister up and over the other side of the teeter-totter, until she was high up in the air.

Katrina Josephina had screamed bloody murder, "Let me on! Let me on! Let me on!" in her most blood-curdling yell. Anything to get attention. So that man had to do something to shut that screaming girl up. He was trying to have a nice time at the park with his own little girls, who were much more well-behaved than that bratty sister of hers. It was embarrassing to be part of such a family, with a sister like that. But Katrina was oblivious to any embarrassment. She could have cared less! The opinion of her family members held little sway over her; so what if she annoyed complete strangers? That girl squealed with delight as her bottom bounced on the teeter-totter. She was always happy when she got her way. Georgina just knew that Katrina Josephina would start screaming again, once her father called them all to lunch. There was no way that brat would want to get off that teeter-totter now that she was happily settled on her side of it. They had to play quickly; soon it would be lunchtime.

Her mother was still holding Peter Martin, who had fallen asleep on her lap in the front seat of their car, long before seat belts and baby car seats became routine. His beautiful dark-haired sleepy head rested on her mother's shoulder. The nurses at the hospital in Kentucky where he was born just adored that kid. They thought he was so handsome with that mop of jet-black hair and those long baby side-burns of his and his extraordinary eyelashes. So, they nicknamed him 'Elvis Presley'.

Daddy was getting the picnic basket out of the car. Her mother was trying to jostle Peter Martin into a comfortable position, without waking him up; while she got the red checkered table cloth out of the back of the car. Proper dining always included a tablecloth back then, even for picnics.

Roger Eugenio, Mr. Independent, didn't think that he needed watching or holding hands. Georgina had tried to hold his hand, but he squirmed unceasingly in his little frustrated, uptight fashion. And then he arched his back angrily, so that he could make his getaway, pulling hastily away from his big sister's extended hand. There was no way R.E. would ever be still, or walk slowly. That boy had been a fast crawler, and he had never even learned to walk. He only ran, ran, ran from the very beginning of his days of mobility; as fast as he could move those scrawny lower limbs of his. There were places to go and mischief to get into. He wasn't about to let his big sister cramp his style. He went running off as fast as his skinny brown legs would carry him, every time he got the chance. There was no stopping that little kid. So, they called him *'Speedy Gonzalez'*, after Grandmother's side of the family. That was her name before Granny knew Georgina's grandfather, who was half of an Indian and half of an Irishman.

Mother, who had gently laid the sleeping baby, Peter Martin, into the baby buggy, was carefully spreading the red and white checkered tablecloth on the picnic table. Daddy was stretching his back with his hands clasped and his arms held high over his head. She could see her father from way up high up in the air where she was on her whizzing, zooming, flying swing. On the one vacant swing, Georgina was going higher and higher. All was well in the world. She was up with the birdies in flight. The girl wanted to go over the tops of the neighbouring houses in flight. She wanted to rise above all of her family and she wanted to fly! Back and forth! Up and down! She pushed her legs forwards and backwards faster and faster and faster so that she would go even higher and higher and higher!

She was on the verge of actually flying off in her imagination on her swing. Then she caught, out of the corner of her eye, her little brother, Roger Eugenio. R.E. had been happily playing on the ground next to the swing set with the dirt, grabbing handfuls of it and throwing it over and onto his head. But he wasn't on the ground anymore. There he was, taking off and running at top speed. When she looked down from her heights, she saw that kid had sprouted wings and taken flight. Flight into danger. He was *'up and at 'em'* as Daddy would say.

That crazy kid is going to hurt himself. He is really going to get hurt, she thought to herself. And she was right. That was when it happened. Roger Eugenio ran straight into the bottom of one of the wooden swings that the man's little girls were swinging on. The hard wood on that swing's seat clipped the boy on the right side of his forehead, making a dull thumping sound as it did so, and leaving behind a sudden rush of blood streaming into her little brother's right eye. A loud, short, sharp bellow followed.

Georgina, in that instant, before Roger Eugenio's small brown head collided with the man's little girl's swing, had thought, *Oh no*, wanting to help her brother. She wanted to, but she couldn't fly off of her own swing and carry that little kid to safety in time, away from the swing she knew was about to swing into him and hit him hard in the head. Away from pain. Away from bleeding. Away from cuts scaring him for life.

Almost as soon as it happened, there was her father, cradling Roger in his arms, frantically trying to calm his son, who was so out of breath that he couldn't even utter another sound. All of the wind had been knocked out of him and there was blood spurting, pouring and gushing from a long gaping cut on his brown forehead. Daddy was saying, "*Mi hito. Mi hito. Mi hito,*" as though his heart was bleeding too. The swing had actually lifted her little brother up off of the ground and when he fell back to earth, he had hit the ground with a thud. She was in shock. She thought, *I didn't 'keep the little kid happy'. I'll be in trouble now.* So, she ran as fast as she could to the car to get a clean diaper so that Daddy could wrap R.E.'s head up to stop the bleeding.

To make matters worse, Katrina Josephina decided at that very moment to see what the commotion that she wasn't the center of, was all about. So, with her side of the teeter totter now settled on the ground for a brief moment, she decided to disembark from the see-saw. This left Gretch suspended high up in the air on her side of the precarious playground equipment. Momentary suspension collapsed into a quick and violent thump onto the hard ground, leaving the girl dazed and in shock. Her instant response was to begin hysterical shrieking at the very top of her young, but powerful lungs. Her baby teeth had clattered together with the violent fall to earth. A cut on her lower lip was not deep, but she had already swallowed some of her own blood and obviously hated the salty taste of it.

Georgina Jane saw it all. Pandemonium had broken out in their family in a matter of seconds. The lovely picnic her parents had planned was over before it had even begun. Until they got to her grandparents' house, everything else was just a blur in her mind. The only thing she could remember was, because of all of the dirt he had covered himself with before the swing crash, that Roger Eugenio's little brown face was filthy dirty. It was clean only in the places where his tears had made brackish streaks down the sides of his cheeks. There were grimy muddy rivulets from the residue of his tears, shock and hysterics covering his grubby brown cheeks. Mother was so embarrassed about having such a filthy child out in public like that. She said that it was a disgrace.

Daddy said that the kid had been screaming bloody murder in the hospital. He said that the boy wouldn't hold still, so he had to hold his son's fragile cut-up head for the doctors. Georgina heard every word he said. And so, as she looked down at Roger Eugenio, now back beside her, she felt sick inside. She felt guilty as sin. She felt responsible. She felt that she should have held his hand no matter what, instead of going up in her swing like that. She felt that it was all her fault that R.E. was cut and hurt.

Her brother's small fragile head was now bandaged like the turban of some whirling dervish. He slept in-between his sobs all the way to her grandparents' house. They never did have a family picnic at the park that day. They had to eat their lunch in the car with her anxious fretful mother, while they waited for the little crying kid with a swattled head and a big stitched-up gash on his forehead to emerge from the Emergency Room exit, carried by the newly promoted off-duty captain, who had frantically disappeared with his bundle what seemed like an eternity before. Her father had to transport Roger Eugenio into the hospital in his arms. Daddy had to hold her little squirming brother's twisting head still while the doctors stitched the kid's forehead back together.

On the Road Again

After they left, her parents were absolutely silent all the way from the hospital to her grandparents' house. Nobody was singing and the radio was switched off. The only sound was the car motor's humming. She knew that the children had to be silent too. Tension was a tangible substance then. Fortunately, Katrina Josephina and Gretchen had fallen asleep on the bed in the back of the station wagon almost at once. Roger Eugenio was in the backseat, his head nestled on a pillow up against her side, next to her lap. He was beginning to fall asleep, whimpering as he did so.

Baby Peter Martin, usually a good baby, was a bit fussy and Mother had to change his wet diaper smelling of ammonia again and give him another bottle of baby formula to settle him down. Finally, everyone was seated in the car. Her father, who usually sang to them as he drove, was completely speechless from his experience in the hospital with her little brother. He stared straight ahead at the highway as though he was mesmerised, driving without thinking. Daddy was like a robot driver, going through the motions.

Granny's Bloomers and Daddy Goes Missing

When they got to her grandparents' house, who had been telephoned from the hospital, by her traumatised and very upset father, the girls were ushered into the backyard to play. They were told, "Be good girls. Don't be too noisy. Don't fight with each other. Try to behave. Daddy and Mommy aren't feeling well," by Grandmother.

Georgina didn't like the sound of that comment. Didn't Grandmother understand that Georgina Jane was a young lady and that young ladies didn't fight? Didn't Grandmother know that Georgina was above that kind of rowdy behaviour? Didn't Grandmother know that Daddy and Mommy weren't allowed to not feel well? After Grandmother shut the screen door, she sat on the back steps feeling frustrated, sad and alone. She'd had enough of those twins by then.

She sat there on the back porch thinking to herself as she stared at her grandmother's billowing knee-length underwear hanging from the old woman's clothesline. Her grandmother sure wore big underwear. It was the biggest pair of underwear that Georgina had ever seen in her whole life! It looked more like a pair of see-through, gauzy pedal pushers, than underwear. George thought of her own embarrassment because of everyone seeing her new red underwear with the special hearts sewn on them at lunch the day before. She thought that was probably the worst day of her whole life. But today seemed nearly as bad as yesterday. Maybe if she wore such long underwear, like Grandmother wore, it wouldn't be so embarrassing to be turned upside down and to be exposed to the whole wide world in the process. Maybe Granny had the right idea wearing those long gauzy modest *bloomers* of hers.

Grandmother told Georgie that those were her 'bloomers'. Those *bloomers* came all the way down to Granny's knees! Seeing her Granny's *bloomers* hanging on the clothesline made George smile, but just for a minute. She realized that she'd had enough of looking at Granny's fluttering *bloomers* and enough of watching those little children. She didn't feel like trying to make them behave any more. It was an impossible job anyway. She wondered where her father was. Amelia Bloomer meant nothing to her at that moment of her budding feminist thought life. *Bloomers* were only funny for a minute. Now she was thinking of her father.

Daddy had been so quiet after taking her little brother, Roger Eugenio, to the hospital. Too quiet. The man had hardly said a word all the way to her grandparents' house. And that was a long way for him to drive and not say a word. Was her daddy all right now? Was he resting or sleeping? Taking a little nap? Georgina felt that she had to go and find him. Find him right now. Right that very minute. She wanted to check on Roger Eugenio too, and see if he was still whimpering.

Quietly opening the back screen door, trying to keep it from squeaking on its rusting hinges, she crept back into the house. She didn't want to attract any attention, and be told off, or made to go into the backyard like a dog put outside from his owner's house. She resented being treated like some kind of difficult little kid. Her mother was occupied in the kitchen talking to Grandmother. She was feeding Peter Martin, who was squealing with delight as mouthfuls of smooshed-up baby food was shovelled into his hungry, opened mouth. That baby didn't understand about their family's trauma. He was happy no matter what. He lived in his own little baby world and reminded her of a noisy, chirping baby bird, smacking his little pink puckered lips, eating what looked like something the color of regurgitated worms. He was surrounded by people who adored him, thought that he hung the moon.

She could hear Granny's new electric washing machine twirling in the background, washing all of the ka ka out of the babies' diapers. Her grandmother was so proud of that washer. She wouldn't let anyone else in the family even touch it, much less use it. Olivia O'Shaughnessy had grown up Olivia Gonzalez, from a big family; where she, like Georgina, was the eldest of a lot of siblings. But when Granny was a little girl, she didn't just have to fold diapers, like Georgina did. Granny had to hand wash them, and a lot of other clothes, in a wash tub with a metal scrub board and lye soap that made her girlish hands go red. That's why Granny loved Avon's yellow hand lotion so much. She never wanted to get red hands again in her whole life.

Before World War II, Granddaddy bought his wife a new electric washing machine with a wringer attached to it, to wring the washed clothes dry. But now, his businesses were doing so well that he purchased a brand-new spin washer from Sears and Roebuck Department Store. Granny still insisted on hanging her washing out to dry, but she loved that new labour-saving washer. It sure was noisy, though, especially during the spin cycle.

Roger Eugenio was sound asleep on the sofa. Granny had somewhat roughly, but carefully, washed the kid's face before rocking him emphatically back and forth in her platform rocking chair to get him to go back to sleep. He was making tiny moaning noises in his sleep, sighing softly to himself. Her old granddaddy was next to R.E., and he was asleep on his special brand new green reclining chair that he was so proud of, with the day's open newspaper spread over his face. He didn't seem worried about anything, snoring noisily underneath the paper which hid his face and torso from her. Only the man's droopy brown arms hung out in plain view, dangling by his sides in limp response to his wheezing fluttering breathing. Glorianna, her grandparents' eleven-year-old adopted daughter, was away at summer camp, and wouldn't be back until next week.

No one saw Georgina sneak in through the creaking back screen door. She was a girl on a mission. She was looking for her father. She crept around and searched the house for him. She looked in all of the lonely empty beds in her grandparent's house, but there was no Daddy anywhere. She looked out the front window and saw their black and white station wagon parked in her grandparents' driveway. Her daddy wasn't unloading suitcases from the car. No one was out by their car. Where was her daddy? She couldn't find him anywhere. He wasn't in bed, even though her Granny said that he *'wasn't feeling well'*. Wasn't that where people who didn't feel well stayed? In their beds? When she had not felt well because of getting the chicken's pox, she had stayed in bed for nearly a week reading *'Little Lulu'* comic books. Where was her daddy? Georgina was beginning to feel frantic inside. Silently, she crept around the empty quiet rooms of her grandparent's house. No Daddy anywhere. A feeling of worry and despair was engulfing her.

Then she heard it. A faint, breathless sound was coming from someplace out of sight. It was a funny, muffled sort of vibration. It was coming from the room she knew used to be her father's room, before he was her daddy and she was his little girl. She could hear something. It was an energetic intonation that sent a shiver down her spine. Still, she couldn't find him. She couldn't see her father. It didn't sound like any sound her daddy would make. That weird haunting noise was coming from inside of the closet. The closet door was tightly shut. What could that noise be? Slowly, she opened the closet door where the frantic blubbering cry was coming from.

There, against the back wall in the closet was her father. The girl saw him plain as day. He was sobbing. His was a lamentation of quick breathless sounds, in his effort to take in big gulps of air. It was almost like he had a chicken bone caught in his throat. Her daddy was breaking down, in rapid, gasping agitation, swallowing eagerly, at a loss for air. He was finally releasing all of the pent-up tension and emotion he had held in so tightly while he drove their black and white Pontiac station wagon to his parents' house in San Antonio, Texas. Back to his safe and sound port-a-call. His homeport.

Having stayed quiet for all of those unhappy hours, he now vomited out all of his anxiety in his secret wailing sobs. That's why he had been so quiet in the car, he was afraid that he would start weeping in front of her mother and his children. His face was turned to the wall. That wasn't like him. Her daddy, tough as brass, was a cry baby. Georgina could see that the skin on his face and neck was redder than usual. He didn't see her or hear her open the closet door. His face was turned towards the wall, away from her.

The girl just stood there staring at her father, listening to his distressing sounds of intense agony. Her father sounded just like a little child, breaking down bit by bit. Piece after piece of his sad heart falling away from himself. He was breathless. In the midst of a heart-breaking wail, he was trying to catch his breath, but unable to keep up with himself, his own breathing getting the better of him. She realized then, that even though they seemed tough and strong, Daddies were breakable, like those ceramic plates in the chicken restaurant. Adults must really be big kids in a kind of over-sized disguise. It was a concept that was really, really hard to take in.

Children vicariously experience their parents' pain, even when their parents try to hide it from them. Feelings find their own way out, even if they are hidden under hats or in closets, like she had concealed her embarrassment underneath that big black hat that her mother had given to her, and like her daddy had swallowed his anxieties by sitting silently in the car after they left the hospital. The girl's emotional sensibilities never allowed her the luxury of being out of touch with the needs of the people in her family. She was not an only child. Sometimes, she realized, even her parents seemed like children to her; children who still needed a lot of care.

The subconscious inner-connectiveness of their souls permeated her young heart at that moment. And somehow, she felt responsible for all of them, even for her mother and her father, who acted like they were always in control, always looking after the needs of their family. They tried hard to act like, because they were big people, they didn't have all of the same needs that little people did. The girl knew now that Mommy and Daddy only pretended to be all right.

She knew that she had to take care of them. Her father's pain, his tears, his anguish compounded her own worry. She was still worried about all of those places on her father's skin where he had been cut when he crashed the army's mean old airplane. Those cuts were healed over, but still those dark slashes looked like mean old jagged stains on her father's skin. She would stare at those relatively fresh marks on her father's face and arms, and she'd wonder about the pain he must have suffered when his plane flew into that big old foggy mountain. As the years went by, he kept saying, in jest, whenever the child questioned him about those terrible marks that hurt her to look at, "Big mean Indian got me with his spear," thinking that somehow Georgina would be comforted by that thought, rather than by facing the truth of what he'd lived through in that terrible night.

But standing there, peering into the dark closet in her grandparents' house, where her father had secreted himself away from all eyes and ears, thinking his pain was unknown to his children, she knew that he had shed what he mistakenly thought were concealed tears. Wretchedness and agony, brokenness and sorrow were impermissible. These were feelings which one had to closet away, so as not to burden the little ones, his wife, nor his parents with them. His Mama and Papa wouldn't see his distress if he hid away in his old closet. Even his wife could not bear this. Anyway, she had her hands full with his five little kids. A child might crack-up if she knew, if she knew of his true feelings of despair.

But it was too late now. Georgina had seen her father in his clandestine meeting with his own misery. With her very own eyes, she had stood there so still and quietly as she watched him cry. She had heard it all pouring out of him with her own ears. Her instincts that her father was upset, even though he had said little or nothing in the car were right. His pent-up emotions could remain disguised for only so long. The girl wondered why there was such shame in crying that her daddy had to hide his tears in such an odd place as the back of his old closet, a closet that smelled of mothballs and was mostly filled now with Granny's winter dresses and coats?

Gretchen had hollered out in anger and shock when Katrina Josephina leapt off of the tetter-totter so nonchalantly, giving her twin sister a bloody lip. Roger Eugenio had bellowed loudly in pain, as loud as he could yell after he caught his breathe, when that girl's wooden swing had collided with his forehead. Like

82

some cruel bludgeon, that child's swing had whacked the side of Roger Eugenio's forehead.

Now that little kid was swathed in a soft white gauzy comforting turban, whimpering to himself in his sleepy state. But where was the comfort for her father? Who, except for his daughter, noticed his pain?

Just then, her daddy turned around, sensing her presence. His tears were almost spent, his sobbing beginning to subside. His alarm and embarrassment were evident when he saw his daughter standing there. How long had she been there? Had she seen his now chagrined performance? His closet drama?

"Go away, Georgina. Go away. Close the door and just go away. Please go away now. Do you hear me, young lady?"

He wanted to shroud the truth of his hurting feelings, the girl could see that.

Feelings must literally be kept behind closed doors. How on earth had she even found him? Better to say no more about it. Better to pretend he felt nothing, not even confess his embarrassment. It was an affront to his manhood to cry; especially in front of his child. His usual bravado was completely shattered now, making the whole upsetting episode even more traumatic.

The experience of holding Roger Eugene's little sandy brown head, watching his dark-skinned son who looked so similar to his own dad, but was barely more than an infant, writhe and cry out in pain as the doctors swabbed him, anesthetised him, and then stitched his tiny forehead back together, was what caused this bursting dam of emotion. It was a pain that the man felt in the depths of his very soul, and even his strong will could not mask nor suppress it. He'd known it was coming. Like some little kid needing to use the bathroom and hardly able to hold it. But he'd managed to hold it in. Hold it in until now. That's why he had hidden in those confines at the back of his pungently smelling closet, where he thought no one would ever find him. Where no one would ever see him.

Her concern rejected, Georgina Jane closed the closet door and regretfully left her father alone. Alone with his tears. Alone with his pain. His pique must be respected. She was subdued by obedience to his rulership over her, which was a bitter pill to swallow at that moment. But it was a glum state of affairs that the girl must accept. Her heart sank like a heavy stone deep down inside of her chest.

Not talking about feelings, especially feelings of raw, convulsing anguish was what was expected. She must accept this way of living, this way of disassembling and coping with feelings out of shame. She was learning about this idea the grown-ups had. Certain things could not be said. Certain things could not be acknowledged. Acknowledging them would only compound the emotional fracture and make it much worse. Exposing hurts to the air was unthinkable.

The realization of this hurt the girl. Her desire to care for her father's aching feelings was unimportant. She could see that now. As she closed the door, standing outside the closet, where her father couldn't see her, she stood very still, waiting to hear if more utterable heaviness escaped from her father's lips into the atmosphere of sound. Georgina could hear his heavy sighs. Sighs that could break her heart if she let them. Sighs that her father didn't want her to hear. A reticence to communicate honest feelings of despair, or agony, or grief, or some awful aching, was not natural to the little girl's heart.

But it was something that her father was trying to teach her, forcing her to learn. And she must learn about it, whether she liked it or not. She hated it. But that didn't matter. This masquerade, this concealment of the truth, not acknowledging or disclosing, always suppressing and stifling was a cruel fact of life. It was like a heavy stone in her heart. This burning scalding cup of galling deception, which in her child's mind was deficient of all reason and logic, was thrust into her small hands, and drink it she must.

The putrefying silence between the girl and her father existed long past this covert incident. It extended into the rest of her childhood, only to surface as a more mature haunting which followed into the years of inaudible quintessential moaning, where the unspoken became the ruling party of Georgina's heart; creating a profound life of its own in her soul. Georgina Jane was not ignorant; though she was forced to pretend to be. Her eyes were opened to what could not even be whispered about.

Like watching strange children in her class, rudely whispering, with their cupped hands over their mouths in the playground; excluding her from their intimate conversations, which were not for her ears; her father wanted to keep her in the dark, to draw a veil over his true feelings of what he saw as weakness; a weakness which must be hushed and kept from his family. Georgina saw her father's feelings as though they were personified. His feelings were like a small, crying child, who needed a pat on the back or on the head, or maybe a hug from a real friend, or a kiss from a mommy or a daddy or a granny to make them all better.

Maybe one of his army buddies in that song he sang so sadly about his long-lost buddy could make him feel better. Maybe that was what her daddy needed right now, a buddy. A buddy who could understand how his friend was feeling and make him all better. It made her feel so sad when she heard her father sing that song about his buddy. She missed Juanita too. She knew all about buddies. Buddies to be missed.

Nights are long since you went away.
I think about you all through the day.
My buddy, my buddy,
Your buddy misses you!

Miss your smile,
The touch of your hand.
I hope and know
That you'll understand
My buddy, my buddy,
Your buddy misses you.

Enchiladas Make It All Better

It was then that the voices of Georgina's mother and grandmother echoing through the house, beckoned her back to another reality. "Dinner's ready! Wash your hands! Come and get it!" The almost melodic, joyous voice of her grandmother rang out. The woman was unable to conceal her ecstasy that her only son, his wife and the kids were at her house. Georgie could hear it in the woman's rapturous voice: the happiness, the delight, the pleasure and the joy of her family's gathering. Granny was just happy to have her only son's whole family together for a meal and some time together. Life didn't get any better than this.

Georgina left her father in his closet. She went to the bathroom and washed her hands with a brand-new bar of her grandmother's perfumey pink Avon soap. Granny had opened it especially for her son, his wife, Claudia, and the grandchildren to use. It was guest soap, not every day white Ivory soap.

It was time to rejoin the rest of her family. Gretchen Gabriella and Katrina Josephina appeared in unison, like Granddaddy's magic, out of the back yard where they had been arguing about who would get to sit next to their beloved

85

Granddaddy at the dinner table. They liked the quiet aging grand-man; mostly because he had a seemingly endless pocket of sweets which he magically pulled out from behind their ears. He called them his *'las angelitas'*; not knowing how bad Katrina Josephina could really be. Angelic presence can be deceiving, especially to a doting grandfather. Even the devil can transform himself into an angel of light.

The girls had argued about who would go to bed later than the other one would go. Their heated discussion entailed the profound idea that frogs could jump higher than bunny rabbits. Disputation traversed the idea that parachutes might or might not break when they opened, causing those who used them when they jumped out of airplanes, to spill their blood and guts out all over the place where they landed.

Were cherry red jellybeans really better tasting than the black liquorice ones that turned your mouth black were? Could Gretchen Gabriella really sing louder than her twin? It was doubtful. Would Daddy really increase their weekly allowance from a dime a week to a quarter when they had their shared fifth birthday? They had debated the very essence of life itself: Who, after all, really loved Grandmother's enchiladas the very best of everyone in their whole family? It was a proposition for which no one knew the answer.

These important arguments were temporarily laid aside. And so, now in from their banishment to the back yard, with faces and hands visibly scrubbed with glistening clarity; the twins presented themselves for their participation in this family festivity. They sat on either side of Granddaddy, who sat at the head of the table. Gretchen Gabriella was to his left and Katrina Josephina by his right side. Side by his side, these girls were like two halves of the same piece of cloth, identical in appearance, their innate and very distinct personalities seemingly hidden from Granddaddy's view. But Georgina knew them by heart.

Looking across the table, glowering at Georgina, the question came, "Where've you been? You were supposed to stay in the back yard too."

Katrina Josephina wanted to know. How could her sister explain to this youngster the feelings of her heart? Their father's heart? Words failed her completely. Georgina just stared at the girl with a blank stare, meant to annoy and to silence. Katrina Josephina frowned back her disgust and displeasure at her elder sister's impertinence and audacity. But for once the girl kept silence. Georgina knew that Katrina's hushed state was only in order to impress

Granddaddy with a charade of pretending to be an angelic being, thus hoodwinking the family's favourite, and only, patriarch in the process.

As all of her family sat down at the dining room table, minus the sleeping boys, Roger Eugenio, still knocked out by the sedative given to him at the hospital, and Peter Martin snoozing on Granny and Granddaddy's big bed after his own feast of pureed, regurgitated baby worms; her father reappeared. His face now washed, and his redder than usual countenance now subdued of its virulence, thanks to Granny's buttery yellow Avon skin cream smeared over the rough spots. He looked humble, even unpretentious.

They all sat there in silence, their mouths watering, waiting with anticipation to savour Granny's delicious beef enchiladas, Spanish rice, pinto beans and soft homemade flour tortillas. The flour tortillas she kept warm by wrapping them in a damp, but clean dishrag and putting them in a shallow bowl. Pretty soon, they could smear great big globs of yummy butter all over them. Granny had even given the girls their own knives to use to do the job all by themselves. It was a real feast set before them, the aromatic fragrance permeating their collective nostrils.

With his head bowed, his hands folded and clasped together and his eyes closed, Granddaddy began his reverent speaking,

"Bless us, oh Lord,
and these thy gifts;
which we are about to receive,
through thy bounty,
through Christ our Lord. Amen."

The words of her grandfather's prayer faded. Georgina's mind was somewhere else. Back in the closet. Back inside the events of the day, which no one wanted to acknowledge. Taking a careful bite of her grandmother's profoundly scrumptious enchiladas, she felt the day's sorrow begin to lift off of her small six-year-old shoulders. Those enchiladas could lift the weight of the world from off of even Atlas himself.

Somewhat hesitantly, she looked steadily across the table at her father's face; now washed clean of his seemingly never existing and apparently long forgotten tears. There he was, bigger than life itself to her. There he was sitting across the table. There he was.

Her daddy, the tough army guy, who was always in control of himself and his family. He seemed at a loss for words. There he was, returning her staring look from across his mother's table. When he had caught her eye, he did what he always did in his seemingly never-ending succession of tough spots. He did the only thing he could do in the circumstance. He did the only thing he ever did, if he had to avoid difficult conversations. He did the most rational, logical, sensible thing he could think to do at that moment. He simply looked across the dinner table.

It was a table that was piled high with platters and breakable plates and bowls and cutlery and dishes and glasses and plastic jugs filled with Cool-Aid and serving utensils all laid out before him. It was a table lovingly filled with the plethora of aromatic Mexican dishes prepared by his mother who adored him, a mother who loved his family.

The man looked into the solemn face of his six-year-old daughter; a small sweet child's face that was gazing into his face with such an intensity that his emotions almost erupted and the floodgates of pain nearly opened again before he could even think of stopping them. She had already taken a bite of his Mama's enchiladas. But when she saw him staring at her, she had stopped chewing. Her tenderness touched him. And for a split second, the man thought that the flood of tears would all come pouring out of him again; producing an unleashing of the remainder of the submerged deluge he knew he still had hidden inside of him.

So wisely. Very wisely indeed. He did the smartest thing a hurting daddy can do in a tough situation like that. The man sighed. And then, he gathered all of the strength that he could find inside of himself; a self that felt insecure and somewhat worried about the future of himself, his family, and the world at large. He did the best, the smartest thing he knew to do in such a tight spot. He did the only thing to even consider doing in the state that he was in. He did not flounder.

He simply gazed into the searching, incisive and diminutive young face of his offspring. He simply looked into the eyes of his little girl. He looked into her eyes. He looked into her eyes without blinking. He looked into her eyes, and then he did what he always did. It was his way of saying that they shared a secret between them. It was his way of swearing her to his bond of secrecy. It was one of the things that he did best. In his daddy-kind of way, he knew how to bring her on-side. So, he put a forkful of Granny's enchiladas into his mouth. He let out a sigh. And then, he winked at her from across the table.

It was a teasing wink. It was a silencing wink. It was a wink to end all winks. He spoke volumes without saying a single word. Georgina hadn't taken her eyes off of his face for even a moment since he came into the dining room. She knew how to make her daddy feel better. And so, without pausing to think about it, she winked back at him. And it was at that moment, that very split second, that suddenly, all of the day's troubles lifted off of her father's shoulders and melted away into the cheese of his mother's enchiladas.

Chapter Three
North to Alaska

Mother and Granny

The malodorous smell had hit Claudia Jane O'Shaughnessy like a solid substance the instant she walked into the rickety old clapboard farmhouse where her in-laws and their adopted, eleven-year-old daughter, Glorianna, lived up on a hillside overlooking the outskirts of San Antonio. *How ghastly! How awful!* she had thought to herself, almost gagging on the spot. These were thoughts she whispered to her daughter, Georgina. "The fumes," she said, "were utterly revolting." The seething mass next to the kitchen sink was putrid beyond belief. "Welcome to Texas!"

"Yeah! Thank you very much! What a joyous welcoming sight!" she had said this privately to her daughter, Georgina. That was last night. This was the morning after the day before. This was the beginning of their stay with the child's grandparents. Mother couldn't believe it. Broth made of used chicken bones bubbled away on the stove. Her mother-in-law had actually collected her own, her husband's and her child's chicken bones. Bones from after they had eaten the meat off of the pieces of boiled, not fried or baked, chicken from their lunch the day before. Bones which had been inserted into the mouths of Claudia's in-laws and their odd little adopted girl (*'The girl'* Mother said Granddaddy called her.) Bones which were now being used to make a healing broth for Georgina and her parents and her siblings and grandparents. Mother was utterly disgusted with those bones. And since Georgina didn't much like chicken bones herself, she could fully understand and sympathise with her mother's feelings. Maybe her mother was right. Maybe Granny really was *'peculiar'*! They had just missed Georgina's young Aunt Glorianna, who had left for a two-week stint at summer's camp. The eleven-year-old was off to a summer camp sponsored by the Knights of Columbus. Glorianna was out in the sticks right now. Glorianna was camping, which she hated. She hated being away from home. Away from her mama and her papa, whom she loved so much. She would get back the day before Georgina left San Antonio to go to Alaska, just in time to say good-bye. Glorianna had left before Georgina and the rest of her family could see her. Grandmother had carefully packed a brown-bagged lunch and food from home for her adopted daughter to take with her to summer camp. In the bag was an array of goodies all wrapped up in wax paper or in tin cans. Included in this splendid take-away-to-camp-feast was nearly the whole entire contents of Grandmother's kitchen cabinet: tinned corn beef, two tuna fish sandwiches, a jar of Gerkin's bread and butter pickles in vinegar (Glorianna's favourite), one jar of Skippy peanut butter (smooth, not crunchy), one jar of Welsh's grape jelly (to add to the peanut butter sandwiches which all kids loved back then), a loaf of sliced white bread from their local Piggly Wiggly, a box of Granny's old Christmas cookies, left over from last Christmas (They were six or seven months old, but Granny kept them fresh by freezing them). And finally, twelve tamales which were homemade by Tia Tenchia, who was Grandmother's little fat brown skinned and brown eyed sister. Grandmother was creamy white colored, with grey blue eyes. Eyes like a partially cloudy and a partially sunny day all mixed together. Granny and Tia Tench looked like they were from opposite sides of the planet, not full-blooded sisters. Glorianna's Mama had fixed the three of them (herself, Grandaddy and Glorianna) boiled chicken, peas, boiled smelly cabbage, potato salad a la Olivia, which meant spicy with herbs, onion, chorizo and hot red chilli peppers. (The house still stunk to high heavens due to that awful, low-class, boiled cabbage. Mother felt that cabbage should only be used in coleslaw, and never, ever, boiled! Boiled cabbage was disgusting, she told Georgina! Only poor people ate boiled cabbage. Only school children had boiled cabbage with those awful school dinners. Smelly pale green boiled cabbage.) Now those picked-over, left-over, grey chicken bones with the gristle still on them, were bubbling away on Granny's kitchen gas stove with its blue flame and hot blazing gas flame, glowing away there underneath her old cooking pot, a relic from one of her many tias. The pot on the stove in their old white house on the hill in San Antonio, Texas. The kitchen counter was the repository of piled up rotting organic matter. Tea leaves, coffee grinds, apple cores, onion skins, garlic paper, banana peels, lemon rinds, remnants of cantaloupe and their hard rind-like skins, egg shells and corn husks all melded together into a putrid gloppy oneness. It was revolting. It

91

was a massive accumulation of decomposing, decaying matter, left to moulder next to the washed dishes. A small cracked and stained tea cup next to the rotting organic matter was full of tiny tomato seeds, watermelon seeds, cantaloupe seeds, longer withering slender marigold seeds and avocado stones being saved for the woman's vegetable and flower garden; almost ready to be planted outside.

Glorianna's Mama had given the girl a big family send-off to camp. With the special lunch she had fixed. And not in the habit of wasting food, lunch's chicken bones were used later to make the healing broth for her son, his wife and the nietos! Those grandchildren just loved Granny's homemade chicken and noodle soup, which the woman had already gotten them in the habit of eating when she stayed in Fort Campbell, Kentucky a few months prior to the brood's visit to her house on the hill overlooking the fields. Mother preferred chicken and rice soup. She said it tasted better than noodles.

The nauseating assemblage on top of some soggy yellowing newspaper was fusing together. The odour permeated the kitchen, overpowering everything else. It had disgusted Claudia on their arrival in San Antonio. And it was too early in the morning for this! Orange carrot peelings and raw potato skins topped the teetering mountain of what to Claudia O'Shaughnessy was just smelly garbage – just old rancid smelly garbage. It had been left there, even deliberately kept and collected by her unusually odd mother-in-law. *His* mother. That said it all. These people were just beneath her. She had married beneath her. And now, she was stuck with them. Stuck with them for the rest of her married life.

To think that this woman was cooking lunch for her family was too much. It was truly worrying. She told Georgina that the child's grandmother's kitchen was so unsanitary. It was like it was the child's fault for having such a woman as her very own grandmother. Like she had deliberately chosen such a woman for a grandmother. Mother told Georgina that Granny's kitchen smelled. Mother said this after she had thought it to herself that the kitchen smelled to high heavens with so great an odour that if she'd been expecting, she would surely have puked on the spot. She knew that even thinking the word *'puke'* was uncouth, but she couldn't help herself. According to Mother, the place was a pig-pen, an utter disgrace. Even associating with someone of her children's grandmother, her mother-in-law's poor breeding was beneath her. And two whole weeks at her husband's parents' home was going to be a great strain on the younger woman.

Mother asked for a clean glass, so that she could have a drink of water to take her aspirins; rubbing her forehead in both dismay and to ease her throbbing headache. Mother's head still ached from the day before. The day they had arrived there. Claudia wouldn't call them clean dishes. Her mother-in-law used the same smelly dishrag for months, using it and then hanging it up to dry over her faucet. She used it to wash everything: glasses, cutlery, plates and even greasy pots and pans. Mother had told the watching and listening child that she never knew if the dishes were really clean or not. The glasses were a bit streaky, that was certain. Mother rinsed the glass out before she used it. The kitchen drain board was piled high with plastic cups and bowls, old cracked and unmatched ceramic plates and saucers and half a dozen metal glasses; all washed up in readiness for the child's Grandmother's noisy, boisterous brood of young grandchildren. They were a rowdy bunch. Claudia had to admit that. But what did you expect when you married into such a family? She should have known! She should have seen it coming. Of course, her children would be a bit wild, just by simple association, if not genetics!

These were the people who meant the most in the world to the older woman. Her heart was in the right place. But to her daughter-in-law, she was in obvious decline. Georgina knew that her mother, Claudia, felt that his mother, Olivia, was a woman who was deteriorating. Mother had told the girl in confidence that Grandmother was *peculiar*. Georgina knew that Mother thought that the child's Granny was like the pile of kitchen refuse and like the old house in which she lived. All of the good dishes, the ones Granny had gotten for selling so many Avon and Stanley Home Products, were put away, and Mother had to use just any old glass she could find. That annoyed her greatly. (Granny had to keep the good dishes hidden away until after this descending litter of niñitos were out of range of all of her breakables. Granny said that she wasn't 'having my valuable things broken by you kids'. Granny said that she had 'seen how you kids treat all of your toys, so you are not touching my stemwear glasses'.) Stemmed glassware with sharp little points all over the outer surface were placed on Grandmother's large family dining table like they were museum pieces; to be looked at, but not touched and certainly not used. The glasses were obtained as a bonus for selling a plethora of Stanley Home Products. Granny had worked hard for those bonus glasses and for other prizes that she got for being such a good saleswoman. Those goblets were precious to her, like Georgina's dolls were precious to the girl. Those precious glasses were too valuable to just risk throwing away on children's usage, and were kept only for grown-ups. But even the grown-ups could only use them for special occasions. Granny wanted to show them off before she put them away in her antique bureau with her other treasures. Mother said that the bureau was only *'antique'* because it was old, not because it was really an antique. It was like everything else in the woman's house, *'junky'*, at least in Mother's mind. Old things weren't so valued back then, like they are now. Modernity was everything. The past was too painful. The past, and old things, were better off being forgotten. Collectibles were thrown out back then, not valued like they are today.

Some small-assorted jam jars, the jam all now eaten on toasted white bread from the local Piggley Wiggley grocery store were to be used by the kids for their milk today at breakfast time. Cool-Aid was to be poured into the children's metal glasses which stacked in high stacks in Grandmother's kitchen cabinets. Red, green, gold, blue and silver metal glasses were there. The woman had plenty of different colors, so that Katrina and Gretchen could always have the color they liked the best. Grandmother knew her girls. She knew that those twins would get into a hellacious argument at the supper-table if they didn't get their first choice. If they didn't get their favourite-colored glass, they'd both start yelling at the top of their lungs and arguing. Grandmother knew her girls!

Claudia O'Shaughnessy just wanted to vomit, right there in the kitchen in front of everyone. She had had a tough day the day before, and hadn't slept well on the lumpy, uncomfortable mattress in *their* house. She wasn't in the mood for the older woman's eccentricities this morning. It was bad enough to be seen driving up to the old house with its tattered unkempt exterior of peeling white paint and red and black trim work. Some of the boards were half hanging off over several of the house's eves. The awnings were slightly torn and perhaps you could say *'battered'*. They had seen better days. The fabric had been nice when her in-laws first had them installed when the girl's daddy, Genio Jr., was a boy. Now they were frayed and unsightly. Now, according to Mother, they just looked shabby and badly needed to be replaced.

All Georgina's Fault

Mother was in a bad mood. The child knew what was the matter with her mother. She knew that the drive down from Fort Campbell, Kentucky had been stressful. Georgina had caused such a scene the day before they had arrived in Texas. It was just awful. That girl. That girl in the chicken restaurant. Upsetting

94

everyone like that. Hadn't Mother taught the girl better table manners? Imagine choking on a chicken bone like that, especially in public! She'd been warned about the dangers of such things, and of the necessity of chewing her food carefully! Napkins were to be placed on young ladies' laps. Hands were to be kept on little girls' laps (on top of their napkins). Knives and forks were to be placed on plates or on the table on the proper sides of the plates; while food was being slowly and carefully chewed. Food was only to be chewed with mouths closed. It was always to be cut into small bitesize pieces and chewed in a lady-like fashion. These table manners were an inflexible part of growing up. Hadn't Mother told the girl a thousand times how to behave at the dinner table? Reminded her of proper etiquette? But no, Georgina had grabbed that drumstick and shoved it right into her mouth! Taking enormous mouthfuls. So, no wonder the girl got a chicken bone caught in her throat!

Little girls were to act like young ladies at the supper table. They were to act as though they had been well-bred. They were not to disgrace their family. They were not to act like savages tearing into their food with their teeth. They were not to chew with their mouths open! They were not to choke in public! Food was not meant to be held in hands either! The woman's daughter knew that. Georgina had been warned about the importance of chewing slowly and deliberately. But would she ever listen? Listen to her mother? So, in a sense the woman felt that her daughter had it coming to her, to choke on that chicken bone like that. If it embarrassed her to be held upside down, well, then, the child was the cause of her own downfall. If she'd been embarrassed, well then, it served her right. Maybe next time, she would listen to her mother and not gulp her food down in such a desperate hurry! Where had she left her manners, after all? Back in Kentucky? Out in the back woods with the hillbillies?

And of course, there was the dreadful trauma with Roger Eugenio at the playground. Georgina knew that it was her job to watch the younger children. Her mother had told her a million times. And though her mother hadn't said anything to scold her afterwards, she had given her *that* look. The girl knew what that look meant. It was a look that blamed the eldest girl for her younger brother's mishap. Thankfully, Roger was not too seriously injured. But he might have been, and then what? Hadn't she already lost one son? How much more could she bear?

Roger was still asleep. He had slept all night, without waking even once. They must have drugged him at that hospital. Good. He'd been sleeping ever since the accident. What if he'd had a concussion? As he was lifted into his father's arms, he had whimpered. But now, the boy was settled on his grandparent's sofa. He had slept all the way from the hospital after his tiny forehead was stitched up. He had slept all night. It was early morning the next day and Roger was still asleep. Mother guessed he was all right. But it was no thanks to Georgina Jane that the accident had happened in the first place. The girl knew that she was supposed to watch the little children. Her mother had told her that. But that girl would never listen. She was off in a world of her own. She was crazy. She was just plain crazy. Disconnected from reality. Living in her own little bubble, like some oddball. Taking her own sweet time, and doing things her own peculiar way. Never listening to her mother, and never doing as she was told. Content to wear raggedy blue jeans like that odd friend of hers, Juanita. Imagine the audacity, the very idea of a young lady wearing dungarees! It was unthinkable! Well, at least they were getting her away from that girl. At least now, maybe Georgina would settle down and behave herself, instead of arguing about whether or not she could wear blue jeans! All of that arguing was putting a terrible strain on the Mother/daughter relationship, which Claudia was trying so hard to build with all of those Mother/daughter dresses she had sewn. But did Georgina appreciate all of her mother's efforts? No! Did she even understand what her mother was trying to do by dressing her up in matching clothes? No, she did not. All that child could think about was wearing blue jeans. So at least now, now that they had gotten Georgina away from Juanita, that low class Mexican, that silly bickering with her would stop. But then, Georgina always did have the strangest tendency to make such peculiar friends.

Nothing was ever easy for the children's mother. But the young woman tried to enjoy motherhood for what it was, a time of feathering her nest and a whirling, nerve-wracking experience. This is what women did. They married and had children. Had them young. No point in waiting. Putting off the inevitable. This was her lot in life, and she had squared her shoulders and gotten on with it. Her life was her family. Nothing less, and perhaps, in some ways, nothing more. Couldn't they all see how trapped Mother felt? Tomorrow mother's own mother was coming over to her husband's parents' home for lunch. Today Nellie would let her daughter and son-in-law settle in with the children; not knowing that what Claudia really wanted was a good cry on her mother's shoulder. She needed comforting. Instead, the stench of her mother-in law's household waste confronted her in a rising, reeking heap. All she'd wanted was a glass of water to take an aspirin. The ripeness of her husband's peculiar mother's garden compost greeted her already tense sensibilities. A glimpse of the teetering mass of refuse had been enough to put her off her dinner last night completely. Anyway, she had been much too exhausted to eat much. Far too stressed to think about food. And his mother always cooked such rich spicy Mexican food, it was unpalatable to her anyway. Claudia would have rather had her own mother's cooking, which she was used to. Olivia's food seemed dubious to her.

Grandmother's Little Angelitas and the Ginny Doll

Katrina Josephina had just come in from the backyard to get a glass of water for herself. The twins had woken up early. That girl saw her mother's face, and a quick glance was all she needed to know that something was wrong. Pointing to the kitchen compost, she said, "Why'd you keep all of that smelly garbage, Grandmother? You're making my mammie feel sick to her tummy. I can tell. Pretty soon she's gonna barf all over your kitchen, and then you'll be real sorry."

Not catching the insults, "That's for my flowers, *mi hita*. Now go outside and play for a while so your mother can get some peace and quiet. You wake up much too early. You kids are the ones upsetting her tummy with all of that racket you keep making. Now be good for Grandmother and go outside and play."

"She's gonna puke all over the floor in your kitchen, Gramma. She hates smelly stuff. You better get rid of it, or else," piped up Gretchen, who looked like Katrina's shadow, she was standing so close to her twin. She'd been watching what was happening with her observant bright little four-year-old round green eyes. Round like Mother's eyes.

"Out! Out! Out! Silencio! On da la pronto!" said the woman with fire in her voice. And like she was scooting two unwanted pussy cats out the back door, she shooed the outspoken and annoying girls out into the back yard where they belonged, locking the screen door behind them. She hadn't been aware that Georgina was nowhere to be seen. So, intent on asserting herself with those unruly twins, that her eldest grandchild's absence wasn't even noticed. Georgina, sensing a family fray was about to start, even before it actually began, had secreted herself away, as she clutched her special *'Ginny'* doll. She was a small doll with jointed legs, and arms that bent too. *Ginny* was her best friend in the whole wide world, ever since Georgina had said good-bye to Juanita, her old best friend way way back there in Kentucky. *Ginny* was a beautiful doll with sky blue eyes that opened and shut, and long curly auburn hair, which was almost the exact same color as Mother's hair. But Mommy's hair was cut in a curly bob haircut that framed her face so beautifully. *Ginny* had been left behind on Georgina's bed at the army base hospital after the child's surgery. Mother had come to visit her daughter, but Georgina was sleeping. So, she didn't see Mother at the hospital. She had sensed her presence, sitting there on her bed looking at her, but the child couldn't awaken herself to speak to her mother. The child had woken up with a sore throat. And all that was left of Mother's visit was the dolly. The child had started to undress the doll, wanting to try on another outfit that came with her. But she was too tired. Too tired to finish the job. And when Mother came back, the doll's clothing had been removed, but not changed. *Ginny* was lying there on Georgina's hospital bed wearing only her underwear. But even on the second visit, Georgina had been back asleep. So, she couldn't thank her mother for the *Ginny* doll, that she loved so much. That was when the girl had her tonsils taken out the year before. Now, both the girl and her doll were hiding. Both of them were safe. They were hiding underneath Granny's kitchen table, where the girl was disguised as a chair leg, but still had a bird's eye view of the proceedings. Georgina knew that if she got in the way, if she was seen just standing there, they might try to involve her in their argument. And she did not want to upset her grandmother. Georgina knew both sides of her family, and she knew there was gonna be trouble. No doubt about it. She had spent enough time around her grandmother to know the woman's fiery temperament. If children were unmanageable, Grandmother would fly off the handle like a whirling forceful tornado. A really and truly Texas twister. Georgina knew how the twins were too. Those two just didn't seem to comprehend that Granny was a very difficult woman, who was set in her ways, and had to be handled gingerly, placating her, not ever getting her riled up. Getting Grandmother mad, (She was only called 'Granny' if Georgina was trying to soothe her, which was, come to think of it, a lot of the time.) was like poking your finger into a big bed of army ants that would bite you like they were the devil himself. Army ants were murderous varmints that lived all around Granny and Granddaddy's house on the hill overlooking the fields and the valley beyond. One of those fire ants had bitten Georgina, the afternoon before. When the child was out looking for Texas doodlebugs to add to the Kentucky doodlebugs' family, which she already had in her purse, an army's ant bit her on her pointer finger really, really hard. Daddy would kill those twins for speaking disrespectfully to his *Mama*. Granny would tell him all about their behaviour in loud angry Spanish, as soon as he woke up and went potty and washed his face and came to his *Mama*'s breakfast table for his early morning (or maybe it would be late or mid-morning by the time he got up) feast of either eggs ranchero with hot picante sauce, or scrambled eggs with chorizo and Granny's homemade flour tortillas with butter smeared on them. But fortunately for the twins, Daddy was still asleep. Daddy was sacked out on the bed in his parent's guest room, snoring his head off! He could snore louder than anything! He sounded like a wart hog. He sounded like a freight train. He sounded like someone making funny loud noises just to make little girls giggle when they heard them. He didn't know how he sounded though, because he was asleep. The louder he snored, the deeper in slumber he was. He was a sound sleeper, and he wouldn't be woken up by anything. Even the twins. Even his *Mama*.

Daddy was dreaming away, wearing his white boxer shorts and a white tee shirt, which was his sleeping costume that he slept in. This was way, way before men wore boxer shorts in bright colors. No respectable man would think of wearing boxer shorts in colors, or boxer shorts with polka dots or boxer shorts with stripes on them. Or boxer shorts in madras or boxer shorts in tartan plaids or with zig zag patterns all over them. Manufacturers didn't even mass produce such garish boxer shorts way back in 1958. Whoever even heard of such a thing? Only white boxer shorts were allowed back then.

Katrina Josephina stood with her nose pressed against the back door screen, giving her pale face a flattened distorted look. Letting the older woman know in no uncertain terms, her displeasure, the girl started her routine disruptive shouting through the now locked screen door. "You meany, meany grandmother. I don't like you anymore. You mean old crabby lady! How dare you lock me outside! Let me in, this very minute! Do you hear me?" The child imitated her father's tone of voice and his forcefulness. She never did learn that it was not her place, to correct the elderly.

"Grandmother! Grandmother! Let me in! I have to go to the potty! Hurry, or I'll wet my pants!" Gretchen implored the deaf ears of the seemingly sour old Spaniard with her beak nose and her sharply pointed widow's peak right in the middle of her forehead. Her long greying hair was braided in two long braids, which were twisted around and around the top of her head like a twisted rope. Georgina had seen the metal *bobbie* pins sticking out from underneath Granny's long braids. Sharp *bobbie* pins holding the woman's long, long length of thick Spanish hair in place. All three of the girls had stood in the bathroom and watched in amazement as their grandmother bent over, almost hanging upside down, and brushed and brushed the tangles out of her long, long hair. Long hair growing almost down to the backs of Granny's knees. Then, they were spell-bound as the woman wound and wound and wound that long braided greying hair in circle after circle, till it was like a funny platted crown amassed on the back of their grandmother's head. To the girls, this woman's granddaughters, that long hair hanging down all over the woman's head, gave Grandmother the appearance of a scary witch. And all of that screeching that she did in a foreign tongue, only added to the false, but genuine, impression the girls had. Their grandmother was not a sweet old lady after all, but a brutish broomstick lady instead.

The old woman was oblivious to the pleas of her granddaughters. She had no intention of letting children rule her life. And because she was busy blowing her pointy proboscis into her *'snot rag'*, she was making her own hullabaloo. Her resounding nose-blowing drowned out the disagreeable din of those two pip-squeak girls.

"I hate you! I hate you! You're nothing but a sour, old, crabby, lady! Your nose is just full of snot and boogers! Let us in! Can't you hear me? You old battle-axe! My mother says that you are a big old grouchy nothing! And I am never ever gonna eat your lousy enchiladas ever again!" rudely yelled Katrina Josephina, still imitating her father's terminology; though not realizing that when she said it, *'battle-axe'* took on an entirely different meaning than when her father used it jokingly and affectionately, to refer to his mother-in-law, Nellie.

Wild screeching chattering Spanish began to spew out of Grandmother's mouth as she heard Katrina Josephina's rude comments. Georgina cringed, hugged her doll tightly and hid even deeper underneath the kitchen table, holding her small dolly for dear life. The girl knew what was coming. Gretchen Gabriella and Katrina Josephina were doing a little caper, and holding their crouches with their hands as they danced a one-legged jig on their grandparent's back porch. "We have to go to the potty. We have to go pee pee in the potty right now! Right this minute! Do you hear me?"

"Come on in, girls. Make it snappy," said their mother, unlocking the screen door and deftly manoeuvring herself and the twins past their glowering Spanish granny, who was not in the least impressed by the twin's shenanigans.

Grandmother said, "Stop bawling like a baby, Katrina. Quit your whining, Gretchen. Big girls don't make such a fuss. And wash your hands when you're finished."

Claudia was annoyed with the woman. But she smiled with her sugary sweet smile, feigning goodness and kind thoughts. Georgina Jane could see her mother's face. But her mother couldn't see where the child was hiding. She knew that, although her mother was smiling, inwardly the woman was not amused. But home for the moment was there in their rickety white farm house with its peeling paint. The house on a hill, overlooking a valley in what would become a big shopping mall in the not-too-distant future. For the next two weeks, Mother had to make the best of it. She didn't want to admit, even to herself what her feelings towards the older woman really were, but she had confided in Georgina, whispering to the defenceless little six-year-old girl in the hallway. Mother was putting on a brave face. Mother was play-acting. She'd even let Granny embrace her when they'd arrived. And now, she'd have to put up with listening to his *Mama* speak to her in that high pitched squeaky voice that grated on Mother's nerves as it petered off into rapid crazy Spanish at the drop of a hat. That voice that gave Claudia a headache. Perhaps it was true; the children could be better behaved. But Mother would never admit this to his *Mama*.

"What's wrong with her?" Gretchen said to Mother, who had let the twins into the house, over the complaints of Mother's mama-in-law. "Doesn't she know that I have a very small bladder?"

Never the Twain Shall Meet

Two weeks passed quickly in Georgina's mind. She learned to love her grandparents during that time, in spite of her mother's attitude towards them. They were so warm and affectionate to her. Chatting away excitedly in Spanish whenever they saw her. They always seemed happy to see her. It was hard for her to take in, to accept. Were they really talking to her? She turned around at first, to see if someone else was behind her. Georgina knew that she was their favourite. And this was both wonderful and it was terrible. It was wonderful because of the closeness she felt towards them. It was wonderful because it felt so good. So good to be treated in such a caring manner. It was wonderful because it comforted the child in a way that only her daddy comforted her, when he had the time to do so, or when Mommy wasn't looking or listening. Daddy's parents seemed to love her even more than Daddy did. They had dared to love her in spite of Mother's disapproval, which they pretended not to notice. Pretended to be too dumb, too Latino, and too culturally different, to grasp Claudia's disfavour towards this child.

But it was terrible because Georgina knew that it made her mother extremely jealous and uneasy. That was the terrible part, making Mother mad. Mother didn't like for Georgina to be treated with such partiality. Mother didn't think that Georgina deserved such treatment. And so, she undermined the child's grandparents to her daughter every chance that she got, knowing how her daughter felt about them, and wanting to change those feelings of affection. Mocking their different ways and imitating their mannerisms was Mother's way of getting her point across. It was her way of putting them down without being direct, but with her use of veiled humour. Surely, anyone would see the comedy in those acts? Those funny scenes would never leave Claudia open to ridicule. Ridicule that others received.

Georgina knew that there was a price to pay for the favouritism of Daddy's *Mama* and *Papa*. The girl knew that her own mother hated the attention that the child's grandparents lavished on her. Mother hated their praise of the girl. Despised their affection for Georgina. Such affection and endearment made Mother uncomfortable. Such feelings: which nearly, but not quite, contrasted with her own meagreness of soul and the inadequacies she felt in her own heart. Such outward displays of love reflected badly on Mother, and showed up the lack of her own maternal affection towards the girl.

Perhaps Granny and Granddaddy compared Georgina to their twin granddaughters and their apparently not so good behaviour. Even Granddaddy knew by now, after two whole weeks with those girls, that they were not the angelic beings he had previously assumed that they were. The older couple weren't used to children's fights at their house. And those two had made themselves right at home. Georgina's grandparents expected better behaviour out of children. Their own three had known better than to act that way. Granddaddy would have taken his leather belt off to his own offspring, when they had been children, in order to control any unruly behaviour. Beating your child was considered the ordinary manner in which to rear children back then. It was not 'child abuse'. It was doing your duty as a parent. No one wanted a brat for a child in Georgina's grandparent's generation.

Granddaddy and his wife knew that their son had no real control over his wife. They both knew that their son's wife had little or no control over their grandchildren; especially those twin girls of hers. Those little terrors! But what could you expect from Claudia? She just spoke too softly with that funny lisping voice of hers and had no authority at all over their grandchildren, never bothering to beat those two naughty muchachas. They had whispered that Claudia let those kids get away with murder. Georgina was the only good one of the bunch. The boys didn't count yet. Babies would be babies. Georgina had overheard her grandparent's quiet conversation from her secret hiding place behind the chair in their living room. They didn't know that the girl could hear what they said about her mother. But since they spoke a few words in Spanish and others in English, the child was able to piece together the gist of what they meant.

But generally, life was a simple affair at her grandparent's house. Crickets chirped happily in the tall grasses where the neighbour's ponies played in the field next door. The air was still, and the summer's sun was hot, real hot, outside. It was hot inside too. And humid. Electric fans were on in nearly every room, but it didn't help. All it did was just move the hot air around in circles. It was early afternoon. Everybody seemed tired, and the younger children and Mother seemed a bit cross. Those little kids were taking *'a siesta'*, an afternoon catnap. Mother was in the back bedroom reading a novel (a *novella* as Grandmother called it) trying to get the twins and Georgina's two brothers to sleep. Because she was older, Georgina was allowed to stay up, as long as she occupied herself with quiet activities. So, she sat at the kitchen table. She sat there listening to her Granddaddy's radio. She sat there listening to her grandparents and her father discuss politics; while she cut out her new paper dolls' dresses. Daddy and his Daddy were talking about baseball and politics. The radio announcer said it would be ninety-six degrees today. There was not a cloud in the sky.

Daddy was happy. Teasing his mother, and pulling her apron strings deliberately to annoy her when she had her hands full fixing supper time food. She responded by telling him off in her mad Spanish voice, and then they'd both laugh! He loved to get a rise out of her. Then he'd smile, and turn to his child, and tickle Georgina to get a rise out of her. Georgina would squirm and giggle and drop her blunt-ended child's scissors, blaming him, and telling him off by saying, "Stop it, Daddy!" He'd respond by mocking her in his sarcastic imitation of her. Pretending to be a six-year-old girl, he'd say, "Stop it, Daddy! Stop it, Daddy! Stop it, Daddy!" all the while still tickling her underneath her arms to force out yet more and more laughter. Making his *Mama* and his daughter laugh gave him great delight. Making them laugh was everything to him.

Daddy was with his Mama and his Papa. There in their home. He loved his parents and the security that he felt there with them. He knew that they loved him too. There was no need for an explanation of how they felt for each other. There was no need for pretence there. There was no reason to pretend to be someone important with them. They loved him just the way he was. He could act like a grown up or act like their child. They just loved him no matter who he was.

Georgina realized that Daddy's old family, before he had a new family with her in it, was different from the family that he had started with Mommy. Mommy was one way. Granny, or *'Mama'*, as Daddy affectionately called his Spanish mother, hadn't really changed with the times. But make no mistake about it. Granny was a very outwardly strong lady. She wasn't ashamed of being tough and outspoken, even though it was considered by the child's mother to be *'unlady-like behaviour'*. Mommy was soft and seemingly gentle, even genteel. Grandmother seemed more in control. Mother did not. But it was all a mystery to Georgina; because no one in their family (with the exception of Katrina Josephina, who often made Mother cry) dared to do anything except what her mother wanted them to do. The woman had her ways. They were subtle, but immoveable nevertheless. Mother was clever and ingenious in a quiet, but shrewd way. She knew how to control people without even raising her voice, and certainly never her hand in a threatening manner. It wasn't necessary to speak loudly or rant and rave. That was uncouth. Well-bred young women did not ever raise their voices or show a clear demonstration of being truly angry. Mother didn't have to act that way. It was beneath her dignity. People just did as she asked of them. In her quiet, polite manner, Mother had real control and even what you might call, a stage presence.

Dwyanne – the Bathtub! I'm Dwowning!
From an Old 'Knock, Knock' Joke

Days turned into weeks. And after they had visited the Alamo, gone to the Spanish Missions, seen all of their Spanish speaking relatives from down in *'The Valley'*, who had come to San Antonio for the family reunion to see Genio Jr. and his family off to Alaska (that's in South Texas for those who don't know about *'The Valley'*), it was time to leave. Those darker skinned relatives did nothing but speak in Spanish with each other, eat Tia Tencha's (one of Grandmother's sisters) homemade tamales and tell each other funny stories or jokes, guessing from all of that loud laughing that those strange family members did.

And after they had all eaten (even that bratty Katrina Josephina) about a million of Granny's cheesy enchiladas, spicy refried pinto beans and yummy doughy flour tortillas, and farted a lot; it was time to go. Roger had recovered from his run-in with that wooden swing and had his stitches taken out. He was running faster than ever now, brandishing that deep scar across his forehead like a branding iron had touched his tiny head, leaving its mark. Nothing could stop that little kid! So now, they could leave Texas and go to Alaska. They were taking Mother's mother, Nellie, with them.

All of the grandkids called Nellie, *'Manga'*. Manga was Mother's mother. Manga had come over to Georgina's grandparents' house to visit a few times in the two weeks that they were there. It was some distance from Myrtle Street where Nellie lived, to Granny and Granddaddy's white house on the hill. And it was hard for her to get there, because there was no bus route going way out there in the country, and Manga couldn't drive a car. Granddaddy had to pick her up in his Chevrolet. Manga was real friendly with Genio Senior and Olivia O'Shaughnessy, Claudia's in-laws. The three of them really seemed to like each other and laughed at their joint grandchildren and at jokes the three of them shared from another generation. Things that were funny to them. Those were their own private jokes.

Or they would reminisce about the hard times they had endured during the Great Depression or World War II, and thank God that those bleak times were now behind them. Granddaddy wondered if Nellie would get a job as an airplane mechanic like she'd had during the War. When they got to Alaska, would she look for work? What kind of job was she planning to look for? Women of Granny and Manga's generation thought working outside the home, and being part of the workplace in the big wide world, was normal. Mother's generation thought that working outside the home was beneath them. No self-respecting woman in Mother's generation necessarily wanted a job outside of the home. They had a job already. It was called being a *'housewife'*. Even secretaries were considered almost morally loose and somewhat dubious in their reputations. Women of Georgina's mother's generation, who worked outside their homes, leaving their families behind, were looked down upon by those who did not work outside of their homes. They were practically scorned! Women of Georgina's mother's generation let their husbands support them. When World War II ended, so did

105

women working outside their homes en masse, end too. That generation's young women considered it more proper to stay at home and raise a family, not get a job and farm their kids out to child-minders, except for very brief periods of time while they shopped or had their hair done. Women of Mother's generation were always going to the Beauty Parlour. Well-set hair-dos were a vital part of good grooming for Mother and her friends. Hair had to be carefully set and permed, or colored if any sign of grey hairs began to show. Then, they would pat their hair into place, perfecting any imperfections, with their gloved, lady-like hands.

The home was where they felt that they belonged, perhaps only engaging in PTA (Parent Teacher Association) Meetings, Bridge Clubs, Country Club events, or in Mother's case, the elite Officers' Club activities. Some country women all got together and engaged in Quilting Bees. Mother did not. She was very particular about certain things, and her personal interests were one of them. And she certainly would never have even considered getting a job which took her away from home.

But Granny had two jobs and Manga worked too. She had a job as assistant pharmacist, and they sure were going to miss her, giving her a small send-off and a cash gift of $30.00 for Nellie's new life in Alaska. Manga would have to work once they got resettled. That wouldn't change once they all moved to Alaska. Manga knew that she would have to find work. But that didn't worry her.

So, when Granddaddy, who admired Georgina's other grandmother's bravado, guts and determination, asked Nellie (*'Manga'*) if she was going to do the same work she had done during the War as an airplane mechanic, (You would have thought that the war had just ended recently.) seeing that there would be so many airplanes on the base in Fort Wainwright, Alaska, Manga said, "No, the last time I lifted parts from those engines, I nearly gave myself a hernia!"

Then the three older people would have a good-natured chuckle together. It was nice to see them all getting along. There was respect and love and a genuine closeness between the child's three grandparents. Maybe because they had all lived through such dire periods of history together. War and money problems are never easy. So, they had mutual respect for what they all had been through.

One day, Daddy pulled up in the dirt driveway with his mother-in-law in the station wagon with him. Some of Nellie's gear was with her. She had a small black and white hound's tooth leather suitcase left over from 1918, the year after the First World War ended. The war to end all wars. It was an old gift from her sister, Rose, when the once eighteen-year-old Nellie left for University. The bulk of her possessions would be shipped to Alaska. But Manga was a 'trooper' and she'd happily manage till then. She was just glad to be included on the family's great adventure to the frosty North.

"Everyone into the car! Time to go to Alaska! Vamos, muchachos! Let's go, kids!" sang out their father.

Today was the day they were leaving for their long trip. Grandmother had washed and ironed all of Roger Eugenio and Peter Martin's diapers. "To get all of the filthy germs out of them," she had said. Georgina Jane's grandmother kissed and hugged all of the children at least three times each, wailing loudly, and speaking in rapid Spanish. She was wiping her eyes and blowing her nariz loudly with her *'snot rag'* as Katrina Josephina had dubbed Grandmother's hankie. The poor ol' lady was trying hard not to be hysterical.

She was going to miss her son and the children, and even that uppity Claudia too. She knew that they would be gone for years, and that she wouldn't see them at all in that time. Alaska seemed like a million miles away. Would they keep in touch and let her know how they were doing? All she could do was hope. And the children would be so big when, and if, she ever did see them again. "God willing." She knew that she would even miss the twin's fighting. She knew that she would even miss her son's teasing and farting. She knew she would miss *'Speedy Gonzalez'* with his twinkling, mischievous blue eyes and Mexican complexion, and those scrawny little fast legs of his, zooming so fast around every corner and nearly knocking her over. She knew that she would miss the baby's crying and kicking and squirming when she tried to change his diaper. She knew that she would even miss Claudia with her soft foreign mannerisms and her odd ways. And she knew that she would miss Georgina. She would miss that shy, quiet little dark-headed girl, so reminiscent of her own mother so long gone from Olivia. She would miss that little girl who hid behind chairs, thinking that nobody could see her. Thinking that nobody knew she was there. There hiding. That little girl who was leaving. Leaving for Alaska in ten minutes time. That little granddaughter who was leaving. Leaving her shadow behind. Olivia would miss Georgina Jane. She would miss her for who the child was. For her being her.

When Georgina asked her grandmother when they would be seeing her again and would she and Granddaddy be coming to Alaska for a visit, Granny let some tears fall onto her cheeks. "God willing," Granny had said. That's what she always said, never really giving an answer. It was as though people had no free will, no choice in such matters. Granny couldn't commit herself to the child. Couldn't answer her questions. How could she answer the girl? How could she explain what their separation would mean to her? Life seemed so painfully hard sometimes. Her son was an officer in the army's Aviation Unit, and so he had a job to do. The Army all but owned him, and he and his family had to transfer to where her son was stationed. Her only son. Part of Granny understood that. The other part wasn't so sure she could really come to terms with it. Grandmother stood there wondering when she'd see them all again. Georgina understood. And she looked behind her as they drove away. She knew that her grandmother was feeling very, very desolate, as she watched the black and white Pontiac drive away from their old white clapboard house on the hill overlooking a valley and fields that would all be so different when Georgina saw them again. The valley and the fields would become the North Star Shopping Mall in just three and a half years' time. In the time it took before she could come back to visit those people again, many things would change. It was a very sad, very hard moment, like a rending, a tearing in her heart. The child felt it. The Granddaddy felt it. Daddy had put a brave face on, feigning bravado. But Georgina knew from her father's real face, not his pretend one, that the happiness Daddy had felt during that two week visit with his Mama and Papa in San Antonio, Texas, had vanished away. Daddy was acting as though he was anesthetised to his pain which the separation from Los Padres caused him. Though Daddy was feeling sensitive to his loss of contact, he pretended not to notice how much he was hurting. Granny was too numb to feel anything. Georgina knew that Granny felt like the plug had just been pulled in the bathtub, and that she, and all of the water, were draining away.

Whenever Georgina's father didn't want his children understanding what he had to say, he would always speak in Spanish to his parents. They spoke a lot of Spanish during the two weeks that her family stayed with Granny and Granddaddy. Spanish with all of those rolling Rs of theirs. Rolling Rs. Rolling Rs. Rolling Rs. Never-ending rolling Rs. The girl didn't know how to speak in Spanish. She could understand a little bit of it though, because she had listened so hard to what they said. But only if they mixed up the Spanish words with the English words. Then she could piece the words together like a secret code. Their words were like a boxed jig saw puzzle all laid out on a table in front of her. Georgina knew where some of the pieces were, and how they fit together. And she tried really hard to find places for the missing spaces in their dialogue. But some words she did not understand. And all of those secrets made her feel strange, like she didn't belong to them. So, even though she was sad to say good-bye to her grandparents, the only good thing was, that she would be able to understand what the big people said in front of the children again.

Westward Ho!

Everything would be different now. Alaska would be a better place, where they would all be safe. It would be a place of new beginnings. Mother had said, "There will be lots of pretty scenery on the way. Look out the windows on the trip and see all of the pretty things, girls. You will learn so much by just looking out the windows."

But nothing could have prepared Georgina for the sights she would see out of the windows of their black and white station wagon with the red interior. The lucky ones got to sit next to Manga, or as the twins thought, in the front seat. But Manga, Mother's mother, sat in the middle of the back seat and read to the children or pointed out interesting things to see in the countryside that Georgina and her family were travelling through.

On their way out of Kentucky, they had already gone to Mammoth Cave, and they saw deep inside of the earth. It was summertime, but Georgina Jane and her sisters and little baby brothers had to wear lightweight jackets into that dark, deep cave; because it was chilly down inside of the earth. That was the place where those poor blind fish, without any eyes lived. Those fish had been in the dark for so, so long, that their eyes had just plain disappeared because they weren't using their eyes anymore.

Georgina Jane thought that she would always use her eyes, so that her eyes wouldn't just disappear like those poor, pale translucent cave fish lost their eyes in that dark, cold, silent cave. The Indians had been in that big cave too. The Indians thought it was a special place, and had buried one of their soldiers, an Indian brave, there a long, long time ago in that deep, dark place.

After they left Texas, they went to New Mexico, because that was the State next to Texas. In New Mexico, they had an even bigger cave there, called *Carlsbab* Caverns. In that giant cave, they had lots of wild bats who lived in that cave in the daytime, when the people visited the inside of the bats' home. Those hundreds of bats were sleepyheads and slept all day long. In the evening, all of those bats woke up from their long naps and they went flying out of the cave to look for food. The thousands and millions of bats flew out of the mouth of that

109

big cave into the night time sky. That was an amazing thing for a little girl to see. Mother didn't like it, to see all of those flying bats. It made her very nervous. Mother was afraid of mice, and bats reminded her of flying mice. Mother shivered even though it was ninety degrees Fahrenheit. Then she shuddered. And then, she shrieked and got back into the car when those hundreds of bats came flying out of *Carlsbab* Caverns. Those bats made a lot of racket and flew and flew and flew out of that enormous cave. They were almost like one big giant bat, the way they all flew so close together.

"We won't go to the Grand Canyon on this trip, but we will go to a place where four States meet. It's called 'Four Corners', and you can stand in four States all at the same time," her father told them.

In *'Four Corners'*, they could stand in New Mexico, Colorado, Arizona and Utah all at the same time. That was an exciting moment. But it was not nearly as exciting as seeing all of those gigantic dinosaur bones at the Dinosaur National Monument in Utah. Her daddy went way out of his way, just to show them the bones of those big, extinct creatures. Those gigantic bones were bigger than anybody's bones Georgina knew about. Those dinosaurs had roamed around the neighbourhood in Utah a very, very long time ago. They had made themselves right at home there, and had even taken over the place. But now, all that was left of them was just a pile of old bleached dinosaur bones. And nobody should be afraid of a pile, even a very big pile, of dinosaur bones. Because those dinosaurs were dead now. They had been dead for a very, very long time.

And after that, Daddy drove them all to a real salty lake where they could float on top of the water without even sinking. That was a place called 'The Great Salt Lake'. It was the greatest Salt Lake that anyone could ever imagine! It was the greatest salty lake Georgina had ever been to in her whole life. She couldn't even imagine that there might even be a better, bigger, greater, salty lake than that place. She knew how to swim, and Manga taught her that it was possible for Georgina to trust the salty water to support her whole body. Manga said that if Georgina would just relax, and lie down on top of the salty water in the Great Salt Lake in Utah, that she wouldn't drown. All Georgina had to do was just to take it easy, lie on her back, and just float and float and float away without even worrying about sinking.

On the way to California, they went to Lake Tahoe and little Roger Eugenio's diaper almost came off. He sat on the shoreline, where the water wasn't too deep, splashing his little hands in the water, trying to get baby Peter Martin wet. But when Roger stood up, his wet diaper was too heavy and it stayed down. That little kid waddled out of Lake Tahoe with his diaper down around his tiny, brown ankles, nearly tripping himself in the process. Georgina and the twins giggled because they thought that it was very funny to come all of the way to Lake Tahoe and then lose your diaper.

But losing your diaper wasn't nearly as bad as loosing yourself and your little sister, Gretchen. That's what happened at the Denver Zoo in Colorado. Georgina and Gretchen were just standing there looking at the lions, when they looked around and saw no one else in their family. Those lions were licking themselves like big, big kitty cats. Those lions were roaring and playing around with each other. The girls were mesmerized by those big yellow pussy cats. Watching those lions was even better than watching the monkeys at 'Monkey Island'. And it was even better than watching the seals at the water park built just for those Sammy the seals to swim in. They could watch those lions for hours.

Gretchen was holding her big sister's hand; trusting her sister to take good care of her. But Georgina Jane was concentrating so hard on those lions, that she didn't hear Mother call her to come to see the tigers, the elephants, the giraffes and the koala bears. Later, when she looked up, no one in her family was even there anymore. It was like the whole family had been raptured away from them. It was like the whole family didn't exist anymore. They had all just vanished. Gretchen started to cry when she realized that holding Georgina's hand wasn't a safe place. Those lions might decide that two little, lost girls would be easy to catch and eat. So, the two bewildered little girls, one four years old and the other six, just sat underneath a big tree for protection, and waited for Mother to find them again. It sure was good to see your mother again after getting lost near the lions' cage at the zoo. But when her parents found them again, Mother was so relieved. She hugged Gretchen and frowned at Georgina.

Everywhere they went, they sang songs with Manga. They drove right through the giant redwood trees singing that song they loved:

"This land is my land,
This land is your land,
From California to the New York Islands,
From the Gulf stream waters,
To the redwood forests,
This land was made for you and me!"

Their childish choruses would sound out loud and clear in the car! How her father could drive with all that racket going on in the back seat of the car, she did not know. Every day, all the way there, the children would take it in turns to ask him, "How much longer till we get to Alaska, Daddy? How many more minutes do we have to go? Are we almost there yet?" The trip seemed to take an infinitesimal amount of time. Georgina couldn't wait to get there and to see what Alaska was really like.

In the evenings, they would stop at motels on the highway, which thrilled Georgina Jane and the twins, who all liked to jump up and down on all of the new beds. Roger and Peter Martin were too little and too tired to care about where they were. They only wanted a bath, their bottles, and to be put to bed. First, they had to have their diapers changed. The twins said baby Peter Martin was a 'kick-a-roo', like the kangaroo they had seen at the zoo. That baby would not hold still to have his diaper changed for anything. He just kept kicking those strong little baby legs of his while Mother tried to change his diaper. Georgina could tell that he wanted to run around like his big brother, Roger Eugenio. That's why he kicked so much.

That bag of diapers was getting stinkier and smellier every day that they travelled. "Next town we come to, we'll wash the diapers," her father said to her mother. Georgina could see that the bag of diapers was getting heavier for her father to lift off of the roof of their car to put more dirty diapers into it. With all of those wet, smelly diapers in it, that plastic bag was horrible. It made her father gag. Daddy had so many suitcases and bags to carry into the motels every night. Georgina thought, *It must be hard being a daddy.*

Her mother had made new nightgowns for the girls to take on the trip. So, after Georgina and her sisters jumped on the bed for a while in the motel rooms, they would take a bath and put on their new nightgowns and get ready for bed. Manga always read to them before they went to sleep.

Georgina's favourite book was called, *Pat, the Bunny.* It was a story of Paul and Judy and their daddy's scratchy beard, which she could feel, like sandpaper in the book. Her daddy didn't have a scratchy beard. She asked him why he didn't have a scratchy beard like Paul and Judy's daddy. Her daddy told her that the reason why he didn't have a scratchy beard, was because he had Indian's blood in him. He said that Indians couldn't really grow beards very well. Their hair didn't grow as well on their faces as it did on top of their heads. Indians probably would never go bald, but they couldn't grow beards as well as Paul and Judy's daddy could. She guessed her daddy got this Indian's blood from her granddaddy, because he didn't have a beard either.

In the book about Paul and Judy, Georgina could put her finger through Judy and Paul's mother's ring, like her mother wore. Mother had a wedding ring that was made out of white gold, that made it look like silver. At the end of the book, Paul and Judy waved good-bye, like she had waved good-bye to her Granny and Granddaddy and Glorianna in Texas. She had waved good-bye so, so hard that her arm hurt afterwards. She had waved goodbye until she couldn't see her grandparents any more. She couldn't see them anymore and they were all gone. They were left behind with Glorianna, standing there on the hill overlooking a field and a valley back in San Antonio. Back in Texas.

Manga was her grandmother too. But Georgina could never make up her mind if she liked Granny or Manga best. How could you like one good grandmother over another good grandmother? She knew that she loved both of her twin sisters, but sometimes she liked Gretchen best. Katrina Josephina was like Granny, except that she couldn't speak in Spanish yet. Sweet little Gretchen was more like Manga. Her Spanish Granny could be very talkative, and she was strong and tough. But Manga was almost always sweet and kind. And when she talked, the girl could always understand what she was saying.

Gretchen was the quiet one, except for when she talked to her twin sister, Katrina Josephina. Then Gretchen could argue and argue, both of the little girls getting louder and louder as the argument continued. And they argued over such stupid things. "He's my daddy!" Katrina Josephina said emphatically, deliberately trying to aggravate her sister.

"No, he's my daddy!" said Gretchen in response to her sister's goading.

"No, he's not. He's only my daddy!" said Katrina, laughing triumphantly. Then Gretchen would start crying, and run to Mother, saying that Katrina Josephina had hurt her feelings again. How her parents had the patience to deal with those two naughty girls, she never knew. She found them very annoying.

Mother Goose was her family's favourite. She knew almost all of those 'baby' nursery rhymes by heart.

Humpty Dumpty sat on a wall;
Humpty Dumpty had a great fall.
All the king's horses and all the king's men
Couldn't put Humpty Dumpty together again.

She thought of her daddy and her little brother, Roger Eugenio. And she was glad that the doctors could put them both back together again after they had their falls. Mother used to sing some of the nursery rhymes in her funny little sweet out-of-tune voice.

Bye, baby bunting
Daddy's gone a-hunting,
To get a little rabbit skin
To wrap the baby bunting in.

Georgina liked that one; because she loved bunnies. Bunnies were so soft. One of Mother's favourite nursery rhymes was *'The Old Woman Who Lived In A Shoe'.*

There was an old woman who lived in a shoe.
She had so many children,
She didn't know what to do.
She gave them some broth without any bread.
And spanked them all soundly,
And put them to bed!

Mother used to say that nursery rhyme to her children if they were naughty and wouldn't go to sleep at night. Georgina thought it was a really cruel mother in that nursery rhyme, and what terrible things to do to little children. She wondered if the mother in that nursery rhyme was so mean to her children, because she was so old and crabby. But her grandmother, Manga, was a little bit old and she wasn't mean. Even Grandmother in San Antonio wasn't as mean as the old woman who lived in that smelly old shoe with all of her children. Mother was pretty nice and she'd never beat them, even that naughty Katrina.

One of their favourite stories was Curious George, that naughty monkey from the jungle who stole the man's hat and finally ended up in the circus. George, the monkey, lived in Africa and liked to eat bananas. He could swing high up in the jungle trees. But George's curiosity made him get caught by the man in the yellow hat, who took poor little George away from his home in Africa. That made George the monkey sad. It made Georgina sad too. She knew what it was like to have to leave your home and go far away, just like Curious George

114

the monkey did. Even though he got into trouble, she was glad that Curious George always stayed curious. That was the best part of the story.

She worried about Curious George when he tried to fly off of the side of the ship like the sea gulls did. It was terrible when George the monkey fell into the ocean. That part really concerned her. She liked the part best where George the monkey put on the man's pyjamas and fell asleep in the man's bed. When Curious George was asleep, he was safe, like Georgina Jane's brother, Roger, was when he was asleep.

Manga's favourite book was *Little Black Sambo* about a nice black family who had lots of pancakes to eat, and the mother and father who gave their little black boy so many nice things to wear. The boy in the story was called, Black Sambo because his skin was really and truly black. He lived by a jungle like Curious George from the other book did. Black Sambo's mother liked to cook and sew. She was like Mother and Grandmother and Manga. They liked to cook and sew too. That's what ladies did. Black Jumbo was Black Sambo's daddy. He smoked a pipe. Daddy smoked cigarettes, not a pipe like Black Jumbo. Sometimes Mother smoked a corncob pipe just for a joke; because she thought that it was a funny thing to do. Smoking corncob pipes made Mommy look like a funny hillbilly woman back on a porch in Kentucky.

Poor little Black Sambo, when he went for a walk in the jungle, had some problems. The bad tigers made Little Black Sambo give them all of his clothes, so that he only had his underwear left on. Little Black Sambo had to trick the mean tigers to get his clothes back. Even though he was so little, Black Sambo was a smart little boy. If the tigers would just fight with each other like Katrina Josephina and Gretchen Gabriella did, then they would forget all about little Black Sambo. Then he could get his clothes back again, and not have to walk home in his underwear. It was embarrassing for people to see you in your underwear.

When he did get his clothes back from the mean old tigers, then little Black Sambo could go home to his mother and father and eat pancakes again. He ate a hundred and sixty-nine pancakes at the end of the story. It was too many pancakes to eat. Georgina could only eat two silver dollar pancakes or sometimes three or four if she was really hungry.

Mother and Manga used different voices when they told the children *Nursery Rhymes* or read stories to them. Manga could read '*The Song of the South*' better than anyone Georgina Jane knew. She could make her voice sound just like a black person's voice. There was a storyteller in '*The Song of the South*' called Uncle Reamus, who was a black man. And Manga could sound just like Uncle Reamus and the animals in the book: Bier Rabbit, Bier Fox and Bier Bear. Georgina would have to look up from the pictures in the book to be sure that it was really Manga reading to her. Manga's voice was so realistic, like a really and truly black person's voice would sound. She hated it when Bier Fox and Bier Bear threw good ole' Bier Rabbit into the briar patch with all of those stickers hurting him like that. But she laughed and thought it was pretty funny when Manga told them about the tar baby and how mad that the naughty, mean animals, Bier Fox and Bier Bear, got with that sticky tar baby guy.

Manga even taught them that song about *Zipadeedoda! Zipadeeaa! My, oh my, what a wonderful day! Plenty of sunshine coming my way! Zipadeedoda! Zipadeeaa! Mr. Bluebird's on my shoulder! It's a cinch! It's factual! Everything is satisfactual! Zipadeedoda! Zipadeeaa! Wonderful feelin' comin my way!*

California, Here I Come!

After a good night's sleep in all of those motels on the highway, they would set out on their north-western journey. Every State that they drove through, when they reached the State borders, her grandmother would tell Georgina Jane and her sisters and little brother, Roger Eugenio, which State it was that they had entered. Finally, they were getting to California, which filled them with immense excitement. The day they were going to the Golden Gate Bridge, at a place called *Sam's* Francisco, a very funny thing happened to them. It was a little bit scary at first, but they all laughed about it later that night when they finally got to the hotel. They were driving on the highway singing,

California here I come,
Right back where I started from,
Where bowers of flowers bloom in the spring.
Each morning at dawning,
Birdies sing and everything!
A sun-kissed miss said,
"Don't be late!"
That's why I can hardly wait!
Open up your golden gates!
California here I come!

They must have sung it a million times; it was such a good song. Daddy had just said, "This is the last time we're going to sing this song, girls." That was when they heard a funny sound, like something falling off of the top of the car. Everyone looked behind them to see what had happened. They could see that something was all over the road. Daddy had to pull over and stop the car, which he hated to do. He had to do it so often for potty stops, especially for Gretchen Gabriella who couldn't hold it.

There on the highway, scattered everywhere, as far as the eye could see, were her baby brothers' dirty diapers scattered all over the road. Her daddy had tied the big heavy bag of diapers on to the top of the car, attaching it to the luggage rack, because they were too smelly to keep inside the car. But the big plastic bag of soggy, stinky diapers had come loose from the luggage rack on top of their station wagon. Every single one of her brothers' diapers was strewn all over the California State Highway. Daddy, who never really cussed, said, *"Ching gow!"* and rattled off what was perhaps, some expletive in Spanish, which Georgina could not for the life of her understand. Her daddy had to walk back there on the highway, all by himself, and pick up all of those smelly *'ka ka'* diapers with his bare hands. He was not very happy when he got back into the car. In fact, he wasn't happy at all. All her father said, when he got back into the car, was, "That's enough singing for a while, girls."

When they got to *Sam's* Francisco, they went to a place called China's Town. It was a good dinner there with all of that white rice and noodles and spicy chicken, in a place with lots of people who all had black hair and tiny slanting eyes. They sure did make good food. And they had lots of big red dragons and paper lanterns hanging up for decorations. Gretchen Gabriella didn't like the food in that place, but her daddy made her eat it anyway. Gretchen starting crying and crying, saying that she hated that weird food and she wasn't going to eat it. She was whining and her father absolutely hated whining. Daddy said that she was a cry-baby and to, "Stop that crying, young lady! Children have to eat what is put in front of them. When my father was a little boy, he was lucky to even have food. They were so poor that they hardly even had any food at all. The only thing that he and his family had to eat were chilli peppers, and pinto beans if they were lucky. Sometimes they didn't even have tortillas. So, eat your food right now. Wasting food is sinful. You have to eat everything on your plate."

Wasting food made her father furious. Georgina knew that.

Maybe he was sorry because he had been in a bad mood because of all of those dirty diapers falling off of the car, and Gretchen Gabriella being a cry baby because she didn't like Chinese food. After dinner, they took a walk around China's Town in the dark; with only the street lights and shop lights on to see where they were going. It was way past their bedtime by then. But no one was whining or being a cry baby, because seeing all of the different things in the shop windows kept them spell-bound and quiet. So, when they were out window shopping and walking around in the dark in China Town, Daddy suddenly got all excited and told them, "Wait here!" dashing back into a shop that they had just walked past. He came out of the shop beaming! Holding something up above the heads of his children. Daddy had goodie bags and was smiling with that bright dazzling smile of his, showing his straight pearly white teeth. He had bought little Chinese dolls with tiny eyes and black hair and pretty clothes on. One for Georgina and one for each of the twins. He had bought two toy monkeys with popping eyes that bashed on cymbals as presents for his sons. He had bought Mother a jewellery box that played a little tune that he said reminded him of Okinawa. He had bought Manga a tea set with pale green Celadon glaze on the teapot and the small teacups, because he knew that she liked to drink hot tea.

Georgina was overjoyed with her Oriental doll, who was about the same size as her other doll. Now *Ginny* could have a friend to play with! This new doll had three changeable wigs with fancy hairdos that could be put on and then taken off depending on how Georgina wanted her to look. She had two different kimonos to wear, in brightly colored silk fabric. Georgina Jane O'Shaughnessy could not have been happier about that, because most of her dolls had to be packed up inside of boxes and go with the movers to Alaska. That was a terrible thing, to have your dolls all alone without you. Georgina worried about her dollies being locked up in that moving van like that. She was so happy having a new Chinese dolly with her to keep her company on the trip to Alaska. She didn't like to think of her other dolls in that box in the mover's van. She worried about her dolls all the way to Alaska. Until she saw them again in Alaska, she thought that those doll babies might be lost forever and she would never see them again.

Sometimes she liked her dolls better than her little sisters, because her dolls never argued with her. And she spoke to them in her own special made-up language. Her dolls were her babies. She'd given each one of her dolls a special secret name, that only she and the dolls knew about. And she whispered to them about all kinds of funny secret things on the trip. "Had they seen that? What did they think of this? Weren't the twins the naughtiest girls her dolls had ever seen? (Then she'd giggle.) Had they ever been to such and such a place like she had been there? Did they know where they were going? Did they know about Alaska?"

In Utah, where they saw a lot of dinosaur bones, she wondered about those giant animals. She didn't understand how such big animals could get lost underneath all of that dirt. It made her think of the other day when she and her sister, Gretchen, had gotten lost at the zoo in Denver. It was pretty terrifying to get lost from the rest of your family; especially with all of those wild animals around you. But she was glad that they didn't have real live dinosaurs in Alaska, because she thought it would be pretty scary to see one in real life. She knew that they did have bears in Alaska, though. Her mother had told her about the bears in Alaska. Soon they would be at the ship in Seattle and they could really go to Alaska. Their black and white station wagon could go on the ship too, now that they had taken all of the dirty diapers out of it and washed them.

Sweet Seattle, the Indians' Old City

In three days, they would be in the city of Seattle, Washington. Washington was two States north of California, along the Pacific Ocean's coastline. That's where they were headed to get on the ship to Alaska. Seattle was named after an Indian chief who was very famous. Mommy had read the Indian chief's speech out to them from a book that Daddy had gotten from the information place about Seattle. Chief Sealth's speech was very, very famous. It was all about the Indians who used to live around Seattle a very long time ago. It was all about how the Indians felt about the white people moving into their home and taking it over. The Indians were not happy at all about having to leave their home. Georgina Jane knew how those Red Skins felt, because she hadn't wanted to leave their home in Kentucky either.

Mommy read what Chief Sealth had said in his famous speech way back just over one hundred years ago. Way back in 1854, Chief Seattle said,

"There was a time when our people covered the whole land
as waves of a wind-ruffled sea covers its shell-paved floor.
But that time has long since passed away
With the greatness of tribes now almost forgotten…

"Our great father Washington,
For I presume he is now our father as well as yours,
Since George has moved his boundaries to the North
our great and good father, I say,
Sends us word...
That if we do as he desires, he will protect us.

"The ashes of our ancestors are sacred
And their final resting place is hallowed ground,
While you wander away from the tombs of your fathers
Seemingly, without regrets.

"Our dead never forget the beautiful world
That gave them being.
They still love its winding rivers,
Its great mountains and its sequestered vales

"A few more moons, a few more winters,
And not one of all the mighty hosts
That once filled this broad land
Or that now roam in fragmentary bands
Through these vast solitudes or lived in happy homes,
Protected by the Great Spirit,
Will remain to weep over the graves of a people
Once as powerful and as hopeful as your own!

"Every part of this country is sacred to my people.
Every hillside, every valley, every plain and grove
Has been hallowed by some fond memory
Or some sad experience of my tribe

"And when the last Red Man
shall have perished from the earth
and his memory among white men
shall have become a myth

*"The white man will never be alone
Let him be just and deal kindly with my people,
For the dead are not powerless."*

Georgina liked it when Mommy read out loud to them like that. And she showed them that the Indians felt sad leaving their old home and having to go to a new home. Some of the Indians were even so mad about it, that they painted their faces with war paint to show the white people that they weren't at all happy about moving. It was like those Indians knew just how it felt to be pushed out of a place that was familiar to them. And they knew how it felt to have to go to a new strange place, like Georgina Jane had to go to one.

For three days and two nights, they stayed at a hotel in the downtown area of Seattle and did all sorts of fun things. They went to Pikes Market and saw raw fish with the eyes still left in those fishes' heads. There were real dead pigs' heads there too. And nice colorful vegetables and pretty, sweet smelling flowers. It was nice to walk around the town. It was nice to look around a new different place. It was nice to get some exercise after being cooped up in the back of the car for several weeks. Daddy pushed the twin's old stroller, where Roger Eugenio and Peter Martin sat up nice and straight and looked all around them. Everyone was relaxed and happy. Nobody was restless and cranky. But after three days, the impermanence of the time in Seattle was something that they all felt. After weeks of travelling, everyone was ready to get on with the rest of their trip. Everyone was ready to go to Alaska. Everyone was ready to get settled. Settled in a new strange place.

Gotta Go Now

So, one morning, Daddy said, "Everyone up and at 'em! We're going to Alaska today!" And at that, the family's wheels were set in motion. The twins jumped out of bed and ran to get their little suitcases packed. Mother was already up and she was changing the baby's diaper. Roger Eugenio was still lying in his baby bed drinking a bottle of apple juice. Georgina rubbed sleepy eyes and felt a bubble in her throat and a butterfly caught in her tummy. "Are we really going to Alaska? Are we really going today?"

Daddy said, "Come on, Georgina. Get a move on, kiddo," playfully yanking the covers off of her and tickling her under her arms, then pulling each one of her toes and popping the joints in the ones he could get to pop.

121

"Stop it, Daddy! Don't pull my toes off!"

"Well, get up then, sleepyhead. Everyone is ready but you. Go and get dressed. It's almost time to catch the ship! It is almost time to leave. So, come on! Get up! Go and get ready!"

Georgina went into the bathroom and closed the door, shutting them all out. She splashed water on her face, like Granny taught her to do. She used the toilet and took her nightie off. Then she put her white gauzy petticoat on, which scratched her legs when she sat down. It was fashionable for girls' skirts to stick out, so net petticoats had to be worn underneath dresses for that purpose. She slipped the new lavender dress on over the uncomfortable, stiff petticoat. It was a new dress that Mommy had especially made for her to wear on the ship. That dress was Georgina's favourite color, and the girl had wanted to wear it sooner, but Mommy made her wait until today to wear it. It was a special 'wearing-on-the-ship-dress', so today she finally got to wear it. She could button all of the buttons all the way up the front. She didn't like dresses with zippers or buttons or bows in the back, because she couldn't reach them and had to depend on her mother to get her dressed, like she was a big baby. She put her white cotton socks on. And she slipped on her stiff, brand new black patent leather 'Mary Jane' shoes, and buckled them all by herself. Last, she put her new white cotton gloves on. All well-dressed ladies had to wear gloves to be considered properly attired back then.

Mother usually had to brush and braid Georgina's hair, but today Manga would do it. Laid out on the dressing table were combs, hairbrushes, rubber bands, ribbons and barrettes especially for the job. Georgina went back to the hotel bedroom and sat on the bed and waited for her grandmother to get around to her. Manga was fixing all of the girls' hair for Mother. Mother had a million things to do still, and Daddy was growing impatient. Daddy was telling Mother that they were going to be late. "Honey, the ship's going to leave without us if you don't hurry up." Mother was still in her shiny nightie and was flustering this morning. And Manga was trying to smooth things over between everyone. Everyone seemed nervous or excited. And nerves were beginning to fray around the whole family's edges. Manga was composed, and her own serene self. Katrina Josephina was grouchy and she was complaining that Manga was pulling her hair too tight in the ponytails. Manga was laughing and telling that girl to "Hold still, Katrina Josephina, and it won't hurt so much." Gretchen already had her hairdo completed and was jumping up and down on the bed, her hair in its ponytails, bouncing with her.

Daddy was telling Gretchen to sit still and, "Cut it out, kid!"

Mother was saying, "I do not have goats. I have children." And she was getting annoyed with Daddy. The only ones, besides Georgina, who were behaving themselves, were the two identically dressed boys; both in the baby bed together and making each other laugh in baby giggles. Before she knew it, they were on board the ship.

'The ship was cheered, the harbour cleared.'
The Rime of the Ancient Marinere
S. T. Coleridge

Nobody could have prepared Georgina Jane for that ship. That ship with its huge hull. That ship with its loud horn, blowing so loudly and scaring her so badly. That horn blasting, and making her nearly jump right out of her skin! Those small cabins with beds neatly made. That ship's potties that they called *'heads'*. That ship's enormous *'hold'* where they put all of the luggage. Those long corridors that swayed and moved from side to side when the ship got underway. That ship with all of the captain's helpers doing all of those jobs. Those helpers all dressed up in their special clean uniforms and shining shoes that looked like they would melt in a bright sun. Those tiny portholes looking out at Seattle harbour the day they left the lower forty-eight States. The day that their sea voyage got underway. The day that the ship took them away. The day that the ship took them up to Alaska.

Daddy said that it would take nearly a week, or was it two weeks, to get there. She didn't hear him very well in the din of the twin's excitement and squeals of laughter. Those two were over the moon with the pleasure of this ship liner's motion and containment. That ship had everything! There was a special padded playroom for children. There was even a movie room for the kids to watch cartoons and *The Three Stooges* and Shirley Temple movies. There was a library with lots of children's picture books to borrow. There was a shop with bubble gum, candy, cigarettes and cigars, books and newspapers and magazines and even some hankies and hats and socks and clothes to buy if you needed them. There was a laundry room to wash the babies' diapers. There was a place to play outdoor games like bowling. There was a huge dining room where they would eat their meals. There was a dance floor. There were chairs inside to sit and have tea or coffee and look out the windows. There were lounge chairs outside to sit and talk or look out at the ocean.

Daddy said that he was tired and wanted to take a nap. He would watch the two little boys sleeping. Manga would take the twins to the children's movie room and they could watch a Laurel and Hardy comedy show. Mother was too excited to sleep. She thought that being on the ship was a great adventure, letting the wind blow in her hair, and closing her blue eyes with a look of contentment and pleasure as they all stood on the deck and watched Seattle, the Indians' old home, disappear.

The Ladies' Luncheon

Mother wanted Georgina to be her friend. Mother wanted to spend time with her daughter. Mother wanted to talk to Georgina. So, Mother took Georgina to the ship's dining hall to have a *'ladies' luncheon'* just for the two of them. But Mommy started talking to a stranger and made some friends right away. Mommy invited her new lady friend and the lady's little boy, Henry, to have lunch with her and with Georgina. Mommy thought that Georgina would like to have a new friend too. But Georgina would have rather just had Mommy all to herself for a change.

That new lady friend of Mommy's had a son named Henry with her at lunch. Henry was a boy. It was supposed to be a *'ladies' luncheon'*. It was supposed to be Georgina's special time alone with her Mommy. But there was this strange woman. And there was her son. There they were. There they were sitting at Mommy and Georgina's table. There they were eating lunch with Georgina and with her mother. There was a boy at the table with them. A boy at the table of a *'ladies luncheon'*. Henry was more than three years older than Georgina Jane. So, that made Henry nine years old. In fact, Henry told Georgina that his birthday was next month, and then he would be ten years old. Henry jabbered on and on about everything and nothing whatsoever. Georgina had little brothers, but she didn't really understand boys. Baby boys were one thing. Nearly ten-year-old boys were another thing altogether. She had never been to lunch with ten-year-old boys before. Nearly ten-year-old boys were like creatures from outer space. Nearly ten-year-old boys were like *Creatures from the Black Lagoon*. Nearly ten-year-old boys spoke in another language, almost as incomprehensible and as foreign as the Spanish spoken by Daddy and Granny and Granddaddy was.

Henry thought that he was very special because he was nearly ten years old. Henry thought that he was a big shot because he was a boy and Georgina was just a girl. He did most of the talking; while Georgina sat and stared at him as she carefully chewed mouthfuls of ship food. She had her napkin on her lap. She had taken her right cotton glove off, so that she could hold her fork and eat her lunch. She had her left hand on her napkin, like Mommy had taught her. She was sitting up straight. She was a real little lady. Henry's mommy and Mother had their own private adult conversation. Henry liked to play baseball, but Georgina didn't play baseball. Georgina knew very little about baseball. So that kid, Henry, explained the rules of baseball to Georgina.

Baseball players used a ball and a bat. They hit the bat with the ball and then ran to things Henry called 'bases'. Anyone who couldn't hit the bat very well got a 'strikeout', which meant that they were a lousy baseball player not worth a darn. Every game had two teams playing and the best players got to have the most times hitting the ball. Because all of the baseball teams wanted their team to win. The goal was to hit the ball with the bat, run to first, second and third base and then back to the 'home plate' to score a point for your team. 'Foul balls' were bad. Getting caught by a player holding the ball was bad because it meant that you were 'out'. Being 'out' was very bad because it meant that you lost getting a point for your team.

Henry liked to collect baseball cards with important players' photographs on them. He had pulled his cards out of his pocket. He laid his cards on the table in front of them, and showed them to Georgina. He thought that she thought that famous baseball players were great too. She didn't see what the fascination with baseball cards was. Even if the men were supposed to be so great, the girl didn't understand the value of Henry's precious cards. According to Henry, these were the greatest baseball players of all time. According to Henry, these were the best baseball players in the whole wide world. But what were you supposed to do with those cards? Play a game like 'Old Maid'? Were you supposed to cut the baseball guys out like paper dolls? Where were the baseball players' paper clothes? Henry, this new boy her mother wanted her to entertain at their 'ladies luncheon' was an authority on baseball cards.

"This one here's my favourite. That's a picture of Babe Ruth! He was with the Yankees. And this one here's Yogi Berra. He's a real winner. That one's Lou Gehrig. And this one! This one's Mickey Mantle! He plays for the Yanks too! He's from Oklahoma though. He's an Okie."

"I'm from Oklahoma too. My daddy says that I was born in Comanche County and that makes me an Indian."

"Oh, yeah, kid. So what? Wanna see some more of my cards? This one is Willie Mays, but he's a *nigger*."

"My mother says that is not a nice word to call people. You shouldn't say words like that. Colored people are like candy bars."

"Oh, yeah? Well, kid, I think that you are pretty stupid. I'll say whatever I wanna say! You're just a dumb girl. What do you know anyway?"

"I don't think that is a very nice thing to say. My daddy says that I'm in charge of the little kids in our family, even if I am a girl. And I am not stupid. I can count all the way up to one hundred and one."

"Who cares about your dumb numbers? Aw, kid, how can a girl be in charge? You don't know nothin'! Like I said, you're just a dumb old girl. Who cares what you say anyway?"

Henry's mother thought that it might be nice if Georgina and her Mommy came over to visit them at their room on board the ship. Henry's mother offered to have coffee sent to her cabin for them. Coffee and cream for the mommies and cookies and milk for the children. How would Georgina like that? Did she like cookies? Wasn't she just the sweetest little girl! Would she like to come over for a visit with her Mommy?

Georgina was feeling bored and tired by then. Tired of Henry's company. Tired of trying to be polite to this boy whom she hardly knew, and really didn't care to know, if she'd had a choice in the matter. But Mother had made other plans, and Georgina had to come along to Henry's mother's cabin for the ladies to have coffee and cream and for the children to have cookies and milk. She had to come. Come whether she wanted to or not. She had to come to Henry's cabin and be polite. Be polite to a rude kid.

"Come on, kid. I'll show you my marbles. Have you ever played marbles?"

"My granddaddy is a champion marble player from Dilly, Texas. He has lots and lots of marbles that he won playing marbles."

"Okay, kiddo, let's go to our cabin and I'll teach ya how to play marbles."

Henry's mother led the way to their cabin in another wing of the ship's corridors. Henry flounced on his bed, showing off his bounceability to his new girlfriend. He dug around in his suitcase and pulled out a wad of dollar bills, bragging about how much money his dad made and saying that he intended to spend the *'dough'* on the trip to Alaska.

Georgina, who knew all about dough from Granny's tortillas, thought that Henry must be a very confused little boy, even though he was older than she was. He was so confused that he thought that money was dough, and that meant that he was a dummy without even realizing it.

"Come on, kid. Let's play on the floor. I bet I can win ya in marbles. I'll even loan ya some of my marbles to play with. Ya roll 'em like this. Ya flick 'em off your fingers like that."

On and on, Henry chuntered and big-noted himself, bragging about what a terrific marble-player he was, probably the best kid on his whole block back in Des Moines, Iowa where he was from. His marbles were going everywhere. He seemed like a real crazy marble player, missing every turn he took. Finally, he decided that it was Georgina's turn to flick the colored marbles around. She took her white cotton gloves off. Her first turn she flicked the green cat's eye marble so hard that it shot straight underneath Henry's bed. So, she, like Alice in Wonderland, chasing that white rabbit, followed the marble underneath Henry's bed. Henry followed her.

Henry followed Georgina Jane O'Shaughnessy underneath his bed. He followed her, and he played a trick on her. He played a mean trick on her. He played a very mean trick on her. Henry grabbed her. He hugged her so tightly that Georgina couldn't breathe. Henry was squeezing the very life out of her. Henry was trying to murder her. Henry was a mad man. Henry was a dummy. Henry was a bad, naughty boy. Henry was like those naughty boys back in Kentucky who liked to look up at Georgina's underwear. Henry was laughing. Henry was laughing at Georgina. She was trying to pull away from him, but Henry was holding her tight.

Then Henry did a really, really bad thing. Henry kissed Georgina right on her lips. Henry didn't know that six-year-old girls do not like to be kissed on their lips. Henry was confused and thought that Georgina was a 'dame'. He thought that she would love to be kissed right on her soft little pink lips by a big ten-year-old boy like him, with so many great baseball cards and so many pretty marbles. But Georgina just hated it. Henry was kissing her. Henry was hugging her. Henry was squeezing her. Henry was killing her.

In her mind, Henry was like that sea turtle back in Okinawa who bit Georgina on her hand that day. That yellow-eyed sea turtle wanted to bite Georgina on her hand and then pull her away into the sea with him. This grasping a hold of her gave the girl a trapped feeling. A bad feeling. A captured feeling. Henry was like that oxygen mask that they put over her face in the hospital. Henry was like that mask mixed with gas and medicine to put Georgina to sleep, so that the doctors could get her tonsils out of her throat. Henry was like that mask that made Georgina feel all claustrophobic and panicky inside. Henry was trying to get a better hold of Georgina and stop her from squirming around so much. He was trying to keep her from struggling to get free of him. Georgina Jane was panicking. She was fighting. Her gloves were off. She was socking Henry in his eye. She was socking him hard. Henry was naughty and she was going to beat him up. She was going to beat him up like Katrina Josephina would of if she'd been there.

All the while, this was happening underneath Henry's bed, where the two children were hidden from the view of their mothers, the two ladies talked on and on about so many interesting things. The latest fashions and dress patterns, hats, shoes, travel, family plans, where they were from, who was important politically at the time. On and on, they chattered, not realizing the terror which was confronting Georgina underneath the very bed on which the two women sat and calmly drank their coffee and cream. "One lump or two?" asked Henry's mother.

Henry would not let go of Georgina, no matter how many times she punched him and kicked him and squirmed around underneath that kid's bed. Henry had her, and he was never ever going to let her go. So, Georgina did the only thing left to do. With Henry's lips pressed against her lips, she sucked his bottom lip in and bit him on his lip as hard and as forcefully as she could bite him. She bit Henry so hard that she drew blood. She knew all about biting from watching Roger Eugenio, who was a very hard biter-boy. She meant to hurt Henry. To force him to let go of her. To make him let her out of the crawl-space underneath his bed. He was really getting on her nerves now. He could have his rotten marbles. She was never ever going to play marbles with that kid again. Never ever as long as she lived.

Henry started crying. He was bawling like a baby. And he crawled out from underneath the bed. He ran over to his mommy and showed her what that awful girl had done to him. Georgina crawled out from underneath that bed with his green cat's eye marble in her hand. She threw the marble down on the floor and stomped out of that kid's cabin, not having any idea where on earth she was going. She left her gloves behind. She could not remember the number that was on her door, where she was staying with Manga and the twins. All that Georgina knew was that she had to get away from that kid, Henry, if it was the last thing that she ever did.

Mother sat there on the bed, next to Henry's mother, both of the women examining the boy's face. Bruising was already coming up on that kid's eyelid. His shins were bruised too. But the worst of it was that bleeding bottom lip that bled profusely all over the carpet in their ship's cabin. Blood running down his neck. Blood covering his nicely pressed white shirt. Blood all over his cheeks and chin. Georgina's mother was completely and utterly appalled. It was unbelievable! Mother was simply horrified. Mother was embarrassed beyond all belief. This incident confirmed her worst suspicions about her daughter. Her unruly daughter.

> *'Instead of the cross the albatross*
> *About my neck was hung.'*
> **The Rime of the Ancient Mariner**
> **S. T. Coleridge**

Georgina could not be found for dust. She had skedaddled. She was nowhere to be found. In her child's mind, she had to run and run and run away from danger. The danger of a ten-year-old boy. A ten-year-old boy who wanted to hold her. A ten-year-old boy who wanted to hug and squeeze her so tightly. A ten-year-old boy who wanted to kiss her. A ten-year-old boy she had wanted to kill. And away from a mother who would never ever understand. A mother who would think for sure that she had possibly the worst little girl in the whole wide world.

When he heard about what she had done, Daddy said, "Good girl! Give 'em hell, baby!" He was so proud of Georgina when he heard about her ordeal.

Mother said, "Don't encourage her." Mother was ready to give her daughter a piece of her mind. She was just plain furious, wanting to kill Georgina herself for what she had done to her new friend's nice little boy. The poor little boy who was now frightened to death, and was refusing to come out of his cabin. Refusing to see Georgina again in the dining hall where all of the families had to eat their supper. But Daddy said let's wait and see why she did it. He was beaming with pride at having such a daughter. He loved boxing and had been good at it. His mother still had his trophies displayed on her piano in Georgina's grandparent's house back in San Antonio. So, to have a daughter who liked boxing, and was as good at it as Georgina, was like winning a grand prize, and Daddy was thrilled. He threw his head back and roared with laughter when he heard about it.

Mother would not listen to reason. She took Georgina by the hand, squeezing the child's small hand as hard as she possibly could, digging her sharp fingernails into her daughter. Georgina was defiant. She pulled against her mother's grasp. Mother was taking her awful, problematic daughter back to the scene of her crime. Mother told Georgina, "You must apologise to Henry. You have done a terrible thing. It was unlady-like. It was undignified. It was a really, really awful bad thing that you have done to that poor little boy. I am ashamed of you. I am sorry that I took you out to lunch if that was the way you were going to act. Aren't you ashamed of yourself? Did you see what you did to Henry? Did you see his poor face? You have given Henry a black eye. He will have a black eye for the rest of the trip. And you will have to look at his black eye every day for as long as the trip lasts. I am so angry with you. I could just pound you. I am very, very mad at you, Georgina Jane O'Shaughnessy!"

Mother pulled Georgina all the way through the ship's long corridors, calmly smiling at strangers they passed along the way, as though she was simply out for a nice little stroll with her cute, sweet, little girl. Georgina's horrible scratchy net petticoat was rubbing against her legs, and hurting her. It made a stupid sound as she walked. "Scritch, scritch, scritch!" all the way down the long corridors. Making that awful sound, that scritching sound, all the way down the ship's long hallways. Mother wasn't interested in speaking to Georgina anymore. Mother wasn't excited about going for a trip on a nice big ship anymore. Mother did not want to be friends with Georgina anymore. Mother had not enjoyed her 'ladies luncheon' with her daughter one little bit. Georgina had utterly 'ruined' their luncheon and 'spoiled' the entire first afternoon aboard the ship taking them North to Alaska. Mother glared at Georgina, and continued to pinch the girl's hand very tightly, and to dig her fingernails into the child's palm.

Mother made her way back to Henry and his mother's cabin. She made her way back, pulling, even dragging, Georgina Jane behind her. Henry sat on the bed with a big bag of ice cubes on his puffy eye. He cringed in fear when the girl came into his cabin. And he moved away from her. Moving closer to his mommy. His bottom lip had stopped bleeding, but was swollen to twice its normal size. Georgina noticed that her teeth marks were still evident. His mother was crooning over her precious, darling son, who would now 'be scared for life' because of Georgina. Because of what such a *'wretched'* child as Georgina Jane had done to his beautiful little face.

"Look at this! Just look! Do you see what you have done, girl? What do you have to say for yourself, girl? Do you hear me, girl? Why on earth would you do such a thing?" Henry's mother glared at Georgina, as if she would like to kill the girl herself, if she could only get her hands on her.

Georgina remained sullen. Georgina remained silent. She stared blankly at all of them. That gang of three. She stared blankly at her mother. Her mother standing there with a look of stern chastisement on her face. A look of disapproval. A glaring look. Georgina was staring without blinking. Without crying. She stared at Henry's mother. His mother who hated her. She stared without emotion as she looked at Henry and his bruises and his big ugly black eye. She refused to apologize. She was the worst daughter that any mother could have. She would never have any friends if she went around acting like that. She was nothing but a spoiled brat who needed to be taught a lesson that she would never ever forget as long as she lived. But Georgina refused to say that she was sorry. Her mother could make her stand there and look at Henry's swollen face for as long as she liked. Her mother could make her stand there forever. She would not speak to Henry no matter what. Henry might take it the wrong way, and assume that Georgina would then like to be friends with him again. He would assume that, she had enjoyed his game. His game of marbles.

> *'Hot diggity dog diggity*
> *Boom! What ya do ta me!*
> *It's so new ta me!*
> *What ya do ta me!'*
> > **Hot Diggity Dog**
> > **Perry Como**

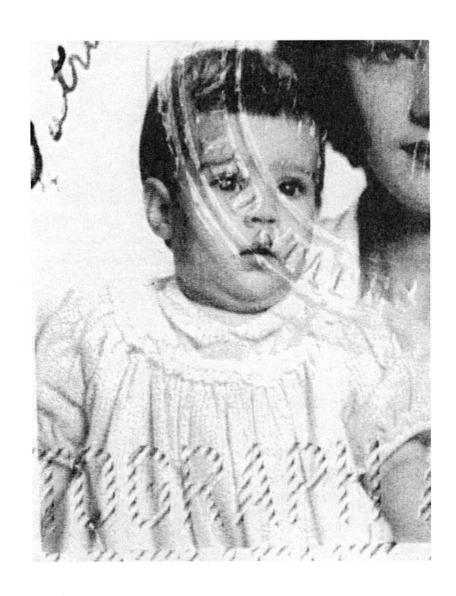

Chapter Four
Deep Waters Turn to Soaring

'Swiftly, Swiftly Flew the Ship'
The Rime of the Ancient Mariner
S. T. Coleridge

It was love at first sight. That first sight of Alaska. That was a day to remember. The day Georgina's family arrived in Alaska was a bright happy sunny day. The Bering Sea, named after a guy called Mr. Bering, had shiny glimmering waves that the ship's bow cut right though with its pointed stern as it headed into the shoreline and the docks of Seward. The child looked over the ship's railing along with everyone else in her family. Almost all of the other families on the boat were there too. Looking at Alaska. Mother had tied scarves, like Russian babushkas around her daughters' chins. The wind was so ferocious and billowy. It nearly knocked the children over as they stood on the deck of their ship. Way, way down there in the swell of the ocean's waves, she saw him! He was her favourite. Her very favourite whale in the whole wide world. She spotted her very own mottled whitish whale in amongst the mostly grey rather boring, ordinary ones. Even Moby Dick could never compare with Georgina's very own white whale, so immense and beautiful. Those giant creatures were very playful, frolicking in the undulating surf and leading, even herding, their ship into its port. Those whales were very excited and exuberant. They acted like they were a bunch of little kids let out for recess at school, having fun in their own private watery playground together.

She wanted to join in with them as they leapt up, and the great force of the sea's breakers was as though it was nothing of any real substance to them. When the weight of the monstrous creatures fell back, onto and into the water, the mighty waves moved out of the way. The girl felt that she was only a tiny dwarf compared with the sheer size and strength of such humongous mammals, who could even blow water and air out of the weird not-closed-up holes on top of their heads. From her vantage point, high above them, she could see inside of those waterspouts. From her lookout station, she could see where the whales were leading them. From her position, daringly bending over the ship's railing, she was able to look right down inside of the top of the whales' heads where they kept their big, big smart intelligent whale brains.

Whales and people were mammals. Daddy told her that, so it must be true. He said that people were related to whales because they were both mammals. How could she and her family be related to such gigantic beings? Did whales really like people? Did those whales realize that Georgina was part of their mammal-family? Were whales really as clever as they acted? Where in the evolutionary chain did she and the whales mesh? She stood there, staring down at the sight of those huge sea mammals, amazed that creatures so enormous and gigantic knew how to play together so happily out in the open sea like that. She thought to herself that those cavorting sea animals were a truly wonderful sight, a great pleasure to stand there, holding on to the ship's railing for dear life and look down upon. Watching them was the best show on earth! It was a scene like no other that the girl had ever seen before that extraordinarily magical moment when they first began to arrive in Alaska. As she watched, in her mind, she knew that what she was looking at was truly remarkable and wondrous. Nobody had to tell her that.

Those whales and dolphins of various sizes and species obviously loved the ship and all of the people who were riding in it. It was like those whales were grandparents or friends of Georgina's ship, excitedly welcoming it back to Alaska again. Perhaps the whales and dolphins remembered her ship from other journeys that it had been away on, when it was out of the Alaskan harbour for weeks or months on end, travelling back and forth to the lower forty-eight States, or off to other far-away places. Out of the tops of their gigantic heads, those monstrous creatures of the deep blue ocean were spouting out tremendous sprays of seawater, full of lots of sea salt in it. Those whales were dancing out on the sea's watery glaucous surface. Those whales were performing an incredible oceanic dance just for the girl and her family.

What great performers those immense, smooth, grey giants were! Roger Eugenio squealed with utter delight when he saw them. When that kid saw those whales leaping up from the ocean beneath them. For an instant, Georgina could tell from that kid's face that he thought like she did. Roger wanted to jump into the ocean like Curious George the monkey in their book did. Little Roger Eugenio, who was named after their daddy, wanted to swim away to Alaska with the whales all by himself. Even a baby could tell that the whales were happy to greet them. Even a little baby-kid like Roger Eugenio, could get excited about whales. Even he could see how special and amazing they were. Those whales were out there having a whale of a time, all working together in unison to get that ship to its place on the shore. They seemed really happy to see the O'Shaughnessy family and their big ship full of people and cargo and cars and sailors.

Those whales were helping Georgina Jane's ship find its way safely to the harbour. Soon they would be nearing their new home. What would they think of the State of Alaska, the brand-new forty-ninth State in the Union? Excitement and a sort of hollow fear grabbed the girl by her six-year-old tummy, making her thoughts leap and race inside of her head like the whales' big tummies must have felt when they leapt up and raced below. She felt safe with her family being all together, like the whales' family was together.

But she knew that her best old friend, Juanita, would not be in Alaska. Juanita was still back in Kentucky. Juanita was probably wearing her favourite pair of blue jeans that her mother let her wear. No one in Georgina Jane's family ever got to wear blue jeans, even though her best old friend's mother, Mrs. Gomez, who made really, really good toll house cookies, thought that blue jeans were just fine. Would any of the new people in Alaska wear blue jeans? Would the natives be friendly? Would they wear clothing that was different from the clothes that she and her family wore? She'd have to wait and see when they got there. A whole new world was opening up before her. Of that much she was pretty certain.

Up ahead on dry land, Georgina Jane could see some mountains. They looked immense. They looked looming and overpowering. Those mountains were enticing her. They were beaconing her to come and have a look all the same. During their travelling up to catch the bulky ship in Seattle, the big city with lots of inland lakes, and even more water on its coastline, where the ships were parked and awaiting their disembarking, the girl and her family had driven a slow climb up and over the Rocky Mountains, so she knew about big mountains. The Rocky Mountains were purplish, but the Alaska Mountains up ahead in the distance had more white than purple on them. The Alaskan mountains had white snow on top and green icy glaciers too.

Manga had taught them those patriot songs about the '*purple mountains majesty*' and the one about '*the redwood forests*' as they drove through those places.

The journey had been, as she would say a decade later, 'mind-blowing'. Too much to take in without batting an eyelid. Going up those stony purple mountains, their station wagon had to be put into a lower gear. Cars in lower mountain-climbing-gears made a different sound from their usual purring sound as they whizzed along flatter, more even terrain. Mountains were bigger than anything. Manga told her that Alaska had mountainous country that was gianter than even the huge Rockies had been back in Colorado. Soon they'd be there and the girl could see for herself what Alaska was really like.

Gross and Disgusting Things

It was a good thing that the ship had a laundry room. The afternoon of the day that they arrived in Alaska that evening, Georgina and Manga went to the noisy washroom in the ship with the twins. Manga fed the machines the loads of diapers, pungently smelling of ammonia and baby dung from her baby brothers,

Manga's grandsons. Her grandmother even handled and touched those soiled nappies that reeked to high heavens and made Georgina nearly puke when she got a whiff of the odour those cute little baby brothers of hers produced so profusely. Katrina Josephina had feigned nerves of steel in order to impress Manga. The girl's phoney stoicism and put-on composure, as though her guts and nasal abilities were not stretched beyond all normal composure when she offered to help their granny load the washer, made Georgina smile to herself. She knew her sister's real reason for the offer to help. Sitting up on the counter next to the big washing machine, that sly, deceptively sweet-looking, little four-year-old cat-girl intensively studied Manga as the sort-of-old grandmother poured the potent laundry powder into the washing machine, covering the smelly tops of those soiled cloth diapers with white powder like snowflakes.

Katrina Josephina, sitting on the counter, overlooking the inside of the washing machine pipped up, "What's that white powder for, Manga? Is that to help you get the smell out of these diapers?"

"Yes, sweetheart. You see, if the laundry detergent mixes with the hot water and gets all over the diapers it will wash and sanitise them and soon, they'll be as good as new. And then they won't be so stinky!"

"That'll be good. Because they don't smell very good right now, do they?" (That was Gretchen, who was holding her nose and talking at the same time. She had a nasal quality to her voice.)

"No, they don't! They smell terrible! But you'll see, later on after we rinse them again and then dry them in that big machine over there (pointing to the enormous clothes dryer) they won't smell bad at all."

The diapers needed an extra rinse cycle just to rinse all of that soap out of them. Babies bottoms couldn't tolerate detergent left in their diapers. Infants and un-potty-trained toddlers would have diaper rash red like the measles, which Georgina and the twins had caught the last year they lived in Kentucky. (That was way before doctors vaccinated kids against diseases like: measles, mumps and sick stuff like that.) Big whelps all over babies' posteriors would grow on those little kids overnight if any of what Manga said was 'toxic' laundry detergent left over from the soap suds came in contact with their soft little behinds. Georgina Jane had learned all about the Chemistry of such things. She now understood why it was that cotton diapers were washed and then rinsed this way from her grandmother, Manga, who told the girls about that, and about so many other interesting things on the trip north to Alaska.

When Manga used to be Nellie Irwin, when she was a young college student, in a time when women didn't usually go to Universities to study, she had been one of two young ladies in her graduating class of 1922. Manga had her University degree in Pharmaceutical Studies, so she knew all about things like Science and Chemistry.

And she could explain everything that was scientific (like smelly diapers) very simply, so that even Georgina could understand it.

Learning about defecation and urination, mucus emission from nasal cavities, farting, burping and belching, belly buttons and umbilical cords, vomiting and diarrhoea, fevers and diaper rash and all sorts of bathroom talk, the reason why people cried and why diapers smelled so bad, infections and germs were among the most fascinating topics of conversation for the curious young children. Grandmothers didn't seem to mind talking about such curiosities like her mother did. Funny old Grannies thought it was amusing. Mother would never discuss anything to do with going to the toilet or what must have been the many other realities of her existence. She even hid her underwear at the very back of her drawers, covering all of that nutty chocolate that she ate secretly. It was like she didn't wear underwear and never even went to the toilet! Mother went to the ladies' room instead. She probably didn't even have to go poop poo or have a bottom that needed wiping, or would never admit it.

Mother only ever went to the bathroom or to the 'Ladies Room'. Conversation of what she did once she got there was personal and private or non-existent, never to be discussed even in confidences. Even the word itself, 'toilet' was unmentionable. The child had never heard the term 'fart' referred to by her poised and refined Madre. Shit was allocated the terminology 'ka ka', which seemed harmless enough.

Although Katrina Josephina learned about the ship's poop deck and rejoiced in her newfound knowledge by repeating the word poop poop poop poop over and over and over again until her mother told her, "That's enough, young lady. Now stop saying that word, please. It's not polite. I've told you before. I've told you to stop saying that. You know that we don't use words like that in our family."

Spitting was unthinkable. But Daddy did it every chance he got, clearing his throat with great vigour, rolling down his car window on the driver's side of their station wagon the whole time they were out there zooming around the countryside, throwing his head back and forcefully puffing the snot mixed with saliva out through his puckered lips as far as he could, to keep his juices, after he had cleared his throat, from blowing back into the car and hitting his kids or his mother-in-law smack dab in their faces. Georgina would brace herself as soon as she saw him even start rolling his window down. There was only one reason for it. Her daddy was at it again. He was up to another unrefined occurrence on the journey, like that crude nose-picking he did all of the time. Her mother would tell her in confidence, whispering so that no one else could hear, that his manners were 'deplorable', whatever that was supposed to mean. Mother didn't like the idea of being associated with someone who did things like that. If Daddy acted like that out in public, Mother would always distance herself from him by referring to the man as, 'the children's father' and not as her husband.

Daddy took it as a matter of course. He and the whales had to emit mighty strong sprays of one sort or another. But her father's spitting was an event for which the girl held her breath and waited with dread until the window was rolled back up. Would this be the time when he didn't blow hard enough and the wind would blow his slimy spit, thick with his snotty reserves, and hit her right in between her squinting hazel eyes?

The man loved to fart more than anything. Farting was not just passing wind to him, it was a comical act, the sole intention of which was the entertainment of his children. Those kids loved the rhythmic quality of the sounds Captain O'Shaughnessy was able to emit from his Latin bottom. All the way to Alaska, they were enthralled by his deliberate control of the upper and lower halves of his body.

Daddy was amazing! Besides farting at will, he could flex and unflex the brawny muscles in his arms any time he wanted to. Pretending to be Popeye the Sailor Man and then bad old Brutus all at the same time, he'd roll his long shirtsleeves up and flex and re-flex away to his heart's content. Impressing his children with his many talents gave his life purpose.

His precise timing for maximum embarrassment was superb. If he knew that Georgina was feeling self-conscious or worried about something, like she was about that kid, Henry, getting a hold of her again, or kissing her again, Daddy would try his darnedest to bring Georgina out of her shell. He would lean sideways, even publicly, and fart like a champion steer or jack-ass at the State Fair of Texas. "Georgina!" he'd say loudly, in that overly exaggerated pretending-to-be-astonished tone of voice of his, as though his lovely, dark-headed, shy and quietly reserved, six-year-old daughter had just been the one to actually pass the noisy wind. It wasn't a matter of smell, it was the loud boisterous sounds he made.

Georgina Jane O'Shaughnessy would sit there astonished. Mortified.

Disgraced beyond belief. She, who was sincerely trying to follow, not his example of very bad manners and crudity, like Katrina Josephina admired so much, but their mother's finesse instead. His eldest child would sit in complete frustration and embarrassment at her indignation. She didn't like him to do that. She didn't like him at all at those moments. And she would give him her stoniest stares, furrowing her dark eyebrows in the process, and frowning at the man. Voicing inaudibly her displeasure with her strongest possible disapproving glare, never daring to say a word in rebuke to her otherwise strict disciplinarian of a father. Nevertheless, she had her own opinions about such matters, and she hoped that her displeasure with the man was obvious to him. She hoped that he knew that she was not amused. If they were out in public, she would pretend that she neither knew him, nor cared one little bit about his unrestricted farting. She would pretend not to be burning up with dreadful face-reddening embarrassment, like she actually was the flaming burning bush in the Bible. She would fake a completely nonchalant attitude if her frowning didn't do the job for which it was intended. Oh, the dilemma of having such a father!

His embarrassment of the family's eldest, self-conscious and bashful child would send Gretchen Gabriella into hysterical fits of giggling laughter, which egged the master farter in their family on to more and more farts and riotous and coarse expulsions. Mother did not pick her nose, like Georgina's father did all the time. It was unthinkable. It was unlady-like. Daddy wasn't even remotely embarrassed to make such a spectacle of himself, and bring such shame on his poor wife and his whole family. He was such an enthusiastic nose-picker that he would even roll his buggers up into little sticky balls and see how far away he could shoot them across the room by flicking them off of his fingers. This was the height of family entertainment! It was like he was inventing a new sport. It was like he thought he was a wonderful skilled athlete. There those *boggies* would go, as he sent them off of the tips of his fingers, soaring at tremendous speeds!

Baby Peter Martin watched their father with the complete rapt fascination which only a six-month-old baby can give. One day that kid would grow up and even outshine his own father. P. M. would grow up to impress an even bigger audience with his ability to spit saliva out of his puckered lips to a distance of twelve feet or even more.

Katrina Josephina thought that her dad's great talent as a nostril-poker-inner, phlegm retriever and champion hurtler of his very own *boggies* was one of the cleverest things he did. That girl encouraged his talent at such a preposterous sport and begged the man to pick more and more and more of his oozing mucus out of his nostrils and see if he could make the adhesive balls stick to walls or any hard surface within the vicinity. Then, she and Gretchen'd double over with fits of laughter, which made Daddy feel like King for a Day. Those girls wanted to be taught about this and other lowbrow pastimes more than anything. Then they could fart, spit, nose-pick, burp and do all sorts of other unlady-like activities which Mother felt were unbecoming or showed poor breeding in her offspring. Katrina Josephina and Gretchen Gabriella weren't tom-boys. They were simply a bit uncouth.

Mother was too well-bred to even think about such things; much less talk about anything remotely connected with such subjects. But her children and their father loved gross topics, and Manga, which is what the children all called their mother's mother, humoured them in all such crude interests. Manga did not care what other people thought or said about them. In her mind, those grandchildren of hers could do nothing wrong. Nothing to cause her the slightest embarrassment.

Everything that they did was perfectly all right with her. Everything that they did was just fine. It was just fine because they were the ones who did whatever it was that they did.

Mother was too highly polished to even fathom such behaviour or discussions concerning it. Behaviour and dialogues which she considered to be very lowbrow and in such poor taste, utterly beneath her dignity. The most the cultured of women, the children's mother, would only ever say, if the smell in the car became too over-powering and odoriferous,

"Katrina Josephina, did you pass wind again, dear? Honestly, honey, try not to do that! It is really very offensive!"

Daddy teased his kids and the sensibilities of his cultured wife by saying, "I bet the Queen of Hearts in Alice in Wonderland farts! I bet the Queen of Hearts burps! I bet the Queen of Hearts even picks her nose secretly when nobody is looking. She's probably even vomited or had diarrhoea once or twice, I bet. What do you think, kids? Do you think that might be true?"

At that, the girls and Roger Eugenio would roar with laughter at the thought of a real Queen, like the Queen of Hearts in the story Alice in Wonderland that Manga was reading to them, really farting, burping, vomiting, maybe even spitting and picking her nose like Daddy said she did. That little kid, Roger Eugenio, was too young to understand. He didn't really get the joke. But he, even at that tender age, wasn't about to let on. And he laughed anyway, just to be part of their gang. Even Georgina laughed at that joke. She didn't think that the Queen of Hearts was a very nice lady anyway. So, Daddy making fun of her was pretty funny.

Time Alone with Manga

After the exciting luncheon with their father and mother and little brothers, everyone was exhausted. There was another leg of their journey still in front of them.

That very night, they would be in Alaska. The twins finally took a nap after Manga had read their favourite Fairy Tale story to them in the cabin they shared with Georgina and their grandmother. Katrina Josephina and Gretchen Gabriella had argued about who got to sleep on the top bunk, but today it was Katrina's turn, and so the relatively more cooperative blond-haired twin was snoozing on the bottom bunk as Manga and Georgina Jane slipped out of their cabin. Georgina had been told to pretend to fall asleep too, otherwise those naughty twins wouldn't take a nap either. It was a secret between their elder sister and Manga, who had put her finger to her lips to signal to Gi Gi (as Roger Eugenio had starting calling his biggest sister) that it was time for them to make their pre-planned escape. And so, the two females, one six and the other fifty-five, were in a conspiracy together as they made their secret getaway, and silently snuck away from the usually bumptious, but now sleeping twin girls.

This was one of the greatest of pleasures. The greatest of adventures, to be with Manga on her own. It was a special privilege to be alone with her grandmother in the midst of a family with so many other family members, all of them vying for her attention at once.

It was just good being in the woman's presence, whatever the occasion. Georgina felt suddenly different about what had previously been the girl's perception of the usual drudgery of her routine task, folding diapers for her mother. Her entitlement to help her grandmother fold the old and new babies' diapers now tumbling and drying in the ship's laundry room changed in an afternoon from being what she had previously seen it as, a boring, repetitive chore. Now, with Manga's enthusiasm for the now-exciting project, it had changed to one of delight, and a sign that in the girl's involvement, she was capable of such a big responsibility. The ultimate thrill for the child was, the attention and the respect of her grandmother.

Once they got to the laundry room, through a long circuitous series of swaying passages, the two females, one a matron and the other a diminutive child, they could finally have a private conversation. It was great to have Manga all to herself for a change. She would do anything for that special, private, individual fellowship and female camaraderie. The girl had begun to see that it was okay to ask Manga questions. With most big people she knew, asking questions was against the social order that kept the baby boomers in line. So, with the spinning machines, noisily whirling in a kind of contented unison all around them, she asked her grandmother, "Do you think we'll like Alaska, Manga? Will Alaska be a good place to live? Will it be better than Kentucky where all of my friends live? Will you like it more than you liked Texas where all of your friends live?"

"It will be very different from Kentucky and Texas. I know that it was sad to leave your friends behind, and not to see Grandmother and Granddaddy O'Shaughnessy again for a long time. But I think you'll love Alaska, honey. It is a very beautiful State. Wait and see. You sure are doing a good job helping me fold all of the boys' clean diapers. Thank you for helping me with all of these. Your help is making the job get done so much faster than I could do it all by myself. See how nice and clean your brothers' diapers are now? They don't even smell bad any more, do they?"

Manga held the sweet smelling, fresh from the dryer, warm diaper that she was folding, up to her pink nose and sniffed aloud. It with a great big almost purring sound, like a cat having milk poured into a bowl in front of her makes under her breath. The woman really wanted to prove a point. She kept the diaper pressed, like one of Grandmother O'Shaughnessy's snot rags, against her lovely straight nose for quite a few seconds. Her dark-hazel eyes had a natural slant, which she closed as she did this. But just because she had narrow slanted eyes, she wasn't Chinese like those yellow people back in San Francisco's Chinatown were. Katrina Josephina had rudely asked Manga, after seeing all of the Orientals in San Francisco, if Manga was really part of their family. Katrina Josephina said that Manga must be from a Chinese family because of her slanty eyes. But the children's grandmother laughed good-naturedly and said that no, she wasn't Chinese.

Her slightly salt and pepper bobbed and wavy hair flared out all over her head in a great profusion of soft gentle natural curls, like the woman's soft and gentle and kind and good personality. Mother said that Manga was 'even tempered'. Boy, she sure was! Even her eyebrows were sweet, with little curly bits on the ends. She had a very low hairline, with her forehead nearly non-existent due to the way her hair grew so low, surrounding the top of her brow. Her whole still largely unwrinkled face was sweetly framed by her thick Irish mane. Mother said that Manga had 'good bone structure' because of her wonderful high cheekbones. That was probably true because it was so obvious that Manga was goodness itself. She was like a special fairy godmother. Like in those stories, she read aloud to the girls, even if it wasn't bedtime. She was the kind of person that you could have for breakfast, lunch and dinner every day for the rest of your life and still never get tired of her one little bit.

Manga was totally Irish. She was the only person in Georgina's family who was totally anything. Everyone else in the family was half this or part something else. Being Irish was special because of the Leprechauns and the fairies that the Irish knew all about. Sometimes, late at night, when the twins were already sleeping, and Georgina was lying next to her grandmother on their bigger bed in the ship's cabin, Manga told her granddaughter fascinating stories all about Ireland and the greenness there, in a place with pots of gold and Leprechauns at the end of rainbows. It was a place where the fairies danced. Her grandmother told her of magical changings of people into swans and hound dogs, antlered stags or wild boars. There were stories of cows and horses and fires and rivers and magical places in the landscape of Ireland where people in the olden days used to gather for magical dances around fires.

Manga's sister, Rose, had told Nellie (that was Manga's real nickname that big people called her) all of the Irish stories that she had learned from their mother before the woman died when her little girl, Nellie was only three years old, still just a little kid herself. Sisters were special if they could take care of you like your mother would of if she had lived instead of dying like that.

Georgina wondered if you would still be liked in Ireland if you were part something else. Manga's parents had moved to America a very long time ago. But they were both dead by now. Her grandmother told Georgina that her mommy and daddy had travelled all the way over from Ireland on a ship too, like the ship to Alaska; just not as nice a one. That newly married couple moved away from their home in Ireland and came to the United States a very long time ago. Manga's mother was named Agnes Hegarty, and that's a pretty Irish name to have.

That's how someone so Irish didn't live in Ireland like Manga's own grandparents used to live there, and her Mommy and Daddy used to live there. Those people that the girl didn't even know, even though they were her really and truly relatives, had disappeared off of the face of the earth a long time ago. Except for what her grandmother told her about them, she knew nothing at all about who they were and what their lives had been like way back a long, long time ago. It made her feel a bit sad not to know such important people, people who had known her Manga when she was a baby and a little girl. They had lived in a place where Georgina had never even been to. They had settled in a place called Pennsylvania, named after a guy named William Penn, who was an important man when the colonists first came to America. Manga's daddy worked in the dark. Manga's daddy used a pick and a shovel to dig black coal out of a cave. Not a cave like *Carlsbab* Caverns in New Mexico. Not a hole in the ground like Alice's Wonderland. Manga's daddy was a coal miner. So that made Manga a coal miner's daughter.

The Irish people were very poor, and sometimes the daddies couldn't find jobs or get money to buy food for their children. So, that's why Manga's family became Americans instead of staying in Ireland like that. All of this was hard for Georgina to understand, because she had never, even once been starving like those poor Irish people looking for crusts of bread must have been. But it made sense in the girl's imagination for people to move far away from their place of domicile and all things familiar. That's what was happening to her in her family's migration to Alaska.

She knew, even as a child, that it must have felt strange and even a little bit scary for her great-grandparents to leave Ireland behind, like she had left the South behind. Had her great grandparents felt the strangeness of their journey as much as she was feeling hers right now?

Manga taught Georgina Irish songs and stories. Sometimes Manga would sing Georgina to sleep. She had such a dear little melodious voice, very much like a little girl's voice. Myrtle the turtle, their dark colored maid back in Kentucky used to sing to Georgina too. But Myrtle the turtle's voice was loud and deep and booming, bursting forth with all of those mighty spiritual songs about the Laud Jesus and the sweet byes and byes. Manga's singing voice was sweet and low, like the glens back in Ireland must be like.

So much confidence in laundry detergent did the girl's grandmother have, that she wasn't even nervous that the fabric of those previously smelly diapers would still contain particles of the boys' ka ka on them.

"We did a good job getting them so nice and clean for Mommy, didn't we? It would have taken me a lot longer if you weren't giving me a hand. You're such a good little helper! I bet you help your mommy all of the time, don't you? What would she do without such a good helper like you?"

A nod and a smile answered Manga's question. That cherished, seemingly old (to the child's mind) sage of a woman always made Georgina feel good about herself. She couldn't explain what her grandmother did for her shy inexperienced heart. All her youthful mind knew was that she needed what Manga could give to her. Not the tangible things. Her grandmother had some funds from her varied jobs as seamstress, airplane mechanic and assistant pharmacist, but she was not well-endowed financially. It was more about the immaterial; the intangible substances of love and devotion to family and kindness to little people, always giving them a healthy dose of freedom and empowering them. Manga was a free spirit; before the term became a coined expression in popular usage. Giving her love and encouragement was one of her greatest pleasures. Her ability to instil a feeling of self-worth, joy and security in her grandchildren is legendary to this very day.

No one who knew the woman could ever forget her. She left her special indelible mark of happiness on everyone who ever knew her good way of being, and ever had her Irish eyes smiling at them. Being with Manga was like being touched with a magic wand by a fairy godmother. All of her fifteen grandchildren loved Manga. How could those kids not value a grandmother who knew how to love them so well? Knowing Manga during a time in life when most big people deliberately tried to overlook and squash children like helpless bugs underneath their feet, seemed like finding gold dust.

The Ugly Duckling and Her Mother

The girl's mother, by contrast to her own mother, did not seem to be able to instil such a good feeling of usefulness in her own child, at least not that particular child. It was difficult for the girl to understand why, or explain those feelings of constant inadequacy which Mommy had. But Georgina knew that it made her feel badly about herself. It was something that the child just knew intuitively was happening to her. And there was nothing that she could do to change the process.

Mother made her feel dizzy about who Georgina was. It was like the girl could hardly ever do anything right. Mother made her feel like she was some odd sort of freak in a circus sideshow. Like an oddball who wanted to wear unlady-like clothes and could hardly even fold diapers the right way. Mother made Georgina feel like she was the ugly duckling in their family. And there was nothing at all that the child could do to change that, though she did try to be acceptable. But it seemed to the girl that nothing she did would please her mother. Nothing she tried to change about herself was ever enough.

Manga, by contrast, helped Georgina to feel strong and capable of doing anything the girl wanted to do. The child didn't have the words for an adequate understanding of it, but it was a subtle process that the girl perceived; though couldn't articulate, all the same. How can a child explain to herself that her very own parent doesn't really like or accept her? How can she even grasp such concepts? Little people; with hearts so naturally filled with openness to the wonders of life, arrived on the planet with such accepting, forgiving attitudes. Separate, yet dependant, needing grown-ups to nourish their souls. Craving love and attention, and sometimes, like Katrina Josephina, who needed to be the star of every show, being naughty just to get attention, even if it is negative attention they get. Georgina felt that if she were someone else, her mother would like her better. But who else could she be? And she really did try to be good, as good a girl as she could be.

Whatever Georgina's mother felt about her daughter, the girl worshipped her mother. Thought she hung the moon. Wanted her attention, but seldom received it. This constant pushing away made Georgina blame herself for her mother's rejection. Mother was perfect. Everyone knew that. Everyone who knew her, thought that Claudia Jane O'Shaughnessy was the epitome of graceful femininity. The beauty, the intelligence, the charm, the social skills, the talent of the woman were noticeable to everyone. The child should have just been grateful for having such a mother who was such an inspiration, a model for the women of her generation.

Mother was the perfect archetypal 'Suzy Homemaker': a great cook, a bottle-washer, an appealing sexy wife to her husband, an outwardly caring mother, an entertainer of friends and colleagues of Captain O'Shaughnessy's military compatriots, a story book reader, a church-goer, a real beauty with impeccable manners, a shapely figure, an interior decorator, even of the drab army housing she was forced to live in. Mother had a talent and flare for almost everything she did. She loved flower arranging and driftwood displays. She craved having pretty things all around her. She liked for her children to be well-mannered and well-behaved. She polished their shoes and the shoes and army boots of her husband tirelessly. She excelled in everything. The one exception to this was her lack of understanding and acceptance of her eldest daughter.

Something was missing from their relationship. What Claudia felt when she looked into the face of that child was just a void of hollowness inside. This emptiness spilled over onto her quiet, but perceptive daughter. The woman gave and she gave and she gave, until there was little of herself left over. Couldn't they all see that? Didn't they see 'how hard she tried'? Her efforts to conceal the truth of her feelings, misgivings about the gender of this child, when a boy was expected, failed. A boy had been hoped for, not this recalcitrant girl. Anger that her college days had ended abruptly when she had such a promising career as a social worker in front of her. Pregnancy with this often difficult to comprehend child had altered her life forever. She was saddled too early with this child. And it left her feeling frustrated and just plain mad.

The others coming so quickly in rapid succession afterwards were more accepted. By the time she had conceived and bore her other five children, she had gotten over the shock to her delicate system that motherhood caused her to feel. By the time that the other children began to be born, she understood the value and status that such little people could give to her life. Like brand name labels on designer clothes, or speedy new sports cars, or the perfectly cooked meals of haute cuisine, children of the 1950s were the crowning glory of those rushed into marriage for whatever reasons back then. Mother, like the women of her generation hadn't even thought to begin to question their roles as wives, homemakers and mothers en masse like their daughters would question such roles. Mother and her lady friends just did what was expected of them at the time. Walking through life like the 'Stepford Wives'. Walking and living without questioning the status quo.

A Difficult Child

'Oh let me tell you about her!
The way she looked…

Oh, let me tell you about the way she looked
The way she acted
The color of her hair…
Her eyes were clear and bright.
But she's not there!'
'She's not There'
The Zombies

But when Georgina had been born, Mother couldn't understand it. She just did not gravitate to her daughter naturally. Her terrible labour and forceps delivery of that baby girl had nearly killed her. Or at least that is what she thought, looking back on the whole dreadful, painful and embarrassing experience. She had been unable to breastfeed the girl. That girl. That girl sitting

148

there at the table questioning her. That girl asking her all of those embarrassing questions like that. Claudia would rather forget that her small, inexperienced breasts had been too tender to do the job of nourishing her very own baby. They had become encrusted, hard and heavy, like two solid rocks, weighing her down. That yellow milk. That yellow milk oozing out of her like that disgusted her. Seeping out all over her lovely blouse and spoiling her appearance.

Her inability to nurse Georgina made Mother feel insufficient. All of that sucking. Suckling like pigs do. It was lewd. It was not something that a young woman of polite society would do without wincing from both the physical pain and the obvious shame of such an act. To engage in such an activity was humiliating and disgraceful. It was downright degrading to Claudia's delicate, enlightened sensibilities. She just knew in her heart that breastfeeding was not something which she wanted any part of. In her mind, it was nothing to be proud of. It was nothing but a shameful, shameful act.

When Mother had gone to lunch with Georgina on the first day of their special journey on the big boat, just before they had met Henry and his charmingly polished mother, the girl had made the mistake of asking Mother what the lady sitting at the next table was doing with her little boy. Georgina had seen the strange woman draping a scarf over her shoulder and inserting her rather large squalling three-year-old son, a strapping lad of a boy, underneath the scarf, hiding his head and her chest in the process.

"What's that lady doing with her little boy, Mother?" Georgina had wanted to know. Mother had turned red in the face, too shocked and too horrified to answer her daughter immediately. Mother had swallowed hard two or three times before she had answered Georgina Jane O'Shaughnessy.

"Well, dear, some people don't have very good manners or a proper sense of decency. What that lady is doing is shameful! Simply dreadful. Something that should not be done in public. But stop staring at her, dear." (Mother shuddered as the nursing neighbouring child was finally beginning to cease his flailing and wailing and was calming down nicely, hidden away underneath his mother's lavender scarf, which was draped over them both so discretely.) "You see, Georgina Jane, people who are common, people who don't know any better, do all sorts of things with their children that we do not think are proper to do in our family. You must learn about these things, dear. They are very important."

Georgina studied her mother's face. This was the answer? Somehow, the child knew that Mother had carefully sidestepped her question. Her distasteful question. She knew that Mother's mind was faraway, like when the child looked out the boring classroom windows back in the old school in Kentucky. Claudia was lost in thought. Her mind was somewhere off in the not-so-distant past of her own motherhood experience. She looked across the table at Georgina sitting there. Sitting there and questioning her. Mother suddenly looked serious and unhappy. What was she thinking? Georgina knew that she had said or done something wrong. She could tell that by looking at Mother's face, so deep and intense, after so much excitement in boarding the ship. Mother's thoughts were some place faraway. Mother was thinking. She was remembering something. She was remembering the girl as an infant. She remembered the child as a tiny pink baby. A crying baby. A baby who had wanted to eat her own mother alive.

That awful baby grasping her bosoms was too obscene. It was something that poor white trash did with their children. Something that low-class Mexicans did.

Folksy Italians or Grecians, Sicilians, Spaniards, Turks or those poor women of African descent nursed their dark-skinned babies. Women who had no pride. No sense of propriety. Women like that odd and ignorant woman seated at the table next to them was doing. That woman was exposing her breasts (which everyone in the ship's dining hall must certainly know existed underneath the woman's scarf) to the world. That woman was breastfeeding her son! And she was doing it publicly! It was a practice that was disdainful to Claudia. She was above all of that.

When Georgina had been born, baby formula was readily available, after all. So, the child wouldn't starve, and even seemed to prefer sucking that baby bottle nipple, with its easily given milky formula, to her own mother's sore tits. A hard labour and difficult delivery, and her failure to nurse the girl, gave her a sense of failure. The widespread knowledge and diagnosis of Post-Partum depression was not clinically understood the year the girl was born, in 1952. Impacted breasts were painful and an embarrassment.

Claudia's hovering mother-in-law, Olivia, gave baby Georgina's mother the creeps with all of her strange superstitious Mexican/Indian traditions. Odd things Claudia found Genio's mother doing with the baby's diapers and peculiar things placed inside the baby's crib. The result of her stress and exhaustion and the soon departure of her husband to Okinawa, gave Claudia nothing but; anxiety. His leaving. Leaving her with his mother. His mother who annoyed Georgina's mother. Got on her nerves and rendered her milk let down reflex inoperable. Mother failed as a breast-feeder.

And Claudia O'Shaughnessy couldn't fail at anything. That very thought was unthinkable. And this arrogance of opinion, and the pride of her life, made her blame those negative, uncomfortable feelings of inadequacy on the girl; never ever on herself. To internalise this deficiency and inadequacy would have been unthinkable. The very idea was completely impractical. It was ludicrous in the extreme.

But someone had to pay for the depression and pain that she often felt. So, the little girl was the likely target. Not that the child's mother would ever admit, even to herself, that she sometimes abhorred her very own flesh and blood. That would make her a monster, wouldn't it? That was a thought that she simply could not, would not, tolerate. There was nothing whatsoever the matter with her! And let's face it. She was never violent towards her daughter. She was never guilty of yelling at her.

Mother always spoke in a quiet, gentle, even tone of voice, telling Georgina to sit or stand up straight. (Slouching was treated as almost an obscenity.) Using a firm, but lady-like intonation, Mother would say, "Georgina Jane, if you continue to scowl at me like that, I will knock your block off!" But these threats never amounted to anything, and couldn't be taken seriously.

All Georgina could think to do was to either scowl, or to just look away. The girl was at a loss for words. Words that she knew that her mother did not want to hear anyway. When she was confronted with her mother's displeasure, she felt very small, very helpless. Mother was big. Big and sometimes angry. That was scary. To be left alone with a big angry lady, even if it was your very own mother, was a terrible thing. Mother would get madder and madder and madder. By the time Georgina had looked away for the third time, in an effort to avoid a confrontation, or scowled or rolled her disdained hazel eyes, Mother would be furious. Just plain furious. Then she would say, "Look at me when I'm speaking to you, young lady! Don't you dare look away from me. Look at my face this minute! Do you hear me?"

There was no escaping the woman. There was no looking away. There was no place of safety. And due to Georgina's seeming indifference to being told off, Mother became annoyed with the girl. She became just plain disgusted with the child.

All of that shrugging of her shoulders like Georgina did so often, only served to put a further estrangement between the girl and her mother. So, over the years, a subtle coldness developed in her manner to that particular child; as though the weight of the world could easily rest on the shoulders of the quiet, timid and shy, but strong-willed little girl. That youngster was the cause of her mother's secret dismay and hidden disappointment that her life and her expectations had been thwarted due to her own offspring's too soon, too sudden arrival. Georgina's inherent personality was a personality that her mother would have preferred that the girl not have. Nothing that the child did, pleased the woman. With a personality like that, who could blame Mother? With a personality like that, all the girl succeeded in doing was getting on Mother's nerves.

Claudia did try her best to be a good mother. She honestly did. Everyone could see that. But somehow, it wasn't enough. What that child needed she wasn't getting. The girl felt her needs out of every pore of her being, but couldn't express them. It was like constantly having her insignificant, unspoken, unarticulated feelings swept aside, so that someone else could have things felt or thought about their way.

The girl sensed the subtlety of the situation. She knew that she was, in some ways, maybe even intrinsically, just an inconvenience. The child's inner voice, though rarely spoken, was silenced before it became audible. She was only to be seen if she were presentable. She must not speak unless it was her turn to do so. (It seemed to the child like her turn would never ever come.) She must sit up straight and behave like a 'young lady'. She must not stare at people when they were out in public. She must not chew her food with her mouth wide open. She must not frown, or her face might stay like that forever. She must learn to have better manners. She must not forget to say her prayers. She must. She must. She must. She must!

She must say 'yes or no, sir' to her father. She must say 'yes or no, Mother' to her mother. Saying 'yes or no, ma'am' was far too Southern. Mother was Mother. Mother was not a ma'am. Mother was not a Mammie. Nor was she a Mama like Grandmother O'Shaughnessy. Ma'ams were too Southern and thus beneath Claudia's northern birth right. Claudia was from Wisconsin, not Georgia! Not North or South Carolina! And certainly not Mississippi! Mammies were too Southern. Mammies were too black and Mother was not like that race. Mamas were either too Hispanic or too poor or too something else altogether. Something that Claudia was not.

Georgina must not question her elders. Her elders and her betters. The list went on and on in seemingly endless dos and don'ts. What the opinionated child thought was unimportant. How she behaved, how she looked, was a different matter. Georgina Jane O'Shaughnessy not only did not act the way her mother wanted her to, she didn't look the way her mother wanted her to look. She looked too much like his side of the family. Too much like her father. With her thick coarse mane of slightly wavy dark hair. Unruly hair. Wavy hair. Not like her mother's lovely naturally curly auburn locks. The child's hair had a mind of its own. A mind of its own like Georgina Jane had.

Georgina's pensive hazel eyes. Not like her mother's gorgeous round clear sky blue eyes, with their curling thick lashes. That child, that difficult child, was so challenging, that although she started off with her mother's blue eyes, Georgina had changed them just to prove a point! That obstinate, wilful and headstrong girl had deliberately changed the color of her eyes after the twins were born! That stubborn little girl had deliberately altered those once lovely aqua-blue eyes when she was all of two and a half years old! She had altered the color of her once lovely blue eyes simply by her sheer will-power. Blue eyes like the ocean. Blue eyes like the sea. Blue eyes changed forever to something else altogether! Why had she done that? Why had her mother's little girl transformed her appearance so radically? It must have been intentional. It must have been an act done with the sole purpose of displeasing and hurting the sensitive feelings of her mother. Eyes do not normally change in a two-year-old like that! Everyone knows that's impossible.

Back in 1954, when Manga wrote to the child's Mother, her own daughter, Claudia, living in Okinawa where Manga's son-in-law was posted by the military, asking, "How is Georgina? And how are her beautiful blue eyes?" Mother had the humiliation of writing back and explaining to the child's grandmother that Georgina no longer had blue eyes. Just like that. Claudia's one consolation in having such a child was the color of the girl's blue eyes. A blue that you could melt into. A blue that Mother liked. Liked very much.

Tolerating that unruly head of hair was bad enough. That hair with its crusty scalp. Crusty baby scalp caused by all of the damp weather in Okinawa. Scalp that had to be scrubbed with a baby hairbrush and olive oil every single day when the child was little. Scrubbed to rid her daughter of such a hideous, yellow scalp. Crusty golden scalp caused by too much hair growing in a place much too damp. An awful crusty scalp on her baby daughter, that had made Claudia feel revolted! Nothing could be worse. Nothing could be more embarrassing.

Nothing could be worse, unless it was fleas jumping out of the top of her baby's head, like one woman she had heard of who had dogs and a terrible flea infestation! Dogs who had given that woman's son, fleas that jumped out of his great mane of dark thick hair like Georgina Jane had.

Her hair and her eyes. Her eyes and her hair. What to do about them? The hair she cut short, like a boys' haircut. Claudia put a bowl on top of Georgina's head and cut the small child's hair around it, using the bowl as a template for her baby's hair design. The child's eyes were another story. There wasn't a darn thing to do to control Georgina's eyes. Eyes changed forever. Now those eyes were a completely different color than the color which her mother had given to her daughter. Now, those eyes were a color that her mother hated. And anyway, who ever heard of such a thing as that? It beggared belief! It was unthinkable. And with that one act of defiance, the little, unknowing, then two and a half-year-old girl had trespassed against her mother with an almost unpardonable sin. Georgina Jane O'Shaughnessy had changed her once 'beautiful, blue eyes', which were the color of the deep blue aqua sea, to nearly the color of the eyes of oceanic turtles that swam in the foreign East China Sea! Now, the girl's eyes were full of specks of yellow mixed with dark green and rimmed in brown! The color of the girl's eyes was as crazy as the girl herself. Those wilful eyes! Who did she think that she was, having eyes like that? Defiant eyes, that thinly veiled private thoughts and attitudes that were always determined to act on the child's opinions, regardless of the opinions of her very own mother!

And so, after this, and other acts of insolence, gradually, almost imperceptibly, there developed a constant pushing away, pushing away, pushing away. Never holding or embracing the child, as though closeness and physical tenderness towards the girl, or a simple act of corporal comfort, was somehow blatantly indecent, and to be avoided at all costs. Holding her little girl might lead to other things. Giving the girl a hug might be interpreted as babying her. And at the age of six, it was high time the child grew up. High time she started to behave herself. High time she thought about her mother's feelings for once in her life.

Claudia feels terribly annoyed with Georgina. Terribly annoyed as they sit there in the ship's lovely dining room with its white table cloths and glimmering cutlery and china table settings. It is such a perfect setting. A perfect place for Claudia to let herself go. Let herself be herself. So, for some reason, which she has not given too much thought to, she reaches across the lovely table set with so many pretty things. She reaches across the table, as though to push Georgina's unruly hair out of her daughter's eyes. She wants that awful head of dark hair to just move out of her way. Out of her way of seeing into the face of her daughter. That hair that prevents her from controlling her child.

But instead of moving the coarse strands of thick hair out of Georgina's face, Mother reaches over and gives that naughty lock a hard tug. The child stops chewing her lunch. Her special luncheon with Mother. Mother is pulling the girl's hair for apparently no reason. Has she not sat up straight enough? Is she using the wrong hand to pick up her fork? What is she doing wrong this time?

Mother senses Georgina's confusion. She thinks that telling a funny story will help the tense situation. She tries to explain how awful Georgina's hairy scalp had been as a baby. (Georgina has heard Mother tell that story a million times already.)

Mother tells her daughter the story about the woman from Texas with the baby son who had fleas in his scalp to try to justify her action, to try to distract Georgina from what has just happened. It doesn't matter. Mother's hair pulling of Georgina's wild strands of hair, hair hanging there in the child's face, propels the girl back into another mental space. A space in her mind, that she has tried hard to shut the door on. But there the child is. Not there at the table with its lovely place settings. Not there on board the wonderful ship taking them to Alaska.

Back into another place. Another space. Back into her baby high chair. She is a baby again. Mother is mad at her. Mother is pulling the baby's hair. Mother is trying to get the baby-child to hold still. The baby is screaming. Her face is red. She has lost her hair. Her hair is in her eyes. Her eyes that Mother is mad about. Mad at. Mad at those eyes. Mad at that naughty hair. Those naughty eyes and that naughty hair of Georgina Jane O'Shaughnessy's.

Nobody talks about PMS back then. No one admitted that exhaustion and exasperation and general fatigue and worry could overcome even the best of mothers. Mothers have to be perfect. Mothers' children have to be perfect. Nobody excuses bad behaviour in 1953. Back when the child sat in her high chair. Sat in her high chair crying. Crying for her lost hair. Crying for her itching eyes. Crying for her mother. Her mother who couldn't stop pulling. Her mother who wouldn't stop cutting her child's hair. Hair that she hated.

Stories that Mother has told her over the years. Six and a half years. Stories of other mothers with problem children, like that lady with the baby son with fleas jumping out of his hairy scalp. Dogs with fleas. Crazy lady going crazier. Dirty dog. Hot Texas dust full of fleas. Poor baby with a thick head full of fleas.

Fleas jumping everywhere. Jumping out of the baby's head of dark hair. Embarrassing the baby's mother. Bad mother with a baby with fleas. Take her baby away. Give her dogs to the dog pound. Leave Texas altogether. Get that baby away from fleas.

The kid with fleas in his hair has a brother. If his mother gets mad and pulls the flea-baby's-brother's hair, that kid says, "Stop it, lady! Don't pull my hair like that!" That flea-baby's-brother pushes his mother's hand away. That kid's crazy mother laughs at the brother of her flea-baby. Laughs at that kid pushing her hand away. Laughs at him telling her, "Stop it, lady!" She was so crazy. She hated hot dusty Texas and its fleas.

Hair and bowl. Bowl on head. Baby Georgina strapped into her high chair. Cries from bowl on her head. Cries from hair in her eyes. Cries from her high chair. High chair tray too tight. Baby cries. Week after week, Mother's obsessive cutting of Georgina's hair. For fear of the thick yellow Okinawan mildewy crust. Crust hiding underneath the baby's hair. Hair too thick. Hair that won't stop growing. Growing out of control. Dirty crust because of Georgina's thick unruly hair. Hair acting like a blanket, smothering her baby scalp. Hair making a mess. Georgina and her head of hair like a mangy dog's hair.

Now, at the age of six and a half, Georgina understands. Mother is bigger and more powerful than the child is. Mother holds the cards from the family's private deck, in her bigger hands. Mother is the Queen of Hearts. Only a few cards from the pack are dealt out to the girl. Only a couple of the available emotional resources are shared and permissible for children back then. This becomes the way the child grows up, thinking such things are normal. This is what the relationship consists of. Always placating her mother. Always agreeing with the woman.

Never scowling. Never looking away when Mother speaks to her. And certainly, never ever rolling those awful hazel eyes of hers. Eyes of the enemy. Rolling dark eyes. It is like living with a Mother Superior. Someone who is to be unquestioningly obeyed in a nun's convent. Life becomes a cloistered event in emotional terms for the child, where freedom of choice in what she will eat, wear, sing, say (the when and the what of speech), think, express in feeling and even silently wonder about, all go through the censorious leadership of her madre.

But Georgina is beginning to see that not all other women are like her mother. And so, the child develops the wayward notion that she has a choice in her thoughts and feelings as a member of the female community in the world. But this was a secret which, she knows, even from a young age, to keep hidden away deep in her heart. Intuition is not something which her mother teaches her. Not like Manga does. Georgina knows from an early age that learning to follow her intuition will displease her mother. It will make the girl too independently minded, so it is not to be allowed. It is not even remotely considered acceptable. Why would any rational adult teach children to question them? Teach them to dispute their authority? That will create conditions of anarchy, something practically unheard of back then in families of the 1950s.

Little girls, especially, must learn to be submissive and nice. Being sweet as sugar and spice, and being everything nice, that was what little girls should be. Their grandmothers had been emancipated and could now vote in elections. The Suffragettes had been disliked, and even imprisoned and treated with disdain in their time. But now (in 1958), things are different. Feminist thought is beginning to take effect. Women can be educated beyond simple domesticated activities formerly allocated to women in even progressive Western democracies. But little girls mustn't let such things, such freedoms, go to their heads, no matter how clever they think they are. They are still just girls, lesser members in everything. The endeavours which women can excel at and still be socially acceptable at the time, are all carefully laid out before them. Even as children, the girls of the 1930s, (Georgina's mother's generation) knew full well what was expected of them. Their daughters must learn the same codes of behaviour. Getting married (at a respectable age, not too young, and certainly not too old, or they'd be called 'Old Maids') is a must. Having babies, babies, babies! Cooking, cooking, cooking! Sewing, sewing, sewing! Cleaning! Cleaning! Cleaning! Running households in an orderly fashion is everything to their mothers, and the daughters must continue in this tradition. Continue or else.

Georgina notices how life is, and she thinks about these stereotypes and ways of being that her mother is trying to teach her. Her mother makes her feel stupid and useless. Her father and Manga make her feel that she can do anything she sets her mind to. Sexist ideas have apparently never even occurred to those two. Daddy tells her that she is the oldest kid in their family (apparently forgetting that she is a girl). Daddy says that it is her job to set a good example and lead her younger siblings. He doesn't seem to notice that her diminutive scale and feminine state might be a hindrance to such an exalted position of authority. Mother would never approve of such a position for Georgina!

Manga just loves the girl unconditionally. She likes her granddaughter for who the girl is. With Manga, there is nothing to prove, no scale to measure up to. But Manga is just an old grandmother. And what do grandmothers know? Daddy and Manga aren't around all of the time to empower and encourage the girl. They are only around sometimes. But the child's respect and love for her father and her grandmother begin to vaguely overrun and subtlety undermine her mother's control. Their kindness is like a Big Mama. It is soft and comforting. It is like manna in the wilderness to the girl's soul. Georgina knows that she is a person, not a robot. So, when her mother tries to force feed ideas of inferiority, without considering the important job that her father has given to her, the child has one thought. Mother must be wrong. And the whole idea that Georgina has to just sit in a lady-like position and look pretty is ridiculous! Sometimes she thinks that what her mother teaches her just doesn't feel right. But the girl knows enough to keep her mouth shut about these things and to conceal those obviously rebellious opinions.

Breaking the established game plan, of what life was all about, was unthinkable. It would make you a social outcast. It would make you not a girl, but something else altogether. But it didn't matter, Georgina thought it anyway. She just couldn't help herself. Something frightful and appalling in her personality just propelled the child onward in that downward spiral of obstinacy. Downward on a path of distinctly 'bad' behaviour. A path of rebellion against the established order of things. And that stubborn tendency in the child, that strong, determined will, aggravated the already existent, but unconfessed and verbally unstated and inarticulated feelings of smouldering inner rage Claudia felt for her own child. Georgina's wilful attitudes did not endear the girl to her mother. After all, their relationship was on tender hooks from the beginning of the child's conception. And the unspoken rules of the game were non-negotiable.

Georgina already, at the tender age of six, showed a quiet determination to feel and think the way the child thought best, and not as her mother wanted her to seem: compliant, submissive and above all, clean. But with her Manga, Georgina knew that things were very different, even as a first grader, the girl already knew her own mind about many things. She had spent a lot of time thinking her own thoughts on the bus from Ft. Campbell, driving into the big civilian town of Louisville near the army's base. That was where she went to the First Grade; while all of the other children stayed at home. The twins had gone to preschool, just a little play school on the base two mornings a week. They didn't even know how to read yet. But Georgina had more independence than those girls did. She knew what it was like to take trips away from home even without her family. Every day, she rode on a big, yellow, school bus for what seemed to her like a very long trip to a strange place away from her family. That gave her time to practice thinking what she thought about. The notions she was acquiring differed from what Mother taught her. So carefully taught her. But the girl knew not to mention those different notions going through her little mind. Not to mention them when she got back home in the afternoon and her mother asked about her day in that wonderfully pleasant tone of voice of hers.

On the large, yellow, school bus, Georgina had time to think about her feelings and about things in general. Nobody controlled her thoughts there in that yellow school bus. At home, or at school, or in church, people told her what she had to do. They told her what she had to say. They told her (all of those towering threatening big people) what acceptable thoughts and attitudes she was allowed to have. But on the big bouncy yellow school bus that came to Ft. Campbell and carried her away from her family's influence, she would think as she wanted to think. And nobody could do one single thing about it.

On the school bus, the child's perception and intuition, her instincts about other people and a whole other world away from her family began to develop. The child watched all of the other children, from different families. She saw how they inter-related and acted, the things that they said, the modes of behaviour, which her father, for one, would never have allowed. Some of the children were even what her mother would have called, 'poorly behaved' or 'badly trained' or 'having no breeding'. Other kids were nice and shared things, or let her borrow a pencil or eraser if she forgot to bring hers to school in her little tartan satchel. It was a scary thing to forget your pencil or a ruler, because that would cause an embarrassing scene in front of the whole class while you were told off for being so stupid. Some teachers were nice. Others were usually crabby and terrible to have the experience of being around. Rules were to be kept, or you got into trouble. Sitting without moving, too quietly for hours on long end, was almost unendurable to the girl. Her teachers didn't seem to appreciate her wild unfettered imagination. Some of the things that she said were just plain outlandish, and possibly crazy. Her innate desire to think very differently, originally, was frowned upon with hard ferocious scowls.

She thought back to the old school and how she felt when her teacher told to her, "Sit up straight, Georgina!" smacking the girl's shoulder with that yardstick of hers. "I've told you to face the front of the classroom every day this week! Can't you hear? Don't you listen when you are spoken to? Stop squirming around in your seat like that!"

Georgina had stared back blankly. *What a stupid, rude woman. How mean of her to hit me for no reason like that. That hurts me when she hits me,* she had thought to herself.

Safe Harbour

Manga was fast becoming one of the girl's best friends, allowing a budding fluency of intuition in the child. She even valued and encouraged it. The seasoned adroit older woman differed from her daughter, Claudia. She was not threatened by the gift of original thought in the girl. She liked her granddaughter for who she was, like Daddy did. That was very comforting to Georgina Jane. Her mother sometimes reminded her of the rolling dark sea they'd been riding over, like a substance which the child could not find a way to hold on to, or to be held by. Her mother's temperament went over her daughter in wave after wave of often-silent censuring disapproval; where just a lofty look of displeasure, or a raised eyebrow of denunciation would instantly cause the child to feel like a worm wiggling under a clod. Just like a big ugly nobody. Manga, on the other hand, was like a sheltered harbour, where you could come ashore and park your watery vessel in safety.

Before they had gotten close enough to see Alaska, after they left Seattle, Washington, the journey was just wave after wave and grey skies that made the sea look grey too. If the girl looked out of her magic round port hole window in their cabin, the scenery was still the same day after day. If the clouds moved away for a while, the sea changed colors and was blue and green again. If the sky was cloudy and rainy, then the sea was like the sky, the same drab color. It was like the sea and the sky were melting into one big fuzzy ocean all around the girl. That Danny boy in Manga's song knew all about sunshine and shadows too. Learning about that Irish kid helped her understand about the light that the yellow-golden sun gave and the mellow grey softness and shading that the clouds gave too.

Her heart felt like it was grey. Her little beating heart felt like the sky and the clouds and the choppy bumpy sea. In fact, she felt grey all over, inside and out when she opened her small black velvet purse to see how the doodlebugs were doing. She had been checking on them every day. But that day she had unclicked her brass clasp on the black velvet purse, and what she saw was bad news. Really bad news. Really, really, really bad news. Her heart felt like a big wave had just grabbed it and thrown her heart high, high, high up into the air and then let it fall abruptly back down so hard that it hurt the inside of the girl's chest and made it difficult for her to breathe. It was like Gretchen must have felt when Katrina Josephina took a quick exit off of her side of the teeter totter that day at the park when Roger Eugenio bumped his small head against that stranger girl's swing. Those big waves could really throw people and small children around when their ship rode over those choppy bumpity waves.

When the girl saw her friends, the doodlebugs again, she felt very sad. At first, she thought that those poor little wood lice were asleep, nestled safe and sound inside of her black velvet purse. They were all rolled up in tight little balls. But when she tried to wake them up, they weren't asleep at all. They just crumbled into grey powdery dust in her hand. That's when she knew that now she wouldn't have any doodlebugs to take with her to Alaska after all. It made her feel very, very sad. It made her feel like a complete failure as a doodlebug keeper. Would they even have doodlebugs in Alaska? This was really, really terrible. She was really, really terrible.

She would probably never lay her deep, hazel eyes on another live doodlebug ever again. Just like she'd never see Myrtle the turtle again. Those doodlebugs were really and truly gone. Turned into nothing. Just like she'd never see her best friend, Juanita, ever again. Just like Mother would probably never change her mind and let her wear unlady-like blue jeans no matter how many times she asked her for a pair. The purseful of doodlebugs was gone forever. Vanished into grey dust at the bottom of her purse.

How was she going to cope with being labelled as a murderer of doodlebugs?

Everyone on board the ship would probably find out about her crime and they'd all stare at her like they did that day in the restaurant when her dress fell over her head when Daddy pulled the stuck chicken bone out of her throat. Everyone seeing her red red underwear or staring at her for being a killer of doodlebugs was about the same. And she couldn't understand it, because she'd been sharing every meal with those bugs, and thought that they had enjoyed all of the ship's delicious meals as much as she had.

But seeing Alaska for the first time, helped her to forget about the doodlebugs for a while. Seeing Alaska for the first time helped her to forget about lots of sad things. Seeing Alaska for the very first time was like going straight up to heaven without even dying first. Alaska was almost too pretty to even be a real place. Georgina Jane O'Shaughnessy didn't even know that the world could have such a good place as Alaska. Probably a few of the fairies from Ireland would like to live and dance in a place as fantastic as Alaska.

The ship gave out a loud blast from its big horn. That was the way the ship's captain, the most important man on the ship, who dressed in his clean white suit, told the people on the shore that it was his turn to pilot his huge ship into its spacious parking place on the dock. It was almost time to get off of his ship. He was a busy, busy man, who had other families to take on other trips; probably away from Alaska, instead of to it.

Daddy told them, "Our car will be brought to us in Anchorage. You're going to take a train ride to Anchorage to see your cousins. The army has a new home for us in Ft. Wainwright, near Fairbanks, but that is in the middle of Alaska. So, the trip's not over yet, kids. You get to go on a train ride next."

Imaginings

Through a dark cave, the train carried them. Deep inside of an Alaskan mountain, it was a vast blackness. Daddy stayed behind in Seward to wait for the ship's cargo to be unloaded. He had to retrieve their car and a few of their belongings. He'd meet them in Anchorage tomorrow afternoon. He had waved good-bye to her from Seward's dock, sensing Georgina's reluctance at leaving him behind. There he stood all alone, waving her on to another journey. After the bright and dazzling Alaskan sunlight, the train's dark passageway, which burrowed into the interior of the mountain, made the girl feel like she was Alice in Wonderland, who had followed that white rabbit into the space beneath a tree.

Manga had read that story to the girls on the ship. She made it seem so real, the girl, the rabbit, the underground Wonderland. Alice had found herself in a secret world, and so had Georgina Jane's family. Caves were the places where Leprechauns lived and hid their pots of gold. If they looked out of the train's windows, they could peer into the dark and maybe they'd see those little people hiding pots of gold out there, Manga told them as she pointed into the darkness. Little people, fairies, girls falling down into rabbit's holes, drinks in bottles with labels she couldn't read, girls turning bigger or smaller, tar babies, curious monkeys who wore hats and fell into the sea, naughty children in nursery rhymes who jumped over candle sticks, might get burned or had to be whipped soundly and not given any food, or stuffed full of sweets and rich foods like Hansel and

162

Gretel, girls with red riding hoods, big bad wolves, three little pigs, Leprechauns, bearded billy goats gruff, ugly ducklings, three blind mice, carving knives cutting tails off, Peter Rabbit hiding from Farmer McGregor, the cruel angry mean old Queen of Hearts, the three bears with chairs that broke, or beds too hard or too soft and their porridge eaten all up by a little sneaky girl, Wee Willie Winkie who ran through the towns crying into people's houses to see if good children were asleep yet. Little Black Sambo, Black Mumbo and Black Jumbo, ships' horns blowing, laundry spinning, diapers drying, Daddy farting, Mother smiling, whales leaping, children laughing. Her mind was full of a rich stew of tales. Her head was full of stories so abundant that her mind darted from one idea to another as she stared out into the blackness of the cave.

Her grandmother had already told her about Alice's journey when that little golden headed girl followed the white rabbit and went on her great adventures underground. Now that Georgina was underground herself, riding in that Alaskan train, her mind tumbled. Her thoughts were like the babies' diapers in that clothes dryer, everything melding together in a rich stew of myths and tales of other places in times long, long ago. All of those once-upon-a-time mixed with her present, and infused the girl with a sense of fact and fiction melding into her own mind's oneness. Fairies could actually be dancing right outside of her train window. And if she really, really looked hard enough, she would see them.

Manga had explained all about Irish myths and the legends of the little people. She was a real Irish person and so she knew practically everything there was to know about those 'little people'. To the girl, these were not make-believe storybook characters. In her mind, there really were little people. Most of her family consisted of little people, so Manga's Celtic stories of faraway lands and the magical abilities of the Leprechauns and their gold, were very believable. Didn't they have gold in Alaska? So, it must be true. Little girls like Alice, who was a girl that fell into an underground tunnel, could really go to another world in their dreams. Being small made it easy to go into another secret place for make-believe things to actually happen.

After seeing their cousins and spending the night in Anchorage, Daddy came to get them. They all piled into their car to drive to the new army base that was going to be their home now. Georgina had butterflies in her tummy. All the way to Ft. Wainwright, Manga told her stories of the fairies and their friends. Fairies could fly. And in a sense, so could Alice. Only she flew downwards instead of upwards. She fell into her tumbled Wonderland. The girl thought about all of these stories as she looked out the car's window on the way through the mountains with their white snowy points on top. She felt herself, like Alice in Wonderland, getting sleepy. The feeling of travelling and the familiar purr of the car was relaxing. She snuggled up close to her Manga. Soon they would be at their new home.

Arriving at Last

They had only a brief visit with their cousins in Anchorage. These were people she vaguely remembered. They were people from a long time ago, before her brothers were born. Soon it would be time for her daddy to become a soldier in the Army again. That morning Daddy had put his stiff, green army uniform on. He was a soldier again. He wasn't off-duty anymore. His month of pretending to be a civilian had flown by and was already over. He was reporting for duty later that afternoon. Now, he was driving them to the army's base in the middle of Alaska. Soon her daddy would be flying over, not driving through these mountains. That was a scary idea to think about, because those mountains were so pointy and tall. It would take forever to find someone who went crashing into those giant mountains.

Alaska wasn't a frozen place when the girl got there. She'd been told it was a very cold place. But it was the end of the summertime, and pretty warm for a place they said was so cold. On the tops of the mountains, it must still be pretty cold, because the tops of the mountains were so high up there in the cold Alaskan sky that they had snowy caps on, like elves' hats. And the sky was even bluer than the day they arrived in Alaska. Even the air in Alaska felt different from the air in Texas felt. Texas air was hot and stuffy in the summertime. It closed in on you. Texas air made the girl's forehead sweat with great big drops of salty perspiration. Georgina's salty sweat had tasted like the ocean's water, or like the salty water in the Great Salt Lake in Utah where you could float on your back and not even sink to the bottom or drown. But in Alaska, the air was so fresh and cool that even in the sun, she didn't think she would ever sweat even one drop of her very own salty water. The air itself opened up and expanded in Alaska, just like the scenery did.

When they arrived at the gates of the army's base in Fort Wainwright, the big shots in the military sent someone to escort her family to their new house. Texas was a big place, but Alaska seemed even bigger. Like a place for giants, not tiny fairies or Irish Leprechauns.

164

"What will our new house be like, Daddy? Will we like our new house?" she asked as they drove through the base.

"We'll see," was all he said. He seemed a bit apprehensive and pre-occupied. Maybe he was just tired. All tuckered out from the long trip up to Alaska from Kentucky.

Moving to a new house was exciting. Since their furniture was late arriving from Kentucky, Daddy said that the Army had loaned them some borrowed base furnishings for the new place. He said that it was a great adventure to camp out on bunk beds and army furniture. But Georgina looked at her mother's face and knew that her mother hated this part of moving. Mother only liked to have her own things around her. Her pretty things. Mother hated the army's 'tacky junk'.

It would be several more weeks before their own things got there. Finally, they pulled up in front of their new house. It was late in the afternoon, but it was still sunny. The sun would be awake for most of the night. The sun was a night owl in the summertime in Alaska. That's why they called it the land of the midnight's sun. The Alaskan summer sun was like Katrina Josephina, it liked to stay awake and play all night long.

The Army wasn't as good of a house decorator as Mother was. Metal cots covered with lumpy mattresses and scratchy khaki green woolly blankets lined up like army soldiers in neat rows in the bedrooms. Stiff white bedlinen covered the mattresses. Boy, the Army really liked to iron their sheets until they are really, really tough! Those rigid sheets were not going to be too soft like Mommy's sheets were. All of the covers were pulled very taut. The blankets smelled like mothballs and were somewhat musty. They were woollen and scratchy. The living room had some folding chairs in a fabric similar to the green fabric on Daddy's army uniform. There were green wooden footlockers with metal hinges that contained some of her families' clothing and personal items. The Army was like the Wizard of Oz, full of people wearing green clothes. The Army liked green too, like the people in the Land of Oz and the Irish people did. Everything seemed to be green, like Alaska was that first summer.

Most of their other possessions weren't there yet, none of the pretty things her mother had collected over the years of travelling with the army's guys. Most of their things were missing. The children's toys and the girl's dolls were still in transit. Georgina only had a couple of special dollies with her, including the new Oriental doll from China Town in Sam's Francisco. That new doll was a real beauty. She was the prettiest one in their family. Manga had promised to sew some new clothes for that special little dolly as soon as her sewing machine arrived in up Alaska. Georgina would introduce that new doll to the rest of her doll family when they arrived with the movers. She hoped that the other dollies, who were still with the movers, would be nice to, and accept the new Oriental dolly, even though she looked different from the dolls Georgina Jane already had in her collection.

The new neighbours at Fort Wainwright were very welcoming. They came on over to the O'Shaughnessy's new house and shook hands with her father. The moms told Mother that if she needed anything to just ask. They had even put cereal, bread and canned goods in Mother's kitchen cabinets; along with some used, but clean, pots and pans. And when the girl opened the army's ice box, there were a couple of quarts of milk, some orange juice in glass bottles, some eggs, and sliced baloney, cheese, bacon and delicious pinkish brown Alaskan smoked salmon caught and smoked by the Eskimos. Manga said the Eskimos were good fishermen. And an enormous bowl of blue and purple blueberries picked by their new friendly neighbours were in there. It was a reassuring and welcoming sight and Georgina let out a big sigh as she stood there with the refrigerator door open, letting the cool air flow over her.

"What are those, Manga?" pointing to the big plastic bowl.

"Those are blueberries, sweetheart. You can put those on your cereal for breakfast tomorrow morning. We'll go blueberry picking ourselves soon and get even more. And then, I can make blueberry pancakes for you. Would you like that? Remember the pecan pancakes with brown sugar and maple syrup I cooked for you in Texas?"

The child silently nodded, her big hazel eyes taking in her grandmother's reassuring facial expression. Manga was fascinated by the new possibilities already opening up to her in Alaska. Familiar foods made you feel like you were still back in the old place you used to live in. All American kids loved good old baloney sandwiches. New foods made you feel sort of strange, like eating it made you part of the new place you'd moved to. Alice in Wonderland ate and drank new things too. She ate and drank them on her great adventure into Wonderland.

"Well, in Alaska, we'll have blueberry pancakes instead!" Excitement filled Manga's voice. She was like a small child at that moment, overflowing with the euphoria of the newness of the place, more excited than even her grandchildren were. The twins were already making themselves right at home, bounding down the hallway and bouncing on the army's metal cots.

166

That was how their new neighbours made them feel right at home in Alaska. They bought smoked salmon from the Eskimos and picked enough blueberries for the whole family. And even Gretchen Gabriella, who was a picky eater, really loved that new kind of berry that she had never even tasted before they came all the way up to Alaska.

Every day, after they arrived in their Alaskan home, the girl watched her father head out the door to his new post in Ft. Wainwright. The Army could tell their soldiers where they had to live. Then the Army would pay movers to move their soldier and his whole family to a brand-new army base almost anywhere in the whole wide world. The Army had decided that her daddy should help them up in Alaska by flying airplanes and cargo helicopters with important supplies to other people with no other way to get things. So, Georgina knew that her daddy was flying airplanes again. She sure hoped that he would do a better job flying in Alaska than he had done in Kentucky when he was first learning to fly at Flight School.

And pretty soon the summer ended and it started to get cold in Alaska. Winter was setting in and soon the ground would be covered with a thick white blanket of snow. Snow geese were flying south for the winter, honking high up in the cloudy skies as they flew overhead. The seasons were making a dramatic new changing in the way it looked and felt and seemed. Alaska was like two different countries. It was a perpetually light place in the summertime, with some warm breezes, soft green grass and too many enormous mosquitoes that bit your arms and legs and the back of your neck. Gretchen Gabriella and baby Peter Martin both had an almost allergic reaction to those itchy mosquito bites. They both had big swollen blotches on their shoulders, legs and cheeks. Mother dabbed pale pink calamine lotion all over those scratchy bites, and that, and smelly witch's hazel helped the swelling to go down faster.

Alaska was a very dark cold place in the wintertime when the mosquitoes and lots of other animals slept. Or as the girl learned about, they hibernated in warm caves that sheltered them from the snow. In the winter, Alaska looked like a forever Wonderland, better even than Alice's secret place. Icicles hung from all of the houses. Icicles hung from every shop. Icicles hung like giant sharp spears from the airplane hangars. Snow began to pile up and to cover the grass completely. And neighbourhood ponds, where cattails grew and where the big Alaskan mosquitoes lived in the summertime, were frozen over so solidly that it would take forever for them to melt again, even once the warm weather finally came back to Alaska.

Flight Patterns

Zip, zip, zip, zip, zip, zip, zip, zip! Daddy's green flight suit was hanging up over the kitchen door. Back and forth, the twins pulled her father's zippers on his khaki-colored flight suit. There were zippers all over that suit, even one so Daddy could go potty on the airplane if he couldn't hold it. When Georgina asked him if the airplane had a potty, he had shown her the special bottle that he took with him in the army's airplane, just in case of an emergency. He wore the zippered suit to work when flight instructions were scheduled for the day's work. Miles had to be crossed, tundra flown over to reach small towns and outposts and settlements in the outback regions of Northern Alaska and the western borders close to Russia.

Her father's skill as a pilot of light aircraft; planes and helicopters, made him a valuable commodity to the military. Georgina knew that Daddy's training had made her father like a part of the military's machinery. He was a significant part of the whole battalion of the units stationed in America's largest and northernmost forty-ninth State. And at his new job in Ft. Wainwright, Daddy got to be the boss of lots of other soldiers, like he was their teacher, father, Indian chief, counsellor, group leader and army commander all rolled into one.

That morning, her twin sisters sat on Daddy's lap. He tickled them and scratched the sides of their soft pink cheeks with his own as yet, unshaven face. He was having a bowl of Kellogg's Corn Flakes, full of the sunshine's goodness. It was getting near the time when he'd have to leave for the day. Next, he would shower and shave, but his night's growth of a few whiskers still shadowed his chin and cheeks. Mother hung his green flight suit up over the top of the kitchen door. She had just ironed it on her horizontal ironing board, which seemed to never be put away these days.

"Why do you have so many zippers, Daddy?" Gretchen wanted to know.

"They zip up Daddy's pockets in his flight suit, honey. That way Daddy won't lose things if his airplane turns upside down. His keys and money won't fall out of his pockets because they will be all zipped up."

"Airplanes don't turn upside down, you silly, silly Daddy!" retorted Katrina Josephina.

"You're my little blond bomber. And I can turn you upside down!" he teased, as he tickled Katrina, scooping her off of his lap and turning her upside down from the waist up, leaving her feet pointed downwards. With her head upside down, Katrina's face turned pink and even her soft little pink ears turned a rosier shade. Her mouth was open wide in both surprise and delight at her father's attention. Her two, stubby, blond pigtails stuck straight out on both sides of her round little girl head. Her head was limply dangling between her legs as Daddy swung the twin in circular motions.

Katrina Josephina momentarily looked like a slack cloth rag doll. She reminded Georgina of her favourite Raggedy Ann doll with her pantaloons and wide button eyes. For a split second, she saw Katrina's face; the wide-eyed startled look of a girl suddenly deprived of control over her own little body.

"Me too! Me too! Me too, Daddy!" chortled Gretchen, hanging on to her father's leg; while she stood on his bare feet without the clompy army boots he wore with his flight suit.

"Fly me around like your little airplane too! I want to be a blond bomber!" begged Katrina's twin.

Georgina hated that game her father played, pretending his children were his army airplanes, zooming them in circles round and round the room. Gretchen and Katrina loved to be suspended in mid-air, held aloft by their father, who clutched a leg and an arm as he spun his girls in turn, round and round. Making annoying noisy sounds like the motor of an airplane, he spun his daughters in circular flight patterns. This wild game was too dangerous. What if Gretchen's arm came off of her body? What if Katrina hit her head against a piece of furniture, or collided with a wall? Georgina marvelled at her father's confidence that he had everything under control, in what, to the girl's mind was an unnecessarily unsafe and bizarre procedure. It was not a fun game to watch. Someone might get hurt.

She preferred the other game her father used to play with his twin baby girls. He seemed to understand his daughters' innate personalities and dispositions, even from the time her identical sisters were infants. Though they looked like cookie-cutter versions of each other, Daddy knew Katrina Josephina and Gretchen Gabriella were little people with dissimilar temperaments and opposite views of the world they found themselves in. His children were as much a part of his mortal priority as his army career was. Without them, his life just wouldn't be worth living. His wife, the love of his life, their offspring, these were the people who made his existence complete. For him there was no such thing as life without these precious beings which his passion had created. His heart and soul were found in their pleasure and security. They were his heart. They were life itself to him.

Georgina remembered watching as her father had held those twin girls back when they used to be babies. With their halos of yellow fuzz. When their legs had been strong enough for those pale-headed girls to stand upright on stiffened legs on her father's lap, he had swayed them back and forth very gently. Holding their baby arms, he would play a game with them.

"*Eres tu payosa. Eres tu payosa,*" he had repeated over and over to Katrina Josephina.

"*Eres tu una angelita. Eres tu una angelita,*" he told Gretchen.

They must have known what the Spanish words meant back then before they could chatter away in English. Because Katrina Josephina was something of a payosa clown girl. And Gretchen was certainly the more angelic of the two. Those Spanish phrases, lovingly, playfully repeated to them so often had moulded their little personalities, or perhaps all it did was reflect their innate beings back to themselves.

But the days of that gentler game were long over. Now he could play games with Katrina and Gretchen that were more boisterous and of a more rough and tumble nature. And Georgina, now that she was almost seven, was relieved to be too big for that crazy airplane game. She had never played that crazy game. But Katrina didn't even care if her splayed legs made her white panties with their lace trim show as her father turned her into a human airplane whizzing around the living room first thing in the morning.

Mayhem and noise. There was too much of both in her family. Georgina preferred to ease herself into the day, quietly composing her thoughts after a busy night of dreams. She had dreams which were hard to decipher, and sometimes nightmares made her shiver herself awake with the fright of them. The girl didn't always differentiate between waking and sleeping thoughts. Her conscious and the subconscious realities blended together and fed off each other; moving from one state to the other, where no curtain was drawn down over what the child did not comprehend. Both worlds were full of the incomprehensible, the seemingly unknowable. A meshing together of occasional night terrors within the relative peace and safety of her own little bed became normality to the child. Her bed, which she felt was like an island of tranquillity in a household of so many people with their numerous commotions, was her retreat from the world, her family and school days. That bed was also a place where she met happy creatures like her make-believe fairy girls and even big giants. Sometimes, it was a place where she faced her night time traumas.

This co-mingling of realities was feasible, because the girl knew that waking or sleeping, life could be challenging. Sometimes in her dreams, Georgina visited faraway lands. These were places of adventures. There she played roles she'd never fathomed she could act out when she was awake, unless she was deliberately day dreaming. In her dreams, she flew everywhere, like her father did in his real life. She flew over high mountains. She flew over vast seas. She flew over desert lands with their scrub brush and cacti. Often in her dreams, the sun was shining brightly and multi-colored flowers danced in the breezes of her slumbers. Her dancing flowers had faces and reminded her of the nursery rhymes that Mother had taught her about a little girl named Mary, who was quite contrary (like Katrina Josephina) and had flowers that were really ringing silver bells. In her dreams, the flowers were planted in neat straight rows, like the children in her class at school who stood at attention next to their desks (also in nice straight rows) when their tall teacher or the stern principal walked into their classroom.

Dreaming became an invaluable tool to the girl. Confronting an ever-increasing scholastic workload of numbers and words she hadn't discovered the purpose or meaning of yet, was like her and her daddy's job of flying. Night and day dreaming were important occupations of her childhood. It was as if, she could leave her place in the world, transcending space and the concreteness of matter, by using her mind. It was a place that was her own private domain. Grasping concepts out of her reach, transcending ideas beyond her kin was a constant and purposeful experience for the child. But nobody could trespass into that spatial mental arena and boss her around. She was the queen there. She was the small girl there. She was like Alice in Wonderland. She was always changing sizes, trying to fit through an infinite array of various sized doors that would lead her out to the great beyond or further into the vast interior space she was learning existed within her mind. Those doors would lead her to who knows where? Sometimes she made conscious decisions, and other times thoughts just came to her like breezes blown her way out-of-doors where the Alaskan wolves, bears and bunny rabbits lived.

She ruled in that place her mind had created. Sometimes she fought raging battles, filled with components of treachery in nightmarish creatures too ugly to dwell on willingly after they intruded into the girl's non-cognisant brainwaves. She would awake with a start; almost jumping out of her skin. Drenching with sweat, her hair and skin damp and cold. She would not willingly entertain those creepy gremlins for a moment longer than she had to. She would will them away and banish them from her mind, where they had to slink off to dark corners of her subconscious, where she hoped that they understood that they were not welcomed guests, but rather rude, scary, tyrannical intruders into the child's mental spaces.

Those bad guys in her dreams could fly away or else she would fly away from them. She would fly away to a place of safety in her mind's eye. She'd go to a submerged comfort zone of wonder, and a miniature fairyland where children could play without getting hurt by anything. Dreams opened up to a place of using flight as a means of escape. But when she woke up from her world of dreams, she thought of her father's job as a pilot with some measure of no small consternation.

The idea of flight was not a new one to the girl. And when your father is a pilot, you tend to think about flying a lot. The idea is never far from your conscious or unconscious thoughts. Will your daddy, like Icarus, fall to the earth if he flies too close to the sun? Or, as was the case with Georgina Jane O'Shaughnessy, will your father barely survive his plane's flight smack dab into an Appalachian mountain, leaving him dazed and broken in a military hospital for weeks? Years afterwards, she wondered if her daddy would return to her when he left for work in the morning. From an early age, the child pondered the real possibilities of losing him to the sky. Flying was his life. But she wondered, *Would he exchange his reality with the child, if the perils of his profession claimed him?* Concerns for his safety consumed the girl's thoughts. But what could a child do about it?

Before her family had moved to this cold, cold place, out in the deep, deep snow, another life had been lived in a warm and sunny spot in the South. Her father's plane crash may have nearly cost him his life, but he was not to give up his career, nor his love of flying. The child's worries had to be put aside, carefully of course, by her father, who evaded the issue of her fear. Whenever the girl discovered yet another scar, previously unnoticed, on his face or arms, she asked her father the same question for all the years of her childhood, "How did you get this mark, Daddy?"

His answer was always the same playful response, trying to quell her, and probably some of his own, fears for his safety. Though he was part, she was told a quarter, Indian himself, he always said in an exaggerated, deep, tough-guy voice,

"Big mean Indian got me with his spear!" pointing to the scars from the plane crash. This became a routine over the years, acting like some of his very own relatives were the bad guys who had caused such scars with their sharply pointed spears jutting into his red flesh. But despite his attempts to turn around with jest, the subject which caused his child so much anguish, a persistent worry was always in the back of Georgina's mind.

Now he would be flying even more often, carrying supplies in the enormous cargo airplanes and helicopters out to the most remote regions of Alaska, where no cars or trucks could travel; because there were no roads to reach them. Everything everywhere was covered with layer upon layer of a mantle of thick continual snowfall, secreting beneath it a world unseen for month after long month. Snowflakes caught in opened mouths. A myriad of snowflakes landing on little girls' tongues. Snowflakes gently covering the surface of the small, outstretched coat sleeves of Georgina and her sisters. Girls pretending to be fairies dancing in the falling snow. Whirling and twirling in the wind. Tiny dazzling snowflakes, each one different from the other; almost like people were different from other people. Snowflakes melded together as a mighty, white, unified force. The snow was like a battalion of freezing whiteness fighting against man's ability to cope with that wild place.

Settlements had grown up, sprouting from what? These were places where the sleek caribou, the giant Alaskan moose with its heavy cumbersome antlers and the polar bears as white as the snow and frost they lived in, made their abode. These were the places where snowbirds and giant white hooting owls found sustenance. These were the places where only the huskies pulling snow sleds could travel. Snowshoes and skies were needed to traverse these blinding frigid zones. These were the places where huge sea creatures lived along the coastlines, and were hunted by the Eskimos for their pelts and skins and the gamey meat they provided.

Cold War and the Facts of Life

Mountain range after mountain range covered that vast and frozen tundra; keeping it isolated. Civil Defence had posted sentries. And watches had to be kept, where the country's boundaries were fiercely guarded during this 'Cold War' period. For a year, during World War II, the Japanese had occupied one of Alaska's Aleutian Islands. America had not forgotten the feeling of its territory being invaded, even in a small way, and good old Uncle Sam was on his guard against further occupations. The Yukon with its close proximity to Russia, meant that stations in the northernmost or western remote areas had to be guarded against possible invasion or spying manoeuvres by those foreign potential invaders, those other people. Those other people who were the bad guys.

Georgina was led to believe that these people from Russia were really really 'bad guys'. She thought that these bad people, who were the ones responsible for her and her classmates having to sit underneath their desks, or out in the hallways with their hands over their heads, were called the *Rushpins* or something like that. It was a tense time. Alaska was a heavily patrolled and guarded area; especially the part of Alaska that was close to these bad *Rushpin* people.

Once her daddy had taken them to a place where the army had a big round circle building with men inside of it who were keeping a close eye on these *Rushpin* guys. Strange things were housed inside of that radar lookout tower. It was almost like a little museum in there. One of the very strangest things which Georgina Jane saw, was a glass bottle with a two-headed goat embryo inside of it. Was this deformity caused by those 'bad guys'? It was a pretty scary place. Her father told her that the army's men were watching the 'bad guys' from inside of that circle building with its moveable radar pointed in the direction of the guys on the other side of the narrow strip of sea that divided them. Those army guys would know if those *Rushpins* tried to come to Alaska to get them.

She wasn't sure if those bad guys would hurt her if they ever did come to Alaska. But she knew that the Army would try to take care of them. She knew that the whole country depended on how well those battalions, which her daddy was a part of, did their job. The Army had Air Defence radars and control centers and warning devices. If the bad guys tried to come to Alaska, the Army would know about it first, before the civilian population was warned. Even the girl knew that.

Now at her new school in Fairbanks, they had 'Air Raid Drills', where all of the children had to hide under their desks or out in the hallway with their hands or books and folders over their heads. It was often during these 'Duck and Cover' drills that she realized that the fear that was being consistently instilled in the children might be doing them more harm than good. What were they actually protecting themselves from? Were their small arms really meant to protect them from falling debris? If the ceiling fell down on them, or the windows broke from the bomb blasts that they told the children were threatening them, would their school folders, religiously held over their young heads, be enough to shield them?

She thought this exercise was like a crazy charade, or a silly party game, kind of like 'Musical Chairs', only without the music. The blaring sound that the school's loud speakers played was a blasting continuous tone of an overwhelming siren. Even though it jolted her out of perhaps one of her silent day dreams, it was hard to take it seriously, like the adults did. Every time Georgina heard that awful siren sound, she thought to herself, *Here we go again!* She felt that the children were performing for the teachers in order to quell, not the children's until then, non-existent fears, but rather to reassure the adults who watched. None of the teachers were sitting under their desks or putting their arms or books over their heads. So, was there really a serious problem to be so worried about? And could all of those children really protect themselves, if those 'bad guys' really wanted to hurt them? The threat of 'the bomb' was ever present in those frozen days of cold, cold war up in the cold, cold North. Up in the Yukon.

It seemed like a sadistic game that the children were forced to play when the loud blare of the school's siren sounded the alarm and made them all jump. It seemed like the adults were just trying to scare the children for some reason. Wasn't it adults who made all of those scary movies for children to watch at the movie theater? Now they were exposing all of those little kids to a frightening possibility, that an atomic bomb or some sort of awful weapon could be used against all of them, to destroy their lives and their very culture. Somehow, she didn't trust those bigger people. Those 'Air Raid Drill' bells were always ringing and ringing and ringing at her school. And the worst of it was, that she never knew when it might jolt or startle her out of a class that she was enjoying. It never seemed to happen during one of those boring classes that she hated. If it had, then she thought that she might even have begun to look forward to those sirens.

To the girl, and her contemporaries growing up in the post-World War II era, it was a time when the Cold War was a real war. The fears of their elders could not be evaporated by using Air Raid Drills. These only served to instil fears in their young. Rather than the desired effect of giving them time to prepare for possible invasion and to avert fears, it practically bred apprehension and terror into the children. A whole generation's childhood was immersed with years of the constant fears and ideas of the Cold War, fighting dread rather than real invasion or bombing. A dread of 'the Commies' had a latent effect. In the countless American classrooms of the 1950s, drills were an obsessional pastime. No bombs were dropping. But the guilt of the American role in the new Atomic Age made them fearful of their own fate in such a world. All of those neutrons smashing together and colliding was a massive danger that had now fallen into foreign hands. But the inflicted trauma on, and later what would be called 'post-traumatic stress' of the baby boomers would only be evident when the girl's generation came of age in the next decade. And that's another story.

Georgina began to like subjects like Geography and History. *How did the mountains get there,* she wondered? But since she didn't even know how she got there, how could she understand how those mountains got there? She could see majestic Mount McKinley from right in front of her own house. If she walked out of her front door and looked to the right, there Mt McKinley was every day, standing across, what appeared to her, like a few fields from her house. She wanted to go skiing at Mount McKinley, but her mother said that it was 'too far away'. How could it be 'too far away'? How could it be 'too far away', if Georgina could see it so well? It didn't look 'too far away' from where they lived.

Sometimes fog or 'low clouds', as her dad called them, would surround Mount McKinley, veiling the monstrosity of what was in fact really a giant pile of earth and stones. McKinley was one of God's biggest towers. Mt McKinley was famous everywhere in the whole wide world for a guy who became President of America a long time ago. President McKinley was an important man who had probably known all about that huge mountain that was named after him. It was so famous. Everyone in the world had probably heard of that big mountain near her neighbourhood. President McKinley might have even walked all the way up into the fog and low clouds and brightness of the snow there. Her father knew about 'low clouds' too. He had learned about 'low clouds' when he crashed into that southern mountain because of all of those 'low clouds' down there. He remembered about them. And so, Georgina Jane would remember about them too.

When she couldn't see Mount McKinley she got worried. Had Mount McKinley disappeared overnight? Could mountains even vanish just like that? She didn't want to bother her mother by asking her. She wasn't even sure if her mother was interested in Geography or things like that. Her mother was too busy for questions asked by a little girl. Her mother had all of those stacks of dirty dishes, clothes and training pants and diapers to wash. Her mother had so many clothes to iron, because, as the child learned, nearly everything had to be ironed in their family. There was no 'wash and wear' back then. So, since her mother was so very busy with so many jobs to do, it was impossible to get her attention for very long. Georgina tried to read about mountains and things like that in books. She needed to understand, but who could she ask about all of these questions she had?

When the cousins from Anchorage came to visit, she learned a lot. Her cousin, Bridgetta, was a year and a half older than Georgina and she knew about mountains and things, because she had been in Alaska longer than the cousins in Ft. Wainwright had been there. One time, when the girl's cousins came for a visit they discussed a lot of these things. That's when her cousins, Bridgetta and Leah, tried to tell the girl where babies came from. Their mother had even more babies than Georgina's mother did, so they must have really wanted to know about how all of those babies kept getting there in their household. She wasn't sure if her cousins had to fold diapers like she did though.

One night, when all of the lights were out and even the grown-ups seemed to have gone to bed, her cousins told her that babies happened because their dad did something to their mom. She wasn't allowed to call her mother 'Mom' like her cousins did. Her mother liked to be called 'Mother'. Her sisters thought that it was funny to say: 'yes, Mother' to Mother, and 'yes, sir' to their father. So, her sisters said 'yes, sir, Mother dear' to Mother. The girl and her sisters and little brothers had to say 'yes, sir' to their father. Her dad liked to pretend that Georgina and her sisters and brothers were his soldiers in the Army. That's why he liked to be called, 'sir' instead of 'Daddy' all of the time.

Insistent that she knew everything, and besides, she was older than Georgina Jane, and so her cousin should listen to everything she said, Bridgetta tried to explain the 'facts of life' to Georgina. In fact, the girl wasn't interested in where babies came from. Like Mount McKinley, she and the 'little kids' just were.

"Your dad gets on top of your Mom and sticks his thing in her. That's how they make babies," Bridgetta said with an emphatic authority.

What his 'thing' was, the girl wasn't sure. She wasn't sure that she wanted to know either.

"My daddy would never do anything like that to my mother. My daddy would never want to hurt my mother like that. I don't believe you. Your dad might do that to your mom, but my daddy would never do that to my mother."

The shock of what her cousin had told her, stayed with the girl for a long time. She tried to put it out of her mind. But every time she saw her father for a while after that, she wondered about it all. She didn't believe what her cousin told her about babies and their mom and dad. All Georgina Jane knew, was that, like Mount McKinley, she just was. At nearly seven years of age, that was all she really needed to know about the facts of life and how babies and mountains got there. Sex was not important to her then.

Finding Her Way Around

In school, Georgina learned that Alaska was a land long inhabited by 'the Real People', the Inuits or Eskimos. They had crossed the Bering Strait from Russia to settle in a new polar outpost a long time ago, searching for game. She knew about the '*Bearing's* Strait' because she saw it on the map of Alaska in her classroom at her school. She knew why they called it that. It was because of all of those bears in Alaska. There were all kinds of bears there: grizzly bears, black bears, Kodiak bears, brown bears and white polar bears, who lived out there on the ice.

She learned that long before the whites knew of this land, long before the power struggles began, the natives controlled their own culture through being careful about who did the right jobs. That was how they stayed alive and fed their families in a place as cold as Alaska. The Aleutian Islands had made it easy for those Eskimos to get to Alaska. Some of those people, with their yellowing skin and their thick black hair and slanting almond eyes, probably still had family over there on the other side. It probably worried them to think of their family members living with the bad guys. Living over there. Living over there with the *Rushpins*. But there was not too much they could do about it, because they were so busy trying to survive in the glacial regions and on the frosty tundra on their own side of the Bearings Strait.

Now, her father flew over these remote regions with important things like food and medicine in the big army cargo helicopters and airplanes. He told his young daughter about the hardships of the job.

"Once," he said, "an army plane went down in the tundra during the summer months. Those guys were lost for hours and nearly lost their minds out there. The mosquitoes were as big as the palm of your hand, and their bite was fierce. One Negro soldier was bitten the worse. He had nearly lost his mind when they rescued him."

The girl knew that it was not an easy place to live, despite the hopefulness for a new beginning she had felt when they first arrived in Alaska. She knew by now, that life could be dangerous. Those giant mosquitoes had bitten her too. And she had seen an airplane with skis on it instead of wheels. That plane was flying off to a place where they didn't even have a landing strip. Those planes could land on water or on the snow. They had skis like she wore when she skied down the mountain close to her house. She knew that Alaska was a big, big place. It would be easy to get lost in Alaska. It would be hard for the Army, or anybody else for that matter, to find someone who got lost in a place as big as Alaska, with all of those huge mountains and dense forests. Alaska had lots of giant pine trees. And those big evergreens would probably hide a lost person pretty good out in those deep, deep forests and wooded areas near her new home. Hansel and Gretel had gotten lost in the woods too, so it must be true.

After her father told her the story about the black soldier nearly losing his mind from those big Alaskan mosquitoes biting him out in the tundra, from then on, she viewed the black servicemen with different eyes, as though beholding survivors of greater rigors than she could imagine. Their dark skin somehow translated into a symbol of overcoming the cold in the winter, and the mosquitoes in the summer. Daddy told her that the Negroes felt the cold more than the white people, because where they came from, it was warmer. Daddy didn't like the cold either; because he was part Mexican and part Red Skin. And he said that Mexicans and Indians liked it better in warm places. Only the Irish part of Daddy didn't mind the cold so much. But Irish people in Ireland never had it so cold, not like they did in Alaska.

Until her father had told her the story of the Negro soldier's plight at being lost out there that summer in the tundra's wilderness with all of those huge Alaskan mosquitoes biting the fool out of him, and how those colored people could get frostbite more easily, she never noticed that these people were even there in Alaska. Soldiers were soldiers, no matter what color their skin was. They were all just soldiers in her daddy's army.

Now she had something new to worry about. And she thought about this every time she saw a black serviceman on the base where her daddy was a captain. Until then, the black soldiers were just the same as everybody else in uniform, only a bit darker. Until then, it didn't seem significant that their skin tones were darker than the other paler servicemen. Didn't her own father have a reddish tinge to his skin? Because of that Indian's blood inside of him? Soldiers' skin tone had never seemed important until she saw the world through her father's eyes. His concerns became hers. This was how these generational thoughts and consciousness were passed on. Passed on innocuously by someone close to you. Someone you love.

Mess Hall Turkey

Next Thanksgiving,
Next Thanksgiving,
Don't eat bread!
Don't eat bread!

Stuff it up the turkey!
Stuff it up the turkey!

Eat the bird! Eat the bird!

— Author Unknown

Mother's favourite poem, which is meant to be almost sung and repeated every year in the month of November for the family's annual Thanksgiving Day feast.

In November, at Thanksgiving dinner, the food was always the same. The girl liked the turkey dinner her mother fixed for this special occasion. She thought that her mother made the best turkey dressing in the whole wide world. She watched her mother jam all of that bread and stuff into the turkey's insides. She thought that it was fascinating that turkeys even had 'insides'! But when her mother explained about '*giplet graving*', Georgina wasn't so sure that she wanted to try it. Usually she would try new foods, but all of that bloody stuff in the bag inside the turkey didn't look very appealing. How could anything taste good if it was made from something with all of that blood in it? Eating something's blood didn't sound too good to her. Was it right to eat the blood of something? It made her tummy feel queasy and funny just thinking about it. That '*giplet graving*' looked all right as long as you didn't know how they made it.

Feeling sorry for his men, so far from their own mothers' cooking, one year her father decided that the whole family would have Thanksgiving dinner at the 'Mess Hall' where the soldiers on the base ate. Daddy thought it was one of the best ideas he had ever had. Instead of having dinner at home, the whole family got to go on an exciting adventure.

Daddy said, "It's something the kids will never forget! Don't you think it's a good idea, Georgina? Wouldn't you like to taste some of the soldiers' grumb? What do you think, *mi hita*? Wanna come to the base's Mess Hall for Thanksgiving dinner? It would give your mother a break from all of the cooking she does every day."

"Genio, I don't know, dear," interjected Mother. "I don't mind cooking. I had planned to make a new recipe this year. Five-Cup Fruit Salad. I think the children would love it. It has marshmallows. You know how the children love marshmallows. And Mother is planning to come over and bring her Rum Cake. You love her Rum Cake."

"Well, I want to take you out to eat, Lambie Pie. You work so hard. Come on, baby, I think you and the kids would enjoy a bit of an outing. And it would mean so much to my men. Your mother could come with us."

So, it was decided. Mother would make her fruit salad another time. The whole family would have an outing. They would get all dressed up in their church clothes and Daddy would drive them to the big 'Mess Hall' where his army men ate. Manga was invited too. But she decided that she'd see them on Friday, the day after Thanksgiving instead. If Mother didn't need her help with the cooking, Manga would go out with her friends from the base's PX and have turkey with them. She'd make two rum cakes. One for her friends and one for Genio and Claudia and the kids. Manga knew that Georgina adored the taste of her rum cake. She said that she didn't mind. She was so friendly. She had already made plenty of friends in Fort Wainwright and in Fairbanks, and she'd have Thanksgiving dinner with them.

Georgina was so excited about going to the Mess Hall to have Thanksgiving Day lunch with Daddy's men. There would probably be some of those Negro soldiers there too, and Georgina Jane and her family could eat with them, so that those poor homesick soldiers wouldn't feel so lonely and miss their mother's cooking in their other homes back in those warmer places. The girl understood the spirit of the thing. She felt sorry for those lonesome soldiers too.

When they got to the 'Mess Hall', in the clothes that they usually wore to church on Sunday, Daddy was right. All of those army men in their drab, stiffly starched, khaki green uniforms were so happy to see their captain, his glamorous wife and all of his children. Her daddy wore his 'dress blues', the special dressing-up uniform with all of the pins on it and the shiny buttons. And her daddy didn't wear his enormous everyday clompy army boots with all of the shoe lace holes in them. He wore his very, very shiny shoes, not his marching boots. All of Daddy's army men smiled at Georgina Jane and the 'little children'. It was Thanksgiving Day, the fourth Thursday in November, and a time for families to be together.

Daddy was so proud of his big family. He knew that all of those children of his would make Thanksgiving dinner more like a family time for those poor lonesome homesick soldiers stationed in Alaska. Those poor soldiers could even pretend that Georgina Jane and her sisters and brothers were their very own family from way back at their homes in the warmer places. And then, they wouldn't feel so sad about not eating their own mothers' food at Thanksgiving.

Afterwards, Mother said that she found the Mess Hall depressing and that next year if Georgina's father wanted to take his family out for Thanksgiving dinner, Mother would rather go to the Officers' Club. At the Mess Hall, all of the soldiers and the girl and her family got trays and picked up their own food from a long line of soldiers waiting to get their Thanksgiving Day lunch. At the Officers' Club, Mother could sit down in her fancy clothes and be waited on by waiters in clean white coats. Standing in long lines of soldiers, getting Mess Hall food, didn't appeal to Mother at all. Thanksgiving in the base's Mess Hall wasn't festive to her.

The girl realized that her mother found life in the Army very hard to cope with at times. Moving around was difficult. And living in a place like Alaska; where, although it was beautiful, the weather was so cold, was hard. Life in Alaska wasn't easy. Life was made even harder if the PX ran out of something Mother needed for herself or for her family. For perhaps the first time, on that Thanksgiving Day, at the army's Mess hall, the girl sensed the friction between the direction her father's job took him and the insecurity and displeasure that this way of life caused her mother. Her father wanted to be one with his men. Her mother thought that these enlisted men, and the Mess Hall and the army grub were beneath her. But these were not topics to be discussed in front of the children, whose young sensitivities had to be protected from such unpleasantries. So, nothing was mentioned until afterwards, when all of the kids were supposed to be asleep.

That Thanksgiving Day, the girl and her family ate with the enlisted men in her father's unit. They ate bland turkey and gravy and lumpy smashed potatoes. They all sat down together with the soldiers at long tables sitting on long backless benches. Sitting there with the soldiers stationed in Fort Wainwright. Soldiers whose hungry glances made her realize what life in the Army was really like. Glances hungry for family life. Men lonesome in a freezing cold outback region. The Army moved the girl's family around together, but not everyone was able to bring their mother and father and sisters and brothers along with them. So, driving home in the dark from the Mess Hall, on that first Thanksgiving Day in Alaska, gave the girl a warm feeling in her heart. She knew they had given those forlorn, homesick young soldiers a family to have around them on that special day.

It was a special day when everyone bowed their heads and said a special grace together and ate turkey, dressing and pumpkin pie. It was a day to stop working and have a family feast. A day to remember about the pilgrims who ate with the Indians. Pilgrims and Indians eating together on that first Thanksgiving Day. Like Mother had to eat and make friends with the soldiers. It was a day when Americans were thankful for America being a country. And it was a very special day for Alaskans, because it was the first Thanksgiving Day that Alaska was part of America for real. It was the first Thanksgiving Day after the Alaskan Territory became the forty-ninth State in the Union. It was a good idea to eat with the soldiers on that day. It was a day to be thankful.

Even if Mother felt uncomfortable about eating in the Mess Hall, instead of at the Officers' Club, it had given those soldiers a lot of pleasure. And Katrina Josephina had had a wonderful time. She had been the center of all of those young soldiers' attention, which that cavorting little blond-bomber girl enjoyed immensely. She sat on their knees, letting them bounce her around. She chattered away excitedly. She and Gretchen sang Mother's Thanksgiving Day song. And all of the army soldiers clapped for them. Clapped for those diminutives Marilyn-

Monroes-in-the-making. Those girls who knew how to make any occasion a celebration of sorts.

The soldiers told Daddy thanks so much for bringing his family to spend the day with them. Thanks for the blessing. Thanks for the song from his two blond-bomber-girls. Thanks for being there. They said it was the best Thanksgiving that they had ever had, thanks to him, and thanks to his wonderful family.

Alaskan Night Skies

It was night time when they left the Mess Hall. All around her, the stars were glistening and shining. The wintertime night skies in Alaska came out early in the day and were a thing of beauty. They were a joy to Georgina every time she got to see them. In the summertime, it never seemed to get dark, and the stars slept all night. A child could get awful tired trying to wait up for it to get dark in the summertime. The girl had tried to stay up all night in the summertime once, so she knew that it was true that the 'midnight sky' in Alaska never got dark in the summertime. But this was late November. Winter had set in good and hard. The sky was dark as pitch early in the day. The sun had been on the other side of the world for hours. It was five o'clock. The stars were sparkling just like in the nursery rhyme about little stars that could twinkle and twinkle up high above the earth. Those stars knew how to sparkle and shine, because they were so, so bright.

They used to sing that song about 'The Good Old Summertime' with her cousins, but it never mentioned about the sun never setting in Alaska's summers. Whoever wrote that song just hadn't been to Alaska in the summertime, or they would have put it in their song about the sun never setting in the summer in Alaska, because it was a special thing not to happen. It was daylight even in the night time. Because there was so much light in Alaska in the summer time, plants just grew and grew. Because the sun never really set in the summertime in Alaska, there was an amazing place where the vegetables grew to be a giant size. Those vegetables were almost like Jack's beanstalk in the fairy tale. The Matanuska Valley was known all over Alaska for its giant vegetables. It was probably even known all over the world, it was so famous. They could grow cabbages nearly as big as Daddy was tall there. Those cabbages were so giant and so heavy, that it took two Eskimos just to hold them up for a photograph to be taken of them. If they hadn't taken a photograph of those big vegetables, no one would have even believed how enormous and giant vegetables really could grow in Alaska's sunlit Matanuska Valley in the summertime.

Sometimes, her parents got all dressed up in fancy clothes, and Mother put on her special earrings and jewellery and they went to the Officer's Club for a party, or out for a nice dinner without all of their children. Lots of their army base friends, other officers who lived in Fort Wainwright too, gave dinner parties for the big people. In the winter, when her grandmother used to 'baby-sit' all of those 'little children' with Georgina Jane helping her, they would get to go outside in the snow and see the Northern Lights, the Aurora Borealis. Manga would let them stay up way past their bedtime, just to see those special lights up in the cold, shimmering Alaskan winters' sky. Sometimes Manga would even wake the 'little children' up and get them out of bed, just so that she could carry them outside, still dressed in their pyjamas with the snap-on bottoms and the rubber soles, wrapped up in a blanket. She would get them up especially, just to show them the brilliant colorful Northern Lights. The girl's little brothers would lift up their sleepy heads and say, "Oh! Ah!" just to please their grandmother, who thought that the Northern Lights were special enough to keep her grandchildren up late, just to see them.

Georgina's grandmother spoiled them. Manga was a good cook, and she taught them all about her special recipes. One of her most wonderful recipes was making taffy. They could pull the hot taffy, just like God must have pulled those bright wintertime lights to make the Northern Lights high up in the Alaskan sky. The kids even put food coloring into their taffy to make different colored taffy, like God put his colors into his very own Northern Lights. Those grandchildren could hold their colored taffy up to the lamp's light, after it cooled down and got hard. Their taffy glowed like the Northern Lights, just not as brightly. Manga even let them stay up late, just so that they could see what the sky looked like when it got darker and darker and colder and colder the later it got at night. They could stay up way 'past their bedtime' when Manga came to their house. Even if she knew that Mother would disapprove of her offspring staying up past their bedtime on a school night, Manga broke Mother's rule and allowed her grandkids to see the Aurora Borealis. She said, "It's too special a show to miss. Get your coats on, kids, and come outside with me. Better wear your boots too, cause its freezing out there."

The girl thought that God must be a really good painter when she saw those colors he'd put up in the midnight sky in Alaska. His lights could shimmer and even move when you watched them. They were even more beautiful than the Alaskan stars. The Alaskan stars were on Alaska's flag. Georgina and her classmates sang about the stars of gold on a blue background. But to see the actual stars up in the night-time sky was different than just seeing them on the beautiful Alaskan flag. She wanted to go to where those stars lived. That was probably where the fairies from her storybooks lived. Maybe her daddy could take her up in an airplane to visit the stars sometime. Could a person even fly to a star? Did stars really fall from the sky? Could you really catch a falling star like Perry Como sang about? Could you really catch a falling star and put it in your pocket and save it for a rainy day? Could you reach out and touch the Northern Lights? Would they feel like Manga's taffy?

She didn't get to see the Aurora Borealis too often though; because she had to go to bed at seven-thirty every night until she was eight. When she was eight, she could stay up until eight o'clock. When she was eight, she had to be in bed by seven thirty, but she could read until eight o'clock. She thought that was a pretty good deal, because all of the 'little children' had to have their lights out and couldn't read in bed. But even eight o'clock was usually too early to see the Northern Lights. She had to wait until Manga came to her house again to show the Northern Lights to her grandchildren.

All of her life, Georgina Jane O'Shaughnessy would look up at the ordinary sky, when she lived in places other than Alaska. She would remember the Alaskan skies, and how God had painted them with his lights. She hoped that the Northern Lights would be there forever. She hoped that the Aurora Borealis would never ever leave the Alaskan skies. She hoped that she could see those amazing lights in the dark, dark sky over Alaska again and again. The colors were so beautiful and glowing. Seeing them made her feel happy inside, like she was overshadowed by beautiful glowing colors and lights. Lights and colors up in the sky. Up in the sky while she dreamt the night away.

Manga showed the girl how to find the North Star, close to the Big Dipper. There was the Big Dipper and the Little Dipper. These dipper stars were a group of stars that were always in the shape of dippers, like her mother used with her special punch bowl for parties. Knowing where the North Star was in the sky was important. Like those runaway slaves travelling on the Underground Railroad before the Civil War, Georgina loved the North's Star. Her grandmother taught her how to find the Big Dipper and the Northern Star, which was really Alaska's very own star. Because it was on their flag, the North Star belonged to all of the Alaskans, but especially to the Eskimos, who had lived there the longest.

"When you can find the Big Dipper and the Northern Star, then you will always know which way is pointing North," her grandmother told her five shivering, half-frozen grandchildren, as they stood in the dark, in the freezing wintry snow with their teeth chattering like mad, staring up at the cold Alaskan sky, dressed only in their pyjamas, robes and slippers. Those kids were in too big of a hurry to run outside with their Manga to see the Aurora Borealis. To see the Alaskan stars shining so brightly. Too big of a hurry for coats and boots. The girl thought that those glimmering stars and fabulous lights were a wonderful idea. God was pretty smart to put a star in the sky that was so bright, that if people could see it, and know it was pointing North; they would never get lost.

Chapter Five
Flight of Fairies: An Interlude

Flight School

That was the year Daddy decided to teach Georgiana how to fly an airplane. It was their secret. Mother might have worried about her seven-year-old daughter's induction into Flight School. But Daddy didn't tell her. He took off with his daughter on Saturday mornings, saying he was taking Georgina to work with him. Taking her to see the new friends she'd made on her first Thanksgiving feast in Alaska. It was so secret, that Daddy didn't even tell Georgina about his plan.

He knew his daughter worried about his flying. He knew her concern for his safety. All of those never-ending questions. All of those night terrors when she awoke from her dreams with a sharp scream at midnight. He had gone to her bedside and she'd asked him about the airplane crash over and over again. It seemed like no matter how much he tried to console her, tried to tease her out of that place of anxiety, Georgina still had that worried look on her little face. What could he do? He'd wracked his brain. Trying, trying, trying. Trying to find a way to help his child. Trying to find a way to heal his child's young mind. Trying to free her.

Being Eugenio, he felt the best way to set his child free of her aerophobia was to make Georgina face the fears down. Somehow, he had to teach her to fight what frightened her. He knew that she had it in her. He'd seen what she'd done to that brat on the ship. Genio knew his daughter was a real fighter. He knew from the fear he'd seen on that kid, Henry's face after Georgina finished with him. His daughter had turned that brazen girl-handling boy into a complete scaredy-cat! And Genio'd watched his child, his little girl, as the tables full of rudely staring, scrutinizing faces gawked at the child when she walked into the ship's dining hall on board the ocean liner. Georgina just looked straight ahead, knowing what those criticising faces meant. Knowing those folks were saying awful things about her. Knowing how those gossiping folk had spoken about her behind her back. Knowing their judgmental attitudes. They stared at the girl whenever she had appeared with her family in whatever part of the ship she, and they entered. Georgina did not flinch. She was unmoved by their stares. Mother had told her that staring was rude, and so the child assumed that as rude people, they, and their stares were not worth worrying about.

Daddy knew that unbothered attitude took courage. He knew that Georgina was a brave girl. And he admired her courage and sheer guts. She was his baby and perfect in every way as far as he was concerned. He knew she knew how to refocus her mind when people misunderstood her. He knew that she knew how to deep breathe herself into a place of inner focus and even peace. He knew that Georgina was not what Henry was. Genio knew that Georgina was not a scaredy-cat.

So, one Saturday morning, as the kids sat with their father eating their bowls of Sugar Pops cereal, Daddy off-handedly said, "I think I'll take Georgina to work with me today."

"It's awful cold, honey. Do you think today's a good day for that?" Mother wanted to know.

"Oh, she'll be fine. She can help me get my office at the airplane hangar in order. What do you say, Georgina? Wanna come to work with Daddy today?"

Georgina had stopped slurping her milk. She always drank every drop, even after all of the floating bits of cereal were gone. Daddy said that wasting milk was a sin. He said that the children in Russia were starving. He said that even if she didn't like a particular food, she should eat what was put in front of her. And if she hated that food, she should eat it and 'offer it up for the sins of Russia'.

"Can I really come to work with you, Daddy?"

"Of course you can, *mi hita*. Daddy needs your help today. I have a big project that only you can do for Daddy."

"I know how to clean! I could help you! Mommy, can I go? I could help Daddy clean his office."

"Well, it's cartoon day, Georgina. But if you really want to go with your father, I guess it will be okay. But put your snow suit on, or you can't go."

Georgina hated that snowsuit. It was scratchy and itchy and very uncomfortable. Her mother knew that the child couldn't stand to wear those snow pants that matched that sweet little blue wool coat with its black velvet collar. It was the most uncomfortable piece of clothing imaginable. And Mother just adored how cute Georgina looked in the snowsuit's matching blue wool bonnet. She said that Georgina reminded her of Little Bo Peep. Georgina hated looking like Little Bo Peep. But to get to go with Daddy to work in his airplane hangar, she would wear anything, even something as itchy as those blue wool snow pants. Even something as stupid as that blue bonnet scratching the sides of her face and neck. So, she wasn't about to argue with Mother and not get to go. So, she would wear those scratchy blue wool snow pants and the matching blue bonnet and not say a word of complaint about them. Just so that Mother couldn't argue.

"All right. I will. I will. I will wear the snowsuit!"

"Good girl. Okay! That settles it! Let's get dressed and get goin', kiddo!"

Daddy drove the black and white Pontiac past snowy mounds on both sides of the streets. He was headed to the base's airplane hangars. Huge half circles full of airplanes in neat rows. To airplane hangars dripping with frozen giant icicles dangling from the hangars' metal awnings. Icicles like sharp, pointed daggers. Icicles like Damocles swords hanging way up over their heads as they walked from the warmth of their station wagon to Daddy's job center, the airstrip on the army's base.

Georgina's father spoke to one of his army buddies, saying something about the guy getting "a plane ready for take-off".

I wonder who's going to fly today, Georgina wondered, as she stood on the snowy tarmac outside the hangar looking all around her at the white landscape. Daddy had gone ahead of her to his office inside the hangar. He had to get his flight instructions for the day's work. Georgina watched his army buddy working on a small airplane with skies. Standing there in her itchy snowsuit and her matching blue wool bonnet, she shivered. The soldier was warming the plane's engine up. The girl remembered him from Thanksgiving. He was one of the guys who had bounced Katrina Josephina on his knee. He was one of the soldiers who had applauded her twin sisters' singing at the Mess Hall. He seemed nice.

Without a word of warning, there was her father. Scooping her up from behind. Daddy put Georgina on his shoulders as though she was one of their family's babies. He took her breath away. Next thing she knew, Daddy had tossed her into the interior of the airplane with wheels jutting out from underneath the skis on the plane's landing gear. Airplanes landing on snow or water had to have skis in Alaska. Wheels were only for tarmac. Wheels receded into the skies after take-off from Ft. Wainwright.

"Where are we going, Daddy?" Georgina asked, stretching to peer over the plane's windowsill.

"You'll see, baby! Buckle up and sit tight!" Daddy taxied the plane onto the runway. Snow plows kept the base's runways free of snow. This meant that wheels could be used for take-offs or landing. Everywhere around them was frosty. Snow. Snow. Snow. Everywhere she looked, there was snow. Georgina was so thrilled to be inside an actual airplane. It was the first time in her living memory she had ever been in an airplane. A real army airplane. And there was her daddy. Her pilot daddy! Dressed in his khaki green flight suit, his soft fur lined cap and his green jacket lined with cream colored fur, her daddy looked so handsome. Suddenly, it occurred to the girl that Daddy was up to something. Daddy was taking her flying. Daddy was taking her flying, and Mommy didn't even know.

Summer Fun

When Georgina Jane was eight years old, her aunt brought the cousins to Ft. Wainwright, near Fairbanks to see their grandmother, and to visit the girl and her family.

"It's like a three-ring circus, around here, with all of these kids!" her father said, the morning they all arrived.

The captain was headed out the door dressed in his heavily starched khaki green uniform and clompy military marching boots. It was the summertime again. The child's seventh summer. Daddy loved the warmer weather. He was in a good mood. Summer meant that life was easier. Summer meant that he could leave quickly, without having to warm up the family's station wagon or put it under all of those insulated blankets and put a heating lamp underneath the engine overnight just to keep the whole darn thing from freezing to a solid unusable block of ice, like he did in the winter.

"Put all of these kids down in the dungeon in the basement and lock the door!" he teased, as Bridgetta, the eldest cousin, walked past him without saying a word, or even bothering to look in Daddy's direction. Bridgetta thought that adults were beneath her. She was the star of the family, a natural born performer. What could this man, with his tacky sense of dress, have to say, that would help her in her job as a know-it-all child? It was beneath her dignity to even acknowledge his presence.

"Do you want to go down to the dungeon, little girl?" he said ghoulishly, grabbing Leah, who squealed with both fear and delight.

"We like to lock up little children down in the basement! We fatten them up and eat them for dinner! Grrr! Grrr!" he said, speaking ghoulishly in order to get a reaction from at least one of Georgina's cousins.

The children's playroom took over just about the entire basement, except for the part filled with shelves of emergency, non-perishable food storage, batteries, candles, canned goods and bulk foodstuffs in their huge chest freezer. It was hardly what you might call a dungeon. Those kids even had swings and their tricycles and bicycles down there, along with all of their toy chests. It was more like Romper Room, than a scary place to lock children up.

"It's summertime, Daddy. We don't have to go down to the basement in the summertime. We get to play outside all day!" said his daughter.

This was said in an effort to alleviate the transparent and obvious, ever-increasing terror of her cousins, who didn't know him that well and were starting to believe the very convincing performance of her father's deliberately idiotic play acting. He could have cared less if he made a complete and utter fool of himself with that dumb play-acting of his. He got his kicks out of teasing small children. Pretending to be something else. Trying to convince them, with a pretty believable act, that he was some sort of frightening ghoul or growling monster.

They must not be used to seeing a soldier in the house. That's why they are getting so scared. They must really think that he is going to lock them in the basement and hold them prisoner, Georgina Jane was thinking. "Don't worry, he's only teasing," she said to little Rachel, who was afraid to come all the way into the house. "He won't really hurt you. Come on in." Taking her younger cousin by the hand and trying to pry her away from her hiding place, behind the front door.

But Daddy made fierce, growling sounds at her cousin, Rachel, who, as an obviously captive audience, was frozen stiff and unable to move an inch. He kept clawing at her, trying to be a grizzly bear who would rend her in his paws the instant she set foot inside of his lair.

"I'm going to get you, little girl. And eat you up! Grrrr!" said the temporarily lunatic man.

"He's only pretending to be a bear, Rachel. He just likes to pretend to frighten little children. Don't believe him. Don't be afraid. He won't hurt you. He won't bite you. His teeth aren't really sharp," trying to calm her cousin's obvious fears.

Rachel continued to cower and hide behind the door, afraid to move forwards or backwards away from this obviously deranged military officer, who had perhaps taken momentary leave of his senses. That was all of the incitement that he needed. "Yes, they are!" roared Daddy loudly, baring his teeth and trying to make the most fearsome face he possibly could make at his small niece, who was visibly shaking and still hiding behind the door. Finally, Mother came to the rescue of the, by then, totally convinced and terrified cousin.

"It's okay, sweetheart. Come on in," said Mother to five-year-old Rachel.

"Go to work! And try to behave yourself!" she said to Georgina's father as he waved his arms menacing, showing his sharp fingernails for effect, at any stray and unprotected children he met on his way out of the front door.

Turning back to face her mother, he said imploringly, *"Dame un beso, por favour!"* swooping Mother up in his predatory arms and covering her face and neck with slobbery, wet and noisy kisses.

"I'm not leaving until you give me a kiss!"

Yielding to the man's embrace, her mother let him smother her with kisses. The romantic love scene between her parents was played out in front of the amazed children, who were, by now, all standing and staring with their young mouths wide open, entertained and engrossed by the saucy scene acted out by these two lovebirds.

Who was her father anyway? Was he a fearsome grizzly bear with sharp pointy claws and a terrifying growl? Was he a loving, cooing turtledove who needed lots of besos just to get the day started on the right foot? Was he a scary monster-man? Was he madly in love with the mother of his bewildered children? Were both just play-acting? He was believable in both acts. That was certain.

The children had become a rapt audience, totally engrossed in the whole scene. They were enthralled by the transformations and change of characters which Georgina's father displayed in a split second: the jailer of the family's dungeon, the growling beast with the scary, menacing teeth and huge waving arms and clawing hands, or the love-sick captain. Whoever he was, moments later he was out the door in his summer uniform and driving away in his car. He honked the car's horn as he pulled away, leaving all of the kids somewhat glad to see the back of the man, so that they could get on with the serious business of being kids. Nevertheless, his antics and fantastic performance set the stage for the summer's activities of these gob-smacked and beguiled children.

"Your dad's a nincompoop!" putting the accent on *'poop'* said the still shaking Rachel.

"We're not allowed to say 'poop', only 'ka ka'," explained Georgina to her diminutive cousin.

"Well, then he's a ka ka head," she said with a big sigh, tossing her head full of blond Shirley Temple curls from side to side.

Georgina already knew that her father was really just a big kid. She had learned that a long time ago. So, his antics, although very convincing, didn't really frighten her, even though his growls were pretty real, and his teeth did look a little bit sharp. Her daddy was like the Wizard of Oz behind that big screen in the movie, using sound effects and lighting to frighten poor Dorothy, the lion, the Tinman and the scarecrow. It took Dorothy's little dog, Toto, to pull back the curtain and reveal the Wizard of Oz's true identity. Like Toto, Georgina Jane knew the truth behind her daddy's shenanigans.

She knew that her father was really just Daddy. But to her cousins, who didn't visit that often, that soldier uncle of theirs might just prove to be a real threat. He sure could be scary and unnerving when he started playing crazy games with them. And the more frightened they became, the more their fears provoked his craziness. Her daddy loved to frighten little children. He thought it was a fun thing to do. The light relief he found in those children's squeals of unrepressed alarm and amusement thrilled her father, each squeal egging him on to more and more craziness. It would wind Daddy up tighter and tighter and tighter, making him go on and on and on with those terrifying games. He didn't know when to stop.

It was like Daddy was a giant child's toy that the children controlled. Their peels of laughter were like the gas in the engine in his car. The children's hysterical shrieks and howls of delight egged the crazed captain on and on in his wild cavorting. The girl thought that he would never stop with his jest and tickling. For just a little while, in his hard-working life, Daddy needed to play with the children, to be like he was one of his own kids. He acted like he was eight or nine at the oldest. It must have made a nice change from all of the worries of the 'Cold War' conflicts and getting lost in the tundra.

Sometimes, her father would pretend that his children were his army soldiers. He would line them up according to age and height and make them stand at stiff

194

attention. "Attention! Shoulders back! Salute! Onward troops! Forward! March!" he would command. No one dared to disobey his pretend stern voice, barking out commands. But if the dinner-time antics of the twins or her younger brothers got out of hand, and especially if someone spilled their milk, her father would suddenly say, "*Silencio! Qiate' su boca*! Come!"

Georgina Jane knew that by this, he meant for them to stop goofing-off and to be quiet and eat their dinner. When he said that to them, he expected instant obedience. It was like expecting a river to stop its flow, its gushing, in midstream, as it tumbled downward, over the side of one of Alaska's steep mountains. Her daddy wasn't always being silly and teasing. Sometimes he could switch in an instant and become a real tough guy.

He never seemed to comprehend that it takes children a while to catch up with adults' change of mood and mind. His children were like the soldiers in his army, made to instantly stand at attention and obey unquestioningly. It never occurred to him that his children might be incapable of making the sudden changes in their moods, like he was able to do. Changing from comedy and jokes at the dinner table, to silence and a sudden, enforced sampling of Mother's culinary endeavours, was not an easy character transition for her siblings.

But usually, her daddy was not very serious. And with his teasing, he displayed a flair as a talented actor. But then, he was used to acting. He had to be a daddy, an uncle, a neighbour, a son, a son-in-law, a husband and a captain in the Army. Georgina knew that her father wore many hats. So, pretending to be a guard for the basement dungeon, or a ferocious bear growling at her cousins, or a lover to her mother, was easy. She could see that her daddy was just having fun, playing wild games with those spellbound children, before he had to leave them all and go back to his work with the Army and do his hard job there. Being a growling bear was easy. Loving her mother was easy. Being a captain in the Army was much harder.

With this introduction to their summer's visit, it was understandable that the girl and her cousins spent the weeks that they were together, imagining, pretending and acting. Being a child was serious business in those days. One week they put on a circus, complete with trapeze artists and clowns. Make-up was supplied from Mother's cosmetic box. Costumes were made from old cast-off hats, shoes and adult clothes which came from footlockers stored in the basement.

Even Mother's old stockings were used as wigs, sometimes worn by the family's boys. Those old stockings of Mother's were worn by those little boys on their heads. Those boys were just happy to have the attention of so many girls at one time. The tights were braided by the girls, or turned into buns which sat on top of the boys' heads. That way, roles could be reversed at a time in their lives when gender was insignificant to their play-acting.

Georgina was taking ballet lessons, and so, for her costume, she wore her black leotard and pink tights with her ballet dancing shoes. She was a trapeze artist and had learned to hang upside down from the swinging chin-up bar. Her little brothers, Roger Eugenio and Peter Martin were dressed up like clowns, in funny hats, with lip-sticked and rouged faces. Unmatched clothes and wigged heads made with those stockings completed their ensembles. They were pulled to the playground in their red wagon, where the circus was to take place. It was impossible to have circus acts and a trapeze scene without the swings, the merry-go-round and the monkey bars. Bravely, the circus performers did their stunts, with Bridgetta, as the ringleader, giving the orders. Everyone performed to perfection and the audience cheered and applauded as each tiny child took his or her bow or curtsey. They even sold cool-aid, popcorn and cookies during the intermission.

Playing was a full-time job for the girl and her cousins and siblings. Much of the time that summer, was spent making forts and tents in the neighbourhood. Making-believe was always easier if you got the props right. Her father had made an Indian tee pee out of a cast-off parachute, which he had salvaged for them from one of the army's airplane hangars. He had two of the servicemen from the base come to their house and erect this giant Indian tee pee in their back yard. There were no fences at the army base housing, in Fort Wainwright, and so all of the neighbourhood children could have a turn sitting inside of the huge tent in the O'Shaughnessy's backyard.

Tall pine tree trunks from the forest around Fairbanks were used as the posts over which the parachute, like the peeling of a huge onionskin, was wrapped around and around the framework of this giant structure. That tee pee was quite a neighbourhood attraction. This delighted Katrina Josephina, who became an instant star, and the center of attention with all of her friends. Everyone wanted to come to their house and go inside of that magical tee pee, just like the real Indians used to live in them on the prairies and the plains of the southern United

States. That was way back in a time when there were still so many buffaloes on the grasslands and plains of the Midwest.

It was a splendid summer. It was a time when the fairies really danced. Imaginations would run wild. All of nature became a stage for the girl and her cousins' grand adventures. They spent their time turning their world into a garden of earthly delights; where they could be anything, anyone they wanted to be. Georgina could even be a beautiful fairy with transparent wings. That whole summer the girl believed that she was a fairy. In her imagination, she could really fly like the fairies could. She knew what it felt like to fly. Daddy had taught her that. Her Irish grandmother had told her about the leprechauns and pots of gold at the end of rainbows. So, it must be true. Believing in fairies was easy that summer.

Fairies were tiny, delicate creatures, who could flitter around gardens, like the girl and her sisters and cousins did. Concentration was everything in these childhood games. Play was an earnest pursuit. Mentally making yourself as small and minute as possible was essential, because fairies were supposed to be so little, that you could hardly see them. You had to have a special way of seeing, or being a fairy wouldn't be real.

Like the girl, her cousins loved creative play, making up stories between them, about fairies mostly, and anything magical or mysterious. Whenever they got together, there would be an exchange of ideas for the original stage presentations they planned to perform for the neighbourhood and for their family. They would even sell tickets to everyone for the show at a dime apiece. It was like a real professional endeavour, with rehearsal after dress rehearsal. Acting was serious business. It was a time when, and a place where, the children's imaginations took them to another reality; where the reality of one world could overlap with the other pretend world.

Nothing was impromptu about the dance performances which were choreographed by Bridgetta, the eldest. Her sister and sidekick, Leah, always thought up designs for the costumes. And using old clothes and sheets, which were draped over shoulders, dressing-up took on a whole new meaning. The fairies' appendages for flying, were made of wire coat hangers, bent into the shape of little wings and covered with sheer fabric glued carefully to the sides of the wires. All of the girls wore wildflowers in their hair and they wore veils of gauzy material which seemed fairy-like to them. They made a stage under the carport with sheets for curtains, and carefully arranged chairs for the seating of the audience. One of the most elaborate of these shows was staged in honour of the celebration of Georgina's mother's thirtieth birthday. It was entitled *'The Fairies' Dance'*.

During these summer vacations, Georgina Jane would spend her time off from school, playing with her friends or her visiting cousins. They would test each other with nature quiz books and spend hours walking through the woods in search of rainbows or wildlife. Or, if they were visiting Anchorage, they'd go over to the cousin's neighbours to see the new baby bunny rabbits which had just been born. The nice man would take tiny handfuls of bunnies out of his hutches and hold up for the girls to see and to pet. Trying to be as quiet as four or five children walking together could possibly be, supposing that this would aid them in sneaking up and then getting the wild Alaskan animals to come close enough to be observed, Georgina and her sisters and cousins would wander freely through their neighbourhood vicinities in search of adventures. Sometimes a moose was spotted in the distance, or they imagined that they saw a brown bear catching a salmon in the nearby stream.

The girls, all five to seven of them would tramp around for the whole morning or the entire afternoon. They had to leave little funny faced Carolina at home with the boys, because she was still too young to join their 'girls' gang'. Out for the day! Out on their own. They would take peanut butter sandwiches with grape jelly, all wrapped up in waxed paper. They would take a big bag of potato chips to be shared amongst them. If Aunt Adie had forgotten to buy apples the last time she went to the grocery store, they would just pick blue berries and eat them straight off the wild bushes that grew everywhere. For desert, they'd take their weekly allowance and spend a nickel or a dime on ice cream or popsicles from the musical ice cream van that visited their neighbourhoods every single day throughout the summer months. Every day was a new adventure.

Every day was filled to the brim with summer reading and books from the library, or books that belonged to them. They wrote book reports just for fun. One of their favourites was about a wild little girl (like they were) named Heidi. Heidi tended goats for her grandfather, who let her be wild. Her wildness could even have a healing effect on that crippled girl, Clara. Heidi was a sort of role model to be followed. *Peter Pan* was another special volume. Wendy was an amazing girl, who was a real leader in her darling family. Wendy was a girl who learned to fly and helped the orphaned boys who were living with that never-to-grow-up boy, Peter Pan. Georgina Jane and the other girls lived in a *'Never*

Neverland' of sorts, so these stories really came to life in their discussions of the books that they were reading.

These sorts of books were brimming with feminist ideas. But people didn't know that then. They weren't aware of the impact on the imaginations that this sort of literature would have on girls. Fairy Tales were the same, showing that old women could be witches, and young women could be imprisoned or oppressed by them. The brothers Grimm and Hans Christian Anderson had a big impact on Georgina and her cousins. Their characters were so believable. Life was found in the imagination, real or imaginary. And books supplied the scripts for all sorts of ideas and performances.

The girls drilled each other with fierce competition and a determination to learn all of the answers at the back of the Nature Quiz book which they carried around like it was very precious, like it was their Bible. Knowing about nature was of the utmost importance to those girls. Georgina and Bridgetta and Leah were the joint ringleaders, who took it in turns to decide how they would all pass their time. Or sometimes, they just let things happen, and waited to see how the days would evolve.

"What'll we do today?" the girls would ask each other. The air was fresh. The sun was shining. The world was their oyster. Nothing could stand in their way. And besides, they had the feeling that Mother would be happier, or Aunt Adie's life would be made easier if they just vamoosed.

There were ponds with leeches and cattails. Ponds that had been frozen over in the long winter months when ice skaters zoomed over the ice every winter. Ponds that were now liquid pools. Ponds in their neighbourhoods. Ponds in their minds, put there just for them to see what nature had supplied with her bounty. They would fearlessly wade into the ponds. Water up beyond their knees. Brown pond water covering their thighs. Water that might have covered the oceans. Water that hid the muddy bottom surface from their eyes. Bare feet cautiously threading where angels never walked. Cold children's feet. Cold unfrozen water. Water where anything could be hiding. Leeches would cling to their shins and calves after they bravely waded in. Their efforts to use their pocketknives to cut the coveted cattails from the banks were rewarded. Precarious places where the bottoms of the ponds were muddy, and the mud oozed between their toes, were unnerving. But these ponds gave them their treasures of furry brown cattails. Mother loved cattails in her flower arrangements. Flower arrangements mixed with driftwood from the shores near Anchorage. She, and the girls coveted cattails and pussy willow branches from near the ponds.

No adults were out in the wilds with those wild, untamed girls. No one was 'watching' them. No one really worried about their children being out and about back then. The worse that could happen was maybe a skinned knee, and for that, Bridgetta had Band-Aids in her pocket. A child at the ages of eight or nine or ten or eleven, was considered a responsible person, who could take charge of her whole gang for hours on end without adults interfering. There were bicycle day trips to be taken. Parks to be visited and explored. And picturesque walks through cool woods, where Hansel and Gretel might still be locked in a witch's house, waiting for the girls to come and set them free! Little Red Riding hoods were always on the lookout for the big bad wolf, or an Alaskan bear or wolverine. But the only animals they saw most days were Alaskan bunnies in their summer brown coats, or squirrels scampering up pine trees. Sometimes, they could hear fox cubs in the distance, yelping at each other. An eagle might soar and coast overhead, calling to his mate.

Fields of wild flowers surrounded them, encompassing the girls with color and beauty. Flowers laughing with the girls as they, and the children swayed gently in the breeze. Anemones dressed in white and a plethora of the Alaskan State flower, the deep blue for-get-me-nots, grew prodigiously everywhere they looked. Time seemed always to be on their side, as though the world belonged just to them. As though time was standing still. Standing still just for them. As though they would always be who they were right then. Right then. Right there. Caught in that moment of time forever, like that boy, Peter, in J. M. Barrie's book *Peter Pan*.

Nature Quiz Book

The girls would take it in turn to ask each other questions from a book that Manga had bought for them. It was called *Nature Quiz Book* by Anne Orth Epple. "What is the largest animal that ever lived? Can any bird fly backwards as well as forwards? Are elephants afraid of mice? What does the camel store in its humps? Do cats have nine lives? What is the name of a baby goat?" That was Quiz A. The answers were at the end of the book. At the end of this chapter, the reader will find the answers. After we are finished asking each other the quiz questions, you can go to the end and see them for yourselves.

"Does a bee die after it stings? What is the difference between a moth and a butterfly? What male fish carries the young in a pouch until they hatch? What is the difference between frog eggs and toad? What animal lives the shortest time? Name three kinds of reptiles? What is a white animal with pink eyes called? Do toads cause warts? Can horned toads shoot blood from their eyes? Is the horned toad really a toad? What are apes?" That was Quiz B. You have to go to the end of this chapter to find the answers.

"Does the hippopotamus really sweat blood? Are snakes slimy? What animal is pictured on a nickel? Do snakes wait until sundown to die? Are dinosaurs extinct? What mammal can fly like a bird? Can snakes hear?" That was Quiz C. Turn to the end to find out the answers!

"What is the difference between a rabbit and a hare? What is a group of cows called? What is a walking stick? What is the name for animals whose teeth keep growing? How long does a giraffe live? What is the smartest animal? What is a zoologist? What is a pollywog?" That was Quiz D. Don't peek. You have to at least try to answer the questions before you go to the end of the chapter.

"Which bird migrates the longest distance? Do ostriches hide their heads in the sand when frightened? What sound does a turkey make? What insect eats its mate? Why is the black widow so called? Do squirrels always find the nuts they bury? How many compartments in a cow's stomach? What animal sprays when annoyed?" That, boys and girls, was Quiz E. That's enough questions for today. How smart are you? Can you answer the Nature Book questions without peeking at the answers and cheating, like some naughty children do? Well, if you are the one asking the questions, like Georgina Jane O'Shaughnessy and her sisters and cousins asked each other in 1959 and 1960, then you may now look at the answers at the end of this chapter and see if you, or the person you are testing is smart or not.

Aunt Adie

Alaska was a place where it wasn't hard to find beauty. Some might say that the grandeur of such fabulous scenery might have seemed wasted on little people, thinking that children do not notice such things. But that's not true. The children revelled in all of the sights and sounds around them. They marvelled in the small and great joys of each new day. Time together was everything then. Georgina Jane spent the last summer with her cousins before she left Alaska. Poppies, orange and bright, and multi-colored snapdragons grew in their mother's garden.

When her aunt had time for gardening, she never knew. But Georgina was glad that Aunt Adie made time for gardening; because her garden was one of the most magical places for fairies and little girls to be.

Her aunt had seven children and another one on the way. But she found time for artistic endeavours and exquisite things like flowers and pretty clothes and a vast collection of shoes. Aunt Adie made everything look so easy. With her happy-go-lucky disposition and unflustered manner, she used her energies to do creative happy things, so no wonder her children were so imaginative too. It was easy to see the connection. Georgina's cousins' mother encouraged the girls especially, to develop their creative sides. Activities like writing, drawing, talking and telling stories, taking long walks and collecting leaves, sticks or pebbles or just sitting quietly and thinking to yourself were encouraged. Somehow Aunt Adie knew that exploring your surroundings and times of quiet contemplation would give those girls a secret kind of strength as female people in a mostly man's world.

She didn't interfere with the children's' play. She let them be in their own space. It was a space in which to explore other worlds and come out the other end having found yourself. Having discovered, with all of your other discoveries, who you were too. Georgina's aunt could do anything she set her mind to. She could do her housework and cook for thirteen children; including her own brood and Georgina Jane's family when they visited. But somehow, she still had time for herself and her own interests. It was a time of learning about what it meant to be a woman: a mother, an aunt, a wife and an artist or gardener all at the same time. Aunt Adie was a flexible woman.

Adults didn't talk to children about such abstract concepts then. Kids just had to absorb these things through their own observations. The girl learned this through osmosis; without being told. Children were like a separate kind of being, distant from the adults' world. What children felt or thought, the impressions they formed, was left to the little people to decide. That way of learning left them more time to think about being fairies flitting around gardens without bothering any of the big people. As long as they weren't sassy, what they thought really didn't matter.

Aunt Adie was a self-taught artist. She hadn't had time to go to school to be officially taught to paint, with all of those children of hers. So, she taught herself about Art. She could paint and draw the most extraordinary pictures of flowers and the beautiful Alaskan scenery. Georgina Jane felt that she could almost take a walk into those paintings of her aunt's. Every day after lunch, her aunt would call all of the children together and say to them, "You are not to disturb me for an entire hour. Bridgetta, go and get my alarm clock and set it to ring in one hour. Whoever disturbs me before the alarm rings, will be spanked. Do you understand me, you children? Bridgetta, go and get my shoe, in case I need to spank anyone who bothers me while I am painting."

With that summons and strict orders for the children to get along and not fight or break anything or do anything naughty, her aunt would commence with her intense and all-consuming task of painting. All of those little kids had to take a nap.

Aunt Adie knew that was the only fair way to make all of those small children be really quiet and good and behave themselves. Georgina knew that her uncle was right in what he said about sleeping children. Naps were the only way to get little kids to behave. The big children were allowed to sit quietly and watch, while Aunt Adie painted. But the first person who let out 'one little peep', was under the threat that they would be 'punished with a spanking'! Aunt Adie kept one of her shoes right there next to her while she painted, as proof that she meant what she said. Those shoes were meant for spanking. And that's just what she'd do. Spank.

To Georgina Jane, this time, this one hour a day, was like heaven. All of those little children either had to take naps or read quietly in their beds. So, it was nice and peaceful. Just the big girls were allowed to sit and watch her aunt perform her wonders on the canvas. Aunt Adie could have painted for hours, probably all day, or even for weeks, if she hadn't had so many children to disturb her. Georgina thought that her aunt was like a magician who could pull rabbits out of his hat. Her aunt could look at an orange poppy growing in her garden, and produce it on paper, making it look exactly like God had made it. Her poppies' petals looked just like translucent gauzy orange paper. Her roses looked like velvet. Like you could feel their soft colors and the creamy texture of the rose buds Aunt Adie put into her paintings. Aunt Adie must have believed in fairies when she was a little girl, to be able to paint like that. To be able to see like that.

Uncle Bubba

Georgina's uncle never came to see any of his children's productions. Her aunt's husband travelled extensively. Looking back, one could see why. How could any man hope to keep his sanity, when his wife kept getting pregnant and having more and more children? He couldn't stand the noise, the disorder and the confusion that they created. It was not a quiet household. Something was always getting broken by all of the running around and playing that the children did, and by the fighting that Katrina Josephina and Gretchen Gabriella and the boys did.

One child would run into one door, in the living room, and another would run out of the other door, in the kitchen banging it behind him or her. It was overwhelming. There was no room for her uncle to even breathe in that place. He could not think his own thoughts there. He was too busy with his job for the government, to emotionally cope with all of these small bodies infiltrating his space. Physically and mentally, it was simply too taxing for him to deal with.

Her uncle had grown up an only child. He wasn't from a large family, and he wasn't used to the chaos brought about by so many small people. To him, children's exuberant playtime, was no fun at all. Until he had one of his own, he had never experienced a large family. By then it was too late to change his mind about having so many kids. They were already there, inhabiting his once quiet world. Already there. Already there, complicating his life.

It was too emotionally complex for the man to take in. All of those needs. All of those wants. All of those dirty finger prints everywhere. Too many glasses of milk split at the breakfast, lunch and dinner tables. Too many demands on his busy life. He couldn't shift from one world to another. All he really wanted, when he came home, was peace. And quiet. Peace and quiet. He never seemed to see the connection between his activities in the bedroom and all of the chaos which was the result of his night time endeavours and amours. All of the noise and confusion remaining after his grunts and groans! Putting his thing into his wife like Georgina's cousins said that he did. He never stopped to consider 'what time of the month' it was. He never considered the cycles of the moon and their connection with his offspring. He just kept sowing. Sowing his wild oats.

So, the confusion just grew and grew and grew. It grew until there were eight other heads to count around the dinner table with all of its split milk and mayhem. Too many people talking all at once. It was deafening. He couldn't hear himself think! And there were too many noisy pitter patterings going on in his house.

And to make matters worse, his eight children all developed the same shoe fetish that his wife had. Aunt Adie had a closetful of shoes, shoes and more shoes. Shoes of ever color and description. Shoes! Shoes! Shoes! Everywhere he looked, there were shoes. Shoes needing polishing. Mismatched shoes. Dirty shoes. Muddy, soiled shoes sprouting in every corner of his existence. And that didn't include the snow boots, ski boots, ice skates and skies that appeared during the winter months.

The seemingly unending pile of his children's shoes tormented the man's mind, driving him slowly towards a sort of insanity, a state of non-reality. He could feel his own heart beating wildly with the sights, the smells, the sounds of his household. Noisy confusion everywhere he looked. His heart was palpitating much too quickly. He could feel his blood pressure rising every time he noticed a new pair of shoes lying around his house.

He had been put into boarding school at an early age, where the pupils were not allowed the freedom to run wild, like his children seemed to. His child bride of a mother, Ethel May, who both loved him, and yet felt that he was a drain on her limited emotional resources had rarely spent much time in his company when he was a child. He was 'farmed-out' to her relatives. He was sent to the swamp in Louisiana, to be influenced by his uncles who took him fishin' or taught him how to fix car engines while they drank their home-brewed moonshine. But he didn't like the experience of putting worms on hooks, or the feeling of having automotive grease underneath his fingernails. Though the home-brew was another thing. His education had given him the chance he needed. And as soon as he could, he'd left that life behind in the deep, swampy, mosquito-infested South, where cotton and tobacco grew and snakes and alligators were his relatives' closest neighbours.

The one thing that he did take away from the swampy alligator country was not the twanging accent of the relatives he had long ago left behind. There was one thing he had learned from those poor, backward, simple folks down home. Those were his people down there. They spent their time: pickin' cotton, spittin' 'baccy, makin' out with their cousins, saying their Amens in their churches, drinkin' their moonshine, haulin' their crops to market, pickin' their noses, and eatin' their booggers. He wasn't like they were. He was a cut above the rest. He was blue-blooded. They were not.

But there was one thing he had learned from them. There was one thing he had learned from those old folks back home, besides how to change the oil in his car and fish for catfish in the creek. There was one thing that those simple folks with their home-cooked dinners – cooked from vegetables grown in their own backyard gardens and served with crispy fried catfish and crawdads from the hollow or the creek – had taught him. That one thing they had taught him along those creek beds and in the backwoods was the one thing that stuck with the girl's uncle all of his life. It was his family heirloom.

That one thing was a special, jigging, rhythmic two-step. Perhaps it was a jitterbug. It was her uncle's special act. It was a real fine dance. It was a dance he always danced solo. It was a dance that belonged only to him. Nobody else the girl knew could dance that unique, swinging dance. It was a dance the man used to entertain his children and their cousins long enough to settle them down for a few minutes of peace and quiet. No one moved or said a word as they watched Georgina's Uncle Buford, Bubba for short, do his fast-foot-moving two-step.

It was an old dance from another time, before bombs were dropped on the world, changing it forever. It was a dance that only the girl's uncle could perform. She had never seen anything like it. Nor would she ever see anything like it again. It belonged to her uncle. It was his alone. It was his captured, secret inner gaiety. It was his only light relief in a trying world. When he danced his animated, spry, joyous, wondrous dance in front of all of the thirteen kids at his no longer tranquil house, the girl knew the real truth about her uncle. The girl knew that really, even if too many shoes annoyed him, and spilled milk got on his nerves, he loved all of those kids. He must have really loved them. He must have thought that they were special. He must have cared what they thought of him. He must have wanted to make them happy. He must have. He really must have, to share his special archaic lively dance with them.

Boarding school had been a great experience, according to him. And as Ethel May's only child, he was responsible for propping up his mother's faltering self-image. He felt compelled to make something of himself. It was his way of repaying her for the great, mind-expanding education that he had received. His success was Ethel May's success. His accomplishments were not his alone, but his mother's as well. Living a life through one's children, even grown children's lives, was considered normal. No one saw this vicarious pursuit as dysfunctional then, and if they did, they kept their mouths shut about it.

Letting it 'all hang-out' wasn't acceptable back then. It was the 1950s and talking about feelings was unimaginable then. It took over another two decades before attitudes would begin to shift, and talking about your feelings became fashionable. Because of the impetuous which the imposition on the country of the 1960s race riots put on society, people were forced to change, to open up to each other. Presidents endorsed these changes and laws were either revoked or passed into legislation, so the people, however resistantly, had to follow their lead.

Albeit, sometimes even the racial tensions in the mid-1960s would seem like nothing more than peaceful gatherings to sing soulful songs and join hands, when Uncle Bubba's children turned into the longhairs of the late 1960s and early '70s. The eventual *'Love/Peace Movement'* produced a drama so intense, that his little girls' plays and productions would seem like peaceful summer picnics. The whole country eventually had to be cajoled or else beaten into submission in order to change.

Fairness for everyone, even in a place where the motto was said to be, *'Liberty and Justice for all'*, was a scarcity before changes were procured by pushing against the rigid systems of inequity. Her uncle's children would want more than surface changes in their world. They'd be moved by more than the sight of shoes on the floor. Like those soldiers in Georgina Jane's father's army, lots of marching had to take place in the children's world to bring about the alterations. There was no way that the girl's uncle or her daddy could have ever prepared themselves for what was to come in the next ten years!

People didn't know then, what later became common knowledge. And no one seemed to understand that a child's upbringing and background would have any effect whatsoever on the way that person eventually turned out. Just the day-to-day survival, putting clothes on their backs, and food on the table, teaching them table manners and to respect their elders were considered enough. Her uncle decided that he'd rather be by himself, after his seventh child was born. But by then, it was too late. Georgina's aunt became pregnant with her eighth child, and, as the girl's father used to say, before the advent of mass birth control, "Children are an occupational hazard," to the job of marriage.

It wasn't until years later that she understood what her father meant. To her uncle, it was an obvious *'occupational hazard'*, that left him with feelings of shock and horror at what his own saucy actions could produce, what his own desires and passion could bring about. The procreation of new lives was, after all, the woman's responsibility in terms of the daily contending with what his own flesh and blood got up to. He had no intention of actually conversing or interacting with, on a daily basis, this small tribe, who inhabited his living space.

His wife felt the full burden of shaping those lives, and sometimes, even for her, it got a bit overwhelming too. Without the day-to-day support of the children's father, it was an uphill battle. Just keeping that many children clean, quiet, and invisible meant that much less time was available for her pursuit of Art and a personal happiness that she felt belonged to her and did not include her children. Even the girl's strong aunt couldn't cope with family life without often feeling at times, frankly, a bit crazed and cranky.

The girl, at a tender age, could see the dilemma her relatives had to deal with. She had learned, by watching her own mother and father struggle with herself and her own siblings, what it was like being a parent. It was not an easy job, even for her own practically perfect mother, and her quite capable father. Uncle Buford, Bubba, they called him, was no match for the ingenious ways his kids used to try to slowly drive their father out of his mind. They could do this with one hand tied behind their backs. They could do this just by the simple act of being who they were; diminutive monsters.

A child's later emotional instability or inability to cope with life, which led to drug or alcohol abuse, because of the world's craziness and the alienation within the structure of their childhood family, were not within the grasp of knowledge that her uncle and most in his generation possessed. He didn't understand himself and his own childhood. Nor did he even think it was a necessity of life to do so. How could he offer to his own children a method of living which didn't include escapism, when that's what he himself wanted so desperately?

"The only good child, is a sleeping child," he used to say.

He wanted another reality all of the time, not the real life, where he lived, in a space invaded with so many little bodies and souls crying out continually for sustenance or something he felt at a loss to give to them. Was it any wonder that his children would grow up to be much the same? They would find coping with life difficult. Their life patterns were being set at this time. But no one seemed to realize that then.

Ethel May, Milk Toast and Myrtle the Turtle

The fact that his own mother had not taken the time to understand him, might have been part of his difficulty. She said that she loved him. She thought that they were close. But too many years apart, and too many grandchildren, made him seem remote and almost surrounded, as if by a moat surrounding a castle. Were his children his buttresses and battlements against his mother's latent over-possessiveness of her only child? She tried to span the failed years of his childhood with her longing to hold on to what was a long past outgrown need for her devotion. He no longer needed parental bonding. He had difficulty enough in bonding with his own children, much less feigning a closeness with an over-bearing mother.

Uncle Bubba's mother had aspired to the stage, so no wonder his mother's grandchildren were so talented! Ethel May knew talent when she saw it. And her grandchildren were amazingly talented – especially Bridgetta. The sun rose and set for that child. All others paled in significance. Her son's eldest daughter would be the most successful, the most brilliant and the most entertaining! On this child would hang hope, that all of her grandmother's failed experience with her own child, could be overcome and finally laid to rest. Bridgetta's grandmother doted on her above all others. None of the rest of her grandchildren really existed. Their grandmother's spotlight was only capable of highlighting Bridgetta's greatness.

It was clear to Georgina Jane that Ethel May's one real gift was making milk toast with white bread. When you were invited to stay with her, she always made milk toast. All of the girls loved Ethel May's milk toast. She made it really, really well. It was one of the most delicious things that Georgina had ever tasted in her whole life, transporting the child to a place in time that differed from her own. It was like the forbidden fruit in the Garden of Eden. Nothing could taste that good and not be sinful! Though Ethel May didn't seem overly domesticated, and never sewed, nor seemed to even clean her house, this one delicacy, was what gave her an obvious and definite value and worth.

Ethel May's milk toast communicated to the girl in a way that mere words could not. Ethel May's milk toast had the power to make known to Georgina Jane, all of those things which were unspeakable. When she ate Ethel May's milk toast, Georgina understood what it was like to be a Southern lady, like she knew that Ethel May really was. Ethel May wasn't an Alaskan. She was not a rough and ready female, who had become that way by surviving her whole life in a place as freezing cold as Alaska. She was from the Deep South, where it was warm almost all year round. And where people greeted you with, "Hi, ya'll!" smiling with either crooked, or else all of those straight white teeth of theirs.

Ethel May knew about Southern home cookin'. It was about who she was. It was not something Georgina Jane could see from looking at the outside of Ethel May, with her tightly permed, cropped, greying hair and her pale ivory skin and her freckled hands and face. It wasn't seen in Ethel May's demure, prim and proper, lady's clothes. Ethel May wasn't about her exterior. She was someone else, like a deep well of information, from things not said, only known and communicated in other more subtle ways, like her way of cooking and her Southern-style food. Georgina Jane knew who Ethel May really was by the food that she served. She was not the lady she pretended to be. Like the fairies' songs, Ethel May's persona was no mystery to the girl's heart. The girl could taste who her cousins' grandmother was in every mouth full of the food that she cooked whenever Georgina visited the woman with her cousins.

Tasting that milk toast transported the child back in time. Back in time to when the child's family had lived in Fort Campbell. The girl remembered their Southern black maid from back in Kentucky whenever she ate Ethel May's milk toast. It wasn't just Myrtle's skin color, or her religious beliefs or her singin' that were not the same as Georgina's family's way of life. That woman could cook up a storm of delicious Southern delicacies. Myrtle's cookin' was different from the girl's mother's recipes. Mother was a wonderful cook. Certainly, nothing to complain about ever came from her kitchen. Mother knew how to cook too, like Myrtle could. So did both of the girl's grandmother's, all in their own different ways. That's what ladies were supposed to do, sew, clean and cook. All ladies cooked back then. Otherwise, their kids would go hungry. And their husbands would get mad at them for being so lazy. Women had to cook. That was before TV dinners were even invented!

But Myrtle's food was unique. Her mother's maid's food was thick and yummy with love. Like a magic potion. Made with an unhurried and good heart. Made with a heart full of soul. Thick with the unburdening of her people's history. Every pot laid it all down. Every burden. Every care. They all fell away from Myrtle when she cooked. Every pot full told a story. Every pot made you feel good. Every pot full told you who Myrtle was. Every pot full made you feel good about who you were. Every pot full said, "*I loves ya, honey!*"

On the days when their colored maid came to Ft. Campbell and did the housework, she always cooked a left-behind-supper too. She left it on the stove in stainless steel skillets, or warmin' on shiny metal bakin' trays in the oven. She left it there so that Missus Shaughsee jest had to serve it up for her family! It was

210

Myrtle's way of makin' Ms Shaughsee's Wednesdays easier. Her way of pleasin' her employer's wife. Her way of minsterin' to that difficult, quietly temperamental, pale, white lady with so many chillin'. Myrtle knew Ms. 'Shaughsee didn't have much stamina. That black mammie knew that her employer's wife's constitution was what they used to quietly, call *'delicate'*. She knew that those fragile, over-taxed nerves were stretched beyond the poor, tired, irritable, white lady's capability.

Sometimes Myrtle'd come on over and fix a warm breakfast of Cream of Wheat with one of her smilin', male, colored friends all dressed up with a bow tie pictured on the box. But usually, it was a dinner of black-eyed peas steeped in juices, cooked with the fat of hogs slaughtered and smoked in the 'Tucky backwoods. Collared greens and ham-hocks laced with spicy onions. Chicken fried steak, which she pounded with a meat tenderiser before dippin' the thin strips of beef into egg and milk, and then into white flour with salt and pepper, plus a dash of red Tabasco sauce, cayenne or chilli powder, but not too much to make it unpalatable for the chillins'.

Gritty grits. Succulent Southern fried chicken, that was finger-lickin' fantastic. Chunky white hominy, tastin' like a chompy bowl of broken up knuckle bones. Or pook chops with the gristle still left on them. Soft, risin', floury, flakey bisquits, smothered with grey-blond cream gravy. Or pats of yellow butter from Kentucky cows smeared onto golden warm brown corn bread. Lima beans, pale green and cooked to perfection with chunks of Myrtle's leftover ham. Soft gooey orange sweet potatoes, peeled and baked, and covered with generous dollops of churned butter and cream, all mixed together and topped with caramelised brown sugar. And sprinkled with chopped southern pecans, that had fallen to the autumnal ground. Pecans collected. Pecans stuffed into Myrtle's worn coat pockets, as she walked to work from the bus stop. Past the big old prodigious tree down the street from the Shaughnessy's drab army base house she had walked every Wednesday.

Past the not-so-colored-blind neighbours she had walked. Khaki green (like Daddy's drab army fatigues). Green, fresh, skinny, string beans, whose strings had all been carefully removed by Myrtle's gentle brown hands, were cooked until tender with bacon's drippin' and small bits of left-over pork chops. Smothered steak stewed with okra, tatters, cubed tomatoes and tiny, chopped-up, sweet, purple onions. Or maybe yummy, spicy, juicy, black beans and steamed rice. Or sometimes, Katrina Josephina's favourite. Creamy elbow macaroni and cheese made just the way she liked it. These were left behind when Myrtle went to catch the bus for her long ride home.

Georgina Jane's mother wouldn't let her eat things like milk toast at home. Sweet potatoes and okra were other banned Southern delicacies. Her mother would say, "That's what poor people eat, dear." Georgina Jane thought that her mother meant that milk toast was what those poor black people the child saw on all of those porches back in Kentucky ate. Those poor black people sure were lucky to get to eat milk toast all of the time. Ethel May's milk toast was one of the best things that Georgina Jane had ever tasted, even if it was supposed to be what *'poor'* people ate. It had cinnamon sugar sprinkled on top of it. That cinnamon sugar just floated on the creamy substance surrounding and engulfing the toast. And that was what made it so special and so delicious. It was like a taste of another time, another place. And like the Southern Belle, her cousins' grandmother wanted to be, it was creamy, but with little nutritional value.

Ethel May always introduced her granddaughters officially to guests who came to her home in Anchorage. For some reason, she included Georgina Jane in that exalted list, whenever the child was present. With panache and admiration, she would pronounce the girls' names as though they must be titled, or at least people of some importance. She had been born and bred in the Deep South, like the heroine in *Gone with the Wind*. Ethel May prided herself on her own innate sense of the melodramatic, overstating her softness and her polished mannerisms. A feigned gentility was all that mattered. A feigned gentility that was foreign, English sounding, to make it appear that the Anglo-Saxon was prominent in her breeding. That was what came across whenever she spoke. Ethel May was not ethnic.

Georgina had overheard her mother and aunt saying that *'the children's grandmother'*, as they referred to her, was orphaned, or was it illegitimate? From what was gleamed from their conversations, it was gathered that Ethel May had been raised by an aunt who tried to make the child fit in with her own family of sons. Georgina Jane overheard them say that Ethel May was really from the swamp. And that her real family had names like *Jethro* or *Jed* or was it *Billy Bob* and *Leory*? She had not been raised as the elitist Episcopalian, which she pretended to be. She was really a Baptist in disguise, and a Southern Baptist at that! But Ethel May didn't want to live in the past. There was too much pain there.

Being a grandmother was not something which Ethel May readily accepted. She preferred to be called by her first name, as if her grandchildren were her equals. A Southern drawl was hidden by articulating each word and putting on an affected English utterance. She spoke each and every syllable in a way that you knew must have been because she was so cultured, so well-bred. It was hard to believe otherwise. Her Southern upbringing in Louisiana was a fact which somehow didn't matter, something left behind in the Deep South. She was Episcopalian, and this was how they spoke. Any educated, cultured person knew that.

Being Protestant was important to Ethel May. Besides, her son had married a Catholic, which made the status of being *'high'* Protestant all the more important. That way she could blend their religions together, pretending that they were nearly the same. Overlooking papal edicts, praying to statues, and being blessed by daily transubstantiation, Ethel May could pretend that hosts were simply what they seemed to be, nothing more. Confessionals were just little rooms on the side. It wasn't necessary to divulge what happened in there. It was all just semantics after all. Religious rhetoric could be swept away, like tucking a child into bed at night. It was all just a fairy-tale in that time of enlightenment.

It was like Ethel May was separate from all of that religious jingo. Her only affinity to that rhetoric was an outward profession of 'faith' in an unknown God. Besides, having a spiritual *'union'* with someone she wasn't married to, even God, would have been improper, even to a woman who had been married and divorced as many times as she had been. She had run through husbands like water runs through a stream, washing away all of the substance of those men, who took her to be a real fine woman, perhaps even a lady. Maybe it was her milk toast that had enticed them too. Like it had Georgina Jane.

Sex and religion, these were topics you didn't discuss. They were taboo subjects. You didn't know then why Catholics had so many children. You didn't know that these taboos were the source of it all. It was something of an embarrassment, not to them, those Catholics, but to the Protestants who happened to be related to them. All of those children meant only one thing. They, those Catholics, were sex crazed. That's why they had such big families. But this was something which was never discussed in front of children or in polite society. The *'Coming Out'* of young Southern and needless to say, Protestant women, was seen as a way of obtaining higher social status, not for the purpose of having babies, unless of course, they were Protestant babies. Even then, only a few babies were permitted. Too many babies meant that the parents of these offspring had somehow broken the taboos and social codes by not sleeping in twin beds, like they had in the movies.

Georgina Jane realized later in her own life that the mentality of the North/South divide between the States was still there. The haughtiness of the righteous Industrialising North, at the time of the great Civil War, and the frustration of the true Southerners, was known to still have existed in visible and invisible ways. Subconscious attitudes within her own family, though not exactly expressed audibly, were evident nevertheless.

Like the United States of Georgina Jane's America, individual family members were physically together, yet separate, in attitudes no one talked about. There was a deep and incisive problem in the Deep South, which affected Ethel May's mind and her concept of herself and her family. The War Between the States, which the Southerners still burned from, had altered forever, a society based on riches gained from the trade in human chattel and the forced labour of those masses of sad black humanity. It had been a fact of life, a foundation stone of their society which was religiously justified, because wealth had been obtainable that way.

And hadn't those black-colored Negroes, those slaves, been almost like an extenuation of the Southern families? Hadn't Ethel May's Southern family treated them real well? Fed and clothed their slaves' dark families? Even given them their own little white children's cast-off shoes to wear? Invited them to the big house for Christmas dinner? Before the War. Before the Civil War. Before that terrible war swept over the land destroying their way of life.

This was how many of the people of the South justified their anger and prejudice. Their forefathers, most long dead, had debased, through the mutilations of war on their hearts and minds; those who came after them. Their theory had been that the Southern land just cried out to be taken care of and tended. It was because of the heat in the South. That hot Southern climate. And all of that rich southern soil. That was the cause of the difficulties. Plants just grew too prodigiously for the whites to be able to manage alone. It was nigh impossible. They just had to get some help brought in from somewhere else.

Those damn Yankees knew nothing at all of the plight of their southern neighbours. Those Northerners didn't have all of those bales of cotton to take to market to be weighed. They knew nothing of the skin blistering heat of their Southern compatriots. The lily-white skin of those pure-bred Southern ladies was not something which could stand the rigors of the parching, scorching sun, in states like: Mississippi, Alabama, Louisiana, North Carolina and South Carolina, not to mention Georgia! It was obvious to the Southerners, even a century later, after slavery had been abolished, that God himself had created those imported captives, with skin blacker than even the soil, just so that they could do the right thing. Those darkies had a special purpose in life. They were meant to work the land. They were meant to be traded at any whim that their owners got into their white heads. They were meant to slave their lives away for the inheritors of God's favour, the Anglo, certainly white, descendants of the founding fathers, even the illustrious pilgrims.

The southerners had earned the right to possess, not just the land, but the flesh and blood of other men and women stolen from distant shores, in order to serve a higher cause. Those *Niggers* would never understand the value of freedom, no matter how many laws were passed by those idiot Northerners who were just pencil-pushers, not real men who knew what it was like to sweat. The *Coloreds* were barely human. They had the same savage intent as the *Injuns* had, scalping any poor old sod they caught out on the plains of the Midwest. *Injuns* and the blacks. Why turn a nation upside down just to share the justice and liberty that the white founding fathers had won for her people, not for those Red Skin renegades or for *Niggers*?

Hadn't those owned people served the great nation, their *'home of the free and the land of the brave'*, best by working the land? Hadn't the growing of crops of; okra, corn, tomatoes, cotton and tobacco served the welfare of the nation as a whole? What about the stringed beans, the butter beans and the black-eyed peas, not to forget the sweet potatoes? That war had ripped their families apart and left behind a rancour which was still, generations later, deeply embedded in the psyche of the Southerners. Southerners left behind to pick up the pieces. Their lives were left in tatters even before they were born. Their hearts were already marked with feelings of injustice and anger, even before they took their first breath.

Generations after the War Between the States, Ethel May's people planted this resentment deep into her subconscious mind. It was who they were, in attitudes too ingrained for her to even know that they were there. The resentment for the wealth and social position they felt robbed of, due to the injustice imposed upon them by manumission, was an intrinsic part of who they were. Who Ethel May was.

It was embarrassing to Ethel May that her son and his wife had given her so many grandchildren. They should have stopped with their first perfect child, Bridgetta. One child would have been plenty. Ethel May's acceptance of the eldest of her son's eight children, Bridgetta, was not a sore spot in their family. They all loved her, admired her, followed her example. Bridgetta was bright and clever. She was talented. She was articulate. Her skin was whiter than white. She was the most like her paternal grandmother. Therefore, she was the most beloved by this doting woman of obvious refinement. All of the other children knew this. They accepted it at face value, never considering any other way as fairer or better.

The younger sisters, Leah, Rachel, Susanna and Carolina were sanctioned conditionally as being assistants to Bridgetta's many productions. The boys didn't count. Beyond Bridgetta, none of the other seven grandchildren were acknowledged to any great extent. It was almost as though they did not even exist. It was almost as though they lived in Bridgetta's shadow. The shadow of Ethel May's one perfect grandchild. The eldest daughter of her perfect son. Her perfect son who was Georgina Jane O'Shaughnessy's Uncle Buford, Bubba for short.

Whenever any of Ethel May's special friends came to visit, she would triumphantly introduce Bridgetta as though she were speaking of a prized heifer at the State Fair of one of the Carolinas. So, to be introduced, especially by name, by her cousins' grandmother, was an immense pleasure to Georgina Jane. It made her feel important and special, not loved, but acceptable at the very least. The fact that Georgina was Catholic, was something which could be overlooked. It was not to be discussed.

Perhaps it was from these honourable introductions that Georgina Jane began to believe in herself around the ages of eight and nine. If her cousins' grandmother, who was not even her own grandmother, thought she was someone to be introduced and acknowledged, then she must be like the magical fairies in the girls' made-up stories. And she began to believe that, like the fairies, she really could fly.

ANSWERS TO NATURE QUIZ BOOK
QUIZ A

1. The Blue Whale. It is called the Sulphur Bottom Whale.
2. Yes, the Hummingbird can.

3. No, this is a superstition. It is believed by some people, however, that mice get into the end of an elephant's trunk and suffocate it or cause injury to the long nose. Mice are often seen scampering about the elephant houses at zoos with the elephant showing no concern. Even if the mouse should get into the end of the trunk, one blow of the long nose would send the mouse running.
4. Fat, which it uses when food is scarce.
5. No.
6. A Kid.

QUIZ B

1. Yes, if it loses its stinger.
2. Butterflies have knobs on the ends of their thread-like feelers. They alight with their wings upright. They are seen flying during daylight. Moths are usually night fliers. Their feelers are feathery and have no knobs on the ends.
3. The Sea Horse.
4. Most frogs have soft, moist, smooth skins. Toads have dry skins covered with warts.
5. The Mayfly lives only 24 hours.
6. Snakes, Lizards, Crocodiles or Alligators, Turtles, Dinosaurs.
7. An Albino.
8. No. This is merely a superstitious belief.
9. Yes, at times when provoked.
10. No, it is a lizard.
11. Large monkeys without tails.

QUIZ C

1. No. The skin secretes a brownish-reddish, oily liquid which protects the skin.
2. No.
3. The American Bison or Buffalo as it is also called.
4. No, this is a superstition. If a snake's head is cut off, the body may move for a short time. This is a reflex action of the muscles. This action does

not mean that the snake is still alive. The snake will soon stop moving regardless of the time of day.
5. Yes.
6. The bat. Some other mammals can glide, but not actually fly.
7. They cannot hear as we do, but they can feel vibrations through their bodies.

QUIZ D

1. The ears and hind legs of rabbits are shorter than hares. Rabbits are born blind and hairless. Hares are born with hair and their eyes open.
2. A herd.
3. An insect. It looks just like a stick.
4. Rodents, Rats, Mice, Hamsters, Beavers, Squirrels are examples.
5. Up to 28 years.
6. The Chimpanzee. (Next to Man)
7. Mostly in Africa, some in Asia.
8. No, some give birth to young ones, while others lay eggs.
9. A baby frog before it develops into a frog. Also called tadpole.

QUIZ E

1. An Artic Tern.
2. No, this is a superstition. This superstition probably arose from the fact that at times the ostrich will flatten out on the ground when danger approaches. However, if the enemy comes too close the ostrich will run away at great speed or if cornered will kick with its powerful feet.
3. A gobble.
4. The Praying Mantis. The female may eat the male.
5. Because at times, the female will eat her mate.
6. No.
7. Four.
8. A Skunk.

Chapter Six
Food for Thought

Tasty Morsels

Memories of rainbows and ice cream stayed with the girl after that summer passed. Time sped past her, running ahead of her, like a wild bunny rabbit making a quick getaway. Days turned into weeks. Hours and minutes had already revolved into those days. Days of discovery. The child's wonder and musing were permeated with the novelties of that time. The newness of her times. Times spent in Alaska's long daylight hours. Her childhood. Sweet child. It was a fragrant time during which the girl lived and breathed to be in the great out-of-doors. Outside in Alaska. Experiences which Georgina's eyes and ears and mouth and tongue saw and heard and tasted, left her full and satisfied and happy during those summer seasons of warmth and pleasure.

Crystal glaciers seen as the girl and her family drove through the scenic terrain on their way to her cousins' house in Anchorage, shimmered like giant glowing emeralds splashed across mountains, dazzling her eyes as the sun reflected their brilliance, and filling her small soul with utter delight. Alaskan glaciers seen as they drove through the scenic terrain on the way to her cousins' house in Anchorage. Alaska's beauty brought her pleasure. Alaska could not be matched by another place she knew of. Alaska could not be ignored. Living in Alaska required her participation. Its scenery was more splendid and glorious than any place the child had seen or could even imagine. Alaska was all she ever wanted. No place could be found that was as glorious as that place. That place that was now her home. Her home forever. Or so she thought back then.

There were blueberries to be picked, walking with Manga through berry patches near their house in Ft. Wainwright, in search of such navy blue treasures. These filled her little hand with fruit the size of small plums. She would remember that her father later said, that this was because her hands were so small then, not that the Alaskan blueberries actually were the size of plums. But she did not accept his reasoning. She knew that no place on earth had blueberries gianter than Alaska did. It was the taste and the feeling that she remembered long afterwards. And it was the seeing of these things which she would never forget.

Vitals were brought home to the girl that summer by her uncle and friends of her father. Fishermen and hunters who travelled in search of game through the far reaches of the Alaskan frontier. While the girl stayed at home, the men hunted, fished and gathered of the abundance they found growing or bounding along out there in the wilderness territories. They brought their takings home to her. Each item she inspected and either accepted or questioned. She imagined that she was like a maître de of a fancy restaurant. And these wild takings, gleaned from the indigenous surroundings, a land of the natives, gave her memories meaning.

Wild mushrooms and berries growing free and plentifully were tasted and scrutinized by her little raspberry pink tongue. Delicious smoked salmon and trout whose flavour was permeated with the taste of the Alaskan woods were her favourites. Tough barbecued caribou steaks sizzled over Daddy's hot glowing charcoals. Huge legs of mountain rams, from wild white mountain critters, shot with a hunter's rifle, looked bloody and disgusting. It was like those strong animals could almost have risen from the dead, and such strong disembodied legs could still run wild and free again. Again, if only they could be reattached to the butchered bodies they (those legs) had once known. Those legs and those bodies which had once run wild and free into the vast Alaskan frontier. Legs and bodies of deer, Dall sheep, moose, reindeer and mountain goats. Creatures climbing high, high up into the great mountains in her neighbourhood. These, she knew were the running part of the bounding creatures she had seen on her travels through Alaska's mountainous regions. Where was the other part? She wanted to know.

She wasn't sure if mountain goats' legs would even taste any good. Bloody legs. Sad cut off legs. Bare bloody legs held over her head so proudly. Raw legs. Big legs. Whole legs. Dubious skinned legs. But once Daddy cooked them, those legs tasted yummy. Georgina had to agree. After Mommy basted, and Daddy smoked them over his barbecue's fire, nothing could taste any better.

Scrumptious king crab with its vivid pinkish orange and white long lanky legs protruding from its sharp armoured spiky shelly. Shrimp the size of her forearms, given to her uncle in Anchorage by his fishin' buddies. One shrimp could make a meal for a girl. A girl like Georgina Jane. Plate-size shrimp were pink and delicious. Chewy whale blubber cut from huge friendly whales swimming off the chilly shores of Alaska. Whales harpooned by native fishermen. Whales whose whole bodies were good for something. Whales caught from the cold seawaters around the Alaskan shores. Alaskan hare caught in snares. Trapped. Skinned. Cooked. And eaten. Wild tasting venison sausages from running deer with sharp antlers were made into sausages, spicy and full of flavour. These were made into gumbos by her uncle, who loved to show off his prowess as both hunter, and chef. Giant round cabbages – bigger than even her short little grandmother, Manga were chopped up and used by Mother for her wonderful coleslaw with celery seeds and carrots and mayonnaise, a recipe imported from back in the South. Enormous vegetables from the Matanuska Valley, all these found their way home to her that summer. Georgina was buoyed up inside herself by these flavours and the new tastes of these foodstuffs. This horn of plenty seemed to make its way almost daily into her mother's kitchen with its red and white checked curtains tied neatly back to let in as much sunlight as possible.

The girl would watch and listen as friends of her mother's, who were always dropping by and swapping favourite family recipes, came over during their husbands' long working days. All of the base's moms wanted to be good homemakers and give their children a balanced diet. It became almost like a sort of competitive sporting event between them all. Food and nutrition were important. All of those precious Baby Boomers, from that new post World War II generation were a relatively pampered lot. Many of the kids' grandparents had grown up in the Great Depression, during a time when food shortages were widespread. Between the two world wars and that depressed time, food became a topic of great importance to housewives and their mothers (the Baby Boomers grandmothers) and future mother-in-laws all over the country. Even a generation later, after the Second World War, women, those housewives who had been little girls during such a hard time, were still talking about food, food, food.

Was such and such good for the children? What was its nutritional value? Was it good value for money? Did they really even want to cook it? Should it be basted? Should it be steamed? Served raw? What was its aesthetic appeal? Would it look appetising? Should it be served as hors d'oeuvre? Served as a main course? Served with what? Was it new and exciting? Did mixing food all-together-in-casseroles (a new idea for these ladies) really take less time to prepare? How long did you have to bake it? At what temperature? What would their husbands think of their great inventive new ideas? The child took it all in. These mothers were always busy coming up with new innovations in cooking, like they were some sort of vastly intellectual rocket scientists working away for hours on new discoveries in the privacy of their own kitchens. Would their husbands appreciate their efforts and compliment them? Would those guys even notice what their wives had done for them? Would those men, those tough soldiers in the army say 'Thanks a bunch, honeybun'? Or would they only grunt and eat their wives' special recipes with more grunts while they chewed their wives' home cooking with their mouths open? Rather than realizing that the candles lit on the table signified a great celebration, like someone's birthday? Rather than noticing what a wonderful and beautiful and clever wife they had? A wife with such an inventive way with food? Would those soldiers in the Army realize that a great ingenious act had taken place that very day? Would they see that right there in their very own households some new and amazing thing had taken place? Would those men see that their wives were *'coming into their own'*? Would they be proud of them?

Mothers talked amongst themselves about their children, all of those 'army brats'. They discussed their husbands and their husbands' jobs in the military. Georgina listened as she sat cutting out new paper doll clothes at her mother's kitchen table. Paper dolls could never have enough clothes to wear. And sometimes Georgina even drew and colored her own paper doll clothes. Paper dolls were very serious business to the child. The ladies on the base talked to Mother about food or some new household gadget just coming on to the market. They said that Alaska was always the last State to get things that their family and friends down South already had. The topic of laundry detergent, and its whitening capabilities was an important issue to them. There were not as many outlets for women outside of their homes. Good wives and mothers stayed put. Good wives and mothers worked in their homes. But they rarely called that position a *job*.

They were like that lady in the children's Nursery Rhyme, *'Peter, Peter, Pumpkin-eater'*. That children's ditty, written long before the 1950s, put its finger on the pulse of those times. Children and their nursery-rhyming-reading-mothers knew these things. They knew that women had to stay put or families would begin to fall apart. And nobody would be there to pick up the pieces anymore. That Nursery Rhyme had a lot to say about the times of flux that the girl grew up in. A time when the roles of women were more static than they are today. But a time when things were beginning to change. Gradually change.

Peter, Peter, Pumpkin-eater
Had a wife and couldn't keep her.
Put her in a pumpkin-shell.
And there he kept her very well.

Being kept in a 'pumpkin-shell' sort of existence and being a 'lady of leisure', a homebody, was not all it was cracked-up to be. That was where it was at, staying at home, minding their own families, doing it so perfectly that these women could actually, if they were so inclined, score points off of one another. They became known for things outside of themselves. But these things were, nevertheless, their accomplishments, just the same.

They would be judged for their prowess in skills such as dusting or housecleaning, their fertility, their children's school report cards and higher grades than their lady friends' kids got. How white their family's clothes were, either made them a success or a complete and utter failure in the one place in life where women were supposed to succeed. Their husbands' faithfulness to them and only to them might revolve around how well they did those women's jobs being the best housewife on the block.

But they actually had very little uninterrupted time, little time just for themselves. All for themselves. Times when they could stop the world and get off. Life should have included more leisure time with all of those labour-saving household devices that their husbands bought for them for their birthdays or anniversaries. But were their lives really easier? Were their lives really easier, or just different from previous generations of wives and mothers? They soon discovered that leisure time was not all that it was cracked-up to be. Life was not easy; at least life up in Alaska was not easy.

Activities which women had done in the past, things like cooking from scratch, were changing. Vegetables weren't grown in backyard victory gardens as a matter of necessity anymore. Life was different for these army wives. Life was too transient. The War was over, so they'd have to find something else to do with their time than their own mothers had to manage doing during the Second

World War. Different than their old grandmothers did during the First World War.

Though pre-packaged foods were coming on the market hard and strong, Mother felt that such items were beneath her. But women who cooked from scratch were becoming the exception, not the general rule, as they had been in the past. Dinner could consist of soup in a can (probably Campbell's, with those cute little twins on the label) and topped with crunched or broken-up Saltine crackers floating away on the tops of that new food serving device, the mug.

They didn't have to make do as their mothers, or their grandmothers, often had to do when they were little girls growing up. Leisure time afforded them new opportunities to relax and put their feet up more to watch the television. The girl's mother didn't watch the new soap operas coming onto the television market. She thought such programs were beneath her. Her world was turning because of her family's needs. In her world, reality crowded out the light of day and didn't give her much time for what she considered corny mindless television shows, shows that made the people who watched them almost like white trash from contemporary trailer parks were. Her family's eating habits were something she thought about instead. Their diet was of paramount importance to her.

"Just look at this! Can you believe the size of the thing?" (You would think that it was something else, something besides just food that the women were discussing.).

"Well, I'll be darned. Isn't that something? What are you going to do with that! Just look at the size of it!"

"I thought that I might make scalloped potatoes with that new Cream of Mushroom soup and cheddar cheese. The children just love that. My recipe calls for a dash of that Worchester sauce in it, and my husband loves that. I want to be sure that they eat their vegetables one way of the other. Food has to be disguised to get them to eat what's good for them. I worry that they'd rather have canned spaghetti than this leg of mountain goat."

"My children will eat anything that I put in front of them. And my husband, Joe, well, he eats like a horse! He has such a big appetite and just loves my cooking."

"Well, aren't you lucky to have a family like that. My children are what I would call 'picky eaters'. They are very particular about the foods that they will and won't eat. So I have to keep that in mind whenever new foods, like these caribou steaks come into the house. I have to fix new meats the same as I would any chuck roast from cows. Otherwise, they won't eat it. If I tell the children what they are eating, what I suppose you would call, mutton, they might decide that it doesn't taste good after all. I am hoping that if I fix this king crab like its canned tuna fish, they won't know the difference. Gretchen loves bunny rabbits. She keeps asking me if she can have one as a pet. I can hardly expect her to eat wild Alaskan hare! I'll just tell her that it's chicken. She'll never know the difference!"

Mother would squeal with the thrill of the sight such potential cuisine gave to her. All piled up on top of her kitchen table, she'd survey each and every item, making another shopping list of things to cook and serve with such gourmet delicacies. Her delight was like that of an excitable little girl. She was so ecstatic about her culinary treasures. Provisions brought to her kitchen were never wasted. The woman was known all over their army base neighbourhood for her dinner parties where she served so many delicious dishes. Mother was like a child, amazed by the size and variety of baskets brimming full of the opulent plenty that was Alaska's bounty.

It seemed that new surprises were brought to them nearly every day. If the girl's father was too busy with his job in the Army, and Mother was too overworked with all of the little boys' diapers and housework, so that they didn't have the time to drive the girl around the country to see all of the sights of that magnificent State; at least Alaska's plethora and its wide variety of foodstuffs found their way to the child at her family's house on the army base one way or another. These things enriched her imagination.

Every morsel brought a story to the girl. Each bit of the stores of food told a tale of fields and woodlands with their wild rabbits hiding under berry bushes, changing from their winter whites to the more camouflaged colors of summer. The fur of the wild animals was like Daddy's army uniform that altered depending on the occasion. The girl thought those speedy Alaskan bunnies were so smart to grow new fur to have a magical way of hiding from the fierce Alaskan foxes, wolverines and wolves. Those predators hunted those lightning-fast rabbits that the girl sometimes saw speeding through the wild areas near their home. Bunnies and foxes were white like the snow and ice during the winter months, but in the summer, they were brown and red to match the dirt in the forests or the bark of the trees.

Near the sides of the mountains where she had seen the glaciers, was the passing sight of mountain goats and Dall sheep steadying themselves as they climbed higher and high up into the precarious peaks. The sight of these creatures stopped her heart. These were animals of the past, not like the present where she lived. When she saw them through the car window, she yearned to join them in their climb. They were free. In her dreams she could fly, so climbing would be no problem.

Sneakin' Out the Window

The days grew longer and longer until the sun seemed unwilling to leave them at all, or to set completely over Alaska. And the stretching of the days meant that there was more time to explore, discover and learn in those prolonged daylight hours that extended way past the girl's usual bedtime. Georgina loved to read. Every night, she read a book to herself. Tomorrow would be a new day. Today was over. Two successive days were never the same, because every day the girl expected surprises to find her. Life was never boring in Alaska. The warmer days grew long and longer until the sun seemed unwilling leave them or to set over Alaska. And the stretching of the days meant that there was more time to explore, discover and learn in those prolonged daylight hours that extended way past the girl's usual bedtime. She loved to read, and read, and read every night by the sun's light shining into her bedroom, which she shared with her twin sisters. Katrina Josephina snored and ground her teeth in her sleep. So Georgina Jane smiled to herself, but tried to ignore the girl, as she read her Nancy Drew books, or the children's picture book of Gulliver's Travels, about a giant man who went to an island of little people, the Lilliputs, who must be related to the real tiny Irish leprechauns.

That was the summer that her cousins taught her to sneak out of her house just by opening the basement window to release the girl and themselves from their slumbering family. With all of them working together as a team, they would move and rearrange the furniture (like their mothers did in their 'pumpkin shells'). They could hoist each other up and go out of the basement window that was way over their heads. The last one out had to be pulled by the strength of the other five girls. The rest of the people in their family were all too tired to use the extended daylight God gave to them all night in Alaska's summer for anything other than sleeping. But that gang of girls had other ideas.

"Let's sneak out the window, George."

That was Bridgetta's bright idea. That girl instigated lots of brazen forbidden things. She was fearless. She was like an adult in a child's body. Speaking with authority, Bridgetta insisted that the girls make a bold escape, like in the movies.

"If we get caught, my father will skin me alive like they did to those poor rabbits. Mother said that it was chicken stew, some make-believe phoney story about an old recipe from her Irish grandmother. But I didn't believe her. I know those were really wild bunny rabbits in that food."

"Ah, come on, Georgina Jane. Your dad will never find out. We won't tell him, will we, Leah?"

Not waiting for her sister to answer, Bridgetta began to move a toy box towards one of the two basement windows.

"Give me a hand, will you? Once we get this over to the window, we can climb up and get out of here."

"All right, but we'd better be quiet, or my mother will hear us. She's a light sleeper."

The girls were all sleeping in the basement, or supposed to be. The rest of their family was upstairs asleep. How they could snooze away the night's daylight was beyond her. It seemed like Alaska was made for night time escapades due to the amount of light shining on the place. For the girls, there were more important things to do than sleeping the night away. That was the summer the girl spent out of doors night after night, sitting or lying on the green grass outside of her home, lit past midnight by the soft night's daylight. She wasn't daydreaming. She wasn't sleeping. She was night daydreaming in the bright summer's twilight. Deep, dark nightfall never seemed to come to her in those summer days, not like it did so early in all of those winter months. There was a lot of catching up to do for those girls who lived in a place that was darker than normal all winter, and lighter than normal all summer. The summertime was the time to get even with the Alaskan sky for getting dark so early in the wintertime. Dark skies gave their mothers an excuse to send them to bed earlier than normal in the wintertime. Mothers pretended it was later than it really was in the winter. Children wouldn't know the difference. But the girl knew how to tell time. She had seen her daddy's alarm clock on his side of her parent's bed when she snuck into her parent's bedroom to sneak a piece of her mother's *Almond Joy* candy bar, a habit that she had for all the years of her childhood.

Mother tried to fool her, but she knew what time it really was when she was told that it was her bedtime. They could get even with their mothers in the summertime when the sun refused to set, and they refused to go to bed early like good girls. They knew even then, that they were not good girls at all. Not good girls like their mothers told them to be. Their mothers obviously didn't really believe that they were good girls either, or they wouldn't have kept reminding them so often to be good girls.

* * * *

Four summers melded into one in her memories. Four summers spent in Alaska. Three winters, three autumns and three springs. They arrived in Alaska in the summertime and they left Alaska four summers later. Like precious stones, summers were small compared to Alaska's long winters. Manga had given Georgina a black diamond and white gold bracelet. Alaskan summers were gone before the girl knew it. Summers were full of light. Sometimes in the middle of the night, she'd give up the idea of even trying to be good and fall asleep. The light from the unsetting sun was keeping her awake and it was useless to even try to travel off to the Land of Nod. When her cousins were there, she had gotten used to the idea of being a night owl. Doing naughty things was normal to those kids. After her cousins' left Ft. Wainwright, or she left Anchorage to go home, Georgina would follow her cousins' example of being naughty. She would escape from their army base house by climbing out of the window all by herself.

With all of her efforts, she would move furniture to the basement window all by herself. She would stack one thing on another, and stretch her way upwards and out of that basement window so that she could climb up up up her great pile of anything tall enough, anything stackable. And like she was related to Jack in the Beanstalk going to another land where there was so much to do, so much to discover outdoors in the middle of the night, she'd simply climb out the basement window without a shred of self-doubt or worry. She thought that if her father had found out about her sneaking out, he might be like the angry giant Jack found at the top of the Beanstalk in that story of hers. But the out-of-doors was too enticing not to go outside anyway.

Then the girl would run wild in her sheer summer nightgown, her cool bare feet touching the soft green Alaskan grass as she ran and ran and ran and skipped and skipped and skipped like a stealthy, quick bunny rabbit. Like an Alaskan doe, a deer. The summer's grass grew green green green, even greener than Irish grass does. And Alaskan grass was as soft as the sweet new baby bunnies' ears in her cousins' neighbours' rabbit hutches. Seeing those new born pet bunnies was almost as good as sneaking out at night.

The girl rationalized her actions to herself. What could possibly be wrong with creating those self-made adventures under Alaska's summertime skies? Skies lit up by a sun that didn't want to sleep any more than she did? It was a sun that stayed dimly bright for most of the night to grow to tremendous sizes all of those vegetables from Matanuska's Valley. It was a summer's sun that shined to give little giggling girls more light to sneak out and sit outside on the night time grass. Time to laugh at their sleeping family's slumber. Time for summersaults and hand-stands. Time for contests of leap frogging and races of great speeds. All of these activities took place on those balmy (by comparison to winter) nights. They weren't about to miss out on the summer's long extra hours of the twilight's last gleaming. Nobody in their neighbourhood even noticed. Everyone in their neck of the Alaskan woods was dozing contentedly in their beds. But the girl and her cousins hardly slept all of those summer nights if they could help it. Half the night they spent out-of-doors.

Family Fun and Georgina Meets a Real Eskimo

Sometimes on the weekends, Daddy would pile his family into the black and white Pontiac with its red interior. They'd head out for the vast unsettled areas beyond Ft. Wainwright and Fairbanks. No matter where they went for the day, it was going to be great to get away from it all and see what Alaska had to offer. Away from Ft. Wainwright and past the borders of rough n' ready Fairbanks. The girl loved to explore new places.

The Klondike was a place where gold was plentiful. Even the girl's grandmother took the day off from her job at the base's PX to see the sights they drove past. Drove through or drove to. Manga came with them to find those golden nuggets washed down the sides of hills by the constant flowing chilly melting streams. She had plans to have some Alaskan gold jewellery made by an Eskimo goldsmith she personally knew in town, in Fairbanks, just as soon as she could collect enough of the tiny nuggets they panned for. Georgina felt that it was important to help Manga realize that dream of hers.

When she got enough gold, she wanted some dangly pierced earrings made for herself. Mother thought that piercing your ears was 'cannibalistic'. But the girl's mother's mother pierced hers all the same. Clip on earrings were more lady-like and let's just say, civilized, in Mother's opinion. Piercing your ears might turn you into a sort of savage. Piercing your ears was too ethnic for Mother's liking. (Piercing any other part of your body was not only too foreign; it was even unthinkable back then.)

"Oh, no, Mother, what on earth have you done to yourself?" Claudia wanted to know. A worried look crossing over her face.

"I've had my ears pierced, honey. What do you think, aren't these pretty new earrings?" Manga was so proud of herself and her new acquisition.

"Oh, Mother, honestly! For heaven's sake! Didn't that hurt you? That is what cannibals do to their ears! Poke holes in them! Wear gold rings or other odd things in them. How could you do such a thing? How could you do such a thing to your lovely ears?"

"I can't stand those clip-ons. They hurt my ears. And I wanted to wear my gold. See, aren't they pretty?"

Mother was unconvinced. "Well, I guess so, but I still don't think that you should have had holes poked into your lovely ears. Pierced ears are for Mexicans. Or for savages."

Manga said that wearing clip-on earrings hurt her ears too much, pinching them and squeezing her thick ear lobes way too tightly. Since wearing earrings was so important to ladies who wanted to feel feminine, Manga had to have them. (Men wearing earrings was unthinkable. Who ever heard of a man wearing earrings?) Manga would rather be labelled by her daughter as a cannibal, than not use her very own panned for Alaskan gold for the original, custom-made danglers. She had her Eskimo friend in Fairbanks make as many pierced earrings as she could afford. She sought after large or small clumps of golden nuggets in every cold stream she could find. Over the years, that dame amassed a wealth of Alaskan gold nuggets, just by her sheer perseverance. And she had quite a few pieces of lovely jewellery made for herself and her daughters and granddaughters.

And whatever her daughter, Claudia, thought about it, Nelly just kept wearing those dangling swinging gold nugget earrings in those savage holes poked into her ears. She had that Eskimo jeweller stack up her gold nuggets, one on top of the other, melding, wielding those nuggets all together. Her dangling earrings were her own unique design, every pair a work of art. Every pair told a story. Every pair of gold earrings told a tale of places she had been to with family or friends. Told a tale about Alaska. Places she had visited. Places she had gone panning for gold, like she was some raunchy old sourdough. Manga was becoming part of the Alaskan culture. And Alaska was becoming part of Manga, or Nelly, as her friends affectionately called her.

Discovering her very own gold helped her to forget past times. Some of her past times had been sad times. Some of her past times, she'd just rather forget. Never looking back at them like Lot's wife did, and becoming a hard and bitter pillar of stone. She'd lay her own markers in the sands of time, thank you. Some of her sad times, she would just rather forget by becoming a new person. She had made a conscious effort to be happy, and she wasn't about to let anything from the past hold her back. Some of her past sad times, she could forget by enjoying herself where she was at that new moment, up in her newfound home. Up in that place of remembering and that place of forgetting what was before, life began all over again. Nell could ignore the pain of those unhappy former experiences by becoming a good ole friendly crusty sourdough up north. Up in Alaska.

Nell knew how to mix with the natives way up there. They liked Nelly, and she sure as hell liked them. Some of Manga's best friends were Eskimos. She thought that they were some of the best people in the whole wide world. She introduced them to her granddaughter, Georgina, so that the girl could see for herself how wonderful those people really were. Meeting that Eskimo was better than eating ice cream. That Eskimo. That shy Eskimo. Whatever his last name was, she couldn't remember. He hardly spoke one single intelligible word to her. He had more shyness than the girl ever thought of having. But Georgina thought that there was no one like him. Whatever he did or did not have to say to her with words, he said in other says.

Manga loved to go into Fairbanks and go to the Indian Trading Post there. She had made friends with one of the Eskimo craftsmen. A tall man with big crafty hands and a love of plaid shirts. Manga wanted Georgina to meet him so that the girl could see what a real Eskimo craftsman was like. The girl's grandmother also had some earrings and a necklace with gold nuggets inside of a glass locket filled with Alaskan river water to pick up. Her Eskimo friend had made them especially for her. He said that they would be ready today. So today was the day that Georgina got to ride the bus with her grandmother just to meet the Eskimo friend her Manga had made.

"This is Georgina Jane, my granddaughter, Will. She's come with me to pick up my jewellery. Is it ready yet?"

"Hum. Hum," Will said in response to Nellie's introduction and question. He was the quiet type.

Georgina stood there silently. She was the quiet type too. So, she understood the lack of his need for words. He noticed her interest in the small items for sale in the glass cabinet next to his cash register desk. Georgina was intrigued by the tiny ivory carvings. Her favourite was a palm size ivory carving of two polar bears facing each other.

"That's for the dog sleds," Will offered. "They (the Eskimos) lash them on to their dog sleds for the races. It brings them good luck."

"Oh, they are wonderful," said Georgina, as Will removed the small ivory carving from his glass cabinet. Manga could see that her grandchild's interest pleased her big yellow friend.

"How much is that, Will? If Georgina wants it, she can have it," Manga asked.

So, Will and Manga haggled over the price of his special creamy white polar bear token and quickly agreed on a price. Nellie thought that he was being over reasonable in his price, and she offered to give Will more than he asked. But Will wasn't having it. He liked Georgina and wanted to give her a token of his pleasure at meeting her. Her grandmother's friend placed the special ivory dog sled toggle in the girl's hand. It was a wonder. Something so small and so beautiful and so perfectly made. Made just for her.

"Thank you, Will. Thank you, Manga. I will always treasure it. I just love it. Wait till Mommy and Daddy see what the Eskimos have made just for me!"

Georgina Jane O'Shaughnessy knew that those native Inuits could do wonders with anything put into their hands. Gold. Jade. Ivory from the tusks of walruses. Or bones from whales or porpoises. Animal bones. Once living skins. Beadwork. Leather goods from tanned animal skins. Skins used for clothes. Skins used for Eskimo shoes and boots. Parkas with fur lining. Leather leggings to keep the intense chill off their people's legs and arms and faces and toes and even fur mittens to keep them from losing their yellow fingers to frostbite. Handbags all made of wild Alaskan animal skins. All made of tanned sweet smelling animal skins. Animal skins that turned people into walking, breathing, living animated wild feral creatures. Even their boats were all sewn together from some part of the wildness.

What did those once living things, like dead animals' skins and bones and tusks have to say? What did wearing animal skins make you? Make you into? Did wearing the wild animals' pelts make the girl wild? Wilder than she would have been if she had never seen them? Never felt them? Never worn them? Wild like the now dead animals were? Is that why the Eskimos wore such things? Wore skins of animals they'd killed? Animals they'd skinned? To become wild and cunning like the wolves, foxes, bears, seals, walrus and bunny rabbits from Alaska's wild frontier places? Ferocious, untamed, wild things?

Big trunks of giant trees were turned into totem poles. Trees carved and painted by those natives with their magical symbols and faces which stared out at the girl with big watching eyes. Eyes that knew. Knew things. Secret things. Symbolism was there, a major part of who they were and how they thought about life. The symbolic was everywhere. Big or small, those Eskimos, who liked to rub noses, surrounded their lives with charming and illustrative arts and crafts. That was where usefulness and beauty met together. Met together there in the kaleidoscope culture of those native Alaskans. Theirs was a culture where animism was second nature to them. Objects de Arte had a life of their own. Carving animals out of ivory, or primitive animistic faces into the tall wooden totem poles had a secret meaning to them. Inside cultural understandings were prevalent within their work. These were things that outsiders knew nothing about. And few could grasp them with outlooks and opinions of openness back then. Like the Modern Art of people like Picasso, their work had to grow on you, like those tall totemed trees once lived and grew in the Alaskan forests.

Nothing, seemingly nothing at all, was impossible for her grandmother's friends, the Eskimos, to do. They knew about being unfettered, about being wild. To them, being wild was just normal. To them, the white man's idea of wild was just the norm, their special way of being. Wildness, wilderness living, was the Eskimos standard way of being. Wilderness and being wild was theirs, and Manga's philosophy on life. And just maybe Nellie's daughter, Claudia Jane, was right. Maybe she was right that pierced ears did actually make you more like a native. If you had holes poked into your ears, you would become savage. Having pierced ears made you a wolverina.

Nelly Irwin LeVision took to Alaska like a duck takes to a pond. She took to Alaska like it was part of her family. She took to Alaska like the whole State was a great old friend of hers. Like she'd known it forever. She took to the place like it was her closest, dearest lover. She took to Alaska like it was the good and decent husband she had never had, but certainly deserved. Manga loved Alaska as though God had created the whole half-frozen territory just for her. Whatever Alaska gave to Manga, Manga gave right back. That old battle-axe, as Daddy called her, gave color and light to the place, simply by just being there. Nobody was more enthusiastic about Alaska than the girl's Manga was.

The girl, the old battle-axe's second granddaughter, saw Alaska like her Manga did. The girl had the same vision of the State that her maternal grandmother had. Nobody could love Alaska more than those two did. Every square inch of the vast and open wild territory, now the forty-ninth State in that great Union, was perfect as far as they were concerned. Nobody thought about pipelines and oil too much to disturb the place back then. Those lucrative projects hadn't brought such great wealth yet. There was no such thing as the Valdez spill yet. So, the pristine wilderness was nothing but God's own place on earth, at least his northernmost place. God must have sat right up there on the tops of those lofty cold Alaskan mountains and laughed his head off, sitting on that part of the circle of the earth like that. Who else could sit up there freezing their buns off day and night, night and day? Only God himself could venture up to some of those freezing elevations. Nobody else had his audacity or daring.

"Hey, you old battle axe! Why don't you come with us next Saturday? Let's go for a picnic and a drive and you and the kids can go panning for gold," the girl's father would say teasingly to his mother-in-law.

"I'll get Joan to fill in for me at the PX and join you. I'd love to come. Can I bring anything? Want me to fix my rum cake for the kids? Georgina loves my rum cake. I promised her that she could have some the next time I made it. Ask my daughter to give me a call and we can co-ordinate what we need for the picnic lunch."

"That'd be great, and maybe could you pick up some comics from the PX for the girls? That Katrina has decided that now that she can read, she wants comics every time we take her to the store. Claudia says that she wants to encourage her to read more, and Gretchen too, so if you could bring some Little Lulu, Popeye, or whatever they have in stock. That would be a big help. See you next Saturday, Nellie."

Her father hung up from his conversation with his mother-in-law. He knew she would refuse his offer to drive over and pick her up in their station wagon. No matter what the weather was like, even if it was twenty degrees below zero, his old battle-axe of a mother-in-law liked the freedom of her walks to their house. That one-mile walk could freeze the toes off of an elk. That is, if an elk had toes to freeze. It was a long walk home. But Nellie didn't care. She would have walked all over the whole entire State of Alaska if she could of! Just for the experience. Just to get to know the place even better.

"The old battle axe says she'd love to come. She wants you to call her if you want her to bring anything," he told his wife who had her hands tied with making sandwiches for the children's lunchboxes.

Manga walked over early Saturday morning to help Mother pack a picnic lunch in their big basket with brown straw top flaps that buckled down to keep small fingers from reaching the covered food. Fingers that couldn't wait to grasp the tantalizing selection hidden inside of their family's picnic basket. Lunchtime wouldn't come soon enough to taste the devilled eggs with their blended spicy innards with red paprika sprinkled on their forked toppings of egg yolks mixed with mayonnaise and mustard and sometimes chives.

Cold potato salad made of boiled potatoes taken out of their skins, with diced hard-boiled eggs, finely chopped onions, pickles and celery with dill seeds and creamy mayonnaise added, that was her favourite. Fruit, chocolate chip cookies, Betty Crocker's chocolate cake made from a boxed cake mix, dill and sweet jerkin pickles, ham sandwiches or peanut butter and grape jelly sandwiches on white bread for the little kids, was all crammed together into that big basket. Manga wrapped everything in waxed paper to keep it fresh, in the days before sandwich bags and cling film replaced it.

That wicker basket was like a part of the girl's family. It was like a special heirloom. What it meant was that the family would be together for the whole afternoon. Daddy would take the day off from the obligations of his job on the base. He wouldn't be flying airplanes that day. He'd be busy driving them all over Alaska so that they could learn about the State where the Army had sent all of them. They'd been 'shipped off' for real. But even soldiers have to take days away from their responsibilities. Those 'off duty' days when her father could be with them, meant that all of those kids of his would have 'quality time' with their father, before the days when it was labelled as such a thing.

Mother would stop her ironing or house cleaning or cooking, to take the day off to be with her children, husband and mother. When Mother rested from all that she had to do, she could just relax and talk to them. Manga made any picnic complete. With that endearing laugh, her being there made the day's outing that much more enjoyable. Even her occasional taking of the Lord's Name in vain if she dropped something pretty heavy, like a bottle of beer or soda pop, on her bare already hurting toes, was tolerated, even laughed about. Probably God understood how much Manga's toes hurt when she said a loud *goddamnit*! Look what happened to Jesus' poor feet with those sharp nails poking into them. That probably hurt a lot worse than dropping bottles of beer on them did.

The very sight of the food hamper on the kitchen table, filled the girl's heart with a rise of joy. She knew what it meant. Nobody had to explain it to her. Today was picnic day, the day they'd take a day trip off the base to somewhere special. Any place you went in Alaska was special. So, it didn't matter which direction her father drove them in. North. South. East. West. What would they see on that day? What would they do to make it an exciting day?

Seeing that basket taken down from its storage place, meant that the family was going somewhere together for the day. These were in the days when fast food and take-aways were harder to come by; especially out in the boondocks. So, Mother's cooking would travel with them in that picnic basket for an outing to the woods. Mother's recipes would go away from their kitchen on the base in Ft. Wainwright. Food taken and eaten away from its usual place had a different meaning. Good food, which Mother sent with Georgina to school, wrapped in wax paper, was like opening a gift, like a special surprise to open when she got there. When she opened the wax paper, she knew that her mother was thinking about her when she made that sandwich.

When she was out in the shady tall piny woods, or in a clearing along the highway, where the State had placed picnic stops for families travelling, that's when opening her family's picnic basket took on a great significance. That's when food from home meant something. Eating it made her feel like she belonged somewhere. Belonged to someone. Even if she was away from that place where she belonged for the whole day, food brought from home, food made especially for her, comforted her.

That's when her father would make a bed in the back section of the station wagon for his children, like he did when they travelled from Kentucky to Texas, and then from Texas way, way up north, way, way up to Alaska. Blankets, pillows, books and toys and games of Old Maid were placed like a shrine to his family in the car's uttermost region. The twins would vie for that prized card of the funny old maid. Who would have thought that Katrina Josephina would take playing that game so seriously, that she would eventually become a real old maid herself someday! Children's games were taken very seriously back then. Long drives had to include more than just the superb Alaskan scenery for all of those easily bored children.

Mother always kept a secret stash of children's prizes for the best child. She would buy things on sale, when things got marked down to half price or less. Then she would hide them on the top shelf in her and Daddy's closet. Georgina had discovered lots of loot that way, by moving a chair to climb up and look inside of those hidden-away goodie bags full of things. Those things, that then wouldn't surprise her when her mother produced them in the car. The one who could behave the best in the car, got the first prize. Bags of special in-the-car travelling treats of new card games like: Go Fish, number games of addition, subtraction and multiplication, vocabulary word games as well as waxed crayons and dot to dot books were for those who could count or were learning to read, finger puppets made of felt and candy bars and other goodies.

Dolls also came along on those trips, because they wanted to see Alaska too. Nearly life-size baby Tiny Tears dolls and small jointed Ginny dolls were like part of their family. So, their travel bags and little pink wardrobes with doll-sized coat hangers for doll's clothes were brought along for the day. Those dolls would miss them if the girls were gone too long. The dolls had their own room in the basement; where a playroom was set up for the children's plethora of toys. The dolls had their own miniature furniture, clothes and wardrobes to hang them in on tiny coat hangers. A doll baby bed was lined up with all of the girls' dolls, there were so many of them. Gretchen Gabriella had given each one of her dolls a name after all five of their Alaskan girl cousins.

Mother used the time in the car to teach her children all of those politically incorrect 'Knock Knock' jokes. Or she would tell them the insulting to the simple of mind, 'Little Moron' riddles.

"Knock knock," Mother would begin. Everyone in the car would put on their thinking caps and try to come up with the answer first.

"Who's there?" the kids would all say.

"Dakota."

"Dakota who?"

"Dakota she fits. But the pants are too tight!" Mother would answer. Then everyone would all laugh together.

"Why did the little Moron put bird seed in his shoes?"

"Why?" all of the kids would ask.

"To feed his hungry pigeon toes!" Mother would say, and then she would laugh and laugh because these jokes reminded her of her childhood.

Daddy rarely drank much in the way of alcoholic beverages. But on picnics, he would always take a few bottles of beer to put into the freezing cold Alaskan streams near their picnic grounds. Drinking beer was like making a special party or celebration out of being with his kids and his wife and his mother-in-law all day. All of the winter's ice breaking up kept those sparkling clear streams very, very cold, even in the warmer months of summer. Soda pop for the kids was a special treat saved for such occasions. Milk was better for children's teeth. Too much soda pop would rot their teeth away to practically nothing at all, like they were old hide-chewing lady Eskimos. Drinking soda pop was saved only for special occasions.

They'd park the car after driving for an hour or more, in some remote spot. Everyone would pile out and run for the hills or woods, or stream or as close as they could get to a glacier. Her father would walk down to the cold stream near-by and wedge his picnic beer and the crate of the children's soda pop in the rivulets that seemed to be everywhere in Alaska. The snow and ice up in the mountains had to go somewhere. So, it became rivers and streams all over the State when it wasn't frozen up in higher elevations. Daddy got big Alaskan rocks and made protective barriers around his beer and the pop. Otherwise, the river's strong currents in some places, would push the drinks down river and somebody else downstream might get to drink their family's special drinks.

Manga took her granddaughter to investigate the trees on a nearby hill, close to where Daddy parked the car. Georgina listened intently.

"Look, that's Eskimo writing paper," she said, peeling back the thin white bark of a birch tree, which came off in curled up sheets of white paper with brown speckled dots randomly placed on its outer surface.

"If you ever get lost in the woods, you could peel this thin white bark off of the trees and make it into paper. You can write on the underside of this bark. See? You'd have to wet it and then flatten it out with some rocks first though. The Eskimos invented their own kind of paper that way. They know lots of things about the Alaskan forests. They know how to set traps for animals they need for food or clothing. Sometimes, the Eskimos put nets across the rivers to catch salmon or trout. They are pretty good fishermen. They are some of the best fishermen in the whole world. They make the best-smoked salmon in the world. Don't you think so?" A wide-eyed nod was the child's response.

"Did you know that the Eskimos even use the animal skins to make small boats to go out to the ocean and catch whales? If the ocean is frozen, they take their huskies and dog sleds out to help them pull the whales back to their village. Remember the whales we saw when we were coming into the harbour in Seward? In South Alaska? Remember the first day we saw Alaska? Did you ever think that Alaska would be as pretty as this? Let's go panning for gold, want to?" was how the informative and at the same time, inquiring conversation with her grandmother went.

Georgina rolled up her pants and took off her green suede shoes and white socks with their lacy cuffs. She would bravely follow her grandmother's example. They'd tread into the edges of the icy streams, walking on smooth river rocks into the fast-flowing waterways. Until their feet and legs were red, raw, colder even than their hands that they plunged into the river's surface to pull up the smooth stones. She'd stay in the water for as long as her Manga would stay. The thought of getting out before her grandmother did was almost like contemplating mutiny on the Bounty. No way would she be such a traitor. As they panned for gold, tiny flecks appeared amongst the grainy sand from the bottom of the stream. Manga put the shiny precious metal flecks and river water into a little chemistry tube with its cork lid for safe-keeping. The girl was busy inspecting the smooth river rocks.

"Any rock that has a white line all the way around it in a circle, is a wishing rock. If you can find a rock like that, it will bring you good luck. You can keep it in your pocket and rub it to make a wish on it," Manga told her grandchild.

Manga waded into the cold streams in her bare feet first. She was the leader of their pack of two. Georgina laughed at her Grandmother's feet when she saw them. Everything about the woman fascinated the girl. She would remember what Manga told her for years afterwards. Maybe telling a child something out of a patient heart of love, helped them to remember what you said. It must be true.

Because sometimes, the girl forgot what adults told her. It was like big people were force-feeding her with information, and stuff that they wanted her to know, and then she was supposed to maybe regurgitate it back to them at a later date, before she forgot entirely what it was that they had told her in the first place. But not Manga. She wasn't like other grown-ups. She was much nicer.

"Manga, why is your toe sticking straight up in the air like that?" Georgina wondered aloud, looking at the wintry woman's bare little tiny feet and her first two absurd toes going up straight up in the air, instead of straight ahead like they were supposed to. The girl wanted to know what on earth was wrong with the

239

woman, to have feet like that. Her grandmother's feet had funny toes and shiny thin skin with its blue, cold, cold blue veins, making Nellie's feet appear to be almost grey. There were so many of those blue veins oddly bulging out and travelling over the surface of them; just below the tracing or tissue paper-like skin on those aging, deformed, cold, freezing cold feet with their disobedient crazy toes.

"It's only my arthritis, sweetheart. It makes my toes poke straight up in the air! Isn't it funny looking? Have you ever seen toes that looked like my toes?" Manga was laughing.

"No. Does it hurt? It looks like it would be hard to put your shoes on with your toes sticking straight up in the air like that."

"I know! But isn't it funny? I have to push my toes down just to get my shoes and socks on! Nobody I know has such funny feet like I do!"

Manga was laughing at her own two feet. Her poor old feet. The woman was always laughing at herself. She said that her arthritic feet and toes felt so much better submerged in the icy water. But she hardly ever complained about the pain. She saw her funny poking-up toes as comical. That acceptance of her own frailties and even amusement with her own body, moving towards decay, gave her a certain charm. To the girl, Manga was invincible. So what if her toes stood straight up? She could walk just fine. Manga could walk for miles. Farther than anyone Georgina knew. Except for those Eskimo hunters. Manga could walk for miles and miles and miles.

The girl's grandmother had a saying, "If I stay at home, I'll feel as badly as I will if I go out. I'm going to be in pain no matter where I am. I might as well go out. I might as well. So, I'll go out and enjoy myself!" That was her philosophy on life. Life that was meant to be enjoyed, no matter how badly she felt the arthritic pain in her shoulders. Or even if her demented rickety toes stuck straight up in the air, making it hard to put her shoes on. Feet were happier with shoes off anyway. And that freezing icy water in the Alaskan stream was easing the pain by numbing her toes.

The child and her grandmother stepped out of the icy stream, and walked gingerly with frozen feet so icy cold that they could hardly feel anything on the rocky surface of the shoreline. This was summertime in Alaska. They both saw red raw toes and feet and ankles below their naked shins. It was no laughing matter.

"Let me dry those frozen feet of yours, Georgina Jane!" Manga urged, drying her granddaughter's rock-like feet while her own were still wet. Still solid blocks of icy blue and flaming freezing red.

Freezing feet never really become dry until they finally warm up again. Putting them back into their socks and shoes just felt like frozen feet with shoes and socks on them. Like blocks of a solid mass that didn't feel like it belonged to you. That's what such cold feet felt like. Walking wasn't easy. It took Daddy wrapping his girl in a blanket and carrying her to the back seat of their car, where he turned the car's heater on full blast for his daughter and mother-in law's frozen solid feet to thaw out. Manga followed slowly and deliberately. With feet that cold you could step on broken glass left over from other picnickers' shattered beer bottles left lying on the ground. You'd never even know it if you cut yourself. You were too numb to feel anything you walked through!

"You gals are nuts! Just crazy! How can you stand that freezing cold water? Are you out of your minds? What a couple of dizzy dames!"

He chided them like they were both his children, trying to rub four rigid feet simultaneously sticking up, red as anything, from the back seat. It wasn't that it was a cold day, the weather was balmy for Alaska. But the rivers and streams never got much above freezing, no matter what time of year it was.

The twins danced like fairies on the shoreline, until they were called to have lunch. They were too sensible to get such cold wet feet. With feet like chunks of rigid wooden blocks, the girl left the warmth of the family's station wagon. Lunch was on a woollen plaid blanket near the rocky shoreline. It was time for the picnic lunch, cold feet or no cold feet. Her mother handed the girl a paper plate with a ham sandwich of chunky, thick slices of freshly baked ham.

Mother's ham was the best in the world. Ham was packaged in ham-shaped metal cans with keys attached to the bottom of the ham can. The ham was like the can it came in, both shaped exactly the same. The best way to cook it was with brown sugar packed around the top and sides and carefully placed (with whole cloves used like toothpicks holding them in place) rings of canned pineapple in equal distances on the surface of the brown sugar topping. The prize was a piece of the cooked pineapple, melded with the brown sugar and heated cloves permeating the pineapples and the meat to give it a browned appearance, like the color of the soles of her school shoes. But the brown part was deceptively dirty looking. It was the best part of the ham, the outside. It was so sweet and caramelised. The surface and rind of the ham was almost crunchy and chewy all at the same time. That was Georgina's favourite part. She could have eaten just the pineapples and the ham rind and been happy. But the meat was succulent and juicy, just the way she liked it.

There was a devilled egg wobbling on its slippery white sides next to creamed together soft, but chunky potato salad. There were carrot sticks and celery with cream cheese and chives. Perfectly sliced carrot sticks. Celery stalks with that filling that Mother made. And a big sliced dill pickle garnished the ham sandwich. If they had been a kosher family, it would have been boiled cow's tongue that some ignorant people took for ham, eating dozens of small party quartered sandwiches before they realized what they had done and feeling like they'd puke at the thought of what they had eaten in their stupidity, eating all of that kosher cow's tongue, which they mistook for ham.

Colored plastic forks were used for their picnics. Roger Eugenio now three and a half was teaching his side-kick of a little brother, now a two and a half-year-old hunter, how to stab his food like they were lancing bears or other wild Alaskan animals. They pretended that ham was the carcass of some hunted creature from the spooky deep woods surrounding their picnic grounds. Deep, deep woods. Forests stretching for miles. Woods and forests full of bears. Wild, ferocious bears. Bears that would eat the girl and her family all up if they could. The boys made sounds like they were ferocious predatory hunters in pursuit of all of those wild Alaskan animals in their imaginations, as they killed their sandwiches. Peter Martin was sticking his tongue out and biting it as hard as he could with his relatively new teeth, as he strained to catch his tricky, slippery devil egg with that white plastic picnic fork he was holding.

Salt and a bit of black pepper had been poured into squares of waxed paper with twisted tops to hold them shut until her father sprinkled salt out on top of her picnic lunch and into his mug of cold beer. The salt caused even more bubbles to cascade up to the surface where the beer's foam sat like a seething mass of the summer's white mosquito larvae. It was a mystery she didn't understand until years later, how her father could drink that golden liquid which gave him a funny frosty moustache. He let her taste it, and compared to her Coca-Cola it was acrid and bitter. Soda pop was bubbly too, but it tasted better than beer.

Leaving the picnic ground behind, after hours of looking for fairies, gold and bunnies or bears, or being chased by their father who wanted to growl at them and tickle them until they laughed so hard that their tummies hurt like anything. They crowded back into their trusty station wagon. Daddy wanted to make them all laugh until they couldn't take it anymore. Tickle them until they were exhausted. Exhausted from laughing. Then they headed back. It was the end of the day, and time to go back to their home on the army base.

Perry Como, one of Daddy's favourites, was singing a love song on the radio. After that, it was Nat King Cole, singing *Love is Here to Stay,* which was released in 1953, the year after the girl's birthday. The skies that day might not be clear, but the guy with the soothing voice on their radio was saying that *'It's very clear...our love is here to stay. Not for a year, but ever, and always'.*

Daddy felt romantic and put his arm around her mother. He was driving with one hand on the steering wheel now. A bit nerve-wracking to watch from the back seat. He needed both hands to drive. Then the announcer said that the weather today would be mostly cloudy, with a chance of some rain later that afternoon. Daddy would try to hurry home before it started a summer's deluge out in the wild Alaskan parkland.

A Poor Dear and a Grizzly Bear

Up ahead, just off the road, was a place where travellers could get gasoline, foodstuffs, fuel and newspapers. There was even an old-fashioned diner counter inside, with backless chairs, what you might call high stools, that spun round and round in circles as the twins walked past them. Those stools twirled to heave chubby bottoms on or off of them. Stopping for gas at a filling station alone on the long road home, the whole family piled out of their car. Like a procession of army ants, marching one by one. Georgina and her family filed past the curious eyes of the people inside. It was a bit scary to see so many children coming at them all at once. Sort of took their breath away. Old-timers and latent discouraged, but not utterly cast down, prospectors, gave sideways glances as one by one all of those little heads walked past them.

The girl had to go badly. That Coca-Cola was going right through her. She got out to go to the ladies' room with her mother, sisters and grandmother. Daddy would take the boys to the men's room, now that they were out-growing diapers. Potty training created a whole new set of responsibilities for their father, who had himself broken the social codes of the times, and had even changed the soiled nappies of his offspring when the kids were younger. He loved to brag about it, like he knew something that they didn't.

It was an outpost or a trading post for rough and ready hunters and trappers and seasoned Alaskan sourdoughs. After their potty stop, Manga bought some bubble gum for the girls. All of that bubble blowing would keep them quiet and busy in the car. And as long as they didn't fall asleep with it in their mouths, they could chew it. Chew it even though Mommy said that chewing gum made them look like cows chewing their cuds. The twins were beginning to get all tuckered out and their tiredness made them cranky, like two small crab apples. Katrina Josephina could be bad-tempered at the best of times, and she had had enough fun for one day. She had been pinching Gretchen Gabriella, her twin, off and on for about a half an hour in the very back of the station wagon.

Daddy talked to the man at the counter, and offered him a quarter to do his usual 'flip you double or nothing' trick. It didn't work with that guy. 'Fraid not' was his only response, not catching her father's joke.

Walking back to their station wagon, Georgina saw him. At first, she wasn't sure what on earth it was up there on top of the camper of that bashed-up, rusty old blue truck. Then she realized too late to save herself. She recognized what it was that she was looking at so close-up, when she went to get into her side of the car. The sight was gruesome and disturbing. It was a huge buck. He was tied to the top of the truck parked next to their station wagon. He was bleeding terribly. He had a gaping hole and a big gash on his shoulder that needed stitches, but would never get them. The huge stag, with antlers nearly as big as her father's whole body, lay with blankly staring, helpless opened eyes. Its carcass tied with cruel ropes to the top of the truck's luggage rack.

The truck had pulled into the outpost while the girl's family was inside. Now, it was parked next to their black and white station wagon. It was not a pretty sight to come back to. That enormous deer would be furious to be tied down like that. The male animal's entire body was sprawled out on top of the other vehicle. He wasn't going anywhere in a hurry. His once powerful legs had failed to run away fast enough to escape the rifle's shot, which had found the deer's heart. Now, his life had bled away, and with his big mouth open, his tongue hanging out of the corner of his red-dripping-bloody mouth, the daddy deer lay silently. He lay there bleeding silently to himself.

It was no use him getting angry with the hunter. He had no way to express whatever it was that he might have felt at being shot like that. His emotions, like his blood, were all draining away from him now. It was too late now. Now he was a silent deer. He was a quiet deer. He was a deer with nothing else to ever say to anyone. Ever. But when she looked up into his sad face, as Georgina bravely passed him on her way to her car door, she could hear him. He was

244

screaming at the girl. She stood frozen to the spot. Those sharp antlers couldn't protect him from the hunter's gun.

"Great gobs of garbage! Get into the car, honey," said her father, shooing his daughter past the gruesome sight and hoisting her back into the interior of their car.

He acted as if seeing a giant dead deer was a sight they saw every day.

"Only blood and guts!" pronounced Katrina enthusiastically, pointing to the bloody mess dripping from the bullet hole near the deer's shoulder.

It was a fresh kill. The sight made the girl shudder. Driving away from the deer was like pulling her heart in two. She stared out the back window of the station wagon as her father drove away. Nothing she could do would help that poor dead dear animal now. Nothing she could do at all. That was life. And that was death. Life and death in Alaska.

When Captain Lewindowski, a friend of her father's, graciously gave them a leg of one of those magnificent creatures, after a successful hunting trip, it was not an easy thing to think of eating that barbecued meat served on a plate to her at suppertime that summer. Her mother had made sloppy joes out of the minced venison meat that Manga had ground finely for the kids. That was what they made of the chunks of the big deer's fleshy leg, southern sloppy joes. They put sweet pickle relish and a flown-in sliced tomato on top of the savoury spicy meat-in-a-bun that they served with those new crinkled potato chips.

These creatures were like kindred spirits to her child's heart. Georgina hesitated when she had first seen the huge raw leg, its skin and hairy bits now removed from thighbone to hoof. They had proudly held the limb up in front of her, as though it were some prized trophy of the man's hunt. Being a girl, she did not see the reasoning behind the man's intrepidity in scaling the mountain, or traversing forests in pursuit of such a kill, to possess this mighty animal's carcass. Those ideas didn't come naturally to her girl child's mind. What the hunter had done did not have the same meaning to her as her dreams did. She could be one with the forests' doe deer or the mountains' mountain goats by dreaming of being with them. Her imagination was everything. And man's culture, she was learning, seemed to require the shedding of blood, or the downing of something or someone, to find achievement. But this was unfathomable to the mind of this little girl.

All she wondered was how could she actually eat this meat from the stag's leg now that she had met so intimately, and known a real dead deer, personally?

Having been introduced to the stag tied to that man's truck, she felt obligated to have some feeling about the loss of life out there in the wilderness. Would she become one with the animal, as the Indians believed they would, by eating its flesh?

That summer she learned to eat caribou steaks cooked on her father's barbecue pit. Mother made the best homemade barbecue sauce imaginable. She ate icy cold whale blubber that was kept frozen in the freezer. She tasted the delights of king crab legs and smoked salmon. She savoured those venison sloppy joes as though they were heaven on earth.

Bear meat was supposed to be greasy, but the Eskimos ate it, like the Indians and the pioneers had eaten it in their times of need. Eskimos made coats out of the fur skin pelts of these great animals and others. Some people used the bears' used coats, heads, teeth, arms and claws as rugs to put in front of their fireplaces. At their local Community Center on the base in Ft. Wainwright, the Army had acquired a huge hunting trophy shot by one of the servicemen on one of his days off. It was a Kodiak bear. The giantest bear in the whole wide world. It was frozen in time. Frozen in space. Standing there enormously. Grimacing at the girl. Holding his big hairy arms out. Holding them out way up there above her head.

At the Halloween just past, her father had taken them to an autumnal celebration. She was dressed as Little Miss Muffet with her spider attached to a string suspended from a stick, which she carried beside her. When they arrived in the hall, her father was thrilled to bits to see that huge stuffed bear. He made her sit beneath that enormous taxidermied grizzling bear so that he could take her photograph. That huge Alaskan bear's claws hovered over her head. His furry pelt was ominous and somewhat smelly. That giant stuffed bear smelled like he was still full of his lost life. He was not a stuffed Teddy Bear, named after President Teddy Roosevelt, from when Manga was a little girl. His teeth silently grimaced, as his tacit throat soundlessly growled under his breathless, open mouth. Georgina's heart momentarily stopped. Her fear was tangible. She refused to let that bear get the better of her. Somehow, she got through it. Fear could be ignored, if her strong determination willed it away.

Whale Blubber, Native Savages and Toilets

Now she could eat the flesh of the ocean giants, the whales who had once escorted her ship coming into their harbour at Seward. This Eskimo 'ice cream', as the Native Alaskans called it, was chewy black 'tar' next to melt-in-your-mouth pale pink moosh. She learned to love it and looked forward to her uncle's travels into the wild country, visiting the Native Americans, the Inuits. What on earth would he bring back next time? He would be sure to bring home more exotic foods for thought and body.

Though he rarely spoke to the children, unless he was shouting, Georgina's uncle, her cousins' father, amazed and astonished her. She felt that she was always learning from him. That he was always feeding her knowledge which seemed too rich, too good to be true. He was authentic, saying just exactly what he meant to say, not trying to fool her, like her daddy usually did when she asked him anything serious. Like Coca-Cola, her Uncle Buddy was the 'Real Thing'. Or as they say back where the man grew up, '*Coca-Cola is the Real Thang*' in that twangy accent of theirs.

Uncle Bubba-Chuck, 'Woodchuck' for short, was an amazing man. He had a knack for putting words together, even she could see that. He was so full of stories when he did speak. Maybe he had learned how to tell a good story during late nights in his earlier boarding school days. Sometimes he would casually mention his years in the school, which had been run by the Dominicans, or was it the Franciscans? He said it had 'built character' in him, that his life would have been unstable without it.

He had been a child without much of a knowledge of his father. But those priests at the school had been his fathers. They had taught him. They had fed and housed him all those years. All those years ago. The girl knew not to ask him about his mother and her life in the swamp with those family members with such odd names. It would only embarrass him and that would make him edgy and cross. She knew how he got when he was angry. It was obvious, even to a child, that it was safer not to bring up the subject of his mother and why she hadn't taken care of him herself.

But he seemed interested in food. And because she was curious about where he got such amazingly immense crab legs, arm length shrimp, succulent smoked brown trout, and where on earth he had found the strange and extraordinary pink and black substance he kept wrapped in the freezer, she asked her uncle how he happened to come by such culinary treasures. What was that pink and black stuff in the freezer anyway?

"The whale blubber is for the baby's teething," he said.

The fact that whales and their blubber, before then, were still a mystery to her, seemed to go unnoticed. She stared at her uncle in amazement that he was, after all, actually speaking directly to her. It had never happened before. She must be special to him, she thought. So, she continued to ask him, as respectfully as a girl could,

"Why would anyone eat the whale's blubber?" she asked meekly.

"The Eskimos eat it! They call it 'Indian Ice Cream'!" he hollered back at her.

Of course, she should have known. But what was 'blubber' anyway? She wasn't sure, but it must be an extraordinarily perfect part of the whale. There must be something wonderful that happened to you if you ate the blubber of such a giant sea creature! Wasn't it the largest animal in the world, now that the dinosaurs were all gone? Georgina felt as though the very power of the seas themselves was right there inside of her uncle's freezer.

"Here, have some!" he offered, cutting off a sliver of the strange, but colorful substance and handing it to the child. It was more of an order than an offer or a request.

His generosity overwhelmed her. Because he had given it to her and she didn't want him to be angry with her, or worse, to stop talking to her, she took a tentative bite. It was obviously something very valuable and awful hard to come by. So, Georgina ate the small sliver of the whale's blubber. It was flubbery.

It tasted like nothing she had ever tasted before. Was it good? She wasn't sure. How could you tell? What would you compare it to? It was rubbery and chewy and gooshy all at the same time. Whales were really unique creatures. There weren't any other animals that she knew of, that were like whales. The girl had seen the whales blowing water out of the tops of their heads. She had learned that they were not fish at all, even though they lived in the watery ocean. They weren't fish, but really large mammals. Mammals were animals like cows and moose and deer and dogs and cats. So, eating a mammal, as long as it wasn't your pet, was okay.

When she and her sisters and brothers had seen the whales in the ocean, even a white one, escorting their ship into Seward's harbour when they first came to Alaska, she thought that they were magical creatures. She thought that the reason that the whales were leaping up in the air when their ship came in, was that those whales were so glad to see her and her family. Georgina had been afraid that her little brothers might fall into the ocean like Curious George did, if they were held

248

too close to the ship's railing when they tried to see those giant whales. It was windy up in the front of that big ship. A baby might get blown far out to sea in all of that wind.

The black part of the whale's blubber made her think of the hot tar on the streets in Texas when it was summer there. They put tar in the cracks of the broken parts of the streets down there. The South was where the Tar Baby lived, in the same neighbourhood with Brer Bear and Brer Fox. Those silly fellas had made a Tar Baby to fool ole' Brer Rabbit, the star of the story. Smart ole' Brer Rabbit had tricked them though, and Brer Fox had gotten stuck in the hat-wearin'-corn-cob-pipe-smokin' Tar Baby instead. You couldn't step into the hot Texas tar because it would stick to the bottom of your shoes. It wasn't a good idea to get hot tar on your brand-new white summer sandals. Your mother would kill you if you did that. Those new shoes, and you, would never be the same again after that experience.

But the black 'tar' part of the whales' blubber wasn't like Texas tar, or similar to the Tar Baby at all. It didn't stick to your teeth like black liquorice jelly beans did. Whales' tar was cold, frozen solid almost. She could see why her uncle said that he gave it to his baby for his sore gums, when his baby's teeth were coming in. She knew that teething hurt babies. Her little brothers only had rubber rings with colored water in them, that her mother kept in the freezer for their teething. Sometimes Manga gave those squalling, screaming, fussy, teething grandsons wet and then deliberately frozen clean washcloths to chew on. They had never even had whale blubber though. Georgina wondered if they would have liked to chew on the whale's blubber like her uncle's baby did.

Next to the black part of the whale's blubber was a soft pink part, Gretchen's favourite color. It reminded Georgina of the *Jello* that her mother put out on the back porch to set five minutes before dinner. If the *Jello* wasn't set completely, her mother would whip it. It would become frothy and cold. Partly congealed red *Jello* turned to a beautiful shade of pink if it was whipped. Whipped pink *Jello* was like the color of the whale's blubber. The kids in her family all loved *Jello*. She wasn't sure if they would like whale blubber though.

After she had eaten the whale's blubber to please her uncle, and only because she had the courage to speak directly to him, her uncle told Georgina Jane about the Eskimos and their ways. She thought that the Eskimos must be the most amazing people in the whole wide world, to think of such a clever thing, like giving their babies the chewy black blubber of the giant whales. Knowing what whale's blubber even was, must have been a great discovery to them. Whoever had tasted black and pink whales' blubber first must have been a very brave person to taste something so new and unfamiliar to them. That was how the Eskimos helped their little yellow, squinty-eyed babies to grow up big and strong.

If their babies ate whale's blubber at such an early age, even before they had teeth, they'd be some of the strongest people in the whole wide world. Wouldn't they? She tried to express these sentiments, welling up inside of her mind. Her thoughts were racing wildly inside of her from just a little taste of the pink and black stuff. That blubber was already giving the girl lots of new ideas about the Eskimos and food in general. Those Eskimos were so amazing, weren't they?

Her uncle wasn't impressed with her opinions of the prowess or intelligence of the Native Alaskans. "Damn Indians! They are not like white people," he said. "The government tries to please them by bringing civilization all the way up here to those uncouth filthy varmints. The United States government went to the trouble to build new houses for them. But do you know what they did?" (Not waiting for her to answer, he continued to speak about his opinions of such matters.)

"Those morons are completely ungrateful. Do you know what they did?"

(In her wide-eyed amazement, she was too stunned to speak.)

"I'll tell you what they did! They wrecked the whole *goddamn* place! They tore down the walls to make one big room!

"They want to cook over open fires. So, they ripped out the cooking stoves!

"They want their whole damn family to sleep together! So, they tore out the new walls we built for them! I designed those houses myself.

"They want to pee and shit into holes in the ground. So, they threw their toilets out in the snow!

"You can't do anything for them! Nothing the government does for those savages impresses them. It's useless, completely useless. It's a waste of the government's money to try to build houses for these useless Indians.

"They'll never understand the white man's culture or appreciate anything you do for them. They're just plain old ordinary *fucking goddamn* savages!"

The child was dumbfounded by her uncle's use of such big words. Her daddy never said words like that. The scathing litany of judgments Uncle Bubba had against the native Alaskans was damning all right. She could see that the clash of cultures evidently really bothered him. And if the Eskimos really were

250

'useless', then she could see why it would annoy him like that. After all, wasn't he always busy? He wasn't 'useless', like he said the Eskimos were. He was always doing lots of things at his job, working for his growing family.

If the Eskimos were really savages, like Uncle Bubba said that they were, was that how they had figured out how to use such a thing as whales' blubber in the first place? Whales' blubber to help soothe their little babies aching gums when sharp new pushing-under-the-gums-baby-teeth were bothering them so much? And making those Eskimo babies cry all of the time? All of those stomach and eyeteeth hurt a lot coming into those small pink mouths. Teeth had to come into swollen little baby gums, ready to burst any minute with brand new baby teeth. Eskimo babies' gums that had never even had holes poking through them before, needed whale blubber a lot. That teething cutting into them would have been dreadful without whales' blubber to soothe and make those babies feel a lot better.

Maybe being savages was a good thing. Maybe being savages was how Native People could survive in such a place like Alaska was. Native people had to be wild, like the animals who were indigenous to these regions. Those canny wild animals needed out-smarting. Feral savages had a knack at knowing things that gave them an advantage in places so ferocious that like Alaska, you and your babies would die otherwise. That was the way it was for those Eskimos in that place with all of its biting arctic regions and desolate times of the year.

She wasn't sure that she agreed with her uncle's perception of such things. And she began to see that her family was separate from other people who had different ways. This had never occurred to the girl before. Until her uncle had taught her that the Indians or Eskimos were not the same as her family, that they wouldn't even use a toilet, her opinion of them had been different. Before that, the child had thought that the Native Americans were just a part of the whole. To her, before that moment, prior to tasting the Eskimo's raw black and pink whale blubber, Eskimos were endearing, new and exciting. It took her uncle's years of vast experience and his phenomenal way with words, to explain to Georgina that these natives from the icy regions weren't so great, even if they did eat whale blubber

But Georgina knew, even then, that the Eskimos were pretty smart. She knew that the Eskimos knew a lot of things. They knew how to live in this cold place. They could even build houses made of ice, and stay warm inside of them when it was freezing cold outside! They could catch slippery fish through holes they cut into the ice to feed their families in the dead of the most icy winter months. The Eskimos also hunted seals and sewed the wonderful sweet-smelling cured skins for their clothing. Their men liked rhythm, and made their drums from animal skins that they used at their gatherings. The girl went to visit the Eskimos with her family. That was when those savages threw the girl high up into the air on their blankets of sewn together Alaskan animal skins. They threw her so high up into the air that the Eskimos made her feel like she was really flying. She had to catch her breath. Her tummy was in her throat. Her all but breathless scream was funny to those arctic people. They laughed out loud like Manga laughed aloud. They thought that the girl was amusing when she screamed out in sudden fear at being thrown up up up by them, so so so high up into the cold Alaska air. Thrown up on their blankets. Up high over the snowy fields. Up in the air so high. Up in the sky so grey.

Eskimos smoked the salmon that zoomed upstream, trying in vain to escape them. The girl's uncle brought home the Eskimos' families' food. He served food to his kids that was caught or hunted by those yellow babies' papas. Nothing wild could escape the Eskimo hunters or fishermen. Nothing wild could escape them because they were wild too. They were wild too, like Alaska was.

They shot the caribou for the steaks her uncle ate and the deer for the venison sausages he loved so, so much. He made gumbo from a recipe his Aunt Lois (who was married to her cousin, his Uncle Leroy, her cousins' great-uncle) gave to him from way back in Louisiana with those yummy sausages. His gumbo recipe was famous all over the State of Alaska. Deer killed by Eskimos was tastier than almost anything they could even think of putting into it back in the South. And the craw daddies back in Louisiana creeks were almost nothing at all compared to the enormous shrimp Eskimo fishermen netted and pulled out of Alaska's frigid, Nordic-like salty waters. Shrimps and venison sausages got added to Uncle Bubba's famous gumbo recipe. His Southern gumbo was a Northern specialty made with big Matanuska onions, fresh greenhouse tomatoes, yellow, red and/or green bell peppers, and that essential imported okra, frozen and then flown in from the South. His spices were a secret that he wouldn't even tell to his wife.

The Inuits supplied him with so much to be grateful for. But Uncle Bubba wasn't grateful at all for what the Eskimos had done for him. They had enriched his life. But he never stopped to think how much better his life was. How much better a place Alaska was. A better place because of those peculiar people.

Peculiar people who tore out all of those government toilets. Tore them out. Tore them out and just threw them out in the cold, cold Alaskan snow. Peculiar people who knocked down walls. Peculiar people who built fires to huddle around. Like those toilets were completely useless. Like those walls were a nuisance.

Uncle Bubba didn't understand why walls were in the way of families huddling together, like they used to do, so that nobody in their families would get cold. They built those open fires so that they could continue keeping their traditions. They wanted to keep spending time together like they always had, telling generationally passed-down Eskimo stories around all of those friendly open fires in the middle of their families' big shared rooms. They lived in houses where walls were bad things, not good *thangs*. Walls kept them apart, when all they really wanted, was to be together.

They caught the whales for her uncle's baby's sore teeth. Whales gave them so much. From those ginormous creatures, they got oil for lamps in their warm houses. Meat to eat. And bones to carve large and small sculptures that were elaborately made with skill that was passed down from father to sons for generations long before the whites conquered their no man's land. A cold man's land. They were so clever, they knew how to preserve food, so that nothing got wasted in a place where civilized commodities had been impossible to come by in the long years before the arrival of those often arrogant, land-grabbing, privileged white men.

Smoking their meat and storing it up high inside of sheds where the bears and wolves couldn't steal it, was a smart thing to do. Even the Eskimos' ravenous husky dogs couldn't bite into that marvellous smoked salmon, much as they would have liked to. Unless their Eskimo owners deliberately gave them chunks of that carefully smoked salmon, or chunks of the meat of other wild animals, invaluable huskies, those sled-pulling dogs would have been dead. How could those Inuits really be 'useless'? The girl realized that she had a lot to learn, but sometimes learning made you feel funny inside.

Funny Feelings

She had felt funny inside, the day her sweet little baby teeth starting falling out of her mouth. That was a terrible feeling, losing your very own teeth. She had gotten used to those little teeth. It was a very scary thing to happen to a little girl. It hurt to lose her teeth like that. Pretty soon, she would look like some very old woman without any teeth at all, who had to eat babies' food all of the time. Then, she couldn't whistle like Daddy did.

Every day, as soon as Daddy came home and walked into the front door, he would whistle for Mother. Whistle! Whistle! That meant Mother would know Daddy was home and she was meant to whistle back. If Mother didn't whistle back, something was wrong and Daddy would go looking for her, whistling all the way through the house. Whistling was his way of calling Mother, like she was his dog. Whistling was important. Without whistling, a whole way of talking would be lost. Daddy whistled all of the time. Every day of his life he whistled.

If Georgina smiled without those two front teeth of hers, she would look like that Goofy dog on the Disney cartoons; except Goofy's teeth weren't non-existent, they were too big for his mouth. Nobody told her that her teeth would grow back, only bigger, next time she had teeth. Until then, all the kids at school would laugh at her and make fun of her falling out teeth, like they did the day she wet her pants. Wetting your pants and losing your teeth were almost like the same thing. Georgina thought that she would never be the same again after those two things happened to her.

When she was seven, she had her First Holy Communion. The children got to eat the host, which was really Jesus' body. The priest was going to put that round piece of Jesus' body on her tongue, and then she could taste it for herself. Only the priest, in his long flowing robes, drank the blood of Jesus, which he poured into a golden cup.

How could he drink that guy on the cross' blood? The girl thought that was gross, even though the nuns tried to convince her that this had a special meaning. To Georgina, this was like some sort of strange initiation rite into an even stranger group of people. Everyone who has high up in this group wore long gowns and spoke in Latin when they performed that ceremony on the altar with all of those cloths and golden cups. That priest kept wiping those cups clean. Were they really all that dirty? Did Jesus' blood make things need to be washed and wiped like that? Drinking blood sounded weird. It was all a bit scary, even though her daddy said it was what her family believed in. But even her daddy's rationale didn't dispel her concerns for what seemed like the oddities that they taught her.

She looked at Catholic crucifixes and wondered, "Why aren't these people helping that guy, that Jesus Christ, off of that cross? They seem like they just want him to stay there, on that cross and suffer forever and ever, never getting to come down. If I really do eat his body, will he get to come down from that crucifix? Will his body taste anything like that mountain goat's leg? Aren't people really mammals, like the whales and the caribou and the goats? Eating people's bodies, even if they are related to God, seems like a strange thing to do. With so many children having their First Holy Communion, would there even be that much of Jesus' body left?"

She wondered what part of Jesus' body the priest would give to her. When she ate her First Holy Communion, would she eat Jesus' arm? How did they know which part of Jesus' body was the best part to give to little children? Georgina worried about this idea of eating the man they told her was God's son's body.

For weeks and months, those nuns at her school worked so hard, trying to instil these things into her hard head. They tried to prepare the girl and the other children for this new experience, this first Holy Communion. Those children had to memorize so many tricky things about Jesus and his body. Georgina was afraid that Father would ask her a catechism question that she didn't understand the answer to. If she gave the wrong answer, Father probably wouldn't even let her taste Jesus' body after that. He'd be so disgusted with her for being so stupid.

None of the things those nuns said about poor Jesus and his body and his blood, made much sense to her. Sister said that she should stop asking so many questions. Georgina was just glad when the nuns told her that, no, she and the other children would not have to drink Jesus' blood, only Father would be drinking Jesus' blood. She was really, really glad about that. It would have been terrible to have to drink that blood like Father had to, even if they did put the blood into a nice big clean golden cup, called a chalice. Drinking blood must be something that only special people, who went to the cemetery, could drink. That Father had to go to a lot of special classes at a place called a cemetery to learn all about how to drink that cup of blood.

She knew all about blood, and not just from seeing the deer's blood all over the truck at that gas station. Right before she heard about having her First Holy Communion, she had even tasted blood. She knew that blood was salty. Tasting blood was not something that she thought was a very good idea. It was a scary thing to taste blood, even if it was your very own blood. Her gums bled the day her tooth fell right out of her mouth when she was eating her ham sandwich in the school cafeteria.

She nearly bit her very own tongue right off once, and that made her get a whole lot of blood in her mouth. She had even swallowed her own blood, and that was a terrible feeling to swallow your own blood. Swallowing blood was one of the most revolting things that she knew about. She had even tasted Henry's blood the day she had bitten him on the ship coming to Alaska. Tasting someone else's blood was really, really sick. That day was a really, really bad day. A bloody day.

The day she nearly bit her own tongue right off was another bad day. All of the kids in her family liked to play 'leap frog'. They would take turns and make a row of crouching bodies and one of the kids would leap over the bodies of his or her brothers and sisters. After the person, whose turn it was, got to the end of the row, they would crouch down and the last person in the row would start leaping over and over and over the other children. When it was Georgina's turn to be the leapfrog, she was having such a great time, bouncing over the crouching bodies of her brothers and sisters. That game was so much fun.

But then, that dumb sister of hers, Katrina Josephina, just decided that the game was over and she stood up, right when Georgina Jane was leaping over Katrina Josephina's crouching body! She was leaping so hard, so fast, so very quickly, like that quick brown fox, that she was lost in all of that leaping. And she was so enthusiastically playing leap frog, that when Katrina stood up, her momentum was too great to stop herself in mid-air. Katrina collided with her sister and Georgina bit right into her very own tongue. Her tongue was gouged into it by one of her own teeth. It had a hole in the middle of it where Katrina made her bite it. Blood was gushing out, bothering her mother, who had told the children to be good while she was fixing their dinner and waiting for their father to come home from work in the cold and in the dark. So, that's how the girl knew about tasting blood.

The only thing worse than swallowing blood, was swallowing marbles. Once she had swallowed a marble. Her mother made her go to the hospital so that the doctors could tell her to take her shirt off and ex-ray her and see inside of her tummy and find that marble that she swallowed. That was way before she grew bosoms like Manga had. But they found out that she was pigeoned-chested without her shirt on, which alarmed the army doctors even more than the swallowed marble did. She knew after that, it was not a very good idea to put marbles into your mouth in case you accidentally forgot that they were in your mouth and you swallowed them. But pretty soon, Georgina Jane would have to swallow Jesus' whole body. Like she had swallowed that marble. Would Jesus' body be as hard to swallow as a marble was?

She had a new dress and a white veil with little flowers sewn on to it. Manga had sewn them especially for her. She even had a new pair of clean mated, white socks, and polished white leather shoes and un-worn white underwear. Everything that she wore had to be white. Had to be brand new. It was important to look her best to eat part of Jesus' body. All of the second-graders at her school had to get dressed up and fold their hands, and kneel down and have some of Jesus' body on the day that they had their First Holy Communion.

When it was finally the special day of the First Holy Communion, she went up to the front of the church, after the priest said a whole lot of prayers in Latin. She waited patiently for her turn to go up to the front of the church and have Jesus finally placed on her tongue. She was very nervous about it. She knew that her tongue was different from all of the other second graders, because her tongue had a hole in it from playing leapfrog with Katrina Josephina. She hoped that Jesus wouldn't mind how her tongue looked. She kept her hands folded in front of her, just like Sister said to do. None of the other children seemed to think that Jesus tasted bad. She knelt there in her pew and watched them. When it was their turn to taste Jesus' body, they knelt at the front of the church, opened up their small mouths as big as they could, and then they just gulped and swallowed Jesus whole.

The girl knew that you weren't supposed to bite poor Jesus' body. If you bit his body, it might hurt him even more than that cross did. She hoped that she could remember not to bite Jesus. The nuns said to just swallow Jesus' body without biting it.

How can I swallow a piece of Jesus' body, without chewing it up first? she wondered. It worried her.

Her parents had been very careful to teach her to chew every single bite of her food very, very carefully. Otherwise, she would choke. Georgina hoped that she wouldn't choke on Jesus' body, like she had choked on that chicken bone in Vicksburg, Mississippi. That was a scary thing to choke like that.

When Sister stood at the end of the girl's pew in church, drumming her fingers on their pew with that solemn look of hers on her face, it was time to go up to the front with her classmates and get some of Jesus' body for herself. Everyone in her row stood up together. It was like they were army soldiers all marching in unison. It was like they had practiced doing at their Religious

257

Education class. Catechism was one of the classes where she had learned about God and Jesus and the Holy Spirit.

Those teachers didn't like it when someone questioned what they taught. Questioning could damn you to hell. And Hell sounded like a pretty scary place. Purgatory didn't sound much better. It was very very hot there too. Only you didn't stay in Purgatory forever. You'd only stay there for a little while. Or if you were pretty bad, you'd stay there for longer. So, she tried to just listen and not make Sister so mad at her.

Finally, it was her turn to eat Jesus' body. When Father O'Brian stood in front of her, as she knelt down in the front of the church, Georgina Jane O'Shaughnessy opened her mouth so that Father could give her the very First Holy Communion she had ever had. Communion wafers, which were the actual body of Jesus Christ. Father would put that round, white, circle on her tongue. She would finally taste what Jesus really tasted like. After all of the anticipation, all of the talking about Him, this was his moment to come to her.

There she was, with her little seven-year-old mouth open as far as she could open it, like the baby birds her brothers had always reminded her of, when they ate their baby food from all of those small baby food jars. Her mouth was wide open. Her eyes were closed. Her neck was very stiff. She could hardly breathe out of that pigeon chest of hers. The palms of her hands were sweating. She could feel her sweaty palms through those white cotton gloves her mother had bought for her. Bought especially for this very special day in her life. Her heart was pounding. She felt fear grip her by the back of her throat. She felt like she was waiting forever and could hardly breath. She was frozen in a stiff kneeling position with all of those other little all-dressed-up second graders from her school.

Her tongue was still scared from Katrina Josephina's decision to jump up so quickly in the middle of that game of leapfrog. Finally, she was going to taste Jesus' very own body, like she had a body. Like whales had bodies. Like deer had bodies. Like bears had bodies. Like mountain goats had bodies. Like bunny rabbits had bodies. Like Daddy had a body. Like Mommy had a body. Like everyone in her family had a body.

Just when she thought that, she would forever be frozen in that physical, mental, emotional, spiritual position for the rest of her life, and probably would be stuck there for all of eternity; it happened to her.

Father said, "Body of Christ," and put the wafer, that was really Jesus, on her stuck-out tongue.

So then, there was Jesus. There was Jesus, resting on her tongue. And Father O'Brian had moved on to the girl kneeling next to her. That moment that Georgina had been waiting for, had finally arrived. After learning so many things about Jesus and his body, she realized that he was really just like a dissolving cracker in her mouth. A wafer. A small, round, crunchy disk of a wafer. A wafer slowly melting away on her tongue. Melting there in her mouth. Melting and melding. And becoming part of her.

Chapter Seven
Native Realities

Seeing with Open Eyes

The girl began to know that she didn't always see things, like the adults in her life saw things. She began to see things with opened eyes. It wasn't anything that happened all at once. It wasn't like she woke up after a night of dreaming and knew something that she hadn't known the day before. It was here a little, there a little, one thing adding together with another that caused her to look with new eyes at her parents' and teachers' and other big people's opinions. All she knew was that with every passing day, she became more aware of what she thought all by herself, without any of those big people helping her.

She didn't like to fight with other people. It wasn't her style. If she said that she had a differing opinion, it was sure to get her into trouble. Heated discussions with Mother were a real nuisance. When she was smaller, it was what her mother said, or what her father said, that gave her a lot of her ideas about what to think. But just like she had outgrown her two favourite pairs of shoes last summer, now she was outgrowing her parents', her teacher's, and her uncle's thoughts. She could see that the adults were very sincere about what they told her. They seemed convinced about what to think. They should be allowed to think what they wanted to think. But sometimes, she didn't agree with them, and she wanted to think about things the way that she thought about them.

She was like the State in which she lived. It was a wild country. Alaska, with its peaks, frozen tundra and clear skies was an untamed place. The animals were feral out in the wilderness areas all around her. In her heart, Georgina was a rustic, feeling happier being outside rather than inside. She somehow knew that no one would ever really be able to tame her. Try as they may, they'd never succeed. The girl just plain was the way she was. Whoever God had made her,

Georgina was stuck with it. Stuck being herself. And to top it off, she had the audacity to feel that it was her right to possess her lofty thoughts, which, like Mt McKinley, were pretty immovable. Her frozen looks when she disagreed with the guidance she was given, confirmed her mother's worst fears about her offspring. The child was just stubborn and difficult. Anyone could see that. The child saw as control, much of what was said to her.

'She's too young for such strong opinions. I just wish for once that she could accept what I say and leave it at that, instead of arguing with me all of the time. Why can't she be as sweet and good as Gretchen?' She overheard her mother telling her father.

Frustration was all that the girl ever seemed to bring to the relationship. Again and again, it was the same old story, like a broken record skipping and skipping as it ran over a scratch on its surface. Her daughter's ideas about clothes or her choice of friends or her strange lack of embracing of the family's religious ideology, was a continual burden on the woman's heart. To her mother's heart. Mother's determination to try to teach the girl to be more lady-like seemed, quite frankly, like a lost cause. This renegade girl, her future would certainly bring her troubles a plenty unless she could be less vocal about her opinions. Her ideas were too radical for the times she lived in; when being a tomboy was the worst insult you could give a girl.

Always being reminded that she was a girl, and therefore certain ways of being were unacceptable and to be discouraged, only added fuel to the fire in the heart of such a strong-willed child. Georgina Jane didn't see that being female should limit her. Her little girl body was all she knew. And at that young age, she never realized its significance to who she was, who she must be. Be because of the dust and water that contained her. The child only knew that having fun was the most important thing. But Mother had other ideas. Seeing her daughter sitting spread eagle to play jacks was something Mother felt was unlady-like. It made no sense to the girl. Winning was what mattered. Picking up the most jacks while the ball was bouncing was what mattered. To her mother, it was a vital part of her education to teach the girl to keep her knees together at all times.

This never made sense. That was just the way things were, no explanation given, except that it wasn't lady-like. Like I've already explained to you that Mother always kept Georgina at an arm's length away from her. Why did it feel like her mother did not really love her? Why should she always be the one to change? Why did she feel that she could never please this woman who was held up on such a high towering pedestal in the girl's heart?

After she saw the movie, a recurring dream frightened her. In her nightmare, her mother kept turning into the Ice Queen. The Snow Queen kept a child locked away in her cold, cold kingdom. The girl would wake up and think about her dreams. She would reason with herself. She must be confused in her dreams. Mother washed and curled her hair. She washed and ironed her clothes and polished her shoes. Mother gave her food to eat. But the child had a vague feeling of uneasiness about her mother. It was something she could never put her finger on. May be that wasn't her real mother after all. Wouldn't your real mother love you for who you were?

Sometimes it felt like a dense fog on the mountains that you could fly into and never find your way home again. Was her mother mad at her because Daddy loved his little girl? It felt like Mother was nervous that Daddy would love his daughter better than he loved his wife. If Daddy called the girl one of the pet names he had for her, 'Punkin', 'Snickers' or 'Brown Eyes', the girl sensed that something was wrong in her mother's attitude. The girl saw the look on her mother's face. It was not a happy look.

It was almost like Mother became a little girl again and wanted the girl's daddy to be her daddy too. It was almost like Georgina wasn't allowed to have a daddy. It was like Mother wanted Daddy all to herself and didn't want to share him with his daughter. If her daddy made the girl feel special, it was clear that Mother didn't like it. Georgina Jane wasn't really allowed to feel special in her family.

The girl felt that her mother would go on and on and on, repeating the same things over and over again, like Georgina was an idiot. Did her mother really think that she hadn't heard her the first time? Did her mother think that she was deaf or stupid or something? Didn't the woman understand that her daughter just didn't want to argue with her? But giving her mother 'the silent treatment' never worked. Occasionally, Georgina would frown, but her mother would always scowl back at her, not willing to lose the power struggle. They were like two children, trying to stare down the other one. The one who looked away first was the looser. It was a game that the girl, though she knew she could stare longer, could never win.

Double Trouble

Her twin sisters, especially Katrina Josephina had it easier. No one ever got the better of Katrina and lived to tell a happy tale about it. No one had ever really successfully controlled the seven-year-old. Even Daddy sometimes felt it was a hopeless job, a lost cause, trying to control that particular child, Katrina. But a semblance of respect for a larger man, especially one in a uniform, was a cruel and loathsome necessity to the kid. And she usually knew better than to cross Daddy. If he told her off, she might want to protest, but she knew that she had to deal with it quietly, at least for the moment. Until she got the opportunity to rattle the man's nerves again at another later moment in time, she would just have to bide her time.

Georgina could only tell her sisters apart because Katrina Josephina was usually the brattier of the two. Gretchen Gabriela was usually sweet and easy to get along with, as long as Katrina left her alone. She could look into those two identical faces of her sisters, like two peas-in-a-pod, and tell who was naughty Katrina Josephina, and who was good little Gretchen Gabriela. Katrina Josephina always looked at her older sister with that I can do what I want to. You can't make me be good look. Being as bad as she possibly could be always made Katrina Josephina happy; because that girl knew her sisters, and her father hated it.

Katrina Josephina could not be controlled by any one; even Georgina Jane's firm and determined father had a hard job trying to do it. That girl was so strong willed she wouldn't even stay in her bed and go to sleep at night. She just wanted to stay up all of the time and be as bad a girl as she possibly could be. One time, when he couldn't take her insolence any longer, Daddy had even tied that girl's ankles to her bed with a diaper, just to keep her in. She screamed and screamed and screamed until her little voice was nearly all gone. It was like torture to her big sister to watch that bratty girl being so naughty. It was agony to listen to Katrina Josephina screaming her head off until she got her way or fell asleep, which ever came first. She was so naughty, that even in her sleep she did what she wasn't supposed to do. From an early age, that girl went sleep-crawling as a baby, and was sleep-walking as soon as she could stand up unaided later on. All through the house, nearly every night, Katrina Josephina prowled their house like a disembodied spirit, like a homeless soul, looking for that place of rest that obviously eluded her. It had been hoped that maybe Katrina'd sleep better at the new house in Alaska, but she still, even there, gave her parents a hard time at bed time.

But the twins' popularity gained them an unchallenged advantage with their demure mommy. No matter how bad their behaviour was, or what they got up to, Mother would always pretend to look the other way, rarely even scolding them. Georgina could see her mother smirk to herself, trying to stifle the laughter that was trying to bubble up inside of her. The worst punishment she would dole out to them, was to thump their pale little foreheads lightly with her middle finger. Occasionally, she might even make them stand in the opposite corners of the living room. But that was only to reinforce their understanding of Arithmetic. The one who counted to one hundred could leave their corner first. Mother prided herself in teaching her children to count. Every time they encountered a step up or down, they had to count out loud. That was supposed to make learning numbers fun and easy to remember.

Another punishment, on occasions when Katrina Josephina and Gretchen Gabriella argued, was to tell them to sit on the floor in the hallway and make them stare into each other's faces. But this was more a game than a punishment to those two argumentative girls. It wasn't long before they were deliberately making funny faces and crossing their eyes which produced peals of laughter and uncontrollable giggling. Mother would wince and say to them, "Don't cross your eyes like that, Katrina Josephina. They'll get stuck looking cross-eyed and you'll look that odd forever. You look very peculiar, Gretchen, when you make that face. Now please stop that right now. Do you hear me?"

But Katrina Josephina loved to make stupid faces, just to be the center of attention. That girl could do so many interesting things with her deceptively sweet-looking face. She could cross her eyes, roll her tongue, make a fish face by sucking her cheeks in and moving her lips. She could even pull her upper lip up and make it stick to the ridge underneath her nose. She was multi-talented. That was obvious. If she wanted to make funny, odd-looking faces, there was no stopping her.

Mother loved the twins' blond hair. Georgina knew that her mother hated her hair. Georgina had a thick raven colored head of hair. Her father loved his daughter's hair. And he told her that hair was called 'pelo' in Spanish. He said that his child had hair just like his own hair, like the wild Indians on the Plains. Those Indians who used to shoot their bows and arrows and kill the buffaloes for their families' dinner had hair like that. Mother didn't like it when Daddy told Georgina Jane that she had lovely hair. It made Mother mad.

Mother had always cut Georgina's hair very, very short, from the time she was a baby. It was strange to think that a girl had to be lady-like with such short hair. But remember that those were the days of flat tops and crew cuts for boys. Georgina's father had so much wild black hair, that he had to force it to be tame by putting gobs and gobs of *Brylcream* all over it. That was the only way Daddy's hair would stay down on his head in a neat hairdo. Otherwise, it would be uncontrollable. Her little brothers looked like copies of Daddy with his clean-cut army haircut. Men and boys wore their hair combed straight up on the top and then slicked back and held in place with that sticky *Brylcream*, which made their hair very shiny, like waxy patent leather shoes.

In Alaska, because it was so cold, Georgina's mother didn't cut the girl's hair so short. Katrina and Gretchen had worn their hair in pigtails since they were about two years old. But Georgina had to wear her hair in a style her mother called a 'pageboy'. The girl couldn't understand why she had to be so darn lady-like with a pageboy's haircut. So finally, when they found out that they were moving to Alaska, Mother let Georgina wear her hair longer, almost touching her shoulders.

From an early age, the girl knew that clothes and hairstyles were very important things. These things said something significant about a person. How you wore your hair, or what clothes you dressed in, said who you were and what group you belonged to. Clothes and hairstyles were like a kind of army uniform. They kept people in line. Ears had to be checked for grime every day. If a child's ears had grime behind them, or inside of them, it reflected badly on their Mommy and Daddy. Having ears full of grime meant that you didn't have very good parents, and that you were a very dirty child. Shiny leather shoes with clean soles were important too, especially as army brats, when kids had to look presentable. Every child in her family had to learn to polish their shoes like Daddy did to his army boots. These were routine things that had to be carefully checked on a regular basis.

One escape that the girl had from such a regimented lifestyle was a very funny television show. It was called 'The Three Stooges'. It was the funniest show ever made in the history of the whole wide world. That show captivated the girl. She would howl with delight and laughter when the boss of the three stooges, Mo, would poke his fingers into Curly's eyes. It was funny that they

265

even called him Curly, because he had no hair at all on his head. Curly was like the hairless bear called, *Fuzzy Whuzzy*. Curly was totally bald-headed. Those three Stooges would make Georgina laugh so hard that she'd nearly wet her pants right there in front of the new television set! Sitting there on the floor, in front of the new television set, the girl would rock back and forth and double over in hysterical laughter. Oblivious to anything or anyone else in the whole wide world, Georgina almost went into the television set where *The Three Stooges* lived. She could run around inside of the new television set with those funny hilarious three guys, pulling hair, poking people that she was mad at in the eyes and doing all sorts of crazy stunts too. Like those *The Three Stooges* did crazy zany things. She thought that it would be very funny to poke someone in the eyes who annoyed her too.

Katrina pulled Georgina Jane's hair. Katrina Josephina was like Mo hair pulling Larry, the other one of the three stooges' hair. Georgina hated that. Getting your hair pulled really did hurt your scalp. That was the only thing wrong with growing your hair long. If you had longer hair and a bratty little sister, like Katrina Josephina, your head would hurt a lot. With longer hair, Katrina had more to get a hold of if she was impatient with Georgina. Sitting in front of Katrina, and blocking her view to the new television, was sure to get Georgina's longer hair pulled really, really hard.

Ain't Learnin' Fun?

Her teacher, at the school her parents sent her to, could sometimes be cross and angry with the children. That nun reminded the girl of that crazy old woman who lived in that big old ugly shoe in the nursery rhyme her mother used to say to her when the girl was little. Obviously, that nun just didn't know what to do with all of those children in her class. Since she was so crabby and mad, like that woman in the shoe, that nun tried to stomp on those children's imaginations in order to control them all of the time. Except at recess.

At recess, the girl was free. At recess, the children could run wild and play any game they wanted to play. Georgina liked to play jacks and *Hop Scotch* the best. And she loved to jump rope, counting every time she jumped high up in the air, to escape that rope touching her ankle. When she jumped rope, her feet left the ground. Jumping rope was almost like flying for an instant. For a second or two, she was suspended above the earth, unattached to anything holding her down. She'd be up in the air, momentarily suspended above all of the trauma of trying to learn things in that classroom. Things that seemed impossible to understand. Maybe being crabby, like that nun could be, made it hard to explain things in a way that children could comprehend them.

When her teacher got cross and angry, she thought, *That's not a very good way to teach little children. Little children shouldn't be yelled at like that, to try to force them to learn things. There has to be another way to teach children things that they don't know yet.* When it was her turn, during a Spelling Bee, or her teacher would try to make her recite her multiplication tables, she just silently stared at that tall, grave, serious nun in that strange outfit. Georgina knew that nun would not even give her time to think about the answer, before she got angry with the girl for not answering quickly enough. So, she would just stare at Sister Margaret Mary. And then, she would look away, and give up trying to think about that nun's question. She'd just shrug her shoulders in resignation that punishment and disapproval were going to come her way. Not knowing the answer quick enough, was a federal offence in Sister Margaret Mary's classroom.

Not knowing the answer quick enough meant that the girl's name would be written on the blackboard. Having her name written on the blackboard meant that her teacher was publicly disgracing her, making her feel less of a person. Spelling words, or knowing her multiplication tables, were far more important to her teacher, than the girl's thoughts and feelings about words or numbers. Because numbers and spelling were too hard for the child to be able to give a quick oral answer, having her name written on the blackboard was her teacher's way of controlling her ability to think in a way that would make Sister Margaret Mary's job easier. Having her name written on the blackboard, meant that something was terribly wrong with the girl's mind. Writing her name on the blackboard was meant to 'mark' the child, making her feel all the more incapable of learning.

If writing the girl's name on the blackboard didn't get her message across to the child, Georgina had to take a note from her teacher home to her parents and get them to sign it. Her parents had to be cajoled that way into making their stupid daughter learn things she couldn't seem to learn. If the note wasn't signed, corporeal punishment would get Sister's point across. Making her parents sign that note, meant that not only was her teacher against the girl, but she was getting Georgina's parents involved. Sister hoped that they would feel so ashamed of their daughter's poor performance in school that they'd be mad at her too. That way, all three adults could be against the child at once. They were meant to be like a crowd of bullies gathered around her on the playground, threatening and menacing. She had better learn or else.

Numbers and Spelling seemed like Mount McKinley to the child, unscaleable, unreachable. Numbers and Spelling were like giant mountains looming up in front of her, making her feel incompetent and incapable. Her teacher's attitude towards what was only later recognised as her dyslexic tendencies, made the girl feel like she was a deficient human being, without value and worth. Learning these things seemed like an immense impossibility to the child, a trial of her stamina, which had to be borne patiently and compliantly.

The girl's only way of fighting the system was to at least act like she was a 'good little girl'. It was obvious, even to Georgina, that little girls had few rights in the world she lived in then. Since she wasn't a 'cry-baby' like her little sister, Gretchen could be; she endured the ridicule quietly. It was only her penetrating, steady, piercing, stare that got her point across. Her disapproval was measured by how long she could stare down the adults in her path. The road to learning, and realizing her personal dignity, was a long one, with lots and lots of obstacles in her way.

Along that road to learning, the girl would meet a number of trolls, like the one *'The Three Billy Goats Gruff'* in her storybook, faced. The troll tried to keep the billy goats from crossing over the bridge. Sister was like a troll. Education could feel like forced feeding in the hands of the wrong person. The girl knew that much. If writing her name on the blackboard didn't make her remember her Spelling list, or learn those numbered equations then Sister told Georgina that she would have to write 'lines'.

'I will learn my multiplication tables. I will learn my Spelling words.'

The girl had to write these sentences one hundred times. Over and over and over, she wrote the same sentences. Each time she wrote those lines, she would say to herself, 'I will **not** learn my multiplication tables! I will **not** learn my Spelling words!'

Sister would give her another one of those corporal punishments, if writing lines didn't work. The nun would find another way of 'marking' her, other than writing her name on the blackboard, or singling her out for the pointless exercise of writing lines, which even the child knew would do nothing to increase her ability to understand Mathematics. Public humiliation was the name of her teacher's favourite game. Georgina understood the rules of that cruel and inhumane game very well, whether she could comprehend how to multiply 6x6 or not. That ruler on the back of her hand really, really hurt. But it still didn't make her learn how to spell or memorize how to multiply numbers until she was darn good and ready to learn those things.

Maybe she'd never be ready to learn those things. Never ever ever. Never ever, even in her whole life!

The girl sometimes felt that nothing she did was good enough for Sister. So, she would just look out of her classroom window and think her own thoughts. She would think about what a cold, grey day it was. She would think about how she could be skiing down a mountain, rather than trying to answer Sister's questions. In her thoughts, she could fly far away from that nun in her funny hat, with all of that tight, stiff, black and white fabric wrapped around her head and neck so tightly.

Sometimes Sister, in her black and white habit, reminded the girl of her family's black and white station wagon. That Pontiac and the nun were both the same colors. The only difference between that black and white car, and Sister, were the tiny black and white hairs coming out of the sides of that nun's helmet. Seeing those short curly hairs was funny. Those naughty hairs would not behave themselves. They wanted to escape that teacher's efforts to control them, like the little children who were in that nun's class wanted to. Those hairs, like the girl, had a mind of their own. Even Sister could not make those greying, black and white hairs stay in their place, underneath her habit. Seeing those hairs, made the girl want to laugh out loud. But she knew that Sister would not think that it was funny.

Sister could not laugh at herself or anything else. She took herself, and her job, teaching children, far too seriously. And so, the girl smiled to herself, just to cheer herself up a little bit, while she waited for the bell to ring. When the bell rang, she could escape her teacher's stern looks and displeasure. When the bell rang, that meant that it was time for the girl and all of the other children to fly out the door of their classroom. When the bell rang, they could go to recess, or go to lunch or, even better, get on the bus and go home.

In the morning, on the way to school, she almost always had a tummy ache. But on the way home, she could relax. On the bus home, Georgina could read and read and read. Reading was much more fun than sitting in a classroom and contending with Sister Margaret Mary. When she read a book to herself, she could fly away to other places, and not let anything or anyone bother her. Flying away, inside the covers of a book, was the best thing about leaving school in the afternoons, when she took the long ride home from Fairbanks to Fort Wainwright. On the bus home, it would get darker and darker and darker under the grey, gloomy, evening skies. That was the only bad thing about taking the bus home, the ensuing darkness of the winter's early dusk. It was hard to read in the dark. And it got dark way too early in Alaska's mid-winters.

The only thing that she could do when it got darker was to close her Nancy Drew book, and think. Thinking her own thoughts was pretty good, like travelling to a faraway land where the fairies lived. In that fairyland, she could imagine what it was like to be loved unconditionally, and accepted as she was. Even if she had a hard time in the other world, where the big people lived, in fairyland, there were no giants besetting her. In the other world, adults ruled the children, sometimes not too patiently or kindly. But in fairyland, children could be free to explore the world on their own terms.

The adult world was different then. In that world, children were on the outside looking in, except during playtime and recess. But in fairyland, no one had to learn how to spell so many hard words, or memorize those awful multiplication tables. And if they did have to learn those difficult things, teachers would be patient and kind to them, while the children worked on such hard jobs. If they were slower learning those hard things, teachers would give the children all of the time that they needed to find the answers, without making the children feel inadequate and stupid.

Escaping into her world of imagining, was not without a price tag. She knew that thinking her own thoughts did not always make her very popular. That was the price she had to pay, for thinking her own thoughts. Sometimes people didn't like it if she thought her own thoughts, and not what they wanted her to think. She knew that. She knew that she had to keep her thoughts to herself. She knew that sometimes her own mother could almost see her thoughts, even though the girl was silent about them. Looking away from Mother was not a safe place to escape to. She was told to keep her eyes on her mother's face, whether she wanted to think Mother's thoughts or not.

'Look at my face when I'm talking to you, Georgina Jane,' Mother would say, as she tried to make the girl see her point of view.

It had never occurred to Mother that if she would take the time and sit and help her daughter to learn the multiplication tables, the girl would appreciate the time and effort taken. But no one understood about dyslexia back then. And the girl, because of her difficulty learning certain things, was an embarrassment to her mother. Like a lot of other kids, Georgina was treated as though she was just plain stubborn and unwilling to learn. How this wreaked havoc with a child's self-image didn't concern people then. Only later did they understand that frustration would permeate so many lives, causing them to feel eternally deficient. Generational gaps, even chasms, developed over this inability of some children to learn fast enough, if ever.

The girl kept hoping that it wasn't true that her mother didn't even like her. It was so hard to understand how someone's very own mother wouldn't like them. So, the girl tried to convince herself that it wasn't true, that her mother did like her after all. She often told herself that she would be liked if she could just agree more often. If she could just become someone else, someone more like her mother, then Mother would be happier with her. Scaling that mountain would take a lifetime, like climbing cold, tall Mt McKinley. Would she ever succeed in becoming that more acceptable person, that better, more likable person her mother wanted her to be?

When Mother would keep repeating herself to try to force the girl to look at her face, it annoyed the child. Her mother was like Curly, who annoyed Mo, the boss of the three Stooges, so much that he nearly got his eyes poked out!

That mother of mine has to have an audience, or she can't even speak, the girl thought to herself. Her mother didn't like it when Georgina looked away from the woman when her mother tried to speak to her 'about something serious'. Georgina Jane O'Shaughnessy started not to even care. Even if it was 'serious'. It might be 'serious' to her mother, but that didn't mean that it was 'serious' to the girl. She had to look away from her mother's face. If she looked at her mother's face, then her mother's facial expression would try to dominate how the girl felt. By the look on her face, Mother was trying to control her daughter. She was telling her child what she was allowed to think. The girl knew that she was only allowed to do certain things, and was not allowed to do certain things, but she preferred to at least think what she wanted to think. She did not want to think what her mother thought about everything. She wasn't concerned, even if these things were 'serious' to her mother.

"Georgina Jane, you've got to learn your multiplication tables, or Sister will be very upset with you again," Mother said in her lisping voice, not knowing how to speak properly, because her tongue was too big for her mouth. But her lisping words, said so seriously, and the long duration of her sombre conversations about education only made Georgina want to burst out laughing, and Mother would definitely thump the girl on the head if the child did that. Sometimes even laughing was against the law.

But the girl didn't like those tricky numbers, and she couldn't care less if Mother or that crabby Sister Margaret Mary got upset with her. Sister getting upset with her was the one sure thing the girl had learned at school. And the girl didn't like that Sister Margaret Mary's attitude one little bit. That teacher of hers, didn't know how to make numbers interesting. So, the child wasn't interested either. Georgina was a stubborn child, and once she made her mind up about something, there was no going back to change it. She had learned about standing still in her opinions and could just look away or pretend that she was Mt McKinley in the disguise of a little stubborn obstinate and immovable girl. At those times, the child's opinions were inflexible.

"You still can't tell the time, Georgina Jane. Aren't you interested in time? You have to learn about time sometime," her mother said repeatedly.

Mother's Little Girl

But time felt shorter, like it had shrunken away to almost nothing in those long winter months. Georgina would rather ignore time, until the summer sun was shining again. Maybe next summer, she would learn to tell the time.

"Mother, I want to wear blue jeans under my dress, not those dumb scratchy snow pants. My friend gets to wear jeans underneath her dresses. Why can't I wear jeans?" she would ask her mother.

In the wintertime, dressing was a major problem. The girl chaffed at her mother's taste in clothes. Her mother's rules about clothes were unbendable, like they were set in stone. Wearing blue jeans was against the law in her house. Her mother would not change that law for anything. She had already told Georgina Jane that back in Kentucky.

"Only poor people wear blue jeans. It's what farmers wear. Jeans are not for ladies to wear. So, you can't wear blue jeans under your dresses. Period. Now I am not arguing with you. So, don't ask me again."

The girl didn't like to hear her mother talk about jeans like that. One of her best friends, Afton, an Eskimo girl at her school, wore jeans under her dress, to keep her legs warm. She seemed all right, and she didn't live on a farm either. Georgina would rather have cold legs, than to wear those dumb old snow pants that matched her coat. Mother didn't think that certain colors, when they were put together, matched each other.

"Purple and orange do not go together, Georgina Jane. You can't wear that outfit. It doesn't match. Take it off and wear the clothes I've laid out for you."

She thought that her mother treated her like she was her mother's little dolly, always wanting to dress her up in clothes that her mother thought were cute, but which the girl hated. Her mother thought that the girl looked so adorable in those woollen blue snow pants, with their matching coat and bonnet. And even if that outfit that her mother wanted her to wear was blue, a color the girl liked, those snow pants were not at all like the blue jeans that she wanted to wear. She couldn't stand those snow pants; they were scratchy and itchy. Sometimes she thought that her mother was wrong about what she thought about things, like jeans and food.

To the child, sometimes her mother's face was like those 'low clouds' that her father had flown into, and lost his way in the mountains of Kentucky. Georgina felt that she could get lost in her mother's face. She felt that her mother tried to dominate her thoughts by that face of hers. The girl didn't like to argue with her mother, so she just looked away. She didn't even say a word to her mother. She was trying to let her mother have her own thoughts too. But she did not like it when her mother told her what she was allowed to think. So, she'd shrug her small shoulders and go back to her dresser drawers and put another ensemble together.

"Those clothes don't match either! Pink and red do not go together!" said her exasperated mother.

With the men in her life, she started to know that it was different. Men were easier to keep happy, because they didn't often tell their thoughts about their thoughts. Even her uncle, who had taught her so much about toilets and walls and whale blubber and the Eskimos, things like that; even he was away with his important job too often to tell her too much.

And her daddy didn't like to tell her about that airplane crash and how he felt about it. Her father still thought that she was his little girl and would believe anything he told her, just because he was her daddy. So, she let her father make-believe that she still believed him about the Indians. She knew that there weren't even any Indians up there on that mountain in Kentucky. She knew that those Native Americans, as they had yet to be called, were on the reservations, not on that mountain where her father's plane had crashed.

Because her mother must have been a little girl once, and must have known that little girls have to be able to think their own thoughts, the girl knew that she couldn't fool her mother. Her mother knew that the reason why she looked away from her mother's face, was because, that way, Georgina could think whatever she wanted to think, and not what her mother wanted her to think. If she had been more like Katrina Josephina, always just wanting to have her own way, then Mother would have let her alone. Her mother didn't fight with Katrina. Katrina had always thought her own thoughts. Mother knew that it was hopeless to try to tell Katrina Josephina much of anything, because she had never listened to anyone but herself. And Gretchen, the only other girl in the family, was just happy looking into anybody's face.

She knew that her mother felt a need to control her daughter. But when her mother said something to the girl that she didn't like to hear, the child just looked away from her mother's face. She didn't think that looking away from Mother's face was a bad thing to do. But when she looked away, her mother got the message. Her mother was a smart lady about most things. She knew that when her daughter looked away, it was because she didn't like what her mother was saying to her. Mother didn't like it when the girl looked away. Mother hardly ever got really, really mad at her. But when that girl looked away from her mother, who was trying to make her think the way she thought, and not like the girl wanted to think, it made Mother mad.

"Look at me when I'm talking to you, young lady!" she said, almost spitting when she said it.

Mother only called her a *young lady* because she had heard the girls' father call Katrina a *young lady* so many times. Mother thought that she could try this out on Georgina Jane, like her father did with Katrina Josephina. Her mother thought that she could make her daughter think what she wanted her to think, and not what the girl was already thinking. But it hadn't worked on Katrina, even when her sometimes stern father said it. And it wasn't going to work on Georgina Jane, to call her a *young lady*, when she wanted to think her own thoughts. The girl knew that now that she was nearly nine, she was a big girl. And besides, her mother didn't even ask her what she was already thinking about something. Her mother told her that she had to share almost everything else, but she wasn't asking her daughter to share her thoughts, so that her mother could see things from the girl's way of thinking about them. Even if she did look at her mother, when she asked her to, her mother would still be mad at her.

"Wipe that look off of your face, young lady!" her mother would say to her.

But this, she found impossible to do. That *look*, that made her mother so mad at her, was all that the girl had to give to her mother at that time. That *look*, that made her mother so furious, was all that she had, that belonged to just her. But if her mother didn't want her to share *that look* with her, then she did the only thing that she knew to do. She shrugged her shoulders and she rolled her eyes. She was beginning to see that adults could be very difficult. Very difficult indeed.

Eskimos and Outgrown Shoes

The girl sometimes felt like the Eskimos must have felt with all of those white people living in their State. The Eskimos were in Alaska even before the Americans bought it from the Russians. The Russians had sold Alaska for practically nothing. They didn't know or care about all of the gold and rich oil hidden there. They didn't value all of that timber from those hundreds of miles of forests. The Russians didn't understand what they used to have in Alaska, just like the girl's mother didn't seem to understand who her daughter really was.

The girl knew that the Eskimos understood about color combinations. She had seen their exquisite fancy beadwork on the items in the Trading Post in Fairbanks. The Eskimos weren't shy about their use of color. They didn't seem to know the rules about which colors could be put next to other colors. Their art comforted the girl. They saw colors like she did. They wouldn't have disapproved of her choice of colors in the unrestrained fanciful outfits she tried to put together. Native art was free of her mother's constraints. The Eskimos, and the girl, heard a different voice. They saw things in a way unlike the disapproving voices that they sometimes heard.

In her mind, she had created another world, where people got along with each other, and didn't care if someone peed on the ground, or threw their toilets out into the snow. In the other world in her mind, blue jeans were just fine. Because if she could wear blue jeans, then she could hang upside down on the monkey bars at the playground, without her underwear showing, when her dress fell over her face.

Even then, she began to question her elders. Were they really her betters? She wasn't sure they always understood things clearly. Sometimes they were just too serious and rigid. Maybe they were too busy to think about the things that she thought were important. Big people didn't think that kids knew too much.

They wouldn't have listened to a little eight-year-old girl like she was, who might have had a different idea than theirs.

It made the child unhappy to hear, that because some people were different from her family, they were wrong. She realized that the world was a place where some people were different. But in her mind, that was okay. She didn't tell her uncle about her feelings though. When he told her about those Indians and their toilets and their walls, somehow she just knew that he wouldn't understand how she felt. Maybe it was because of the boarding school, or his relatives from the swamp. But when her uncle talked to her, and she didn't like what he said, the girl didn't even bother rolling her eyes.

When she was younger, Georgina Jane had met the Eskimos. They had tossed her up, up, up, high into the clear Alaskan skies, on their blankets of sewn together animal skins. They had taken her for exciting rides through the snow on their dog sleds, pulled by their frisky husky dog teams. They were a refreshing and exuberant people, full of the joys of just being alive. They knew how to work together to survive. The men would hunt for seals, fish and walrus, or even big whales in their kayaks. The women would stay at home, and cook Eskimo food, and sew all of those animal skins into clothing or blankets to keep their families warm.

The old grandmother Eskimos would chew on those animal skins, to make them nice and soft for their baby Eskimo grandchildren. Those old grannies nearly chewed their poor, old front teeth down to nothing, by gnawing on those animals' skins so much. The more that they chewed on that leather, the more supple it would become. The Eskimo grannies' lives were important. Who else would love their families so much, that they would grind their teeth down to almost nothing, just to make softer, more comfortable clothing? And the most amazing part was, that the Eskimo grandmothers peed on the tough animal skins to use their own urine as a fabric softener. That was before they then chewed on those wild animal skins afterwards.

Those Eskimo women were tough ladies and true feminists in a time when only people like Virginia Wolfe had really understood about such things. Native women in Alaska didn't talk about being feminists. Words didn't matter so much. They were interested in other things. Other things like cooking and sewing and sweeping out their husband's hunting trip igloos or the family's log cabins. Other things like chewing on animal skins. Those Native women had plenty to do to keep them busy. Their days were full with the job of taking care of their families. The Eskimo women helped their men smoke that delicious salmon, that the girl's uncle liked so much. The Indian women made fur parkas. They wore their little babies on their backs. Little Eskimo babies looked so cute inside of their mamas' parka hoods lined with all of those soft Alaskan bunny pelts. If they had to take them outside in the cold Alaskan winter weather those little Eskimo babies would stay extra warm that way. Their tiny black eyes would poke out from behind their mothers' heads, trying to find a way to see the world their own way too.

How could the Eskimos be wrong, just because they wanted to pee on the ground instead of into toilets? Her uncle hadn't even listened to the Eskimos' reason for throwing those toilets out into the snow, just like Mother never asked her why she looked away. If Mother had asked her why, then she would have known. Maybe the government should have asked the Eskimos what kind of houses they wanted, before the government spent all of that money that her uncle was so mad about. Maybe it was really the government's fault about the walls and the toilets, and not the Eskimos' fault at all.

The girl had worn the shoes the Eskimos made, called mukluks. In the winter, all of the neighbourhood dogs had barked and followed her home from the skating rink when she wore them. But she ignored those barking dogs like she sometimes did with her teacher or her mother. Those mukluks were made of seal skin and rabbit fur, and tied with the sinews of caribou. To the girl, they seemed like magic shoes that could attract attention and make her feel special. Those Eskimo shoes, that Manga, her grandmother, had bought for her at the Eskimo Trading Post, were like enchanted shoes. Those Eskimo shoes could give the girl special powers. They kept her feet warm too, with all of that bunny fur sewn inside of them by those Eskimo ladies, who sewed like her Manga did. Georgina didn't realize why the dogs were attracted to her. She didn't know those dogs were drawn by the smell of the leather skins, and not to her. Not to her, because of who she was.

The Eskimos' practicality and use of animal skins to make their clothes seemed to be the best way to dress in Alaska. They caught so many animals to eat and use for sewing into clothing. If those animals could stay outside and live in that cold, cold place, think what their fur would do for people? The Eskimos had reasoned this out in their minds. The Eskimos knew how warm and durable animal skins really were. Seal skins, wolverine, deer, fox, rabbit pelts and even bear skins gave them a variety of textures and outfits and shoes. Wearing those skins on their backs, and covering their toes, would keep them warm as toast. Wearing those skins was sensible. That way, the Eskimos and their children wouldn't freeze when they went walking in the snow.

During the previous summer, the girl and her cousins went to craft classes given by the Eskimos at a local YMCA. They taught the children to string beads and sew the beads onto leather. They beat their drums and sang Eskimo songs for the children. They showed them tiny carvings they had made from the tusks of walrus. Everything those Natives did seemed magical, and fascinated the child. In her eyes, they could do no wrong. Those different people liked their drums and the cold Alaskan weather, like the girl did. They had so much courage to live in a place as cold as Alaska. She liked them. And she respected them and their ways. She knew that it wasn't easy to be in a place like Alaska.

Her uncle might not approve of the Eskimos, but she thought that they were very exciting. And so, a love of hand-crafted things was birthed in the girl that summer. She saw the value of the Eskimo's way of life and the beauty of the things that they made. Their artistic things, things made with their own hands, made the Eskimos feel better about life. From their giant totem poles, to the tiny ivory or jade carvings, everything they touched became almost like magic to the girl. She was especially drawn to their beaded work and carefully stitched and sewn garments and unusually beautiful apparel. These people spoke to her heart. The Eskimos whole way of life seemed surrounded by beauty and purpose and meaning. The girl liked their simplicity. And as a child, without realizing it, she identified with their humility.

They explained the way they lived, as though it was the only way that they could survive the harsh climate and the lonely desolate regions in Alaska. By and large, Eskimos still lived separately from the new Alaskans. They had their own lonely spaces, far from the booming new centers where the whites lived. When they did integrate, they were looked on with some degree of fascination, apprehension or perhaps even fear. Theirs was a frosty, icy, frigid world. A sometimes-desperate world. A world where snow had to be melted, just to wash their dirty dishes. The girl knew about the Alaskan weather. She had survived that last winter too. When the temperatures dropped to seventy-two degrees below zero for a whole week Georgina was there. She was there. There. Living there in Alaska with the Eskimos. She was a member of the 'Seventy-two Below Club' in Fairbanks. And she even had a badge to prove it. She was very proud of it and kept it pinned to the front of her parka.

Those Eskimos had to huddle together as families to keep warm. And they couldn't afford to get cold bottoms sitting on all of those toilets. That's probably why they threw all of those unwanted toilets out into the snow. No one asked them if they liked those houses that the government for the Bureau of Indian Affairs built for them. The government agency had specially designed houses that the Eskimos didn't like too much. They didn't like those houses any more than the girl liked her mother's choice of clothes for her to wear. The Eskimos were forced to live in houses they didn't like. The girl was forced to wear itchy snow pants. It was kind of the same.

But just because the government tried to make the Eskimos live in houses they didn't like, those Native Americans made it clear to the bureaucrats their true feelings about those houses. The Eskimos made their opinions perfectly clear to those house builder guys. The Eskimos did more than look out the window, or shrug their shoulders or roll their eyes, like Georgina Jane O'Shaughnessy did. Like Georgina Jane O'Shaughnessy looked out windows at school that year. Like Georgina Jane O'Shaughnessy shrugged her shoulders when her mother or her teacher got on her nerves. Like when they got annoyed with her. Like Georgina Jane O'Shaughnessy shrugged her shoulders when she felt that the situation was hopeless. Hopeless. Just plain hopeless. Like Georgina Jane O'Shaughnessy rolled her eyes and shrugged her little girl shoulders to let people know that she was unhappy with them. Like she knew that they were unhappy with her. Like Georgina Jane O'Shaughnessy, the Native Alaskans did not believe in putting up with what to them was nonsense, without a show of protest. So, the Eskimos let their feelings be known to the government. They made it very clear what they thought about those unwanted, unliked houses. On the day when the Eskimos deliberately trashed those houses, the government, and everybody else in the whole wide State of Alaska, were left in no doubt whatsoever about the Inuits' feelings about the brand spanking new habitations built especially for them. The Eskimos remodelled those houses that the government made especially for them. They remodelled those houses to be what they wanted those houses to be. Not houses that the Bureau of Indian Affairs wanted.

The government's agency built all of those houses with walls inside of them, keeping those Native People separated from their whole family. If the government had asked the Eskimos what kind of houses they wanted, then the Eskimos wouldn't have torn out all of those walls. The walls weren't there in the first place. The Eskimos were there, in Alaska, first. Maybe the government should have asked the Eskimos about what they wanted for their families. Maybe they should have tried to let the Eskimos teach them something, like the girl had done.

The Eskimos and her uncle reminded Georgina Jane of her grandparents speaking in Spanish to her father. She knew what it was like to hear people speaking a language that you didn't know. There were voices all around you, but they didn't mean anything if you couldn't understand them. She remembered her mother learning to drive, and not understanding Daddy when he tried to teach her feet to push the right peddles. Maybe the people from the government should just sit down with those Eskimos, like the poor black people in Kentucky, on all of those porches did, and talk to each other. Then the walls wouldn't have been there in the first place.

Those Eskimos and their beating drums, like the constant rumblings of the earth beneath their feet, had a certain feeling of sadness about their beat. The Native music was reminiscent of the tremors of the land itself, like it was trying to speak to you. The earth could quake sometimes in Alaska. Was it only the Eskimos who heard and understood the sounds of the earth? Sometimes, the girl would wake up in the middle of the night to the whole earth shaking, even inside of her house. It felt like someone was trying to shake her out of her quiet warm bed. She wondered if the rest of her family felt the earth move with its night time tremors. Or did they all just sleep right through it? Her house was usually so quiet and still in the middle of the night. She thought that she was the only one who noticed Mother Earth rocking all of those Alaskan babies in their cradles in the middle of the night.

You had to get used to the earth shaking in Alaska. That's what the earth did in Alaska. The earth did what her mother's congealed *Jell-O* did when you hit it with your spoon. It wiggled on your plate. The earth wobbled in Alaska. If the earth shook during the day, everyone would freeze, standing still until the earth stopped shaking. It was like that game the children liked to play at recess, *Frozen Statues,* where you had to momentarily stand completely still, just like you were permanently frozen all of the time. In a way, the Eskimos had been standing still for a long, long time in that frozen, shaking place. That place of earthquakes.

But even the Eskimos, who had lived there for such a very long time, were having to adjust to the ways of the new people in Alaska. The ways of the Americans, who had bought the Eskimos' home from Russia, were not the same as the ways of the Inuits. The new owners of Alaska, made the Eskimos feel that their old ways were not the best ways. The Eskimos were made to feel that they were like stupid children, who couldn't learn their multiplication tables or something else the government people wanted to teach them. Teach them about important things like toilets. Teach them about great room dividers like those walls the government insisted on putting up. Teach them about special things. White man's things. But even though the Eskimos had been doing the same things, living and surviving, the same way for a long, long time, their ways weren't always respected. The new people in Alaska didn't understand the Eskimos' old ways any more than Georgina Jane's mother understood her daughter.

The Eskimos' ways must change, or there would be problems. The girl thought that this might have made the Eskimos feel sad, like they didn't even belong to their land and ways anymore. Maybe that's what they were saying in their drumbeats and the sad moans that went with those Eskimo drums and songs. Like the Eskimos, the child was learning to wait for someone to listen to her. Even if her mother wouldn't let her wear blue jeans under her dresses, like her Eskimo friend at school wore them, she could pretend that those terrible snow pants were really jeans. She could make-believe. Even if her teacher at school, Sister Margaret Mary, would scowl down at the child's little face, and frown at her for not understanding her Arithmetic, the girl could survive, like the Eskimos did. The girl could beat her own drums, in her own little heart. And that would help her to be happy, being herself and thinking her own thoughts.

That was the year that Georgina Jane O'Shaughnessy outgrew two of her favourite pairs of shoes. There would be even more shoes to be outgrown. There would be shoes that didn't ever need to be polished. Shoes like her favourite mossy green suede pair. Shoes like her black suede shoes. Shoes that were almost identical to her green suede pair. Shoes that she loved. But shoes that her feet didn't fit into anymore. Shoes that made her feel that she was one of Cinderella's mean and ugly stepsisters, with feet that were too big to fit into her shoes. Shoes that would never fit her growing feet ever again. Shoes that she hated outgrowing. That growth would cause a feeling of melancholy in the child's soul. She could not stop her feet from out-growing those shoes, even though she loved those shoes so much. She wondered if she would ever have that feeling again, like when she had worn those mossy green shoes that were the color of the moss that grows in Alaska. That comfortable pair of shoes was gone now. She could not wear them again, and she could not even look at them anymore.

Her mother had given her two favourite pairs of shoes away, because they didn't fit the girl anymore. Her mother said that she had given the child's favourite shoes 'to the poor people'. Those shoes were probably given away to some poor Eskimo child with smaller feet than Georgina Jane O'Shaughnessy had. The girl wondered if that Eskimo child would love those shoes as much as she had loved them. She wondered if the new owners of Alaska could love Alaska like the Eskimos did. Transformation was something which could not be bound or halted. Time would not stand still. Impermanence and change were a part of life, which the Eskimos, and even that strong willed girl, could not escape.

Chapter Eight
Green Biscuits

Kid Stuff

She awakened to the smell of soft fluffy biscuits rising in the oven. What the aroma meant drifted into her subconscious even before she was fully awake. Saturday morning! Manga's here! The other children were already up and watching Saturday morning cartoons – their favourites: *'The Road Runner Show'*, *'Bugs Bunny'* and *'Little Lulu'*, followed by *'Mighty Mouse'* and then *'Mr. Magoo'*. Georgina Jane preferred the 'Three Stooges'. That was because she was older and more mature than they were. At the age of eight, she thought cartoons were beneath her. Being the eldest of five children, she was responsible for setting the example, and in her mind, keeping them all in order. Someone had to do it.

Mother was always busy washing and ironing their clothes, cooking their meals, or decorating the house by moving their furniture around and around to various new spots in their solid, but basic and unaesthetic army base home. Now that she was expecting her final child, Mother had to rest and take naps with the little kids. Mother didn't have time to make these children behave themselves. The girl's father always told his daughter that she was 'in charge' of things when he left for work. She was 'in charge' because Mother had to 'take it easy'. Being 'in charge' was her job, and her father's. But being a military officer, he had too many men under his command to be at home for enough hours to make his children obey all of the time.

And her sisters were always getting into fights with each other. Those two *'Blondies'*, like the lady on the comic strip with Dagwood, her funny husband, were strong willed. Gretchen Gabriella was strong in a quiet, but persistent kind of way. Her twin, Katrina Josephina was just out right naughty and loved being that way. Katrina would just as soon pinch, kick, shove, trip, pull your hair, as look at you. She'd jab you with her stuck-out elbow. She'd fart in your face. She'd spit in your hot chocolate. There was nothing Katrina wouldn't do to someone she was mad at. There was not too much subtlety with that girl. She always had to be top dog, the leader of the pack. It was her way, or no way at all. She was such a tough cookie, that sometimes Katrina would even bully Mother and make her own mother cry like she was a hurt little child. Gretchen, on the other hand, was nice to everyone for the most part, but she'd take no nonsense from her twin. And Katrina had a way of winding Gretchen up, and getting that sweet, usually quiet, girl's goat.

Sometimes, now that they weren't babies any more, her brothers, who loved to be buddies together, were even starting to fight with each other too, punching the other in the nose, tummy or the sides of their little faces. Peter Martin could really get on Roger Eugenio's nerves. That little kid was too placid and complacent for Roger's liking! And with his runny nose, which he was always picking by sticking his small fingers into his already inflamed nostrils, and then plopping the contents of his retrieval into his mouth, Peter could be a bit gross. That four-year-old boy just hadn't learned proper etiquette yet, and it showed.

Daddy had a funny poem that he said to Peter Martin every time he saw that kid pick his nose:

Peter is a nose-picker from a long time ago!
Peter eats his buggers ever so slow.
Eats them and eats them,
And that's why we say,
Peters picks his nose,
Wherever he goes!

Daddy encouraged the boys' boisterous, laddish behaviour. And to make matters worse, he was teaching those two kids to box. He had been involved in the sport of boxing when he was a teenager and in his early twenties. Now a captain in the army, he had no time for boxing himself. But he was so proud of his own accomplishments in the sport, that he was certain it was the best way to teach his sons to get along better with each other. He had won awards for his talent in the Golden Gloves, quite an accomplishment for a boy from a neighbourhood of mostly Mexican roughnecks who routinely practiced their fighting skills on each other's bodies inside and outside of the boxing ring.

So, Georgina's little brothers were being trained by their father to fight, and to fight well. It was an art form as far as Gene O'Shaughnessy was concerned. Boxing could teach Roger and Peter the agility that Daddy thought was a necessity for any growing boy, who was gradually growing into manhood by laying punches on his opponent's cheek bones. So, their father bought little miniature boxing gloves for those two boys and he would tie the gloves on to their small wrists and take them down to the basement to fight each other on top of a pile of Okinowan tatommies placed in the middle of the floor for just such a purpose.

The only problem was that those two kids didn't leave their fighting in the specially designed 'ring'. They transferred their skills of precise and trained punching of each other's body parts to any arena in which they found themselves. So, fights broke out everywhere in the house. No place was a sanctuary away from such violent scenes. Mother seemed to have no control whatsoever over the antics of her children. Mayhem and fighting were a constant in their household.

"When I grow up and have children," Georgina told them, "I won't let them behave as badly as you children misbehave."

Georgina knew about the word 'misbehave'; she'd heard her mother use it often enough.

"Stop misbehaving, boys. Be good for mother. No fights in the house," she'd say in her soft lisping voice.

On Saturday morning, while their parents slept in, the kids could do the unthinkable. They could watch cartoons and eat their breakfast in front of the television. When Georgina walked into the living room, she saw that first servings of biscuits with gloppy pats of butter and spoonfuls of strawberry and grape jam were already in front of her younger brothers and the twins. Plastic glasses of Nestlé's strawberry milk were half-full, with mouth marks on the rims and sticky pink finger prints on the sides of the glasses.

Roger Eugenio, who was five, had a heavy pinkish moustache on his upper lip. He ignored her when she slowly ambled into the room, stepping over his small child's body, wrapped up in his yellow blanket and stretched out on his belly on the carpeted floor in front of the television. He was engrossed by what that naughty Road Runner was doing. There was no way her entrance could distract him from such an interesting and engrossing bird, speeding along the vast southern roadways in search of new adventures.

The Road Runner made that annoying sound, *Beep! Beep!* all of the time. That bird was from the desert, from hot places like Arizona and Texas. Roger liked to act just like that big bird, who could run so speedily on the roads in those hot places, picking up his long legs in order to keep his toes from burning on those long and winding roads with their scalding hot asphalt and melting tar. With his skinny brown legs, Roger Eugenio was the fastest runner in their family. He was always running away as fast as his pencil thin little brown legs could carry him.

She was not an early riser like he was; he had been up for hours and was already wearing one of his favourite hats. Roger Eugenio was a collector of hats. He had a different hat for every occasion. Roger was always busy becoming someone he thought was powerful and important. Perhaps he wasn't really sure who in the world he was. So, he had to have the hat and also costumes to go with whatever his mood might lend itself to for the day's activities. Dressing up was who he was, always pretending to be someone important, so that he didn't lose himself in such a big family. Roger had a whole trunk full of every kind and style of hat imaginable. And since he slept with his clothes on, underneath his pyjamas, he could be ready to go outside at a moment's notice.

But not in this weather. Getting ready to go outside in the Alaskan winter involved a whole drawn out process. First, he had to wear at least three pairs of heavy woollen socks. Next came two tee shirts. Layer three was a pull over turtle neck. Then he put on a pair of long john thermal underwear, followed by a pair of corduroy trousers. And finally, his one-piece snow suit which zipped up in front like Daddy's flight suit. After he put on his snowsuit, with all of its accompanying paraphernalia of hats, mittens and scarves, he could go out to hunt bears with his brother and shadow, Peter Martin. But the morning's cartoons would keep those boys occupied for some time before they even thought about going out into the cold, deep snow.

Peter Martin, who was four years old, was sitting on the sofa, wrapped in a blanket too. Georgina could see his funny little kid feet poking out from underneath the covers. He usually had on his pyjamas with the snap on bottoms with their feet of rubber, non-skid soles on them. But today, he was wearing two unmatched socks, one green, the other blue. It didn't bother him. Her mother said that Peter Martin had a 'placid temperament'. She wasn't sure exactly what that meant, except that it must be true if her mother said it. What she thought her mother meant was, that Peter Martin couldn't care less about his socks. As long as he was looked after by everyone and anyone, he was happy.

He had been an adorable, cuddly baby. Georgina remembered how her mother had said that at the hospital when he was born, all of the nurses had cooed over such a gorgeous baby boy. Those nurses loved that baby, and they had called Peter Martin, 'Elvis'. This was because he had lots of dark black hair and long sideburns on the sides of his cheeks. He had fabulous eyelashes that framed his beautiful, hazel eyes. Even as a new born child, Peter was a wonder, an exquisite sight. She was surprised that Peter Martin was even awake yet, he was such a sleepyhead. But if Roger Eugenio got up, Peter Martin had to follow him. Wherever Roger Eugenio went, Peter Martin would be there. They did everything together.

Roger Eugenio and Peter Martin thought that they were 'tough guys'. That's what being little kids meant to those two. At the ages of four and five, they thought of themselves as mighty hunters, real he-men. They were intrepid and fierce. The fact that they had no facial hair or deep voices didn't seem to alter their impression of themselves as being the toughest of the tough.

Bear Hunt

Once, they decided to go out and 'kill a bear'. It had taken them about half an hour to put on their snow suits with the snapped-on mittens, their extra socks to keep their toes warm, and woollen scarves to wrap around their faces until only their eyes showed. Between the scarves and their ski hats, you could barely see their eyes; they were all bundled up, snug as two bugs in a rug, against the cold Alaskan day.

As the boys were getting ready to go out for the big hunt, padding themselves with layer after layer of protective garments – or rather, Mother was up, and she was dressing them – the boys talked about how big this doomed bear would be, how fierce it would look when they saw it. What enormous teeth it would have. How they would kill it with their knives, and stab it with their spears. That gigantic bear would not escape them. Of that, they were certain. No way would that grizzly bear escape their clutches and prowess at being hunters of savage, ferocious grizzly bears. They would get that big, gigantic bear no matter how tough that bear thought he was. They were tougher. They were mightier! And they were stronger! They were really going to get that bear! Grrrr Grrrrr!

287

Her little brothers seemed to remember a real bear, a giant stuffed grizzly bear which had made quite a considerable impression on them when they were taken to an airplane hangar on the army base, for the annual children's' Halloween party. They had been dressed, by Mother, as scary creatures with make-up added to their small faces to make them look more authentic. They even wore bonnets with ears sewn on to them. Roger Eugenio, with his dark skin and tiny limbs, was all dressed in red and was holding a long pitchfork. He was that wicked fellow, the devil. Peter Martin, who was still a chubby little boy, had been disguised as a black cat. His little dimpled face was painted with long black whiskers to match his long gorgeous eyelashes. Katrina Josephina and Gretchen Gabriella were also in disguise. That was the year that Katrina pretended to be an evil witch. Gretchen was a dancing girl. Georgina Jane was Miss Muffett.

Some of the costumes at the party were pretty frightening. She wondered why her mother would let those two little boys see such scary creatures. Wasn't she concerned that Roger Eugenio and Peter Martin would be frightened? Apparently not, because her mother proudly pushed the twin stroller, where the brothers sat enthralled with the excitement of the occasion, into the converted airplane hangar with its appropriate orange and black streamers and other seasonal decorations.

As if the costumes weren't terrifying enough, when Georgina Jane, her sisters and her brothers arrived at the entrance of the hangar, there was a gigantic grizzly bear standing erect, and larger than life. The taxidermied bear, preserved for all to see, had its huge arms with its sharply clawed paws, held out in front of its face and huge body. Its menacing teeth made her certain that she heard an audible sound from its ferocious jaws. Her heart stopped when she saw it. But how would this giant bear affect her little brothers? Fear was definitely an important ingredient to add to their fun. Fright, dread and apprehension were all part of their script.

Now she knew. This 'bear hunt', which they were so carefully planning, detail by gruesome detail, was the culmination of the effect of the bear in the airplane hangar. It was enough to give small children nightmares for years. She had wondered that previous Halloween why her mother didn't seem to realize how scary these things were to her own children. But these boys knew how to attack even bears, and to act out their fears from an early age. Admitting fear was impossible, fears had to be hunted down and killed, like the target of their bear hunt would be.

For the hunt, Peter Martin would take a long stick and stab and stab the bear they were planning to kill to make sure that the grizzly bear was really and truly dead. Roger Eugenio had his gun holster strapped on to his skinny waist, now padded out with his snowsuit, tee shirt, turtleneck, and two sweaters. He looked very *rolly poly* in all of that snow gear. He just knew that he would shoot that fearsome bear and then Peter Martin would stab it and kill it dead.

Poor bear! Poor, poor bear! Those boys would stab it and stab it with their plastic knives and Peter Martin's 'spear'. Then they would skin it. After that, they would bring home its skin, and somehow drag its heavy carcass, to Mother who, judging from the girl's innate knowledge of her mother's facial expressions, did not look overjoyed at the prospect. By now, Georgina Jane and her mother were feeling sorry for the bear whose fate was sealed. A bear who was about to be killed so gruesomely by these two small boys, might run away when it saw them chasing him. They had so graphically described the intended pursuit of this giant ponderous hulk of a beast, that it seemed a sad fate was sealed for the lumbering, but large creature they planned to return home with that very afternoon.

When Roger Eugenio and his shadow and sidekick, Peter Martin, finally did go out the front door to 'kill a bear', they had worked themselves up into a frenzy for their planned attack. But once outside they stood silently shivering and motionless, frozen, not with cold, but with dread. They stood outside on the front porch, too afraid to move or to speak for a moment or two. It was obviously too awkward to admit to your own brother that you didn't have the courage to kill a bear. Within three minutes, the hunt was off. The timorous little hunters had frightened themselves so much, with all of their bold talk of the prospective 'bear kill', that they had scared themselves stiff. Their sister watched them through the window.

She had worried that her own mother had let these two small 'hunters' brave the cold alone. Her own mother had even encouraged this bear hunt, by listening excitedly to her brother's wild speculations about this proposed tracking down and slaughtering of one of Alaska's biggest and most fearsome beasts. How could her mother allow her own children to face an immense bear unaccompanied? Wasn't the woman even concerned for the safety of her own children? Where was Mother's protection of her progeny? Did the potential slaughtering of her own offspring by a huge bear not terrify the boys' mother?

The boys stood there, in all of their winter garb, in the freezing cold arctic temperatures, all by themselves on the front porch, looking at each other and obviously wondering what to do next. For what seemed like an eternity, she watched her two little brothers on the porch. Would they brave the dazzling white neighbourhood, as she herself had done so many times on her own walks through the snowy adjoining fields in her own searches for sightings of wildlife? Would they even be able to really find a bear today? Did real bears even live in their neighbourhood? They discussed their options. Should they stay on the porch? Or should they go out beyond their snow laden front yard, out into the wilds of Alaska? Out in search of that giant scary bear?

But no, thankfully they couldn't face the reality of a prospective bear kill. She watched as they rang the doorbell and timidly asked Mother, "Could we come back in, please? It's too cold to kill a bear today. We'd better wait until it's warmer to kill a bear. We'll kill a bear another day."

"All right," her mother had said, not wanting to offend their male dignity. They had done their best. They had proven their powerful young manhood at least in their minds. And back into the warm living room, they came. They were safe and sound. The 'bear kill' could wait for another day when they were older and maybe a bit braver. The two small 'hunters' enacted what they thought grown up men had to do. Hunting was what the Eskimos in Alaska did. Proving yourself by some feat of daring, even killing, was important to them.

Women were different. The girl was beginning to see that. Mothers and grandmothers didn't want to go out and kill big old scary brown, black, white or grizzly bears. Mothers and grandmothers took care of small children, cooked the food and cleaned the house, while the men went out and battled with the elements to bring home 'the bacon'. Even the Eskimos used this idea to survive, so it must be right. Sometimes the Eskimos and the old-timer Alaskans, the Sourdoughs, might even eat bear meat if they had too. But she had heard that bear meat was very greasy, so she didn't know if she would like it too much with all of that bear fat in it.

The Eskimo ladies stayed home and sewed warm clothes for their families and cooked Eskimo food and made pretty things. Those Eskimo ladies could make wonderful, soft clothes, even out of rough animal skins that their husbands and sons brought home to them. She had seen a few of the old Eskimo grandmothers, whose teeth were worn down from chewing on the skins to make them softer for their little grandchildren. After those tough Eskimo men had killed the animals, who the skins used to belong to, the ladies and old women had a hard job, working on all of those killed things to make nice, soft skins out of them.

The girl knew, was just beginning to know, that boys and girls were different. Mommies and Daddies were not the same either. She realized that if her brothers had an Eskimo Daddy, he would have taught them how to hunt and kill a bear, or some other wild animal. The boys in the Eskimos' villages went out into the cold especially to hunt with the men. Those boys would kill, kill, kill! If they got the chance, some wild creature would be brought home to their mothers for food or clothing. It was something in their blood, the need for more and more blood! Georgina knew that ladies were not the same as men and boys. Ladies didn't want to kill bears and see all of the blood and guts spill out.

Season's Greetings

She knew that her mother liked pretty things. That was part of her mother's job, being pretty for Daddy to look at. Dressing up when Daddy took her out to church or to the Officers' Club, was one of the things that Mother did best. Daddy had even bought her mother a musical jewellery box with painted flowers, to keep the treasures he gave to her in it. That jewellery box played a Japanese tune. That was Mother's special box from Okinowa where Katrina and Gretchen had been born. Her mother had lots of jewellery, some of it from Alaska. The jewellery from Alaska had pearls on it and some was made from jade. She had a sterling silver bracelet with a big black diamond on it. Manga gave Mother a necklace with water and gold nuggets in it, and a ring made with three kinds of Alaskan gold. Some of her mother's jewellery was made of ivory by the Eskimos. Mother wore clipped on earrings when she got dressed up to go to church or to a party at the Officers' Club.

Christmas was an important time for getting dressed up and looking nice. Even Mother's house had to look nice and get dressed up for Christmas. At Christmas, Georgina Jane and all of the 'little children' got to help their mother decorate the house. Her mother got an Advent calendar for them to open every night. And on December the sixth, when it was St Nicholas' Day they could put their shoes out in a row for St Nicholas to bring them each a little present and some candy. They had a nativity scene with baby Jesus and Mary and Joseph, the angels, the shepherds, the three wise men and also a few of the animals. The 'little children' could play with the nativity scene made out of fabric characters.

291

But they weren't allowed to touch the breakable scene, because like Georgina Jane, Mother had learned that the 'little children' broke things.

One year Mother, who tried to be practically perfect at everything she did, got little gold stars and meticulously strung them on strings of various lengths.

"I'm going to string these stars up in the hallway so that the little children can see them for Christmas."

The girl knew how special stars were to Christmas. At church and at school, she had learned some Christmas carols that told everyone all about the little star of Bethlehem, lying so still and silent up in the dark sky where there was everlasting light. They sang about the star of wonder, star of light, star of royal beauty bright, guiding people with its light. She sang about how the stars in the sky looked down on sweet baby Jesus when he put down his sweet little head on the day he was born. She even knew that Jesus had his own special star at Christmastime when he was born. That's how those three wise men found the baby Jesus in his manger, and brought him some nice presents, like kids got if they were good boys and girls. Not having stars at Christmastime would be like having a very dark cold time of year, not a celebration when you really needed it.

Mother had lots of friends who also had husbands in the Army, the same as Daddy's job. Sometimes her mother would make special meals for her friends that were 'not for the little children to eat'. Her mother might let Georgina have a taste of what she cooked for the luncheons for the army wives. Georgina could set the table and put the tiny little pies with smoked salmon or things too spicy for 'the little children' on the dining room table. Mother had ironed the green and red and white tablecloth very carefully. She had pressed special seasonal napkins used only at Christmastime, because they had a special Christmas flower on them, called a poinsettia. Mother had bought special Christmas candles for the table setting.

Every year, she'd make a wonderfully delicious cheese ball with grated yellow Cheddar cheese, cream cheese and Worcestershire sauce sprinkled into the blend. Then Georgina got to help roll the somewhat sticky cheese ball around in sunflower seeds that stuck to the cheesy mixture. That cheese ball was eaten with tasty crackers that she put in a circle around the cheese balls for her mother.

There were peanuts and cashews on a pretty ceramic dish. There was Mother's special fruit salad that she made every year, with mandarin oranges, grated coconut, walnuts, tiny marshmallows and bite size pieces of pineapple all stirred together. There was roast beef wrapped in a pastry Croat, or ham for those who didn't eat kosher. There were roast potatoes and roast carrots. There was broccoli and frozen peas cooked to perfection. There was celery soup and hot soft rolls with curled pats of butter.

There was a relish tray with curly carrot sticks, radishes, dill pickles and sweet jerkins and celery that had cream cheese stuck on it, were all arranged carefully next to the black and green olives. Things like that were served to Mother's guests. The 'little children' didn't like the taste of olives, but Georgina loved them. Every year she got a jar of olives in her Christmas stocking and she ate the whole jar before they even had their breakfast.

A pine tree, cut from one of Alaska's forests was center stage in the living room; all decorated with breakable ornaments Mother had collected on her travels with the Army. Manga had helped the twins string popcorn she had popped especially for the tree. The boys got to put silver tinsel strips on the tree as long as they did it carefully, and not in gloppy handfuls thrown on all at once that stuck to the higher branches in clumps. The youngest person in the family got to place the special Christmas tree star on the very top of the tree, being lifted up by their daddy high up over everyone else's heads to do it.

And every year, Mother and Manga would make new ornaments using seasonal cookie cutters shaped like circles for babbles, drummer boys, peppermint candy canes, angels, stars, triangle Christmas trees, reindeer, Santa's face with his white beard, and Santa carrying a bag full of toys and presents to come down the chimney. Every year, they'd make salty hard flour and salt dough ornaments and bake them in the oven and paint them with the children. After the ornaments were painted, Manga would varnish them with smelly shellac down in the basement. The ornaments had been baked with wire stuck into them before they went into the oven, and so they could be tied with string or have hooks put through the wire to hang them on the tree.

Windows were decorated with lights and stencils sprayed with fake snow. Everyone in the family had a Christmas stocking with their name embroidered on it. Those stockings were hung in a long row next to the fragrant pine tree. Soon they'd be filled with small goodies and stocking stuffers that were almost more fun to get then the big Christmas presents of new dollies and their houses and new dresses, socks, underwear and ribbons for the girls' ponytails or braids. Santa thought of everything a kid could possibly want and brought it year after year. Somehow, no matter where the Army had moved them, Santa still always found them and brought bag-full of gifts.

One time, one of the army wives brought her children over to their house to see the Christmas decorations in the O'Shaughnessy's house. Georgina was supposed to play with her mother's friend's children. But she didn't like these children. They made her nervous because they were so wild and unruly, misbehaving every time they'd come to the house. They were even worse than the twins and her brothers. But her mother told her that she 'had to be nice to them' because their mother was her mother's friend. The girl just knew those children would do something naughty when they came to her house. She had seen them in action before, and she knew what they were like. Her father wasn't even going to be home, so there would be no one there to yell at those naughty children when they came over and did something bad.

The smallest of that woman's children was a naughty little boy. You could see it on his face. That kid always sassed his mother, talking back to her in the rudest voice possible. It was appalling! That spoiled brat ran wild in their house from the minute he got there. He liked to break things even more than her brothers did. When that bad kid saw those stars that Mother had hung up so carefully, he went wild. That boy acted like those stars were put up just so that he could attack them.

He started charging back and forth in the hallway and jumping up and down so that he could hit Mother's stars. Mother had pinned the strings holding the stars to the ceiling. She had hung them at different heights so that they were almost like the soon expected new baby's crib mobile, hanging over the baby bed waiting for the new baby's arrival.

Georgina had seen the expression on that kid's face. Even before he had attacked Mother's hanging stars, the girl could read that bratty boy's thoughts. She just knew that he was on the verge of doing something really terrible and unruly. That uncivilized, undisciplined kid jumped and jumped and jumped. Every time he jumped and jumped, he would hit Mother's stars with his chubby little naughty hand.

The girl thought that he was perhaps the most disgusting little brat she had ever had the misfortune to meet. He was an uncouth, moronic rascal. He was a total scallywag without even trying. How her mother could be friends with someone who had such an awful child, she would never know!

Finally, when those people left, Mother saw what that boy had done to her stars. Her stars were a big tangled mess. All of the strings were wrapped around each other. The Christmas stars would all have to be completely taken down and then restrung. That boy's mother had seen him do it and she didn't even try to stop him. She even smiled at his mischievousness in a coy smile that Georgina caught out of the corner of her eye. That boy's mother encouraged the kid by her silence and her smile that spoke to her son's heart and told him that it was okay with her if he wrecked the place. That lady must have been jealous of Mother's Christmas decorations. That's why she had let her child act in so badly a destructive manner.

The girl was so relieved when those people left. Nothing could have made her feel happier at that moment when they walked out the front door and it was firmly shut behind them. Now she hoped that her mother would never let those people come back again. She thought that her mother should have listened to her in the first place. She knew that lady's kid was up to no good before he even arrived.

Back to Baking

But it was Saturday morning, and Manga was there. She could bring order out of any chaos. And Georgina felt sure that Manga wouldn't have allowed her grandsons to venture out, into the cold, under a grey Alaskan sky, to kill a bear. Manga wouldn't let bad little boys tangle up her strings or act badly. Manga had a way of making the girl feel protected and sheltered. Nothing much ever seemed to faze her grandmother, but if she was pushed, she could react in a way that put everything back in order. Manga was very calm about everything, but she'd stand for no nonsense. Everyone respected her, though she never raised her voice, hit anyone, or belittled them.

She didn't let problems get to her, even though her life had been pretty hard, from what Georgina Jane knew of it. All of her thirteen grandchildren loved Manga. Nobody had a bad word to say about her, she was so good-natured. Sharing her was a hard thing to do. Everyone felt better when their grandmother was around. Somehow, without even really trying, the woman's calmness permeated everyone she was around. The kids just all wanted to please her. She took care of them all.

That's why she had moved to Alaska with them. She had to help Mother, who Manga said 'had so many children'. For some reason, her grandmother always looked sideways at the kids' father and smiled, when she said that. Georgina wasn't sure why. In her child's mind, she thought that the reason her parents had so many children was because she was the household queen, and her sisters and younger brothers were there to wait on her. The wish of her heart was that 'the little children' were born to serve her. It was one of her favourite things to think about.

But this was all imaginary, none of them actually waited on her at all. She was the one who had to help her mother with them, because she was the oldest. That was her job, being the oldest. Another one of her jobs was 'mating socks', which she hated. She wasn't sure why her mother said that socks had to be 'mated'. What was 'mating' anyway? She just knew that she didn't like the job of putting 'the little children's' socks into matching pairs. They seemed to have dozens and dozens of pairs of socks. It was a never-ending job.

"Good morning, sweetheart!" giving the child a tight hug, said Manga as Georgina entered the kitchen, still feeling a bit groggy.

"Did you sleep all right?"

The girl nodded.

"I was waiting for you to get up, so that you could help me make some green biscuits. Would you like to use the cookie cutter?" handing the sleepy girl a large four leafed clover-shaped cookie cutter.

"Why are the biscuits green, Manga? How did they get to be so green? Did you make them green?" she asked her grandmother, as she looked into the large mixing bowl half full of sticky dough which had a distinctive green tinge.

Her grandmother showed her a tiny plastic bottle of green food coloring which she had stirred into the Bisquick baking mix. Her grandmother entrusted, what seemed to the child, like a magic bottle, into the palm of the child's hand. It felt smooth against her skin as she held it.

"Squeeze a few more drops into the mix to make it greener," her grandmother told her encouragingly.

The idea of making green biscuits fascinated her. She liked colors; she had made a color wheel for the Science Fair at her school. She liked the way the colors on her color wheel had turned magically into a white blur when the wheel was rapidly spun around. She had carefully set her wheel up on the table at school, after painstakingly coloring in the triangles, which formed a circle of colors. It was amazing that the 'wheel' had survived so far. She had been afraid that the twins and her younger brothers would break it, before she even got it to school. They had been fascinated by the colors which turned into a blur of white the faster the wheel was spun.

Roger Eugenio and Peter Martin had wanted to spin her color wheel again and again and again. She just knew for sure that they would break it. They were always breaking their own toys. But she had been told that she had to share. She was the oldest and had 'to set a good example for the little children'. How many times had she heard that? It was something that her parents drummed into her, like the monotonous tone of the Eskimos' drums. But why did setting 'a good example' have to jeopardize her color wheel? She just knew that they would break it, after she had worked so hard getting the colors just right, keeping inside of the lines. Those little kids didn't seem to know the meaning of the word 'gentle'. And it seemed that nothing really belonged to her, everything had to be shared. But she was used to it by now. It was just the way her life was. Sharing her color wheel was just part of it.

"The biscuits are green, because today is March 17, St Patrick's Day!" said Manga, who had walked two miles in the snow to take care of Georgina Jane and the other children, so that her parents could have one morning to sleep late.

Usually, Mother woke her up early for school. It seemed like the middle of the night then, because the sun was still asleep when she and the twins had to get ready for school. Her mother always said a poem to the girls to help them to get up so early in the cold and dark Alaskan mornings.

A birdie with a yellow bill,
Hopped upon my window sill,
Cocked his tiny head and said,
"Ain't you shamed, you sleepyhead?"

Every morning, it was the same, except on Saturdays, when the girl could sleep late. But it was hard to sleep late when your sweet old Irish grandmother has walked over to your house for miles in the freezing cold, especially to see you and to fix your Saturday's breakfast.

Cold Feet and Life's Lessons

The child worried about Manga. She was afraid that Manga would fall over and hurt herself on the slippery ice. Her grandmother had already fallen over three times, dislocating her shoulder and breaking two fingers once in the process

297

of pointlessly trying to stop her fall. Once she really hurt herself and had to wear her arm in a sling until it stopped hurting. But Manga was not afraid of anything. She'd never complain about the cold or about her broken fingers wrapped in gauze and stiff wide Popsicle sticks to hold them still. And Manga didn't seem to even feel the cold. It would be thirty degrees below zero, with ice and snow everywhere you looked, and Manga would go outside in the snow to pick up the newspaper for Daddy, wearing only a short-sleeved shirt, and sometimes in her bare feet.

"Manga, put your coat on! It's freezing out there!" the girl would say.

But her grandmother brushed the child's worries aside. She found the cold bracing. She had discovered that the ice energized her tired old system. Manga's the one who taught the girls to lie on top of the snow and wave their arms up and down and make snow angels. Manga had never lived in any place she liked better in the whole wide world. She liked life better in Alaska than anywhere else she'd ever been before.

Manga would get together with her friends and go to their Indian sweat lodges and old-fashioned saunas and get all hot and stuffy. Then those old-timers would race half-naked out into the frigid Alaskan blizzard-like conditions. They'd rub the frosty snow all over their shrivelling, shivering, half nude bodies. Some of her rickety, doddering pensioner friends would even lie down in the frosty conditions and come up with a coat with ice sticking to their still sweating bodies. That was to stimulate their blood flow, before their next retreat into the sweat lodges for more warmth. Then the whole cycle of sweating heat and invigorating, stimulating cold would start all over again.

Manga told her granddaughter all about her wild, unrestrained rompings. The girl knew all about her grandmother's escapades in the snow. All of those exposed old people, out in the freezing snow with very little in the way of clothing on, must have been quite a sight! It was a pensioners' group who went blueberry picking together. They rode on rafts and canoes down white-water rivers. Those retirement age persons were fearless of the cold. They were like the girl's grandmother, who thought that the snow invigorated her. Manga said that the snow stimulated her circulation and she just loved it.

"Oh, I'm not cold, Georgina. It's a dry cold. See how powdery the snow is?"

And Manga would pick up a handful of snow to try to make a snowball. But the snow would just fall from her grandmother's hands, like the Bisquick mix into a bowl for making biscuits. The snow would not even make a snowball, because the air was so dry in the middle of Alaska's winter. They'd have to wait for a fresh snow to make another snowman with fresh, wetter snowfall.

"Manga, can we go ice skating after breakfast?" she'd asked her sweet old Irish granny.

"Of course you can, dear! I'll come to watch you and the twins," said Manga.

The twins, Katrina Josephina and Gretchen Gabriella, had double blades on their ice skates because they were still little. But Georgina Jane only had a single blade, because she was able to keep her balance better than those little sisters of hers. All of the girls had white skates. Georgina had really wanted black ice skates. She thought that black was a better color. With all of that snow around, you could see black skates better when you looked down at your feet on the ice-skating rink. But Mother told her that only boys wore black ice-skates. So, she had to wear white skates because white skates were more 'lady-like' than black skates.

Manga made some hot chocolate in a big insulated thermos, and brought some blankets, four mugs and a bag of marshmallows and freshly baked chocolate chip cookies to the skating rink. After Georgina, and the little girls, skated round and round, in the cold Alaskan winter air, on the frozen pond close to their house, they went into the cozy skating hut with its warming heater. Once inside, there would be hot chocolate poured over marshmallows that melted in their mugs. Manga thought of everything! The girl's feet were like blocks of ice after doing all of those figure eights, and skating around the rink a dozen or more times. Even wearing two or three pairs of heavy socks, her feet still got cold. Her feet felt like they were frozen solid after half an hour.

"Take your skates off, Georgina Jane, and I'll rub your freezing toes and warm them up for you. Your little toes are just freezing!" Manga would say.

Taking off her granddaughters' socks, Manga would rub and rub. Georgina's socks had changed from the pliable soft items they once were, full of warmth and comfort, to something else altogether. They had become stiff and cold, hard as rocks. Manga would remove them and put them close to the heater to defrost her granddaughter's socks. Then she would rub and rub and rub life and warmth back into Jane's frozen solid feet and toes, as the girl sat on one of the benches that lined the walls in the cozy shack for the kids who skated at their neighbourhood rink.

Georgina thought that her toes were just frozen stiff and that they'd remain that way forever. She'd never be able to wiggle her toes again. Toes were important. Losing a toe or two to frostbite would have been disastrous! Toes were all important members on her young body. Toes were significant, and not to be lost due to the devious and insidious work of Mr. Jack Frost. She could pick up things with her toes. And she could even pinch that naughty Katrina with her toes, if she pulled Georgina Jane's hair. So, as Manga rubbed and rubbed, Georgina and Katrina Josephina and Gretchen Gabriella sat all bundled up in blankets and drank in unison from the mugs of nice hot chocolate with marshmallows floating on top of the comforting brown and white potion.

Walking home with Manga, she would ask her grandmother about what it was like when Manga was a little girl. Manga was one of the few adults the girl knew, who would take the time to talk to her. If she asked her grandmother questions, Manga would always have an answer. Somehow, even with her job at the little PX, all of her zany friends, and all of those thirteen grandchildren; Manga somehow made the girl, and each one of her grandchildren, feel that they were the only person in the world. Manga made you feel validated, before that became the popular thing to do to someone insignificant.

Manga knew how to make a child feel unique and important, without having to do much. She was a good listener and a good talker. George knew that Manga had had a hard life, but Manga never felt sorry for herself. She was a very unusual woman. She was a model for the women of her generation.

"Remember I told you about when I was a little girl? We lived in the countryside, in Pennsylvania. My parents had moved to America from Ireland to find a better life. We lived out in the country close to a farm. My brothers and sister took care of the cows, and they used to let me ride on the back of the cows when they took them back to the barn every evening from the fields. The cows wore bells around their necks and we would make a ringing sound, all the way home. My brothers and sister took care of me because my mother died when I was only three years old. My sister, Rose, was the eldest. She was thirteen when Mother died. She took care of me and the other children. We had a big family too. There were nine of us in my family.

"My father worked so hard to feed us. Every day he went down into the coalmines, deep inside of the earth. But when I was just fourteen, he got sick with emphysema. (Manga pauses here to sniffle. Must have been the cold.) That was a very hard time. For a long time, we tried to make him get better. But he just coughed and coughed and coughed. He had been down in the mines for too long for his lungs to clear. All of that black dust had done irreparable damage to him. When my father died, we didn't know what we would do without him.

"My older brothers had to work in that same mine from dawn to dusk. They would be so tired when they came home. And dirty. Black as soot. But my sister took care of them. She taught me to read, sometimes by candlelight. She worked hard milking cows and washing and sewing and doing odd jobs so that I could go to school and study. We always had food to eat and a place to live, so we were lucky. My brothers and my sister taught me about what hard work really meant. They didn't get the chance to go to school and study because the only way we could all live was if they kept their jobs. They worked hard so that I could study and go to school. Did you know that I even went to college?"

Georgina couldn't understand how anyone would get to not go to school. Going to school was mandatory. Compulsory education had been legal for many years by then.

"I finished college in the 1920s. I was one of only two girls who were in my graduating class that year. I studied Pharmaceutical Sciences. But a few years after I finished at school, and by then had a job, everything in the country turned upside down. Lots of people were poorer than we had been and didn't even have food to eat. Some of them even lost their homes and their jobs.

"During that time, it was called the Great Depression; lots of people were out of work and they had long lines of people waiting in the cities, just trying to get a bowl of hot soup and a piece of bread. If they hadn't had that level of subsistence, I don't know what they would have done. Lots of people had to leave their homes and travel the country trying to find work. Some of them even lived in cardboard boxes, or 'tin cities' as they used to call them. The country was in a bad way back then.

"In New York, the Stock Market where lots of people had put their money had crashed, leaving lots of rich people penniless. They were very, very poor then. My sister, Rose had taken care of me and she gave me a good start in life. I don't know what we would have done without her."

"Is your sister, Rose, the one who taught you how to make green biscuits?" Georgina asked Manga, hoping that she would find out more family secrets.

Manga told her so many things that she wanted her granddaughter to know about. Most adults didn't have the time, or disliked questions from a child. It was like they seemed to resent children, who took up enough of their time already. But when you are a child, there is so much to learn, and so few people who can tell you what it felt like for them to be little once and to grow up. Were these big people ever even small? And did they even think about life when they were children? Did anyone answer their questions, or were they ignored?

Later in her life, the girl realized that generational gaps, when they are made, are sometimes made from the top down, from a constant pushing away of the young. The young naturally look up to the older generation. It could not be bottled. But when she had her own children, she knew that patience was an essential ingredient to the recipe of family life, like the green food coloring was to Manga's green biscuits. Without patience and communication, there would be difficulties which gained momentum as time went by. Without these essential ingredients, family life would disintegrate, and rifts would exist which never should have been there in the first place.

Love and understanding just came naturally to Manga; it was who she was. She never pushed the girl, or her other grandchildren away. She took the time to talk and to explain about life and green biscuits to them. Her dialogue was a vital strand. Because of it, they'd understand what life used to be like in the olden days. They'd be grateful for what they had. They'd know that sometimes the older generation had had such a hard time when they were growing up, that they lost patience with the younger generation, who had everything handed to them on a silver platter.

But if these hard times were explained to them, the next generation would understand. The kids would know down deep who they were. They'd know where their people came from. They'd feel connected to, not separated from the older generation. They'd feel linked even to the dead, who had already left the planet and taken up their eternal abode somewhere else. A thread of awareness would continue to be woven with that knowing.

Through her example, Manga taught the girl that generational gaps and dissension in families were not naturally part of nature, or inherent to human design. Being appreciated, like Manga cared for her children's children, gave them a sense of their own essentialness. Their self-worth came from their grandmother's care. Appreciating those too young to understand about their own history, much less about the history of the older generation, helped them to value themselves.

Unless they were carefully taught, children could not understand the pains or joys of the preceding generations. Manga knew how to communicate with her grandchildren. She understood their innate needs. She knew that learning to make green biscuits was a very important recipe for Georgina Jane to remember all of her life. Looking into her granddaughter's little face, which lit up whenever the girl saw her grandmother, Manga just smiled and gave her granddaughter a big bear hug.

Chapter Nine
Under Cold Alaskan Skies

'And now there came both mist and snow,
And it grew wondrous cold:
And ice mast-high came floating by
As green as emerald.

And through the drifts the snowy cliff
Did send a dismal sheen;
Nor shapes of men nor beasts we ken –
The ice was all between.

The ice was here, the ice was there,
The ice was all around;
It cracked and growled,
And roared and howled
Like noises in a swound.'

excerpt from The Rime of the Ancient Mariner
by **Samuel Taylor Coleridge**

It was the wild rabbits that signalled the changing of the seasons for Georgina. She could see them as they scampered about here and there, munching on the vegetation and shedding their summer clothes only to don snowy white coats instead. This was one of the mysteries she saw during those years of transformation. Season led into season. She was beginning to realize it, and saw the truth of the flux of time in her childhood. It was part of the magical quality of her life at that time.

Time was donning wings and beginning to 'fly by', as she heard someone say. She conjured up a picture in her head of a clock with the wings of an airplane. Time became almost like a tangible substance to her. She felt that she could hold each moment in her mind, shut away in a great labyrinth of mystery, beauty and the joy of her own wonderland out in the Alaskan great outdoors. Every day there were new discoveries to be made, unspoilt sites to see. The place where she lived was marvellous and stimulating. Every day there was so much to find out about and to see for herself.

The joy of the moment was always with her, except for the times when she felt sad. Her knowledge of adults meant that she could see their sadness, as though it was a discernible substance. Sometimes the oppressiveness of the adults' depression affected the child greatly. It was like a weight that they put onto her young and inexperienced shoulders. She thought that they used their sadness to try to keep her from flying. Their depression or unhappiness was like an anchor to the child's soul, making her feel motionless inside. Their despondency had the effect on her of making her feel anchored in a deep sea of melancholy emotions.

Her only escape from the rigors of family life was her time spent walking in the unspoilt wilderness near their home, where she could clear her head. It was during those treks that she saw the rabbits, who ran past her with the speed of lightning. Foxes couldn't catch them. But even the foxes changed color to become like snowy chameleons in the forest. Wolves could turn white too, but she hadn't seen them in real life, only in pictures. She wondered how the rabbits and other animals knew when it was time to change colors to hide themselves in the snow or turn back to browns or reds in the summertime. She kept forgetting how to tell time, numbers were so confusing to her. But these animals were clever. They knew when it was time to change.

Often a feeling of isolation would creep over the child like a veil or fog. Growing up so far north, where it was cold for so long, and winter winds bit her cheeks making them red and raw if she didn't smear them with *Vaseline*, and where the cold stiffened her fingers if she forgot her mittens, was not always easy. Unlike her younger brothers, she did not have her mittens snapped on to the cuffs of her jacket. So sometimes, she lost them. She knew that pockets were the only thing that saved her from certain frostbite. She had heard frightening stories about people lost in the snow whose fingers or toes blackened and just fell right off of their bodies. Her own sister, Katrina Josephina, had nearly lost

305

her tongue because of the excessively cold temperatures, before the girl's sister understood about the dangers of what the frost could do to you.

The family's black and white station wagon, with its red interior, was parked out in their driveway, blanketed over every night with heavy covers and a heat lamp underneath its hood run from an extension cord to the house, in an attempt to spare the car's engine from freezing solid in the night time temperatures, which plummeted way below freezing every evening. Her father had started the engine to warm it up in plenty of time to get the automobile going.

He would leave for work soon. He had his dress uniform on today because of a meeting with the colonel and he had to look his best. The girl thought that he was a handsome man and she was proud to have him as her daddy. He was a captain and had lots of shiny pins on his dress blues. He wore a special navy-blue hat with gold braid over a black bill in front, and gold braiding going around twice on the main part of the hat. That army hat even had a red line going right around the middle of the gold. It was a very flashy hat, or so the girl thought.

Daddy had to look his best for work. All of his uniforms were heavily starched and had to be sent to the cleaners to get the job done just right. His shoes were always very clean and shiny. He let his daughter help him polish the brass pins. Her brothers helped him to shine his heavy boots. They used to hide their toy cars in those boots, because they were such good hiding places with their high sides.

One morning, as he was getting ready to go to work, her father had removed the blankets and heat lamp from above and beneath the car's chilly bonnet, and started the car's engine. Georgina Jane's younger sister, Katrina Josephina, was fascinated by the small icicles that stayed on the car's fender for most of the winter. Katrina was always trying to pull the icicles off of the bumper of the car. She was too small and not strong enough to pry these solidly frozen popsicles off of her dad's car. Georgina's sister really wanted to eat those icicles.

On one of those freezing cold mornings, Katrina's impatience got the better of her. The girls had been put out of the house, like cats let out for a pee. They were supposed to be walking with the rest of the Catholic kids in their neighbourhood, to the school bus stop. In a flash, before Georgina could stop her, Katrina got the bright idea that she could just lick the flavour off the icicles, like they did in the summer with flavoured popsicles or iced lollies. Instantly, her wet tongue was stuck to the ice. Screaming out in pain at the grabbing cold against her pale pink tongue, Katrina struggled to free herself from the fierce villain who had a hold of her tongue. Georgina saw that her sister's tongue was beginning to bleed quite profusely. Frantically, but pointlessly, she tried to get Katrina's attention, to tell her not to move, to get the girl to hold still.

A feeling of hopelessness came over her while she watched her sister, who was forcibly ripping the tender flesh of her tongue in an effort to be free of the icicle. She was only making it worse. Small strips of skin, from her sister's tongue were stuck to the icicle which was still attached to the car. There was little Georgina could do, except agonize over her sister's pain. She stayed with her sister and talked to her and tried to calm her down. But she felt at that moment, that her sister's tongue would be permanently stuck to the ice on her father's car, or that the desperate girl would tear her tongue in half trying to get free from the vengeance of the blood-covered icicle. Frost was taking out his fury on her sister, while Katrina Josephina screamed as much as anyone with their tongue frozen to a car possibly can do letting out almost inaudible sounds.

At this point, many of the neighbourhood's Protestant children, on their way to the local army base school, were gathering with the O'Shaughnessy girls' Catholic friends from their school in Fairbanks, around the screaming girl with her tongue stuck to her father's car. Mass curiosity amongst the neighbourhood children, on their way to catch their school buses, was evident by their gathering. Hysteria was setting in between Georgina Jane and Gretchen, who felt that they could do nothing to help free Katrina. Gretchen Gabriella was in an utter panic, dancing around in wild circles. She was crying hysterically, not knowing what to do to help Katrina. The girl's twin was beside herself.

"Go get Daddy! Go get Daddy, Gretchen. Quick! Run! Run!" yelled Georgina.

And at that, Gretchen was quick as a wink. She dashed into the house, yelling at the top of her lungs!

"Quick, Daddy! Come quick! Katrina Josephina's gonna rip her tongue right out of her mouth! You have to come quick and save her! Hurry, Daddy! Come and help Trina! She's *bleedin'*, Daddy! Her tongue's hanging out of her mouth. Her tongue's almost completely ripped out of her mouth!" Gretchen was reverting back to her old accent from the South, confusing Daddy with 'Myrtle the turtle'.

"*Mi hita, mi hita*, okay, okay," was his calm, but hurried answer, not realizing the seriousness of the situation. Those twins gave him so much cause for concern, making much over little that he assumed that it was what to them seemed like another catastrophe, but was nothing of any great importance.

Running out the door to check and see if Katrina Josephina really was ripping her tongue out of her mouth, the captain pulled on his jacket and hat as he ran. Mother, clothed only in her long flannel pale green nightgown and dark green chenille robe with its matching slippers, followed with a pan of warm water. Finally, when the pan of warm water was poured over the child's tongue by her obviously dismayed, but outwardly calm father, the girl was free. At last freed, Katrina's tongue was still bleeding heavily from her struggle with the monstrous fingers of her icy captor. Blood and tears came from her terrified face. Katrina Josephina, and her tongue were bloody, but they were finally freed from their car's fender.

The crowd of children began to disperse. Katrina Josephina could stay home today. Dad would probably be late for his meeting with the colonel. His dress blues were splattered with the blood of his daughter's ripped tongue. Gretchen was told by Mother that she could miss school too. The girl was crying, and obviously too upset to try to learn today. Georgina Jane would have to run to catch the bus by herself. So, as she ran to the school bus stop, she thought about the morning's ordeal. When would Katrina ever settle down and fly right? It was useless trying to tell her anything. Maybe now, she'd listen to her big sister. Hopefully this would teach the silly girl about the perils of the Yukon winter before anything worse happened to her. Now she'd know about ice. She'd know that ice and moist tongues don't mix very well.

Science, Parkas and Ski-Flying

This was at a time in her life when science fascinated her. She was learning about cold and hot and about metals and magnets. When she watched the steam rise from her mother's boiling vegetables, she was proud of the fact that she understood why this happened. She had learned about these things at school. The boys in her family didn't understand these things. They didn't even go to school yet, like she did. They were too little to go to school. The 'little children', as her mother called them, didn't have to wait for the bus with the other neighbourhood children, in what seemed like the middle of the night, to go to school with Georgina Jane and the twins.

Alaskan winters meant shorter days, where the sun was almost non-existent. So, waiting in the icy darkness for the school bus, and coming home when it was practically already dark, were things that 'the little children' didn't know about. The twins had just started school the year before and were learning how to read. But they didn't know hardly anything about science. That worried her and made her feel responsible for their safety. What if they got frostbite and all of their fingers fell off?

That's another reason for her long walks, even risking the threat of frostbite. In her mind, there were too many children in her family. She liked to be alone so that she could think about life, not just play all of the time like her brothers and sisters did. Their house was like a continual feast of play, play, play! It was enough to make her feel wheezy and dizzy sometimes. Her father had even turned their big basement into a playground! Her dad told her that it was because it was too cold for the 'little children' to play outside for too long at a time. It was too cold for Mother to go outside with them. And besides, Mother was pregnant and he was afraid that she would slip on the thick ice.

The girl's grandmother, who lived nearly two miles from them, had moved to Alaska to be near her daughter and her grandchildren. Manga's real name was Nellie, or actually that was her nickname. Her real name was Helen. She had learned to sew her own clothes as a child. And when her daughters had children, Manga sewed for them. Georgina wanted a parka like the Eskimos had. "They're too expensive," her mother had told her. So, Manga sewed parkas for Georgina and for her twin sisters, Katrina and Gretchen.

Georgina's was purple, lavender really, her favourite color. Gretchen's was pink because she liked everything to be pink. Her parka was trimmed with pale pink ribbon with rosebuds on it. The hood and deep pockets were lined with white winter Alaskan bunny fur. Katrina's was green, to match her eyes. It had green rickrack and speckled seal skin, like a ribbon along the hem of it as a decoration. Katrina's hood and pockets were lined with an Alaskan bunny pelt that was caught in-between the seasons and was speckled with white, brown and tan fur.

Manga said that she couldn't always tell what color Georgina Jane's eyes were, they kept changing color. Some days, if she'd been crying or felt sad, her eyes were dark green. Other days those eyes of hers would be brown. Another day they'd be a combination of green and brown and yellow, and be hazel. Manga said that Georgina had 'Irish eyes'.

When the girl had been a baby, Daddy had to go a very long way away and live on the island of Okinawa with the army for a while. Mother and baby

Georgina went to live with Manga in San Antonio for about eight months or so. Finally, after months of separation, her father's little family could re-join him in Okinawa. That's where the twins were born, in-between two typhoons. When baby Georgina left San Antonio, her eyes were blue. They were blue like the ocean or blue like the sky. But when Manga had written to Mother and asked how was Georgina and her beautiful blue eyes, Mother wrote back and said that the girl was fine, but her beautiful blue eyes had changed color and were brown.

So, when she made the girl's parka, Manga picked her granddaughter's favourite color, not the color of her eyes, to make it. The parka was a pale lavender. It was a perfect coat for the child. Georgina had deep pockets to stuff her hands into if she forgot her mittens. The hood and deep pockets of the parka were lined in a black rabbit's pelt and trimmed with wolverine fur, which Manga got from the Eskimo traders in Fairbanks. There was even enough of the black bunny's left-over coat to make a black rabbit fur hat for her. She could wear the black rabbit hat to church, where ladies and girls' heads had to be covered. On Sunday, Georgina had to wear her dress coat with a hat or scarf, not her parka with its hood. The parkas were for everyday wear. Her parka's hood was trimmed with a strip of wolverine's pelt, and curved around her face and head.

Wolverines were fierce, wild animals. Wolverine fur was stiff and long, each area of the long strands of fur striated with varied colors within itself. The extravagant wolverine's fur framed the girl's pale face. It gave her courage to brave the cold and her teacher every morning when she wore it to school. The fur was like the animal itself. And it was like that wild animal was talking to the girl as she walked through the cold, surrounded by the fur of that flesh-eating, dog-like mammal. That fur empowered the girl with a sense of strength. It endowed her with, what to her were almost magical qualities, even powers. That carnivorous beast's fur melded with the child's own thick mane of dark hair and filled the girl's head with ideas, saying to her,

"Be like me. Be strong like I was. Don't let the hunters get you. Protect your kit and kin like I did. Show your teeth and bite if you have to. Don't turn your back on an enemy. Face them head on with courage and be brave!"

This was long before the days of protest over killing animals for meat or their pelts by animal rights activists. Worries about cruelty in taking the lives of wild animals would have been laughed at then, especially in Alaska. Hunting was an integral part of the culture in Alaska, initially among the Eskimos, but eventually by many people who became Alaskans. Being an Alaskan made you different; it made you special, like the wild animals that lived there. Being politically correct was not an issue then. Public awareness of such ideas like 'killing animals is morally wrong' was practically unheard of then.

Georgina learned to ski, wearing her new parka, in those years in Alaska. It made her feel like she was flying. She left her fear at the bottom of the slope and rode the rope-tow up as far as she could. She held on to the rope-tow all the way to the top of the beginner's hill. Sometimes she rode all the way to the top of the summit, to the advanced skiers' even higher hill. She would ski down on the snowy covering of the fresh white surface. With her feet positioned pointing inwards, as she had been instructed to do, and her knees partially bent, she sped down the ski slope.

It was a freedom that nothing came close to. She was all alone, the only one in the whole universe. As her velocity increased, and she was speedily pulled downwards to the bottom of the slope, a feeling of total disconnection, except with herself, came over her. It was like she was detached from the whole wide world. For all she cared, there was no one else around her for miles; she was so absorbed in the experience of the moment. Wheezing past other skiers, she wanted to shout out a cheer for herself. She was faster. She was better. She was the best! Not until she was older and learned about other facets of life, did she feel anything near that exhilaration again.

Once, after much entreaty on Georgina's part, Manga agreed to come to the ski slope with her granddaughter. They would ski on the beginner's slope, since it was Manga's first time. At the age of fifty-five, her grandmother was excited too, and was getting ready for the great event, donning ski gear, putting her diminutive, unusually small feet into rented child-sized ski boots, wearing ski goggles and a brightly colored ski hat with a big bobble on top. The girl was delighted with the prospect of skiing downhill with her grandmother. To her, skiing was like flying. And to fly with Manga would be the best thing in the world. Like herself, she felt that Manga knew about being free.

With her grandmother waiting in line, right behind her, Georgina raced up the ski slope, propelled along by the rope tow she held tightly on to. She let go of the rope about mid-way up the slope, thinking that would be a safe height for Manga to take off in flight alongside her thrilled granddaughter. One by one, other skiers came up the slope, but there was no sign of the child's grandmother. Worry began to set in to Georgina's heart. Where was Manga? Had she changed her mind? Didn't she want to come fly with her granddaughter down the side of the nominally challenging slope? Had she become afraid at the last minute? That seemed like an impossibility, because Manga was so brave.

Skiing down the slope, and reaching the bottom of the hill just in time to see an ambulance drive off in the distance, Georgina asked anyone she could find,

"Have you seen my grandmother? She was right behind me, but she never came up the rope tow. She is an old lady, do you know her? Do you know Manga?"

None of her family was there either. Finally, she found her mother.

"Where is Manga? Why didn't she come up the hill to ski with me?"

By the expression on her mother's face, she could see that Mother was trying to disguise the shock she felt.

"Manga had an accident, Georgina. She's been taken to the hospital. She fell backwards on the wheel of the rope tow," she said, lisping worse than ever, and breathing in between each and every syllable she uttered.

Disbelief crept over Georgina's face. This could not have happened. Not to her grandmother. But it had happened and it must be all her fault. Her heart was sinking fast inside of her. She knew that there would never be another moment when her grandmother would be able to experience the joys of ski flying with her again.

Mo, Larry and Curly of *'The Three Stooges'* were involved in slapstick comedy, falling over, walking into doors, hitting each other over the head with boards, punching the other one in the eyes and doing crazy stunts that she thought were hilarious. Georgina loved those shows. She laughed hysterically every time she watched them. *'The Three Stooges'* were the funniest three people in the world. Low humour was the best way to get a laugh. And the girl loved to laugh. Laughing made her happy. Laughing made her forget altogether anything that made her feel sad. Laughing was like taking a kind of medicine that made you feel better all over as soon as you swallowed it.

Georgina even laughed when she watched one of the kids in her class fall over and hurt themselves. Once a dog chased her friend, Debbie, down their street, the other girl screaming in terror. She laughed so hard, as she watched that fantastic scene with her good friend so afraid of the chasing, snapping dog and running away so fast. She laughed so hard, from a place deep down inside of herself. She laughed so hard that she wet her pants. She had to go home and change her clothes; she laughed so hard, doubling over with tears streaming down her cheeks. She couldn't help herself. That kind of low humour just seemed extremely funny to her.

But she knew that this was no laughing matter. Her very own grandmother had fallen over and really hurt herself. Her very own grandmother was in that ambulance. That ambulance that was driving away. Driving away with poor old Manga inside it. Her very own grandmother had two broken ribs, another dislocated shoulder and a slightly mangled hand. All of these were to recover, but in her heart, she felt responsible for her grandmother being injured. That feeling of guilt and heavy responsibility stayed with her for a long, long time.

Life in Fort Wainwright

Her dad had thought of everything for his children. He had screwed in swings with round bolts from the beams on the basement ceiling. He had bought a ping-pong table for them. There were chests full of costumes and toys, toys, toys. The kids even had their bicycles down there in the basement, and they could ride them around in circles or in-between the swings. The girls' side of the room had a kitchen where they could cook make-believe biscuits in the pink metal oven and fry plastic eggs on the stove. They had a table and small chairs where they would seat their dolls. The girls used their tea set and served their dolls tea and cookies.

They had a whole nursery for their baby dolls. All of their dolls had special names, like special little people. Her dolls were like real friends to the girl. She and her little sisters had several doll beds apiece for their baby dolls to sleep in. Once, she scratched her leg by walking too close to one of the beds, leaving a deep gash. Her brother's fingers sometimes got stuck in their toys. Small pieces could be swallowed by the toddlers. Once Gretchen even got two of her toes caught in her bicycle. Safety rules for children's toys were lax then. It was all part of the uncertainty of the world, a place where even your toys could hurt you.

No child would have designed toys that would have injured them when they played with them. It would take the Mr. Tonkas and Mr. Hasbros of the toy world a while to learn from that generation's rough play with their toys. Those baby boomers arrived too fast for the toy designers to keep up with their antics. Past generations took better care of their toys and passed them down to even their grandchildren. Even paper dolls were handled carefully by her grandmother's generation. Georgina Jane's generation didn't always play as quietly or thoughtfully as the older generation had done.

The children had a cash register with fake money. Her father had even installed a 'commissary' and a 'PX' like they had on the army base, where his children could buy and sell little boxes of make-believe food and canned goods. Though they had a freezer full of frozen food, canned goods were important in Alaska. She learned about that in their early days in Alaska. Everyone she knew had a whole pantry full of canned goods, powered milk and other non-perishable necessities. If the electricity went out because the lines were too heavy with ice, no one on the base would have electricity until they fixed it. She had seen those repair men climb those poles. She knew what a hard and lofty job they had. It must be pretty scary up there where those guys worked. When the electricity went out, she worried more about those men climbing up those high poles than she did about their freezer full of food.

If the electricity was out for too long, her mother would just put the frozen food out on the back porch where it would stay frozen solid. It was so cold outside, that the temperatures outside were lower than those in the freezer! Her mother used their back porch to make congealed *Jell-O* for the children's dinner. She said that she put it out there, because it would be ready in time for dinner. The *Jell-O* would set faster on their back porch than in their freezer; where in five minutes the *Jell-O* would be ready. That's how cold it was.

One of Mother's special secrets was her way of making Alaskan ice cream. Georgina was fascinated as she watched Mother put sugar and eggs and cream or even powdered milk made extra creamy by doubling the ingredients in an emergency. Maybe Mother would add some stewed or cut up fruit or some vanilla extract or canned chocolate, or crumbles of a chocolate candy bar blending it all together in an empty coffee can, maybe even leaving some of the coffee in the can too. Then Mother would tape the top of the can shut nice and tightly. She would take it outside and call all of the children to help her. She would get the twins on the top of the driveway, and she and Georgina would get at the bottom of the drive. Then they'd roll the coffee can up and down, back and forth in the snow. Next thing they knew, they'd have real Alaskan ice cream without even going to the PX to buy it. It was a better way of making ice cream than anything!

Sometimes the lights would be off and they would have to use candles to see anything, even in the afternoon, because it got dark so early. And since there was no electricity, the stove wouldn't work and her mother wouldn't be able to cook dinner. One time, when all of the electricity was off, her father brought home bags of 'mess kits' full of supplies for the soldiers in the army. The children had a picnic by candlelight in the dark hallway, eating that strange food. Neither of her parents wanted to join in on the fun and eat those sea rations. Her mother and father just stood there watching their children huddled together in the twilight, tentatively eating their cold canned army food dinner.

Georgina thought that the soldiers must have a hard life. The sea-ration food in the funny cans with their own keys tasted so bland and almost like paper food, not real food. There was certainly no meat loaf like her mother made. There was no macaroni and cheese, Katrina's favourite, in those narrow cans of food that the soldiers ate when they were out on the field. The military personnel didn't even have broccoli, or *broccolia*, as her brother Peter Martin called it. She knew that the young soldiers must have missed their mothers' cooking, especially if their mothers could cook as well as her mother could. Sea-rations tasted like cardboard compared to Mother's food.

Growing up so far north gave the girl a kind of cut-off feeling, like being marooned. It was like the whole world was moving on without you in it. Stories of the South filtered up to the child. In the military, neighbourhoods don't move together; much of a unit the families felt when they lived together on the base. Friendships made, could be friendships broken, if fathers got stationed anywhere else. Your whole life could turn on a dime. That's how fast it could change if the Army made its mind up that your daddy was needed someplace else, anywhere else.

Tales of sun and warm weather, where people could wear peddle-pushers all year round, sometimes gave her a desire to experience removal vans pulling up in front of their house. Moving vans could come to load her family's furniture, and carry them all away to the South. Sometimes she felt the need to be evacuated to warmer climes, back down to the South where her grandparents lived. The knowledge that life went on somewhere else, somewhere she wasn't, gave her a feeling of isolation.

Maybe it was the almost continual cold. The air became dry, and the snow powdery, as the winter months went by. Too cold and dry to even make a snowball or a snowman. Everyone on their street had snowmen. Some were very smart in their dressing up clothes and even smoking pipes or wearing hats and scarves. But if you hadn't made your snowman earlier, when the snow first fell, too bad. Because the snow lying on the ground was just way too dry and powdery to make one. Piles of snow banked high up like heaps of double, even triple decker scoops of ice cream lining the streets until late May or nearly June. She needed to see the green grass underneath the snow. If she could just see it, she'd be happy. She hoped that summertime would come again soon.

Show Time

To beat the boredom of the winter months, Saturday afternoons were spent at the movie theater. It only cost fifteen cents for the younger children. It would cost Georgina Jane a quarter to go to see a show, when she was older, at the age of twelve. She was supposed to take her little brothers and her sisters to the movies and to watch them as well as watching the movie. She both loved and hated the movie *'The Snow Queen'*. It was cold enough in Alaska without seeing a movie about a frozen place with a mad queen in charge of it. That movie made her nervous. Would she freeze like the boy in the movie, and become like a stone for a long time? She knew what it meant to be 'frozen solid' or 'cold as a block of ice'. Knowing that wasn't a mystery for anyone who lived in Alaska. Georgina loved going to the movies. But she wondered what these movies were trying to teach her. She knew it must be something, but she was uncertain exactly what was being said through the coded messages in the shows.

Once she had taken the little kids to see *'Bambi'*. It was supposed to be a children's movie. But her brother, Peter Martin, started to cry at the part where Bambi's mother was shot by the hunters. Georgina had seen a dead deer tied to the top of a car. She'd seen a dead moose thrown into the back of a pick-up truck. Hunters had shot them. They were some fawn's father or some moose's mother. She remembered seeing the blood still pouring out of a freshly shot stag with enormous antlers. She found it very sad and disturbing after seeing *'Bambi'* and listening to her brother wail in the cinema. Her little brother had to be taken out of the theater. Lots of other children were crying too. But Peter Martin was the loudest.

Then there was the time when they all went to see *'Dumbo'*, the flying elephant. Never mind gravity. Dumbo was not affected by his hefty weight. And if he could make money for the circus owners, doing crazy, dangerous stunts, so much the better. But when they chained Dumbo's mother up and she went crazy, Georgina felt almost overwhelmed with sadness. She had been kept away from her own mother several times, and she knew how disturbing that could be.

And if that wasn't bad enough, when Dumbo went up the ladder to the trapeze, agoraphobia took over. It reminded her of the time her parents had foolishly taken her and her younger siblings to a mining site. The little boys went right up to the edge of the ridge overlooking the mining site. And there was no railing. Georgina and Mother almost fainted when they looked over the ridge of the site. They both were nervous of heights. But Dumbo wasn't letting his fear stop him. In the movie, baby Dumbo could fly! There were no nets for him either. Good thing he could fly by holding that incredible feather!

But these were happy 'children's' movies. That genius, Mr. Walt Disney, was the guy who made the story of Bambi and other kid's movies, like *'Snow White'*, *'Sleeping Beauty'*, *'Lady and the Tramp'* and others. Those Walt Disney movies were usually funny, but they could be frightening too. Like Fairy Tales could be. The beauty who fell asleep because of the jealous wicked fairy's mean-spiritedness ended happily. Snow White fell asleep too, but she was looked after, even while she slept, by the seven cute little dwarves. And finally, a handsome cartoon prince gave her sleeping lips a big smoochy kiss, and she woke up. Once Snow White woke up she could hear those seven dwarves with all of their singing they did down in the mines, like where Manga's daddy and brothers used to work in Pennsylvania.

Lady was a sweet little cocker spaniel dog, who reminded Georgina of her sister Gretchen. Lady was a real feminine dog. She fell in love with a rough street dog called the Tramp. But Lady retained her dignity, in spite of her friendship with such an urchin-dog as Tramp. In all of those children's movies, the characters got romantic and kissed a lot. Even the two dogs, Lady and the Tramp kissed each other accidentally with the long spaghetti noodle they were both sucking at the same time.

Mr. Walt Disney's movies were entertaining. And Georgina thought that all of the kissing was funny, because she had been kissed on the boat up to Alaska when she was six years old. She didn't like that boy named Henry kissing her underneath his bed on the ship to Alaska. That boy hadn't wanted to let her go, and that made her feel upset. But she thought that maybe when she was older, kissing might be okay. Daddy kissed Mommy, and she didn't seem to mind it. Mr. Walt Disney's movies were pretty good. His movies were not as bad as some of the other movies the kids saw back then.

Years later, she would think about these things. The girl and all of those little kids went to see movies like *'Moth'ra'* and *'The Lost Continent of Atlantis'*. No one told her about the idea of Science fiction. The strangeness of atomic bombs and the threats of nuclear war were spoken of in concealed codes and muffled messages by these strange films. Were they trying to make light of the terror people felt at such things? It was almost as if the filmmakers and the writers of this genre used mass hysteria and tried to divert the attention of the masses from issues like the Cold War and the threat of bombs by making scary films to occupy the time and minds of the general public.

No one thought to explain these things to children before they saw a film. There was very little in the way of ratings and adult scrutiny. The idea of child psychology was a relatively new field, with indulgence being the order of the day. After World War II, people were just glad to be alive and having children. The change of world ideology, due to the stresses of that terrible war, had not caught up with the consciousness of the masses. Science fiction was one way of forming a discourse in the new world order, and either addressing or allaying people's fear. Encapsulating terror, marketing it to the masses of theater goers, was one way of capitalising on what were prevalent feelings at the time.

In 'Mothra', there were giant moths that carried off two virginal young girls to some faraway place. This was not an enchanting land of make-believe to the girl. It was all too real. And the people in the movie were so calm about all of these dreadful things happening! The obviously deranged miniature girls in the movie were singing as they got carried off by creatures bigger than they were. She wasn't sure if it was meant to be a show about giant moths or tiny girls. Whatever the plot, it literally scared the hell out of her for years to come. Was this sort of twisted logic supposed to be safe for children to see? Even though she loved the idea of flying, she did not like 'Mothra'. She thought that it was a very disturbing movie. Flying with her father or imaginary flying was all right, but to be taken faraway by huge moths was another thing!

And it wasn't just that Georgina had to face her own fears. She had been told for as long as she could remember that she was 'responsible for the younger children'. That was the worst of it all. Her fear was one thing, but these little kids couldn't reason as logically, like she could. What must they be thinking? She vividly remembered for years, Roger Eugenio with his little head of streaked brown and blond hair hidden underneath his arm, hiding his eyes from the horror of these shows. Why did her parents let their children see these appallingly horrid movies? Didn't they understand how disturbed little kids could get?

Fear didn't feel like a good feeling, even to someone who wasn't afraid of flying now, like Georgina. Daddy had been teaching her to fly an airplane ever since they moved to Alaska. She knew that there were things that were scary and startling, especially to little kids. She half expected to see counsellors, or some sort of comforters of children with emotional trauma out in the theater lobby, when they came out of these shows. She thought that but she felt too stunned to speak. But if she had felt a need to talk to someone about it; no one was available to take her call.

She decided early in her life, that children's entertainment wasn't all that it was cracked up to be. Seeing the movie *'The Lost Continent of Atlantis'* was one of the worst experiences in her young life. Movies were like real life to the girl. In that film, a lot of people were tortured in varying degrees. Somewhere along the way, the characters in the film began changing from enslaved people to chained up animals little by little. This drove these, what to her were real people, totally mad. Then the whole place blew up! And to Georgina, living in a place where earthquake tremors were a regular occurrence, the idea of the island of Atlantis shaking and shaking and shaking until the whole place blew up and vanished under the sea, made the cross-over between reality and imagination an impossible line to distinguish.

And they called these 'children's' movies? She was just happy to get out into the freezing cold air and walk home afterwards. She was never sure if her trembling was because she was cold, or because she was suffering from the shock of these 'family' films. Stopping in at Manga's little PX, which was close to the cinema, was her only comfort then. Sensing something was wrong with her grandkids, Manga told them to sit in her office. She brought in bubble gum and silly comic books to comfort them. They'd sit in their grandmother's office in the back of the small store and put their booted feet up and feel happier. Then Manga would walk them home to their mother.

Snow Time

Theirs was a religious family. At Easter-time, when the whole family would go to Mass together, it was still freezing. Whoever heard of such a long winter? She just knew that it would never be summertime again. She felt like she was going to live in a frozen Iceland forever and ever, with the seasons staying stuck in perpetual freezing temperatures. There was no let up to the masses and masses of snowdrifts encircling their house. Like an avalanche of snow coated with ice and hoarfrost; they lived in an incessant deluge of snowfall.

Mother was always dressing them alike, even the boys wore the same color as the little girls did.

"That way, I'll only have one outfit to remember."

So, there they stood on the icy steps of the Catholic Church, waiting to have their photograph taken. They'd been picked as the best family in Fort Wainwright. Their family's photograph was going to be on the cover of a magazine. Shivering in the cold, wearing their new look-alike Easter outfits with their new white patent leather shoes, ankle socks and new hats made of pressed crunchy fake white straw. Their thin white, spring gloves, worn in readiness for more temperate, milder weather, hardly gave a warm feeling to their cold hands and fingers. Their flimsy spring coats, which certainly did not keep out the cold, were a fashion statement, but did not shield them from winter's still remaining, though receding, ire. They stood there on the porch of their church shivering in the cold, frost still nipping their noses, having that family portrait taken, wondering if the winter would ever end.

There were forts made out of snow in their neighbourhood. The snowdrifts were piled up so high that when water was poured over them, they turned to ice mountains. Someone had the bright idea of carving out tunnels into these ice hills for the children to play in. All of the neighbourhood children crawled in on their bellies, through the ice tunnels, dressed in those slick, one-piece waterproof ski suits they all wore. Freezing temperatures meant that a wet coat would turn to ice and the person inside of it would freeze along with it. When she was older, a fear of being locked inside a meat freezer became a part of her psyche, but she never made the connection between these two experiences. One was real and the other imaginary. But only when she was older could she know the difference between the two.

If you weren't small, you wouldn't fit inside of the icy chambers. But to the girl, these frozen, secret tunnels were too terrifying to enter. Except to try it once, at the insistent coercion of her friends, she remained a watcher in that game of concealed or secret slip and slide. Even the one time she did enter the maze of glassy tunnels, she wouldn't go very far into the interior of this translucent temple to some ice god. Once inside of the icy chamber, above her she could hear the calls of the other children. Above her, and outside in the chilly freshness of the frigid air, she could see the outlines of the figures of the other children, running and sliding about on the glassy frozen snow. That snow had been sprayed with water, compressed and frozen in order to make an icy playground for all of the army brats in their neighbourhood. Some adult had carved out the insides and made long tunnels and little chambers. Soon those children on the outside would

320

want their own turn to penetrate deep into this icy region. She knew that light penetrating into the interior of her hidden space, did not mean that escape would be an easy or quick option.

Claustrophobia set in and worked against her usually free spirit. She couldn't fly in here. Probing deeper wasn't worth the risk. It would only be even harder to escape. Who could tell where the tunnels went? Would they go farther and farther, ever falling downwards into this icy space? Would she, like Alice in Wonderland, keep going downward too, falling into that cold enclosed space? Would she ever know free flight again? Would she get lost inside there and not be found until spring melted the huge pile of frozen snow? Would the snow ever even melt?

Massive icicles formed on the awnings of the huge airplane hangars on the army base where her father worked. Ice was a constant concern to the pilots who flew into the wilderness of Alaska. Soldiers and civilians living out in the nether regions of the icy wasteland, awaited the arrival of her father's and other pilots' planes and the big cargo helicopters. Those people were cut off, without roads. Those inhabitants were without a way to even receive mail or food supplies and fuel, except by dog sled or ski plane. Trucks couldn't reach them that time of year.

Whiteouts of treacherous high winds and blowing gusts of snow made it impossible to see the difference between the land and the sky. Places like Nome, Barrow and Prudhoe Bay took on the very essence of remoteness in the girl's mind. These settlements could be cut off, trapping the trappers and other territorial settlers. Even the dog sledders of the Iditarod Trail, couldn't get through, if the winter weather got too bad.

The arrival of Spring was heralded by betting on the exact day the ice would break up on the Yukon River. One Spring an entire, huge icicle, the size of a truck, fell off of the base's biggest airplane hangar, as the ice melted in the warming, late springtime, early Summer sun. This immense pointed spear of ice, like the giant lance of some long-ago primitive caveman, fell on top of a car parked directly underneath it. The car was completely smashed – flat as a pancake. Spring had finally arrived at long last!

Wild as an Alaskan Rabbit

In the Spring, Georgina would have no more ice caverns to explore and tunnel into, like some kind of snow bunny, obscured from view in its burrow.

Adventures and escapades had to be found in other places in their neighbourhood. *Dipsty dumpsters*, where all of the families took their bags of trash and dumped them into the large, room-size metal cubes were natural places of curiosity for the children. The metal doors were meant to stay shut, but one of the older kids learned how to open them.

"What a great place to explore!" said one of the army brat boys, one of Georgina Jane's new friends from the base.

"Come on, Georgina! Let's climb in and dig around in this stuff! I bet we'll find some pretty neat stuff in here!" The boy could hardly contain his excitement and was poking his arms into the waist deep junk and trash in the dumpster.

"How do we get in?" Georgina asked.

"It's easy! I'll give ya a boost in. Come on, girl, put your foot here in my hand," said the friend of the boy who was already scavenging in the muck of the *dipsty dumpster*.

One kid was already inside the big metal garbage storage box. He was digging around fearlessly with his bare hands in all of the junk.

"Look what a neat contraption this is, you guys! It's an old radio with the bulbs still inside of it. Why would someone throw such a valuable thing away? I bet I can fix this up pretty good."

Georgina was on her way in. Into the dumpster with her friends. Half of her body and her head were hanging there, suspended between the outside world and the inside world of that smelly dumpster. That putrid place full of a wonderful array of various treasures, each one more interesting and intriguing than the next. The girl had made great pals with these guys in their neighbourhood by then. These were kids she knew from the ice-skating rink and from the ice tunnels and the playground. The past winter they had bumped into each other more than once.

As she was suspended over the edge of the dumpster, it occurred to her to wonder what her parents would think if they knew what the boys were enticing her to do. What she wanted to do. What she was doing. What self-respecting adult could imagine their children doing such a thing? Why would their children want to climb in and dig around in such a filthy place? The smell was awful. If Mother knew of her activities, she would have been mortified. If Mother had known that her daughter, whom she dressed up in frilly taffeta springtime dresses, with their flowing, feminine gauzy sheer material, descended into the dregs of those dumpsters, she would have probably died of embarrassment. Such a disgusting and unpleasant habit. But it was true. Her daughter had such a bad habit. Georgina plunged into those foul-smelling metal containers in search of buried treasures with her exceedingly odd group of Protestant boyfriends every chance she got.

There would have been no end to the lectures that the girl would have received for such unbecoming, unlady-like behaviour. Mother would have been disgraced for the rest of her life to have such an awful, filthy daughter. It was one thing to have brothers whom the girl's mother said, "Smelled like dogs," from head to toe, but to have such a daughter as Georgina had become, was certainly a real humiliation. The girl's contentment, and almost joy of discovery in climbing into those army garbage dumpsters with such ease and delight, would have only added to the consternation of her mother. That girl sure did have funny ways of making herself happy. She was already showing signs of a certain peculiarity and utter disregard for conformity at such an early age. She even took pleasure in soiling her mother's carefully selected wardrobe for her. Where the child's tendencies would lead her, was anybody's guess. She certainly was an oddball. There could be no doubt that there was a deficiency somewhere, hidden away in her genes, probably stemming from her father's side of the family. His mother, with her piles of revolting kitchen refuse, was one example of that woman's oddities. Georgina, whose nose was just beginning to grow with the maturity her face was taking on, did look somewhat like that pointy nosed grandmother of hers. The one on her father's side of the family.

But climbing in and out of dumpsters was not nearly as bad as the girl's other wild tendencies. This was a girl who showed major signs of obvious mental disturbances. It was plain for anyone to see that for themselves. It was plain for anyone to see that if they knew how crazy she had become. Georgina Jane should be branded on her forehead with a sign that said, 'Renegade' or 'Oddball'. Who she even was, and why she did the things she did, was a mystery to her mother. But the child's curiosity and zest for living in her odd little way did not allow her to sit still and play with her dolls forever.

She was as wild as the rabbits she saw tearing through the woods close to their house. Perhaps it had been a mistake to let Manga sew that wolverine fur onto the girl's parka hood. Maybe that was the reason her daughter kept coming home in such a filthy dirty state with a peculiar assortment of treasures found from who knows where. Her mother hated to ask her where the girl had found such things. Dirty grimy things all piled up in a neat collection in Georgina's bookshelves next to her bed. This assortment of junk was displayed right there next to her *Nancy Drew* books, *The Little Princess* book about Sara Crew who lived in a dirty cold attic. The book about *Heidi, Black Velvet, The Grimm Brothers' Fairy Tales* and other wonderful literary volumes bought for the child by her mother who was concerned that Georgina settled down and thought quietly as she read, rather than gallivanting all over the neighbourhood the way she did. The answer to Mother's ponderous questions was something she didn't want to hear.

Did wearing that black rabbit fur hat so unashamedly to Mass give the girl those strange ideas? Maybe it was all of those games of jumping rope, rising off of the earth and finding herself suspended between heaven and the world for a blissful split second, that did it. One thing was certain, the girl, the bad and naughty, squalid girl was too radical and too curious for her own good.

Mother's fear for her own dignity and place in society could be shattered if her daughter's activities became known by the women's groups on the base. A supposed, though shallow, concern for the well-being of the child grew inside of her mother. It would grow and grow in intensity, along with efforts to control and belittle the girl. As the child grew into an adolescent, then a teenager, a young woman and on into her middle age, the generational struggle would continue and even expand. Mocking disdain would replace questioning. The mother would never reach a satisfactory level of control over the child, though she would not cease to try, no matter how old her 'little girl' became.

Frustration would lead to attempts to castigate her daughter for being herself, never accepting the person the girl just naturally was. The girl just was herself. She was herself and nobody else. She couldn't become someone else, even to please her mother. She couldn't become someone more suited to her mother's disposition. No matter how hard the questions. No matter how sour the looks of disdain. No matter how cruel the shunning and dislike for her own flesh and blood, Georgina Jane would always essentially remain the person she was born to be. She would be herself, though more bruised and battered by her mother's displeasure and rejection. She would be the person she was intended to be by someone with a design for the girl's life that her mother would perhaps never understand.

Mother didn't even know about Georgina's midnight rendezvous with the summer's ever-present sunlight. That had been going for years. Mother didn't know that her daughter was not asleep, but frolicking away in the night time hours out on the green, green Alaskan grass. The girl had already been slipping outside in the middle of the night for two summers in a row, wandering the neighbourhood with her cousins, or alone, in search of adventures that were better than dreams. Unable to sleep because of Alaska's uninterrupted summertime daylight in the middle of the night, she had to go exploring outside where life was happening. She might be missing something. Something big. Something real. Something better than sleeping. She was a child. She was not waiting for life to happen to her while she made other plans. She was living life to the full. She was rejoicing in every moment. She was being fully existent on the planet while she was on it.

Besides the ones her mother knew about, Georgina Jane had developed another bad habit as well. She was so curious, always wanting to know things that she was either too young or too simple in her child-like abilities to understand. Mother loved to window shop. The girl loved to look into other people's windows. Mother was like a shopaholic, who couldn't keep away from the shop window dressings even when the stores were closed for the day. Window shopping wasn't a sin. But the girl's inquisitive mind was another thing. She was nosey and curious. She liked to look into, and even study the interiors of their neighbours' houses. Like theater stage sets or settings described in books, these visual aids were Georgina's ticket into her imagination. Into her imagination where other people's lives took place. Into her imagination to imagine how other families lived. What they did with their army houses.

How did they arrange their furniture? Did they collect beautiful ceramic vases from the Orient like her mother did? Did they have a teak coffee table too? Were their houses tidy or grimy? How many kids did these people have in their families? Did their mothers cook elaborate food, or TV Dinners? Did other people's families have arguments?

Early one summer's morning, when she was out on her dawn walkabouts, the girl got more than she bargained for. Georgina Jane did her window peering exercises as her whole family was sleeping in their beds. She went from window to basement window and looked inside. Those windows were almost at ground level, and she had to bend down to see what was inside. She would squat down and take a peep inside of other people's houses, at least into their basements. Did they have swings in their basements? Were their basements full of toys and a big freezer to keep frozen food? Were their basements clean and tidy, or messy and cluttered? Did they have a clothes washer?

She could see if her neighbours lead interesting lives by the way their basement rooms looked. Usually curtains blocked her vision into the interiors. But curtainless windows almost begged the girl to see for herself what was going on in there. For a small curious girl, the desire to look inside and check out the contents of those spaces was overpowering. Those spaces, which were like small stage sets to her, where her neighbours, like performers, shoved their junk, were too great a temptation to resist.

Every basement had a big stainless-steel sink, like a deep washbasin for a puppy dog's bath. And it was there that she saw him. The neighbour's basement had a light on. So, she looked in. There, in the early morning light was a boy she knew from the ice tunnels. He was her friend who liked exploring in *Dipsty Dumpsters* too. There he was. She looked. And then, she looked again. Looked just to make sure. He was like a dog-boy, a puppy dog, in that sink. That dumpster boy was stark naked. He was shiny. He was wet. He was staring back at the girl. Staring back. Both of them too stunned and embarrassed to move their locked eyes from each other's faces. So, they both kept staring at each other. Staring as Georgina's gaze lingered over his male body. His buck-naked boy's body. He saw her face peering into his darkened basement room. A room that he had foolishly thought was a private space. His private space. Foolish because he didn't know about Georgina's night time rendezvous with the twilight and the day's dawning.

But too late, he realized that he was not alone. Not alone now. His private act was no longer his secret. Washing himself in that deep steel sink, like the smelly dog she thought he probably was, was no longer a secret. Most boys did smell, as far as she knew. She knew this from being around her brothers, who smelled like dogs when they had played hard outside in the summer's daylight hours. That morning, that early morning, her act of voyeurism, in the dawn's early light, brought a change in her. And Georgina Jane O'Shaughnessy became even more like an Alaskan rabbit, changing colors when the seasons altered.

Chapter Ten
In and Out of Hot Water

A Bath, a Dog and Diapers in Her Hair

"Take a bath, girls! You've been outside all day and you are really grimy." 'Grimy' was one of Mother's favourite words. So many things got 'grimy' – like behind and inside the refrigerator and behind and inside her little brothers' ears. Dirt seemed to effortlessly find their ears, like their ears were flowers with pollen inside of them. Dirt, mixed with their sticky golden yellow earwax, was like the bees searching for the flowers' pollen. Flowers weren't just pretty; they helped the Alaskan bees make yummy Alaskan clover or flower honey all summer long. The bees could always find the pollen in those flowers, no matter how well it was hidden. Dirt could always find and stick to the insides and the backs of her brothers' ears, no matter how often they were washed with soap and water and those rough washcloths or flannels.

Those boys really did smell like dogs sometimes. Georgina Jane knew how dogs smelled. Her family used to have a husky dog, like the Eskimos used to pull their sleds. But they had to get rid of their husky puppy, because that bad puppy was always biting the children's ankles. Her dad gave it to an Eskimo he knew. It probably was helping that man pull a dog sled by now. She hoped it wasn't biting the ankles of that man's children.

Now they had a new dog. This new dog didn't bite their ankles at all. The new dog's name was 'Frisky', because she moved around a lot. But 'Frisky' had never bitten them even once, so Daddy said that they could keep her, even though 'Frisky' did smell a little bit. 'Frisky' was not like that husky puppy who bit their ankles. They had to run from sofa to sofa in their living room, to get away from that husky's sharp little snapping teeth.

The sharp little teeth of Beowulf, the husky puppy, were painful. That puppy their father had brought home, thinking his children would be delighted, was like having ten bad guys in the house all at once. All he ever did was to bite them and play rough, even biting the head off of one of Gretchen's favourite dolls and putting sharp little teeth marks all over the doll's back. Nobody could control him. Beowulf needed a new home almost as soon as they got him.

"He can pull your sled when he's bigger," promised Daddy.

But if he got any bigger, so would his teeth get longer and sharper. There was no way they could keep such a wild dog in their house, even down in the basement. He had to go and find a new home somewhere else.

In Mother's living room, they had two sofas because there were so many people in her family. That husky still had short legs and he couldn't get them if they were up on the sofas, even though he tried to grab the screeching group of half scared, half excited children huddled together in their efforts to protect their ankles and toes. Her brothers, Roger Eugenio and Peter Martin and her sister, Katrina, loved to run back and forth and jump up on those two sofas, making that little snapping husky puppy chase them back and forth. They thought that it was a funny game to play with that husky dog. But she and her sweet little sister, Gretchen, didn't think it was funny at all. Georgina and Gretchen didn't like the way their brothers and their naughty sister, Katrina Josephina, were training that husky puppy to be as bad as they were sometimes. Now Beowulf, the husky, had gone to live with someone else, someone who could train him to behave and not be such a naughty puppy all of the time, biting people and eating their dolls' heads.

When her cousins came for a visit, like the Alaskan scenery, a vast expanse of imaginations could take over. A continual feast of playtime could begin from the moment that the cousins arrived. Days and days spent outside, where dirt had to be dug into looking for bugs, and when small sweat found its way to the girls' foreheads and backs. The sun was shining. The days were long. Endless games of 'tag-you're-it', 'kick-the-can' and 'hide-and-seek' occupied the hours, the seemingly endless hours of each happy day.

Swinging open the door, the words of her mother rang out.

"Time to come inside, girls. Time to take a bath."

To wash off the day's grime, into the tub the two cousins, Georgina and Leah, went. Two girls could take a bath together. That way they could play with their toys and wash their dolls' hair together in all of those bubbles in the tub. It was

328

the night that hair had to be washed, because the next day was Sunday and a church day. Georgina had a thick dark mane of coarse straight hair, with only a slight wave in the back. Leah's hair was a gentler color than her cousin's. Leah's hair was like her sweet disposition. Her hair reflected that inner gentleness and good-heartedness that she exuded without even trying.

Her natural goodness was not something that she had to work at. She just was good. Like Manga. That was the way she must have been born, with that pure nature. Leah was kind and gentle. She was easy to get along with. Her character seemed faultless. Georgina couldn't think of one thing that Leah had ever done to anyone that was the slightest bit mean or naughty. She was like the poem said, 'sugar and spice and everything nice'.

And so, when Georgina looked at her favourite cousin's short curly, curly hair with its soft brown tightly curly locks that showered the girl's head with a kind of natural radiance, she knew that Leah was very dear to her. She knew that she really loved her cousin very, very much. Sometimes she felt closer to her cousin than to her own sisters. It was just that Leah never gave her any problems, so she was pretty easy to love and to like, both at the same time.

In their hearts, they thought alike, both often blurting out the same things at once. Georgina knew that she and her cousin understood each other in a way that went far beyond words expressed or the length of time spent together. Somehow, a thread of care, or a ribbon of respect and devotion existed between them that even distance and time couldn't irradiate. Though life would move them eventually to opposite sides of the globe, never in her heart could her feelings of safety and trust and love be broken when she thought of her cousin. When she thought of her cousin, Leah, the bond would always be there. Her feelings towards her soul-sister-cousin would always remain.

The two girls were the first ones to take a bath. Bridgetta got to have her own bath because she was bigger. But Georgina and Leah's birthdays were only two weeks apart. They were about the same size too; except that Leah's feet were a size bigger than Georgina's. Leah and two of her younger sisters, Rachel and Carolina, had curly, curly hair. Leah's mom, Aunt Adie, never had to curl Leah or Rachel or Carolina's curly, curly heads of hair.

The girl wished she had curly, curly hair like Leah and Rachel and Carolina's, because then her mother wouldn't have to curl her hair on Saturday night after she washed it. Now that Roger Eugenio and Peter Martin were big boys and not wearing diapers anymore because they wore 'training pants', mother used their old diapers, that she tore up into narrow strips of cloth, to curl the girls' hair. Georgina hated having those baby diapers in her hair. What if those diapers still smelled like ammonia or had 'ka ka' in them? But her mother said that she had washed them and that they were 'fine'. What was so 'fine' about them, she didn't know. She didn't trust those diapers being wound and wound, around and around, and tied into her hair every Saturday night.

But her mother said that the curlers made out of diapers would be softer than bobby-pins sticking into her head. That really hurt your head to have bobby-pins all over your head all night, poking into you like that. Her mother was right; the diapers were softer, even though they might have been embarrassing to wear, sticking out all over your head like that. Gretchen Gabriella and Katrina Josephina got their hair curled with diapers too. Gretchen never complained. Katrina Josephina wanted a 'curler cap' to wear over her diaper curlers. She was too spoiled to wait until her mother could buy a curler cap for her.

Katrina Josephina wore her best red underwear on top of all of those diaper curlers. She had two holes in that 'curler cap' of hers where her legs were supposed to go. Georgina was just glad that none of her friends from school could see how silly that girl looked with those strips of her brothers' diapers all over her head, and she was especially glad that they couldn't see how Katrina Josephina looked with that red underwear 'curler cap' on her head.

"This way," her mother said, "your hair will look pretty for church tomorrow morning."

Mother really seemed to want a little girl with curly hair. Georgina Jane thought that her mother wished that Leah and Rachel and Carolina, her cousins, were her mother's little girls instead of her. She thought that her mother didn't even like her straight to wavy hair. The only way to help Mother to like her raven headed daughter better was to have her hair curled with strips of old diapers.

But Georgina really wanted to have long fat braids. Daddy said that her hair was thick and dark and straight like his hair because they both had that Indian's blood in them. She wished that she had long braids like those Indian girls she saw in 'The Lone Ranger Show'. The Lone Ranger and his friend, Tonto, his Indian friend, were always riding again and again. They always came to the rescue of all of those poor people in the wild frontier. The Lone Ranger had a horse named 'Silver', who was white.

Mother told her a very funny song about Tonto, the Indian.

"Hi ho silverware,
Tonto's got no underwear.
He say, "Me no care,
Lone Ranger buy me 'nother pair!"

She thought that was a very funny song, especially that part about Tonto's underwear. But her cousins told her that, "Indians don't wear underwear." She thought that her cousins' dad probably told them that the Indians didn't like toilets or underwear.

They had some Indian girls on the Lone Ranger's Show. Those Indian girls would keep Tonto company. Indians had to stick together. She knew that the white settlers in the Lone Ranger's time didn't always like the Indians, even an Indian as nice as Tonto, the Lone Ranger's best friend. Some of the bad Indians in the Lone Ranger Rides Again, and in other cowboy and Indian movies, were pretty mad at the white people, who the Indians thought were stealing their land. The girl even knew that those wild Red Skins would get so mad at the white men, who the Indians thought were stealing the Indians' ancestral homes, that the Indians would do a little noisy war dance in circles around big campfires and paint their faces with war paint to scare the white men. Then the Indians would sneak out and surround the white people's houses on the prairie and shoot arrows with fire on them onto the roofs of the white peoples' houses. All the rifles in the world, shot through sod house or log cabin windows, wouldn't stop those wild Red Skins. And if those settlers stole the Indians' land, or killed most of the Indians' buffalo food, then those white people would really get it. Kind of like when Katrina Josephina went on the warpath. There'd be no stopping that girl if she lost her temper. She could really pull and pull your hair if she was mad at you, and then you might end up bald headed like the people in the prairie did.

If those white people ran out of their house, that was already set on fire by the Indians' firebrands, they would really, really, really get it then. Those angry Indians would pull their razor-sharp tomahawks out of their back pockets and grab those screaming white people. Those Indians would then grimace to themselves as they scalped those screaming, frightened white people. That would serve those white people right for trying to steal the Indians' land. Getting scalped would probably kill most of those white settlers. Because when those wild Indians scalped somebody they didn't like, some of the Indians' enemies' skin came off of the tops of their heads with their hair. And who would want to go through the rest of their lives with the tops of their heads and all of their hairy scalp missing? That was the problem with getting scalped; your hair would never ever grow back with your skin missing from the top of your head. She knew that having any hair at all was a good thing, even if you wished your hair was already curly like your cousins' hair that they had been born with was.

When all of the kids were gathered around the television set, watching cartoons or the Lone Ranger Show, sometimes Katrina Josephina would act like she was a wild Indian, because she was so inspired by the shows. If Georgina sat in front of the TV, and that girl, Katrina couldn't see her favourite show, that wild sister of hers would explode, just like she imagined the wild Indians did. Katrina would stick her tongue out and bite and bite it as hard as she could, till it looked like it might even start bleeding red blood. Then Katrina Josephina would pounce on Georgina, just like those wild and crazy Indians had once pounced on all of those brazen, frightened white people invading the Indians' space on the prairies down south. Katrina would grab Georgina's mane of thick hair and swing Georgina's head back and forth with such a ferocity that was almost unimaginable in a girl of such a tender age.

Someday, I'll lose every bit of my hair if that girl doesn't calm down and stop pulling it so hard! she thought. And even diaper curlers wouldn't protect a kid whose sister wanted to pull her hair out. Georgina Jane knew that by now.

Leah and Georgina played and played in that bath. They were having so much fun. It seemed like Mother and Leah's mom must be very busy with all of those 'little children'. They left Georgina Jane and her cousin in that bath for so long. It seemed like hours and hours had gone by. Nobody had come to wash their hair yet. Nobody came to the bathroom when they called. All of the hot water was gone and the water was so cold. She thought that Leah, who was a guest at their house, needed some more hot water or she'd be too cold. Leah might even get sick and die. She might even get frostbite and all of her toes would fall off. The girl knew that she was supposed to be nice to guests in her house.

So, she reached over Leah's shoulder to turn on the hot water for her cousin. Leah couldn't turn the hot water on, because she was facing backwards, away from the faucets. So, she turned the hot water on for Leah. It was very hot water. It was really hot water. It was scalding hot water! Poor Leah! All of that hot water hit her on the shoulders! Georgina Jane could not get the faucet to turn off either. That hot water just kept coming out and coming out all over her cousin! Leah just sat there and screamed bloody murder!

Leah looked at her cousin, and Georgina could tell from the look on Leah's face that her favourite cousin was wondering why she would want to hurt her. Georgina felt so terrible at that moment, realizing what she had done. She would rather Leah had accidentally burned her, instead of Leah getting burned like that. She made her favourite cousin get burned on her shoulders. But Leah was so sweet about it. She didn't even get mad at Georgina. She only cried about her burned shoulders. Her shoulders were really red. Mother and Leah's mom had to put lots of cream all over Leah's shoulders and on her back. She felt very badly about her sweet cousin's shoulders and back getting burned like that. Georgina got in trouble with her mother. She deserved it. But Mother didn't know that she just didn't want her favourite cousin to get frostbite and die, or lose all of her frozen toes, or she wouldn't have been so mad at her.

When she went to confession at church, Georgina told the guy behind the screen in the secret little room about how she burned her cousin's shoulders. After making the sign of the cross, which she worried about doing the right way, because telling her left hand from her right hand was a taxing mental challenge, she told the concealed priest,

"Bless me, father, for I have sinned. It's been two weeks since my last Confession. I burned my cousin with scalding hot water in the bathtub. I hit my brother, Roger Eugenio, for smelling like a dog and for annoying me. And I yelled at my sister, Katrina Josephina, twice for pulling my hair like a wild Indian. I'm heartily sorry for all of my sins."

That holy guy behind the screen told her to say four 'Glory Bees', three 'Hail Marys' and two 'Our Fathers' for burning her cousin. That guy didn't even mention her hitting her brother or yelling at her sister. That guy must have known her little brother, Roger Eugenio and her sister, Katrina Josephina. That's probably why she didn't have to say any 'Glory Bees' and 'Hail Marys' or 'Our Fathers' for them. If she did something really bad, she'd probably have to say millions and millions of 'Hail Marys', 'Glory Bees' and 'Our Fathers'. But burning your favourite cousin is a bad enough thing to do when you are only a little girl and can't turn the faucet off. And the water in the bathtub is freezing, freezing cold because there are so many children in your family and your cousins' family, that you get forgotten in a tub of freezing cold water.

Once a Catholic, Always a Catholic

Georgina went to a Catholic school in Fairbanks. She had to travel off of the army's base to get to her school. In the winter, she had to wait for the school bus in the pitch dark, when it was freezing cold. Early morning seemed like midnight to the girl when she was standing there shivering, waiting for that bus to get there. She didn't even have her mukluks on because her mother said that she couldn't wear them to school. Her mother said that the nuns wouldn't understand if she wore her favourite furry magic boots to school. Going to school was serious business to Mother. Wearing mukluks was serious business to her daughter. But it didn't make any difference. She still wasn't allowed to wear her mukluks to school.

Georgina couldn't understand why it would bother that teacher of hers. Those nuns had to wear funny costumes like they were dressing up for a Halloween party every day. They reminded the child of black and white penguins. She'd seen black and white penguins at the San Diego Zoo on the way up to Alaska. Sister Mary Gertrude was so tall, and with that hat of hers on, she was even taller. The girl didn't really like her, even though Sister Mary Gertrude was supposed to be working for God. Somehow, she didn't trust that nun. But in those days, children weren't allowed to have opinions about such things. So, she never told anyone how she felt. She just knew that if she could have worn her magical furry Eskimo boots, she would have felt braver facing that stern teacher of hers every day.

Her cousins told her that the nuns were really bald-headed underneath their hats. That made her laugh and laugh and fall down laughing. She almost wet her pants laughing so hard, envisioning all of those secret bald heads hidden away underneath the veils those teachers of hers wore. Those nuns were bald-headed like Curly of *'The Three Stooges'*. And that show was hilarious. Her cousins knew a lot. One time when her cousins' mom took all of her children to church, the guy up in the front, told her aunt to keep those loud, squirming, bored, boisterous, unhappy, vociferous children of hers quiet – right in front of everyone in that church!

How embarrassing! Her aunt would never get over it. Didn't that priest know the sacrifices she made to be a good Catholic? She had to wake all of those seven or eight children of hers out of a good sound sleep early Sunday morning. She had to see that those kids were hurriedly feed some kind of cold cereal, because there was no time for a hot breakfast. She had to force that brood to get all dressed up in clothes they complained about. Then she'd have to drive those kids to Church. And her husband wasn't even a Catholic. He was out of town, so she had to get all seven or eight of those kids ready and take them to church, driving them there in the cold Alaskan slippery snow, all by herself.

Those kids hated being all dressed up in their tight new church shoes that they only wore once a week. The smelly dog-boys couldn't stand the cute little bow ties and stiff collars and ironed dress pants and blazers. The girls chaffed at the scarves, bonnets, chapel veils or hats. They loathed the starchy frilly dresses, or new woollen sweaters with their scratchy cuffs and neckbands. Those squirming kids didn't even listen to the sermons and they hated sitting still.

They'd all just rather be somewhere else, instead of sitting in church, not listening to that guy go on and on in Latin, a language that none of them understood. Stand up. Sit down. Kneel till your legs feel like they're gonna fall off. What was the point anyway? Nobody even wanted to be there singing all of those 'Ave Marias' and repeating all of that Latin lingo. Next thing you knew somebody in their family group would fall asleep, fall off their pew and bump his or her head and holler out in pain or anger. Then the other kids would either giggle or laugh or start talking in too obnoxious and loud a tone of voice. They had no volume control. They were an impossible mob to control, even for two parents. For one mother, all by herself with so many children under the age of ten or eleven, it was a feat she could never achieve, keeping them all quiet in church.

Bridgetta said that her mother took them out of that church immediately, when the priest scolded her and told her off in front of the whole church and everyone in it. That man was upset with the kids' mother for her noisy children's disturbance of his Mass. Aunt Adie was so disgusted with the guy's rude attitude that she was fed up with the whole idea of even going to church at all, dragging all seven or eight of her loud, restless children around behind her. Aunt Adie was so completely offended and mad at that priest for embarrassing her and her family like that. So, she had decided that they were never ever going to go back to that church again. Georgina thought that her cousins were lucky, because sometimes her brothers wouldn't be quiet in church either, but her parents still made them go anyway. Her parents just made them all sit in the baby 'Cry Room' with its glass wall and incoming (but not out-going) speaker in a place on the side of the altar. That way, no one could hear her noisy brothers or giggling sisters causing trouble in church. The only good thing about the baby 'Cry

Room' was that she could keep her eyes on Father O'Brien better from the side of the altar, rather than from the back of the church. It was like hiding in the bushes near her house, just to spy on that huge mother moose and her young moose-ling that grazed and then trotted by her without seeing or hearing her. Those moose, and Father O'Brien never even knew she was there, so silent and so concealed behind bushes or one-way glass partitions. But she could certainly see them, and knew everything they were doing, from up close behind the bushes serving as a moose blind or inside that silly baby 'Cry Room'.

Sometimes, they sat at the back of the church, kind of like the *colored* people used to have to sit at the back of the bus or had seats designated specially for them in the balconies of churches and theaters. The girl knew how they felt. Sitting in the baby 'cry room' or at the back of the church was almost like a mark against you for being a part of such a big noisy family with so many disorderly squirming kids.

If Peter Martin fell off of the wooden pew and cracked his head and howled out in pain, Daddy would grab that little kid and rush to the back of the church to the vestibule. He'd hope that his son would be silent while he was having to catch his breath, until they got outside. Once a kid was taken out to the vestibule, and the doors closed behind them, he could holler as much as he wanted to and it didn't matter, because no one could hear his angry cries of discomfort and pain. That kid was still mad because he was little and couldn't do everything that the big kids in his family could do yet.

At early morning Mass during the school week, before any of the children older than seven, who had made their First Communion could eat their breakfast, every child had to hold their missiles and keep their hands folded. Folding your hands kept you out of trouble. The Mass was still said in Latin in those days, like the ancient Romans spoke a long time ago. Those Romans, who put him on one of those crosses of theirs, originally didn't even like Jesus very much. But there was the girl, and there were her classmates, all reciting words in Latin to Jesus.

So, every morning during the school year, and on Sunday all year long, there would be phrases said by the priest in Latin. Then all of the children in school, or the people in Mass on Sunday, would respond in Latin too. The girl knew what Corpus Christi meant. That was Jesus' body being talked about in Latin. She knew how to sing 'Ave Maria' to Mary, Jesus' mother, who needed some attention too because that way she'd go to talk to Jesus for the children. Before you got to go to your pew, you had to dip your hand in holy water in the little dish/fountain near the door. The priest would sometimes sprinkle holy water all over you, getting you spotted with droplets of that blessed water. He'd wave a golden incense burner around and smell up the whole church with the stuff.

And you'd genuflect and make the sign of the Cross in the aisle before you sat down. Genuflecting was like being polite to God. Everyone knew that God lived inside of the Catholic Church. Jesus had a special little place, like a kind of tent with a curtain over it, in the front of the church on the altar. Georgina thought that Jesus would probably rather live on the top of Mt McKinley, because it was such a beautiful high place, so big and powerful.

But her teacher told her that, "No, Jesus does not live on the top of Mt McKinley." Jesus lived inside of the small tabernacle on the altar in the front of church, with the little curtain covering him. Maybe the curtain was kind of like the clouds that went over the top of Mt McKinley sometimes.

She had learned that Jesus was so amazing that he could turn into a white host with his real blood in a golden cup next to his body in the secret tabernacle. That was after the priest said a special blessing over those round white circles he put on their stuck-out tongues at Communion. She knew about holy water too. The priest used the holy water to wash out the special golden cup used for making Jesus' blood in it. Jesus' blood had to be made from red, red wine. The priest, in his long flowing robes, all pressed and ironed so carefully, was like Daddy's army uniform that had to be so clean and stiffly starched.

That priest sure was a good dishwasher, like her mother was too. After that priest washed and washed and wiped and wiped those golden cups, like he was teaching all of the mothers in his church how they should wash their own dishes too, the priest wiped every one of his special cups and the chalice until they were shiny and dry. If you didn't sit in the baby 'Cry Room', it was hard to see what he was doing, because father had his back turned to the audience. The Catholic Church hadn't learned about turning the altar around so that everyone could inspect father's dishwashing after Communion. But Georgina could watch him from her seat in the baby 'Cry Room'.

Those nuns and father taught Georgina about Jesus' body magically turning into a tiny wafer that was so small, that it could even fit on a child's little tongue. Even though she couldn't really understand how Jesus could do this transubstantiation, and be transformed like that, she had to believe it anyway. If she didn't believe it, she'd go to a place worse than *Pearlatory*. If she didn't believe it about Jesus' body, tricking the devil like that, by the priest's magic Latin words, she would go to hell for ever for sure.

So, she tried not to argue with Sister about it. Sister said that God hated children who asked so many questions and would Georgina Jane please be quiet or she'd have to stand in the hallway for the rest of the morning and all of the afternoon. The girl wasn't too crazy about that idea. The last time she asked questions during Catechism, Sister made her stand out in the hallway, and even miss recess, which was like torture. She had a terrible accident when that happened. Sister made her stand and stand and stand in that hallway, for what seemed like forever. Sister just forgot all about her, entirely wiping the girl out of her mind as she taught the more willing, quieter students in her classroom.

Her teacher made Jesus and God so hard to understand about. But the girl didn't think God was so mean about little children who really did want to know about him. She didn't know why her questions annoyed her teacher so much. It was hard for a little kid to understand about God and Jesus if she didn't ask questions about them. But she knew, after having to stand out in the hallway for so long, that Sister hated her questions.

And eventually, the day she stood and stood in the corridor, the kid just couldn't hold it anymore. Sister made her stand in that hallway for asking too many 'sacrilegious' questions. She said that every time Georgina Jane O'Shaughnessy asked so many questions about Jesus' body and blood, it confused the other children who were trying to learn. Georgina was obviously a troublemaker, and would she either shut up or leave the room. She only had one more question to ask. So, that's when the girl had to stand out in the hallway for what seemed like an eternity in Purgatory. Sister made her stand out in the hallway, with her legs aching like that, and the milk she'd had with her breakfast, got the better of her. Sister made her stand out in the hallway for so long that she wet her pants and made a big yellow puddle outside of her classroom door.

That made Sister really angry with Georgina Jane. Wetting her pants proved Sister's point: the child really was a problem child. She was such a baby, who deserved to have to sit in the baby 'Cry Room' with the little kids. She asked those stupid questions just to cause trouble in class. So, it served her right to have wet her pants and have to wear some stranger's used underwear and dry socks from the *'Lost and Found'* box the principal kept in her office closet. Maybe now Georgina would keep her mouth closed and not ask all of those confusing questions of hers, that even Sister, who thought she knew everything, didn't know the answers to.

So, she tried to sit quietly in class from now on. She tried to understand about the special golden cups and father's chalice for Jesus' blood to get mixed up with the holy water that was blessed by the priest, turning it to blood. Or was it the bishop who blessed the holy water? Maybe that holy, holy water was even blessed by the cardinal who wore red and was going to slap her on the cheek when she was confirmed in front of the whole church soon.

That cardinal must not know her mother. Her mother said that slapping children, especially on their faces, was common. Mother sometimes thumped her brothers on top of their heads, with her fingers, if they were naughty. But she would never have slapped their faces. Slapping children's faces was what common people did to their children. And Mother was not common. But even though it was common to slap children on their faces, Georgina would still have to put up with being slapped on her face when she was confirmed in the big ceremony at church.

Her godparents gave her a beautiful gold and silver cross with a pearl in the middle of it. It was made out of Alaska's gold, and so it was really, really special and very, very shiny. She got to wear it when she was confirmed into the Catholic Church. Her whole family would be there watching her. They'd all know if she had learned her Catechism and could answer the Cardinal's hard questions. Every child had to answer questions about his or her religious training.

When it was time for Georgina to have her turn being confirmed, the cardinal, who had come to Fairbanks from out of town, especially to slap her and her classmates on their faces, asked her a question about St Peter. The cardinal wanted to know if she knew who had the keys to heaven. She knew the answer to that easy question, because she had a little brother named after St Peter in her family. Heaven was where Jesus lived when he was allowed to leave their church after everyone had eaten most of his body. She was even surprised that Jesus had much of a body left at all, after so many people came to church to see her get confirmed and to have a taste of Jesus' body.

At their Confirmation, all of the children got to pick a new name for themselves. It had to be a saint's name, or you couldn't use it. Mother said that she should pick someone special's name, like a martyr. Did Georgina like the name Joan, after Joan of Arc, who was burned alive? What about Bernadette, who saw Jesus' mother in some rocks called a grotto? Mother said that was a good Irish name.

But she hated all of the names her mother suggested. She wanted to be named after Manga. So, she picked the same name as Manga. She picked Helena as her Confirmation name. St Helena had been a saint from a long time ago. She had lived in Rome, where the Pope lived. She had become a Christian, after worshipping pagan Roman gods for a long time. And she taught her son, Constantine, about Jesus, so he'd believe in Jesus too. That way, the Romans wouldn't go around being so mean to the Christians who lived in their city. Sometimes those pagan Romans would crucify them or feed them to the lions in their big arena. That wasn't a very nice thing to do to people, just because they believed in Jesus. Helena helped to make life better for all of those Christians back a long time ago. So, hers was a good name to choose.

Even though Sister Mary Gertrude was supposed to be working for God, she was not very nice to some of the children. Georgina thought that God was probably a lot nicer than Sister Mary Gertrude. When she couldn't learn her multiplication tables for the hundredth time, Sister Mary Gertrude hit her little hand with a ruler three times. The girl decided that no matter what, she was never ever going to learn the multiplication tables, she'd just pretend to know them, but she would forget the multiplication tables as soon as the tests were over.

When she was nine, she had to learn a lot of stuff about what those nuns thought of God. She thought that they sure had some funny ideas. They told her and the other children that they would all probably go to a very hot place called *'Pearlatory'*. It would be really, really hot there, but if someone prayed to get them out of that hot place, then they'd go to heaven. But the nuns didn't think that too many of the children were good enough to go straight to heaven. Georgina needed to know about all of these things that the nuns taught her, because pretty soon she and the other kids at her school would be having their Confirmation at the Catholic Church.

Manga even made a new white dress for her, like she made the parka for the girl and her sisters. Only Georgina Jane was old enough to have her Confirmation then. Gretchen and Katrina had to wait another couple of years. And her cousins wouldn't even get new dresses, or get to have their Confirmation, since their mom had taken the whole family out of church and they were never ever even going back.

Every weekday morning, she had to go to Mass at her school. That meant that she couldn't eat breakfast until after Mass. The school served you breakfast, as well as lunch, unless Mother packed your lunch in a red and yellow plaid lunch box. You had to fast before you had communion for three whole hours. Jesus didn't like it if you had any other food in your tummy when he got there. Maybe if she went to Mass often enough, she would go straight to heaven, instead of that hot, hot other place.

Mukluks and Fairies in the Snow

But her favourite thing about school, was riding the bus home, because that's when she got to read her library books. The girl liked Nancy Drew stories the best. She thought that Nancy Drew, the girl in those books, was a really brave little girl to go into all of those dark rooms and other spooky places. Nancy Drew was smart too, because she could solve all of those mysteries that nobody else could find the answers to. She read every single one of Nancy Drew's books. She read so many of those books, that Nancy Drew became almost like a real person to her. On the bus, no one would bother her, and she could read for nearly an hour on the way home.

Sometimes, during those long cold icy months of her last winter in Alaska, a very sad thing started to happen to the girl. Sometimes it would take place during the daytime hours, and she'd want to run out of her house as fast as she could go. Other times, and more often, it could be heard at night, when all of the children were supposed to be asleep. But she couldn't always get to sleep as easily as the other kids could.

Maybe she had a Spelling Bee quiz scheduled for the next day at school. Perhaps it was her worries over her inability, try and try as she did, to learn those dreaded intimidating multiplication tables. In the morning for sure, her vacant, fasting tummy would be worried sick about those approaching tests. Her empty tummy was doing somersaults inside of her. It made her feel queasy and sick on the bus to school in the morning. She felt like a child strapped to a railway line or train track with a looming locomotive fast approaching her and ready to run her over. She knew she would be held like a prisoner by that teacher of hers. All of those difficult and impossibly tedious lessons would not go away until next summer. Then she'd be free again.

Until then, she'd just have to put up with all of it and suffer in silence. It seemed to her that no one was interested in her dread. Her fears were not a topic of conversation ever heard in their household. Too many other people had too many other things to say. Morning would come, with all of its anticipated projects ready to fall on her undeveloped, fragile self-esteem. Her ego would be shattered then.

Like a Damocles sword hanging over her, she knew she would suffer because that homework Sister had given to her just wasn't done right. No one seemed to understand this. No one helped her. So, she suffered silently, alone with her fears and her worries. Like the stars in the Alaskan sky, she was silent, alone in her bed, staring at the ceiling. Shadows in her room, which the hallway's light cast on the walls in her room, were like goblins ready to gobble her up. She wasn't sure which was scarier, those shadows or tomorrow's tests.

While she lay there, still awake, thinking about these ideas, turning them over and over and over inside of her young mind, seeing no way of escape, and knowing she'd be forced to face these gigantic fears, that even her night-time terrors could not surpass, it was then that she began to hear a distant rumbling. There it was again. Be still. Do you hear it? Listen to your heart beating instead. Watch the shadows. No, make them disappear if you keep your eyes closed tightly.

But no, there it was again. And again. There was that sound that she hated more than anything in the whole wide, scary world. More than anything except for her sister Katrina Josephina's blood-curdling war cry, as she leapt on Georgina's head of hair. That girl would fall on her with her full force, with all of her enormous fury at being deprived by Georgina of a clear view of the new 1960 television set's programs.

That sound, that insistent sound that nothing could make go away, was a terrible distressing sound. She dare not move one inch. Every bone was locked into place. She was like a rigid skeleton with only a heart beating, beating, beating inside of that fragile, terrified little frame of a girl. Nothing she could do. Nothing she could think or feel, or hope about, would make that dreadful sound go away. She knew. She knew what to do. The idea was like the proverbial light bulb in her head. She had to stop that sound, that hated sound late at night and sometimes during the daytime too. If they heard her get out of bed and patter down the long hallway to the bathroom to go potty, then they'd hear her and stop. Stop it right now. Do you hear me? Do you hear me go to the potty? Do you know that I'm awake and I can hear you? Hear every word you two are saying? Every cruel word you say comes into my head. Every ugly, mean thing you are

342

saying makes my ears and my head hurt so badly that I want to run screaming into the night, into the cold, cold, freezing cold, dangerous Alaskan night.

Into sub-zero temperatures, I'll run. I'll run in my bare freezing cold feet until frostbite turns them into solid masses of black, rotting flesh. And they'll fall off of my legs for good. I'll run, run, run, run, run, run, run, until I get to Manga's house. I'll run, run, run, run, run, run, run and never come back to even see or hear you again. You and your cruel, icy words are too cold for my little ears to hear. They are too mean for my little beating heart to bear. I cannot, will not, listen to you again. I'll close my ears to everything you say to me. I won't even bother to roll my brown eyes at you again.

As the child slipped silently out of bed and crept down the hallway to the bathroom, she could hear the sounds of her parents' voices even more clearly. She stood there staring at their firmly closed bedroom door, wondering what to do next. And then, it happened. Like a thunderclap when the air is full of tension and lies heavily over everything and everyone in that environment. A tension is there of what they all know has to break sometime and surely will break. Soon and very soon, it will break in great claps of thunder, like bricks falling into their ears and hitting them like batons inside of their very heads.

The door to her parents' bedroom quickly jerked open with a mighty, furious force of inward movement, almost sucking Georgina into that vast, troubled chasm. Still angry after his prolonged argument with her by now distraught and crying mother, there stood the father the little girl loved. But at that moment her daddy was not very lovable. He didn't even look like the same happy daddy she ran up to every day when his black and white Pontiac station wagon pulled into the driveway in front of their grey army base house. This was not the daddy who sang so nicely to her in Spanish with his deep baritone voice.

He could hit such low notes as the sounds of his parents' native tongue uttered forth in melodious song from his lips. His straight white teeth, like obedient schoolchildren, all in straight rows, were evident to the girl as she looked into his opening mouth as he sang to her in Spanish. Standing there in the hallway, looking up at him she had a thought. This guy is not my real daddy. This is a mean, mean, bad, bad man who is making my mommy cry. There she is, sitting with her hands over her head, not seeing her daughter, not hearing her either. She is just a sad, broken, pregnant lady sobbing into her own two hands, not seeing a little worried girl outside of her room, standing in the hallway pretending to be on her way to the bathroom.

"What do you want?" he shouted at her.

"Just what the hell do you want, little girl?" said the strange angry man, now standing before her.

"I… I… I…had to go to the potty, Daddy," was the barely audible answer from Georgina's quivering lips.

The over-stressed, underpaid, part-Irish, part-Mexican, part-Spanish Jew, very confused, over-tired and just plain angry man just glared at her. At the moment, he was no one she knew or wanted to know. A captain in the Army he may have been. But at that moment, she knew she had been like one caught behind enemy lines. It was not friendly fire she was getting either. This angry man was not her friend. Her goose was well and truly cooked now. She'd be washed and hung out to dry after he had thoroughly wrung her out. She'd be taught a lesson she'd never forget.

Fear was a tangible presence then. Inside of her, out of her, all around her, like an overflowing wave that almost physically knocked her over and washed her out to some vast ocean somewhere – out to the Bering Sea, out to the whales, out to the Russians waiting to engulf her very soul with their bombs and weapons of mass destruction. Fear came upon her like a tidal wave flooding through her.

"Well, go then! And get back to bed and stay there! Do you hear me, Georgina Jane?"

A very quiet 'yes, sir' was all the sound that emitted from her lips. A sigh and a great exhalation of air, her warm, soft breath, like angel's dust left behind after a strange long-ago visitation, came out of the girl's mouth. She suddenly felt that she didn't belong to anyone. All of the security and sense of belonging in the world she lived in left her at that moment.

The door slammed behind him and he was no more. For years afterwards, it was almost as though her father did not exist in the same way he had before. She remembered that his body was still around. From time to time, he could play and be a funny daddy again. But whoever he had been, he was not any longer. Like a balloon loosing air, her daddy just seemed empty and unhappy. He and Mommy didn't seem to like each other very much for some reason. Everything had changed on that cold dark scary night out in the hallway in their house.

Here it was another day and her parents were arguing again. She had to get away from them or she felt that the oppressiveness their fights brought, even from behind their closed bedroom door, would bury her heart underneath such a mountain of grief and oozing sorrow, that even Mt McKinley would seem minute by comparison. There on the brass coat rack, was her lavender parka hanging next to Gretchen's pink one. The parka's sleeves were beginning to be too short. It was sad, because she needed that coat, even if the sleeves couldn't be lengthened. She loved that coat better than anything. Manga had made it and put wolverine fur from the Eskimo Trading Post in Fairbanks all around the edge of the parka's hood. Manga had brought home strips of fur, like some ladies bring home strips of ribbons or liquorice whips. Manga let Georgina pick exactly the kind of fur that the child wanted to go all around her face.

It was still very cold outside, even though Easter was almost there. Though it had started to thaw, and the snow was melting into messy slush. It was a chilly, chilly day. Spring comes to Alaska in late May or even mid-June some years. When piles of snow and ice begin to gradually, day by day, disappear, until one day you wake up and can't believe it. The seemingly never-ending snow is gone for a while. But only for a few short months. That's when the world in Alaska turns to the fairies' and the leprechauns' favourite color. That's when the world turns green again, putting hearts back into that easy settled time of summer vacations.

But that day, it was only late March or early April, and the ground was still cold. Even though the sun was shining and the day would soon warm up by dozens of degrees over and above what it dropped to at night. The permafrost would still exist down underneath the top soil, which would thaw out gradually, only to refreeze in a few short months. She felt safe in her mukluks and parka, so she put them on, tying the leather sinews round and round the tops of those Eskimo boots. She tied neat little bows at the ends of the strands of caribou hide strips. Now was the time to escape to the outer world, the world beyond her home. That angry home.

So, quietly she left the house, that drab grey army base house with its basement full of toys and swings. Its Commissary filled with shopping items in Katrina and Gretchen's toy store with its canned goods and empty cereal boxes saved by her mother for their imaginative playtimes was vacant. No one would miss her. The kids were all watching some show on television. They had a holiday from school today. She was free to roam at will all day long. With a mother so busy with washing and ironing and cooking, and arguing her head off with Daddy, she wouldn't miss her daughter.

That girl went out all by herself. She walked and walked, even though she was a little bit afraid of getting lost. It was Good Friday and there was still snow on the ground like there was every Easter in Alaska. So, in mukluks which absorbed the melting snow, rather than repelling the wet cold, she walked through the mush with feet that grew colder and soggier with each passing step. Where was she going? She didn't know herself. She walked and walked for ages. She was in the colonels' and generals' neighbourhood now. That was where her good friend, Claire lived. Claire's father was a lieutenant colonel. She knew that because the size of the houses changed. The higher your father's rank, the bigger your house got.

Somehow, she found herself in front of their church. It was Ft. Wainwright's Catholic Church, where they drove to Mass on Sundays, no matter how cold it was outside. She had never walked there before. People were going in. Her feet were wetter and soggier than ever now. So, why not go inside the church and sit on one of the pews for a minute with all of these people? She could sit still, in the dark vault of a building and think about life. Maybe her feet could warm up and the mukluks would dry a little bit. The service was starting. The usher came up to her and handed her a white Kleenex for her head. She put her hood up. She wanted to hide, so that no one could see her. If they looked into her face, they'd know her thoughts. That wasn't what she wanted.

Her dripping, spongy leather mukluks left wet sodden footprints on the church carpets. She felt like a funny old woman at that moment, out of place and foreign, carrying the burden of the whole wide world on top of her shoulders. What was she doing there? It wasn't even Sunday and they were having church in there. It wasn't Easter yet. But Easter was a special day, so maybe father needed practice getting ready. Maybe this was like a dress rehearsal for Sunday's Easter service.

Things said in Latin mixed with English readings from the Gospels and talk of Jesus' passion proceeded. It seemed like all new stuff to learn about, like she'd never even heard about it before. It was like a play, with guys all dressed up in costumes walking around the church and stopping at the pictures of the Stations of the Cross and saying things. It was sad about Jesus falling down underneath that heavy cross. It was mean of those bad Roman soldiers to make that sharp crown of thorns and put it on Jesus' forehead. It was meaner than the angry words she'd heard her father and mother saying to each other.

Jesus must be sadder than she was. When those soldiers put nails into his hands and feet, it must really have hurt him. She thought that soldiers were supposed to be good guys, like her daddy's army men were. But those Roman soldiers must not have been very nice to act like that to poor Jesus. The only nice people to Jesus were the ladies standing in the crowds as he walked past them. Those ladies even washed Jesus' face for him while he was so busy carrying his heavy cross. And his mother and some of her friends felt sad for him too, standing by his feet while he died like that.

Somehow, all of those words said in church that day made her feel better. It was like Jesus knew about how mean people could be. Like he even knew how she felt. When she came out of church, after the guy in the front had washed all of those other costumed guys' feet and they all marched around the Church saying 'The Stations of the Cross', she saw the sun shining on the church. It was a very bright sun, reflecting on the snow that was still left on the ground. It made her eyes hurt after being in the dark, shadowy church for so long. She thought about how beautiful Alaska was. She thought about how wonderful the world was. And she thought that God must be good, to make it such a good world. Even if her teacher, Sister Mary Gertrude, who should have been working for God, wasn't doing such a good job, she didn't think it was all God's fault.

On the way home, as she walked through the refreezing slushy snow, she realized that she missed her mother. She wanted to go home and find her. She thought that if she could just see her mother's face, she'd feel better. When she got home, she laid down in their melting snow. She'd make one last Alaskan snow fairy in her front yard. Soon the snow would all melt and there would be no more of that soft white cold bed in her front yard. It was disappearing underneath her coat and warm body. The only snow left would be on top of Mt McKinley.

That girl who wore a lavender parka with a muff of wolverine fur all around her face and tied soggy mukluks to her feet to wear to church on Good Friday so she could get away from her angry parents would always remember making angels in the snow in Alaska. She would lie on her back on the cold, cold powdery snow. Then she would wave her arms up and down to make her angel 'wings'. Then she would move her legs in and out to make a skirt for the snow fairy. When she stood up, she could see the fairy was still there in the snow, almost like a shadow. She sometimes believed that she could become a true fairy if she just believed hard enough. She was always trying to get off the ground with those make-believe wings of hers. But soon, the snow would melt and the winter snow fairies would all be gone.

Chapter Eleven
Saying Her Good-Byes

Blue Lips, Black and White Photos and Chewing Like Cows

One of the things that her teachers at the Catholic school taught her, that Georgina Jane did agree with, was that God made the world. She went on blueberry picking expeditions for days at a time. That summer she ate blueberries all summer long. She ate blue berries until her mouth turned blue. Her lips and tongue were dyed such a dark navy blue to purple, that it made the girl look almost foreign, like henna had discolored the entire insides of her facial orifice.

Those colors in the rainbow might even taste good, as well as being so vibrant and beautiful, she thought. The rainbow was made up of lights. And Alaskan light was the best light in the whole wide world. In the winter, Alaska didn't have too much light, but when the State had any light, like it did in the summertime, it was lit up all of the time.

Georgina Jane agreed with Sister that God really did make the world. She could see the logic of that idea, especially in a place like Alaska. One time, when her family had been driving on the Alaskan Highway, a different time than the one when she saw the mountain goats, she saw an enormous, green glacier. She thought that God had put that amazingly beautiful glacier right by the side of the road, like an enormous piece of precious Alaskan jade, just so that she and her family could see it and think of him.

That glacier was the color of Katrina Josephina and Gretchen's cat-like eyes. The glacier looked like an enormous jewel, like a big, big shimmering emerald. The sunlight went right through it and made that enormous mountain ice cube glow like an immense green light. She had to squint, just to look at that fabulous, slick glacier easing down the side of that mountain. It was like that glacier could

348

store up the light of the sun and then flash back its radiance at anyone who looked at it. It was obvious to her that God made that gigantic green glacier. It was too fantastic and pretty for someone not to have made it.

The other thing that proved to her that there must be a God, besides glaciers, were rainbows. In Alaska, rainbows have a lot of room to grow to be a giant size, like the gigantic cabbages from Matinuska's green valley. Rainbows would stretch from one mountain to the other in Alaska. Manga said that the leprechauns hid their pots of gold at the very end of the rainbows. That was easy to believe, because there was so much gold in Alaska for the leprechauns to pan for and hide at the rainbow's end. They had even had a big gold rush in Alaska a long time ago, when lots of people came to her State especially just to find all of the hidden gold at the ends of so many rainbows. A lot of those sourdoughs were still around, prospecting not just the State's minerals, but the beauty of the place and the essence of its wildness as well.

One time her aunt drove all thirteen of the children right underneath an enormous Alaskan rainbow on their way to get ice cream. That rainbow was glowing with red, orange, yellow, blue, green and purple lights. It dazzled Georgina Jane's eyes; it was so bright with all of those glowing multi-colored lights. As her aunt drove right through that giant rainbow, everyone in the car was jabbering away. It was like nothing too special or out of the ordinary was happening. But her mouth dropped wide open. She was dumb-founded to come so close to a real live Alaskan rainbow with its enormous arc and so many of her favourite colors. She was close enough to that mammoth Alaskan rainbow to almost reach out of the car window and touch it.

If so many other kids weren't in her way, she could just roll down her aunt's car window, then she could probably even feel that rainbow. She wondered if those different colors would each feel like they looked, distinct in color and distinct in feeling too. Orange sherbet was her favourite ice cream, but lime sherbet was pretty good too. Grape jelly was yummy, especially mixed with peanut butter smeared on a couple of slices of bread. Strawberry jelly was even more delicious; it tasted so good if she spread it on Manga's biscuits. Lemonade tasted both sweet and sour at the same time, like Gretchen and Katrina Josephina mixed together. But blueberries would always be her favourite. Alaska was full to the brim with millions of blueberry bushes. That last summer the girl and her cousins and sisters filled a plethora of buckets and bowls full to the tops with sweet, tasty delicious Alaskan blueberries that grew the size of the palms of the girls' hands. What a fantastic thing to have happen on the way to get some ice cream with twelve other kids. Nobody was paying attention. They all missed the rainbow as Aunt Adie drove right through the middle of it.

The girl knew about light and how it could travel. She knew about colors too, and had a kaleidoscope that she could hold up to the light and turn the end around and around to cause all of those little colored chips to make extraordinary, varied designs. That kaleidoscope was magic. It was like a thousand different rainbows and patterns all jammed into a small cardboard tube you could hold in your hand and wind up to create orchestrations of colored lights. The combinations were endless.

The girl thought colors were the best thing. Only old photographs and TV programs were in black and white. The rest of the world was filled with color. Manga had a lot of old black and white photographs, but they got ruined. It was like Manga's whole family, her mother and father, her sisters and brothers, and her children when they were little, all just got washed away in that flood that swept into her flat. Manga cried and cried about losing her families' photographs in that river's flood. The woman was just heartbroken to lose those memories and images of the people she used to, and still did, love so much. That was her way of holding on to those long-lost relatives; looking at their black and white photographs was all that she had left of them.

Because Georgina, the twins, Roger Eugenio, Peter Martin, the new baby Roraigh Arthur and her mother and her father were all leaving Alaska, Manga had to move away from Fort Wainwright into Fairbanks. In Fairbanks, there was a flood of water from too much snow and ice melting all at once. There was not any other place for all of that melted ice to go, except for down into Manga's basement, where she kept all of her foot lockers, bought used from the army surplus store. Those army green wooden trunks were filled with her dead relatives' images on black and white photographic paper. Flooding happened in Alaska a lot in the spring, because the snow and ice melted together, but the ground was still frozen underneath the first part of the surface. That frozen ground couldn't absorb enough of the thawing rivers to keep them from flooding houses and other buildings in some parts of Alaska.

Manga stored all of her family photographs of people who had already died by now, in those footlockers. Georgina just worried that there might really be a Pearlatory, and that those relatives of Manga's might still be there in that hot place, instead of in the flood in Manga's basement. She knew about dead people.

She wondered what it would be like to not have skin on her bones, and look like those paper skeletons at the Halloween party at the airplane hangar; with their paper bones and accordion legs hanging down. It must be strange not to have any skin at all left on your bones when you died. One of her friends at school used to have a grandmother too. But her friend's grandmother had died. Now, her friend's grandmother probably didn't have much of her skin left on her bones either. If the floods came too quickly with strong currents, would they sweep away the coffins and wash away the people buried underneath the cold Alaskan ground?

She was really glad that Manga was still alive then. Manga would be harder to replace than even old photographs. She was so nice to her grandchildren, even to that naughty Katrina Josephina and to her wild little grandsons. Manga obviously loved her grandchildren a lot, no matter how they acted. That was obvious to Georgina. Because when Manga's grandchildren came to the PX, where she had an important job selling comic books and bubble gum, she let her grandchildren sit in her office and chew gum and read those comic books. Her brothers' favourite comic books were *'Superman'* and *'Popeye'*. Georgina liked *'Lil Abner', 'Little Lulu'* and *'Archie and his Friends'* better. And Manga's store had every comic book a kid could want. They'd all go tramping into the back of the PX, where their grandmother was in charge. Their snowy boots making minions of small footprints from so many feet, so many youngsters who liked to take over the back office. Their grandmother was gifted. She let her grandchildren put their snowy boots up on her desk and then chew as many pieces of bubble gum as they could cram into their jaws. If they wanted to chew too many pieces all at once, that was just fine and dandy. They could smack, even with their mouths wide open, blowing huge bubbles, and chewing away like cows. Manga had to let her grandchildren chew that gum when Mother wasn't around though.

Mother said, "Chewing gum is common. It makes you look like a cow when you chew gum, especially if you chew gum with your mouth wide open. It's not lady-like."

So, Manga had to secretly give her own grandchildren bubble gum, so that their mother wouldn't accuse Manga of teaching Georgina Jane, Katrina Josephina and Gretchen Gabriella to be common and unlady-like. Nobody said anything about boys who chewed gum with their mouths open though. The rules seemed to be different for boys, than they were for girls.

Those girls really knew how to blow bubbles. Blowing away with the covert bubble gum that Manga secretly gave to them. They could blow really big, enormous bubbles. They were so proud of all of those bubbles they had learned to blow, practicing over and over again with huge wads of the sweet pink stuff crammed into their jaws. Georgina's bubbles could cover nearly her whole face when they had air in them. It was bad if all of the air came out of her bubbles though, because then the bubble gum would deflate and get stuck to her nose. Manga taught her to use ice and rub it on her face, to get all of that gum off of her chin and her nose. The girl thought that was a good idea, because that way, her mother wouldn't know about them being so *unlady-like* and so common by chewing gum behind their mother's back.

Katrina Josephina liked to chew gum the most of anybody in their family. She didn't even care if it was *'common'*; it was still one of her favourite things to do. That girl could chew, chew, chew! Katrina Josephina never listened to Mother when she told her to throw that gum away before she went to sleep at night. Katrina thought that she could just chew that bubble gum all night long, even in her sleep. That girl was too attached to that big wad of bubble gum that Manga gave to her to throw it away like Mother told her to, before she went to sleep. That girl had no intention whatsoever of throwing that bubble gum away.

So finally, Mother realized that there was no point in trying to stop her kids from chewing gum. Even if it was common, and they all looked like cows chewing their cuds, they didn't care one bit. Bubble gum had tiny comics inside of the wrapper. All of the kids wanted those literary surprise stories, and the gum, no matter what. So finally, Mother got the message about their bubble gum. She taught them this funny little ditty and sang it to them. She said that she used to sing it when she was a little girl chewing gum and looking common herself.

My mom gave me a nickel,
To buy a pickle.
I didn't buy a pickle,
I bought some chew gum!
Chew, chew, chew, chew, chew gum!
How I love chew gum!
I do not want a pickle!
I want some chew gum!

So, that settled the argument about chewing gum, even if they did all look like moo cows while they chewed and chewed and chewed that gum with their little mouths wide open, smacking and popping away like that on their grandmother's bubble gum!

Mother had to cut Katrina's bangs really, really short because that kid's gum came out of her mouth at night and got stuck to her hair. That kid would never learn. She didn't even care if she looked funny with those short, crooked bangs of hers, she would still chew gum in her sleep if she ever got another chance. Katrina Josephina was so proud of herself, because she had learned a little catchy tune at school. She loved to recite this poem, just to prove her point about chewing gum and picking her nose too.

Everyone is doing it,
Doing it,
Doing it!
Picking it,
And chewing it,
Chewing it,
Chewing it!
Everyone's doing it!
Doing it!
Doing it!
Doing it NOW!

Kid Stuff

Mother didn't like it when Georgina Jane called the little children 'kids'.

"I didn't have goats, Georgina," her mother would say to her, "I had children."

That year, Mother had another baby again. Now they had six children in their family. Mother told her it was 'better to have an even number of children, because that way, you can have a fair fight'.

Georgina didn't think that fights could be fair. She hated it when her brothers or her sisters got into fights. She hated it when she heard her parents get into a fight. She heard her parents get into fights in their bedroom with their door closed. They thought that she couldn't hear them if they had their bedroom door shut. But she could hear almost every word, even though her mother tried to speak so quietly. Mother could speak very quietly if she wanted to. Other kid's mothers yelled at their children. But Mother didn't yell at her children.

Mother said, "Yelling is common. Only ill-bred people yell at their children."

The girl knew that yelling was *'common'*. And she knew that it was common to say 'shut up' too. But sometimes she just couldn't help it. That sister of hers, not good little Gretchen, but Gretchen's twin sister, Katrina Josephina, was so annoying and naughty, that she couldn't help saying "Shut up," to her. Sometimes she just had to tell that brat Katrina to 'Shut up', even though Mother told her, "Saying 'shut up' is common." But she thought Mother had never had a sister as bratty as Katrina, or her mother would understand why she said 'shut up' to Katrina. Even though Georgina knew she would have to go to Confession and tell that guy in the long dark robes about how she said, 'shut up', again to Katrina, she still did it, no matter how many 'Hail Marys' she would have to say. Saying 'shut up' was like Katrina Josephina and her bubble gum. They both just had to keep saying it and doing it over and over again.

Gretchen was very different from her identical twin sister, Katrina Josephina. They were like the different colors in the rainbows, like sweet strawberry and sour lemons. Gretchen loved the cousins' kitty cat. She would sit for hours with that soft grey cat on her lap, talking in a special kitty language to that pussycat. Only Gretchen Gabriella and the little cat, called *Asher*, or *Miggins* for short, knew that foreign language. Gretchen would say funny things to that cat for hours. She'd say odd made-up words like, 'Kitsabitsamitsa! Kitty middy biddy!' and other cat words to that grey pussycat. The kitty would look up into her face, and she seemed to know what Gretchen meant by those words, gazing into the girl's lovely pale face, with her green eyes, and purring back to her. That cat had green eyes too, like the twins. Gretchen Gabriella's favourite plant in Alaska was the pussy willow, with their soft little cat paws sprouting all over the bushes growing near their house. She would break off boughs of the pussy willow branches and take them home to Mother, who would put them into water. Gretchen collected pocket-fulls of pussy willow paws in her pink parka's coat pockets. Daddy even called Gretchen his little 'Pussy Willow'. That girl reminded him of the soft little cats and tender little plants she liked so much.

When Mother was away having the new baby, it was a very sad time. Mother was in the hospital for a very long time trying to have that baby. That baby had a terrible time trying to be born. Mother needed lots and lots of help from the doctors and nurses at Ft. Wainwright's army base hospital to get that little baby out of her tummy. Mother's tummy looked like it was filled with an enormous watermelon, like the ones that grew in Texas. Watermelons grew in Granny and Granddaddy's vegetable garden in San Antonio, Texas. She couldn't understand how her mother's tummy could get that big and not explode, like an ever-expanding bubble popped all over your face when you blew bubbles with your gum. She thought her mother was pretty amazing. Even with that enormous swollen belly of hers, she would get out and ride up and down their street on her bicycle without any training wheels. Up and down that street in Ft. Wainwright, she would go, with that big gigantic tummy of hers. That baby brother was learning how to ride a bicycle and learning how to sing songs about bubble gum and pickles, before he was even born.

Manga had to come to their house and make lots of biscuits for Georgina Jane and her sisters, Katrina and Gretchen and for her brothers, Roger Eugenio and Peter Martin when their mother went to the big army base hospital to have that singing, chewing baby of hers. The girl felt very lost when her mother was away trying to have that baby. They wouldn't let children under the age of twelve go to the hospital even to see their own mothers or the new babies. Kids had to wait until their mothers finally came home with the new additions to the family, to get to see them again.

Twelve must be a better age, she thought when she was nine.

She could see the hospital from close to her house, so she used to sit on the curb and stare at the hospital. Just staring and staring at that hospital from blocks away, made her feel closer to her mother. But it wasn't as good as having your very own mother at home. But at least you could see where your mother was, even if she wasn't home yet, if you lived close to the hospital.

When her new baby brother, Roraigh Arthur O'Shaughnessy, was born, Daddy took all of the children to see their mother. Even though the army hospital wouldn't let 'children under twelve' into their hospital, the children still wanted to see their mother. They kept bugging and begging their dad to take them with him, when he went to see their mother. So, Daddy piled all of his 'troops', as he called them, into their black and white station wagon with the red interior. Daddy took them all to see their mother at the hospital.

"You can't go inside, kids, but you can wave to your mother from the parking lot. Your mother will wave back to you, from her window in the hospital."

Her father called them all 'kiddos', but not in front of Mother, because Mother said that they were 'children, not goats'.

Georgina couldn't understand why that hospital wouldn't let her into the hospital's maternity wing to see her mother and the new baby, even if the 'little children' couldn't come in.

"I've been in that hospital before, Daddy," she said to her father.

"But that was when you were hurt, Georgina. You were a patient then and so they had to let you go in," her father told to her.

She had nearly cut one of her big toes off the summer before. It was her left big toe that almost came off. In the winter, she always wore three pairs of socks to keep her feet warm. That way she wouldn't get frostbite. If you got frostbite, your toes would turn black. Then they would either fall off, or the doctors would even have to cut those black toes off, because they'd be rotten to the core with the Alaskan frost's ferocious bite. So, she always tried to be very careful about those toes of hers and protect them from the frost's bite.

But in the good ole summertime, when all of the deep, deep snow finally melted, she could play barefooted on the green, green grass in her neighbourhood.

She was even allowed to take the 'little children' to the playground all by herself. The playground was where her mother couldn't see them, because it was behind the houses across the street from their house. When Georgina Jane took those little kids to the playground, she would be 'in charge' of all of those little kids. Her father told her that she was 'in charge' of her younger sisters and her little brothers. It was like her dad had made her part of the Army by putting her 'in charge'. She liked to be 'in charge', but her father told her that sometimes she sounded very bossy and he was the boss in their family.

The girl never wore shoes in the summer, except when she went to church on Sundays. So, all summer she could just run around like a wild girl, and feel that soft green grass growing in Alaska, underneath her feet. That was the best feeling in the whole wide world, all of that soft green grass without any shoes on. Grass would someday take on a completely different concept. The grass growing in the South was not soft like Alaska's grass. The bottoms of Georgina's feet would turn green like the grass in the summer.

One time, when she was put 'in charge' of all of those 'little children', she took those kids to the playground. That was when Roger Eugenio got his leg caught underneath the merry-go-round the summer before that, when she was eight. She had to dig that kid's poor little skinny brown leg out from underneath that twirling merry-go-round. There was sand underneath it, and all of the sand

356

had gone around Roger Eugenio's leg when he fell off the merry-go-round and got his leg caught. The other kids on the metal and wooden merry-go-round were having so much fun, that they didn't want to stop going round and round and round. And there was poor Roger Eugenio, screaming out in pain and near agony, with his leg almost being buried beneath the sand underneath that piece of spinning playground equipment.

That round-about was a big dangerous toy. Georgina had to jump off that spinning contraption as it spun almost out of control. She yelled at the neighbourhood's children to STOP! But still, they went round and round and round, oblivious to Roger's plight. That kid was screaming out in pain, but they thought he was having a great old time, like they were, yelling out in their excitement. She had to pull with all of her might, and make that thing stop going around. She grabbed the spinning bars and jerked the thing to an abrupt halt. Then she had to try to pull Roger's leg free, from underneath all of the sand that had buried it. She had to dig that kid out of that sand. His scrawny leg was stuck in there, being scraped by the spinning not so merry-go-round.

Somebody had run home to get help, so Daddy dashed back to the playground and came to the kid's rescue. One of the neighbourhood kids had run to the O'Shaughnessy house to tell the captain that his kid was buried underneath the dirt and the merry-go-round. Daddy had to come and carry Roger Eugenio home and then load the kid into the back seat of the black and white station wagon and take her little brother to the hospital to get thirty stitches in his leg. Like the Eskimo ladies sewed leather, the doctor had to sew Roger's skin on his leg back together. Roger Eugenio had skinny brown legs that could make him run so fast. He would have to give that little leg a rest for a while until the sore scabbed over and started healing. That kid was always running away, because he was the fastest runner in the neighbourhood, out running all of their friends. They called him their 'little brown monkey', because he was like Curious George, Roger was always running around up to something.

But the summer that she was nine, she got to be 'in charge' when her father wasn't at the playground with the children. Even that naughty Katrina Josephina had to obey what Georgina told her to do or Georgina would tell her dad when they got home how bad Katrina had acted. Her dad might even get mad at Katrina. He might even yell at her. So, in their bare feet, Georgina, who got to be the boss, played with the other children at the playground for hours on end.

Games of catch me if you can, hide and seek, softball, hula hoop contests, and mad dashes around and around on the merry-go-round kept the kids busy.

The girl's favourite piece of playground equipment was the swing set. In Ft. Wainwright, Alaska they had rubber swings that curved around your bottom, not like the wooden swings in the South. She still remembered Roger Eugenio's head getting smashed and hurt by those wooden swings. The Army had thought of everything to keep all of those army brats safe and happy. Those army generals must have had daughters who loved to swing, like she did. She loved to swing high up into the clear Alaskan skies. Up in her swing with the rubber seat, she could fly up to the sky. She could see over the tops of the houses. She went up so, so high. She could almost see her house with their black and white station wagon parked outside in the driveway. Up and up and away. She was off into the clear blue Alaskan sky. She had never gone up so high, nearly seeming to go over the top of Mt McKinley in the distance. It was like she really could fly, she was up so much higher than even the clouds! Every time she bent her legs backwards, she pushed her swing up even higher than the last time. It was a process she had learned to do when she was little. Higher, higher, higher she went. One more time and she'd finally reach her goal of a great height, far above everyone else in the world. Soon she would hurl herself off of the rubber swing and actually fly through the air! Her brother, Roger Eugenio, had taught his big sister Georgina how to do this.

If that little skinny kid can fly off of his swing, so can I, she thought.

Finally, she felt brave enough to fly off of her swing in mid-air. Georgina leapt out of her swing as it swung forward, and she flew and flew until she hit the ground with a thud and landed on an empty Cheetos can.

Cheetos were like crunchy orange potato chips. But all of the kids in Alaska liked Cheetos better than anything. Cheetos were a bright vivid orange color. They came in pretty blue metal cans that you had to open with a key, like a can of coffee or a can of ham. They put Cheetos into cans to keep them fresh longer, because Cheetos didn't taste good unless they were real crunchy. Until she flew off the swing and onto this empty Cheetos can, she never realized how sharp the rim of those cans could be. It was fun flying off of that swing. She had believed for an all too brief moment, that she was a fairy with real fairy's wings. A fairy flying through the air! Now she could really fly off of her swing into the air, without anything holding her up but her belief in the powers of flight. She had done it, flown all by herself! Up in the air was a wonderful place to be, with the wind in your hair, suspended above the earth and all of its cares. Landing was the problem.

There her foot was, all covered with blood. Her big left toe was hanging almost completely off of her foot. That nasty Cheetos can had sliced her toe to the point that only a little bit of skin on the top of her toe was holding it on to her foot. And just like her cousin, Leah, had done in that scalding hot bath, Georgina started screaming her head off. She was screaming bloody murder! She was screaming as loud as she could! She was screaming even louder than Leah had screamed, when all of that scalding hot water hit her on the back! Her toe was dangling there. Blood was oozing out of her and going everywhere. She wasn't sure if she liked Cheetos very much now. She might never eat Cheetos again after what that blue and silver Cheetos can had done to her toe. Georgina, who was always the one 'in charge' at the playground, was suddenly not in charge any more. With your toe almost cut completely off, it's hard to be in charge. But she yelled to Katrina Josephina, "Go get Daddy! Hurry! Run! Run, Katrina, run!"

And before her startled sister could think twice about arguing, she took off. Katrina had suddenly been promoted to being 'in charge', and the girl liked the idea. She took off running with all of her might. Katrina Josephina and Gretchen Gabriella always got to be the little girls, who could just play and be happy with no responsibilities. They never had to understand how hard it was to be a little kid yourself, and yet, because you were the oldest, have to be responsible for all of the other little kids in your family.

Katrina Josephina was like someone whose bubble had popped all over her face. It was like a sudden bursting of a gigantic popping wad of stretched out pink gum burst all over her nose. Seeing Georgina's toe nearly cut off, had really startled that kid. Nevertheless, that girl could really run, nearly as fast as Roger Eugenio could go. Katrina Josephina was the heroine that day, tearing across the playground like lightning, and dashing through their neighbourhood to go get Daddy for her big sister.

It seemed to be taking her father a long time to get to her, and carry her home, with her bloody toe spurting out so much blood. Georgina thought that she better try to make it back on her own. All of the other kids stood there and watched her clamber to her naked shaky feet, one of them now deformed and gushing with pulsating messy squirts of blood. Somehow, she hobbled back to her house, surrounded by a dazed crowd of confused and overwhelmed children. She couldn't make it all of the way home though, and the house across the street had to be her resting place, bloody toe and all. The most she could do was just sit on the driveway across the street from her house, and scream her head off until her daddy came out to get her. At first, when he heard all of the commotion, her daddy was mad at her for screaming her head off. Until he saw all of that blood on their neighbours' driveway, he came angrily over to his daughter, like a big grouchy angry grizzly bear. She was making too much racket. You weren't allowed to scream and yell in their family. And besides, it wasn't 'lady-like' to scream and yell like that. Mother had told her that. But she couldn't help it. She had to scream, with all of that blood and guts gushing out of her big left toe. She knew it was her left toe that was coming off. She had finally learned her left from her right.

"You hold a pencil in your right hand when you write, Georgina," said her daddy. "Because you are right-handed. I hold my pen in my left hand, because I'm left-handed. That's how you can remember your left hand from your right hand." So, she knew this dangling toe was on her left side and not on her right side where she held her pencil when she wrote.

After Daddy realized that she had a good excuse for screaming her head off, even her brave daddy, who had been cut up by those Indians' spears back in the mountains of Kentucky when his airplane crashed, knew Georgina's bloody left toe was very serious. All of the usual red color drained out of her father's face. He looked like someone who had seen a ghost, the fright knocking the sense out of his normal military self-control. His disconcertion was evident to his daughter as she searched his face for some semblance of reassurance. Would her toe really and truly fall right off, as she feared? Would she bleed to death, like some wounded grand adventurer? Like a hunter cruelly attacked by a wild bear or some other savage beast? And not just a little girl cut by a sharp metal Cheetos can? She had flown through the air, and she loved it. But her crash landing into that sharp can was very costly. Her daddy picked her up and carried her across the street to the black and white station wagon.

He told Katrina Josephina to 'run inside and get me a bunch of clean diapers'. Even that mean Katrina felt sorry for her when she saw all of Georgina's blood gushing out of her, and her toe almost coming off of her left foot. Blood was spurting out of her foot, where her toe should have been securely attached. Everywhere, blood was everywhere, draining away from her, and making her dizzy at the sight of it. There was blood oozing out of her toe at an alarming rate. Pretty soon, she'd probably lose all of the blood she had.

Daddy tried to calm her down. "No, you're not going to lose your toe, Georgina. No, *mi hita*, it's not going to fall off. They can sew it back on at the hospital. Now stop all of that screaming. It'll be okay, I promise."

She remembered how terrible it was to nearly loose her biggest left toe like that. And she remembered that hospital where her mother and her new baby brother, Roraigh Arthur O'Shaughnessy were.

Katrina Josephina came running back with a bunch of old diapers. Her father gently wrapped his daughter's big toe, and her whole left foot, up in those baby diapers. He tied a diaper around her thigh to try to stanch the bleeding. But her toe would not stop bleeding, and the diapers wrapped around and around her foot were getting redder and redder by the minute. She was like a faucet where someone had left the water running. Her blood would not stop pouring out of her. Her red blood. She didn't know that she had so much blood in her. Some of it was probably from that Indian's blood that she and her father had inside of them. A lot of her blood was going away from her. It was all over their neighbours' driveway and all over those diapers. It was a good thing that their car had a red interior, because her blood was all over their car's seat, making a big mess. She had been to the hospital where Roraigh Arthur was born. She had to have her left big toe sewn back on there.

Frisky's Farewell

Not only did they have a new baby now, but *'Frisky'*, their dog, had eight puppies. Dad said that they could keep one of the puppies. They had to give all of the puppies away to other children, except for one puppy. They couldn't keep all of the puppies, because they had so many children. Their daddy said that they would have to share the puppy that they kept. One by one, the puppies went to new homes. Finally, they only had one puppy left. But why had her father let another family come to their house to look at this last puppy? This puppy was the one that they were supposed to get to keep. They had even picked out a name for *Frisky's* last puppy.

"They're going to make us give this puppy away too," Roger Eugenio whispered to them when he came back into the bedroom. That kid had snuck down the hallway to overhear what the grown-ups were discussing, even though he had been taught that it was rude to eavesdrop. He didn't care; he had to know what was happening in the other room. All of the kids had a funny feeling that something was up. So, the children took the puppy and hid him in her brothers' closet. Frisky was too big to put into the closet, but at least the puppy would be safe there. Then Daddy couldn't give that puppy away now. There was a knock on the door.

"Where's the puppy, kids?" said her father.

"We don't have it," lied her sister, Katrina Josephina, keeping a straight face like some kind of totem pole Indian.

But Dad could hear that puppy whimpering in the closet where they had hidden him. "We have to give that puppy away too," said her father.

"But you said that we could keep one of Frisky's puppies, Daddy. You promised. Why can't we keep it?" implored Georgina.

"Because we're moving, kids. We're leaving Alaska," said her daddy with a very long, sad look on his face.

"These people want Frisky's puppy and they want to have Frisky too. That way the dogs can stay together. We can't take the dogs away from Alaska. This is their home."

She was in shock. They were leaving Alaska? No one had mentioned this to her before. Alaska was her home too, like the dogs. She had no plans for the foreseeable future to leave Alaska. He must be out of his mind. This was their home. How could they leave Alaska? Where were they going? How could they find a better place to live than Alaska?

"Is Manga coming with us when we leave?" she asked her father.

"No, *mi hita*, Manga's staying in Alaska. You kids and Mommy are going to Texas to see Granny and Granddaddy after you go to Anchorage to see the cousins."

She couldn't see how this could be true. They had brought Manga up to Alaska with them. How could they leave her there without them? She had to leave Alaska with them, if they left. It had never occurred to the child that her grandmother had a life of her own in Alaska, a life that didn't always include the girl and her family.

This was unbelievable. Her father must be wrong. But he didn't have a look on his face, like he did when he teased her sometimes. They couldn't really be leaving Alaska. But it was true.

Mother, hoping to conceal the truth, told her, "Daddy is going to the new place in Oklahoma to get it ready for us."

Georgina Jane and her mother and her sisters and little brothers were staying in Alaska for the summer. They were going to spend the summer with their cousins. And wouldn't that be fun? They would leave Alaska behind at the end of the summer, on the twin's birthday in August. She felt like her heart was like her big left toe had been, cut and dangling inside of her chest at that moment. Her heart was chopped and gashed like her toe had been, nearly cut off of her foot. Her father's words went through her like a sword, cutting her to the quick, and making her feel queasy, dizzy and sick inside.

Like God's words to Adam and Eve, expelling them from the Garden of Eden after the fall, her father's words meant that she had to leave her earthly paradise. It felt like she was told she would have to leave life itself. She knew she would never find a place she liked as much as she liked Alaska. Baby Roraigh Arthur would never know the Alaska he was born into. He would have to leave before he grew up to appreciate the beautiful place he had been born into.

Her parents made it sound like a wonderful new adventure was about to start for them. But the child could see through their transparent cheerfulness. If her father was going one way, and her mother another, couldn't she at least get to stay in Alaska with her cousins or with Manga? She remembered all of the uneasiness she had felt at their arguments. Now, this was the result of all of their angry words to one another, not finding a solution except that they had to leave Alaska.

Not finding a solution but to uproot Georgina from a place she loved. Uproot her from Alaskan soil. Uproot her from Alaska and transport her into the unknown. To places she'd rather not go to. That was what they were doing to her. The inability of children to control their destiny hit her squarely in the middle of her chest as they spoke to her and to her twin sisters and to her little brothers. Now her brothers would never get another chance to kill that bear. Katrina Josephina and Gretchen would never get another chance to whiz down the snowy hill in their flying saucer again. Georgina would never get to lie on Alaska's cold, cold snow and make another snow fairy there.

It was the beginning of the summer's vacation, when she usually felt so happy. But inside, where her bleeding, cut-up heart lived, she felt desolate. It felt like she'd never be happy again in her whole life. She thought she'd wake up from this horrible nightmarish scenario. She hoped that none of her parent's words were true. She prayed that they weren't really leaving Alaska. How can a child distinguish between made-up stories and reality, when they seemed both so real and so imaginary? In her heart, Georgina was hoping that this was a dream that she'd wake up from. That it was only like a story, or like the scary shadows on her bedroom walls at night, making her too afraid to even get to sleep to dream. She just hated the whole idea her parents had of leaving Alaska. What was life without living it in Alaska? It was unimaginable.

That summer, she and her cousins wrote a play about fairies. The girls performed the play for her mother, her aunt, the boy cousins, her brothers and all of the neighbours. Her daddy was already gone somewhere, maybe to Oklahoma; she wasn't really sure where he was. Nobody was talking to her about her daddy. Saying the word 'Daddy' was like saying a bad word. A word that nobody was allowed to say anymore. Her uncle was away on a trip to see the Eskimos. The play was written and performed for Mother's birthday. To the girl, it was a farewell dance to Alaska. She was leaving the State of Alaska, the greatest place in the whole wide world, the place she loved the best. Their dance steps and the songs, she and her cousins made up for the play, *'The Fairies Dance'*, were not just for Mother. That time of enchantment, when the fairies danced was coming to an end. Georgina knew that she was saying her goodbyes to the place where she, her sisters, her cousins and the fairies, had all danced together.

A Final Dance

But before she left Alaska, before that time of dancing with the fairies was over, the girl saw wonderful things in the south of Alaska where her cousins lived. She held gentle new-born bunnies in the palm of her hand. She picked so many blueberries and ate them right off of the bushes that she thought that, not just her mouth, but her skin would turn blue. Like if you ate too many carrots and turned orange. She saw rainbows that covered the road where they walked or when they drove in the car with her aunt. They drove right under that rainbow in her aunt's car. They went panning for gold nuggets with Manga, one last time. She saw whales in the ocean by the coast of Alaska, spouting all of that salty water out of their lungs. She went to Ethel May's house with her cousins to have some more of that wonderful, delicious milk toast that her mother said 'poor people' ate. She waded into the thawed-out ice skating rink and picked cattails to her heart's content from the edges of the unfrozen pond and got bloodsuckers stuck to her ankles. She and her cousins and siblings went to a park in downtown Anchorage where there was a house with a roof that looked like a witch's hat.

Aunt Adie watched all thirteen of those children that summer: all of her aunt's own children, Georgina Jane and her twin sisters and her three little brothers, including their baby brother, Roraigh Arthur. And her aunt even had another baby in her tummy, when she did it. Her aunt already had seven children of her own to watch. When her aunt had her next baby that would give her eight children. Then they could have fair fights in their family too, because they would have an even number of children to do the fighting.

Mother worked at the Eskimo hospital to earn extra money to pay for milk and groceries for all of those children. As far as Georgina knew, they hadn't heard a single word from her daddy. How could he go away and not write a single letter to his girl? Why did he even bother calling her endearing names like '*mi hita*, punkin, snickers, brown eyes and kiddo', telling her that she was '*muy bonita*' and then just leave without hardly even saying good-bye? It was a worry. It seemed like both of her parents were away from her that summer, which made the girl feel very sad, even though she did have all of her cousins to keep her company and to play with.

It was a chaotic household at the cousins. Sometimes one of those thirteen children would break something. Then Aunt Adie would try to make them tell her, "Who did it?" She'd get eyeball to eyeball with each one, but either the girls would look away or just giggle. Nobody was scared of the woman. Even if she did have a closet full of shoes to spank them with, none of the children would tell who did it. Sometimes they didn't even know who did it! Something would get broken, and it was just considered by the children, as a natural part of being such a big family. It was the adults who expected nothing to get broken after having so, so many children running around messing things up and destroying property.

When something got broken, her aunt would say, "Bridgetta, get my shoe for me. Either you children tell me who broke it, or I am going to spank all of you."

And Bridgetta would resign herself to a group spanking and go into her mom's closet and get the softest shoe she could find, not those pointed, high-heeled ladies' shoes. Then all of those children, who wouldn't tell on each other, would have to line up in a long line, and get spanked by Aunt Adie, who sat on her brand-new sofa, that was still wrapped up in its plastic cover.

Aunt Adie was not like the mean old woman who lived in that shoe, and had so many children, she didn't even know what to do. Georgina could see that her aunt thought that spanking all of those children, was really a hilarious thing to have to do. It was like her aunt was acting like Mo, the guy in charge of '*The Three Stooges*'. Her aunt almost laughed out loud when she spanked all of those children's bottoms. She could tell that her aunt thought it was a very, very funny thing to have to do, to spank all of those children. She could tell that her aunt thought that spanking so many children was funny, by that smirk on her aunt's face when she spanked them one by one with her slipper. Georgina thought that it was funny too, but she only laughed when she and Leah were by themselves, not in front of her aunt. If she'd seen them laugh, they might have gotten spanked all over again for not telling and for making fun of a grown-up.

But usually, her aunt was nice to them. She didn't treat them badly, like that crabby old woman in the nursery rhyme had treated all of her poor children. Her aunt took them all to get ice cream cones that summer. Thirteen kids piled into her aunt's car. Aunt Adie was brave enough to take all of those children to the drive-in restaurant to get ice cream cones. It only cost a nickel apiece to get an ice cream cone then. It was one of the best things about the good old summertime, eating ice cream cones from drive-ins.

All of the kids were in her aunt's car eating their ice cream cones that they got from the drive-in when it happened. Peter Martin, who was still a little kid then, was just placidly eating his nickel ice cream cone. He licked and licked and licked that ice cream cone. Peter Martin loved that ice cream cone so much. He loved that ice cream cone. Loving it. Licking it. Loving it and licking it. He licked so hard that he licked the ice cream right off of that cone and on to the seat of his aunt's car. Aunt Adie saw him do it from her rear-view mirror. Her aunt just turned around and grabbed that kid's empty ice cream cone away from him, and threw it right out of her car window!

Poor little Peter Martin! All twelve of the other children were eating their ice cream cones, but his very own aunt had thrown his cone out of the window! Now he just had to sit there and watch the other kids eat their ice cream cones. But he was so placid, that he didn't even cry. Georgina's sweet cousin, Leah, let Peter Martin have licks off of her ice cream cone as long as he didn't lick it right off of her cone like he had licked it right off of his own cone. The next time her aunt was nice enough to take all thirteen of those little children to get ice cream cones, she made the kids all get out of the car and eat their ice cream cones sitting on the curb!

Her aunt had gotten a new sofa that summer. It came wrapped in clear plastic. You could see all of the pretty orange and yellow flowers, on the fabric underneath the transparent plastic wrapper, but you weren't allowed to touch the sofa or to sit on it. It was the adults' sofa. It was not for children; even Bridgetta could not sit on that flowered sofa. Her aunt would not take that plastic wrapper off of that sofa all summer long. After Peter Martin licked his ice cream off his cone, and right on to his aunt's car seat, Georgina knew why her aunt kept that plastic wrapper on that new sofa.

Her little brothers were always up to something. One day they got into their aunt's car, the one where Peter Martin had licked his ice cream off of his cone right onto the seat.

"Let's drive away and go find our mother. She'll buy you another ice cream cone." Georgina Jane overheard Roger Eugenio say to his kid brother, Peter Martin. So, before she could bat an eyelash, they were at it again, doing something dangerous. Doing something naughty. Doing something crazy. Sitting in the front seat of her aunt's car, Roger sat behind the steering wheel, hardly able to see over the dashboard. He was wearing his favourite green and yellow foam cap from his hat collection, like a comic book gangster's hat pulled down over one of his blue eyes. Those boys were planning their getaway. Peter Martin had climbed into the front seat, and was seated beside Roger. They had persuaded the youngest of their five girl cousins, Carolina, whom they called 'Katie-Kat', to come along too. She sat in the front seat next to the passenger's door. They were the trio who were always getting into the most trouble. They were always egging each other on to worse and worse feats of daring and naughtiness. They were always up to no good. They'd never sit still for one minute. Maybe her uncle was right when he said, "The only good kid, is a sleeping kid." He must have had those three crazy little *munchkins* in mind when he said that.

Helplessly, before she had time to think, much less act, Georgina watched as the car sped backwards out of her aunt's driveway. Roger Eugenio was in charge. He was taking his little brother and his cousin Carolina, to get another ice cream cone. He put the car into gear, releasing it from its parked position. Whether in neutral or in reverse, the automobile her aunt was so proud of, moved. It moved quickly. It moved very quickly. The car zoomed across the street and into the cul-de-sac.

The whole street suddenly filled with people of all ages. It was like they knew those three kids would plan something so outrageous for that afternoon's entertainment. This was as lively as it got around there in that once quiet street. Amazingly, no one was hurt too badly. The curb across the street slowed the car down enough to help it come to a moderate standstill. Katie Kat bumped her forehead against the glove compartment as the car jerked to a cessation of movement. That funny, deliberately cross-eyed kid had a bump on her head. But fortunately, it was a bruise that an ice pack brought rapidly down. No serious injury happened to either of the boys.

Aunt Adie had learned that summer that it was pointless to yell at these three little kids. She just breathed a huge sigh of relief that they had survived another escapade in a long line of their adventures that summer. Soon Georgina's mother would take her six children and leave for good. Their days of causing their aunt's heart to nearly jump out of her body were nearly over. Their opportunities to give her one more throbbing headache were soon to end.

No more ice cream would be licked off of cones in the back seat of her car again. Her children could have homemade ice cream at home from now on. She would teach her children how to eat their ice cream properly by licking in circles around and around their cones. Licking their ice cream in circles would even out the glop of mushy ice cream on top of their cones. The sticky mixture would stay on their cones and not fall off onto their mother's car seat. Georgina's brothers could sit on the curb and eat their ice cream, if she decided they even got ice cream again. They were not allowed to get into her car again for the rest of the summer. And if anyone whined or complained, there'd be no ice cream again. Ice cream was a special treat. It was not for naughty little nephews who thought they could drive their aunt's car out of her driveway!

And furthermore, their aunt was not impressed with the *meany-meany* look that Peter Martin had taught her youngest daughter, Carolina. Katie-Kat was a girl, not a scary monster. Those kids had been trading demented, distorted facial contortions like people traded jokes. They had been doing this all summer long, and she was really fed up with them now that they had dropped ice cream in her car and then driven it out of her driveway, crashing it in the street. The fact that Peter Martin had taught his demure little cousin to spit was also not very much appreciated either. He was proud of the fact that he could already, at the age of five, spit four feet in front of him. His spitting contests with his little feminine cousin were disgusting and he had better stop doing it while he was at his aunt's house. Maybe some other mother would be happy to have a spitting, funny-faced daughter, Aunt Adie was not.

Georgina could tell that it worried her aunt that her beautiful little daughter, with her sweet radiant head of auburn curls and her gorgeous milky white complexion, would be permanently disfigured by those ghastly twisted scary faces those boys were teaching their cousin. Their squeals of delight and doubled-over laughter only egged that diminutive girl on to make even more and more frightening faces. Their admiration was everything to that kid, with her funny, funny demented little faces.

Finally, the summer ended, and the twin's birthday arrived at the end of August. Katrina and Gretchen both got new dolls for their birthday. Katrina Josephina got a *'Poor Pitiful Pearl'* doll that even looked like her. Gretchen Gabriela got a *'Baby Tears'* baby doll that, cried real tears when you gave it bottles. It even wet its diapers, like her little brothers used to. Nobody in their family wore diapers anymore. Even little Roraigh was in training pants. The morning that they left Alaska, Manga got up early and made a big pink and green birthday cake for Katrina Josephina and Gretchen Gabriella's birthday. That was the day that the twins were seven years old. All of the kids got to have birthday cake for breakfast on the morning that they left Alaska, because by lunchtime, Georgina Jane and her family would be gone from Alaska. They were moving to Texas.

The saddest part to the girl was saying good-bye to her cousin, Leah, whom she loved like she was her own sister. She wished that she could take Leah with her to Texas. She did not want to say good-bye to Leah. Even though she had accidentally burned Leah's back, her cousin still loved her. That was the best part about Leah. You could accidentally even burn her back, and she would still love you, just like it had never even happened. So, she cried when she had to tell her good old buddy, and kissin' cousin, Leah, good-bye for the last time, before she left Alaska. Leah cried too. She gave Georgina a big, big hug, like she didn't want to let her cousin go.

"Here are some 'forget-me-nots' for you, Georgina," Leah said, handing her a small bouquet of Alaska's State flower. "Please don't forget me."

That really made Georgina cry, and cry, when the sweetest cousin in the whole wide world gave her those pretty little purple-blue flowers. How could she ever forget someone as dear as Leah?

"Thank you, Leah. These are my favourite color. You are so sweet. Of course, I won't forget you. I'll never ever forget you."

All of the memories that she had of her family's lives in Alaska came flooding back to her at that moment. The drives through the beautiful Alaskan scenery were still clear in her mind. The glaciers. The mountain goats. The white rabbits speeding past her in the woods. The mountain where she had skied every Saturday. Sisters Margaret Mary and Mary Gertrude's baldheads and funny veiled hats. Manga's green biscuits. Her color wheel for the Science Fair at her school. That biting husky puppy. Her little brothers' bear hunt. Her magic Eskimo mukluk boots and the parkas that Manga had made for Georgina and for her sisters. All of these were indelibly engraved upon her child's mind. There were other things that she could still see in her memory too. Like the bottles of beer and soda pop that her father had put into the edge of the Yukon River, to keep icy cold for picnics in the forest, where they had gone together as a family. Like her daddy's songs. Like her daddy's dancing. Like her daddy's smile.

Like the tiny bunny footprints and the moose tracks and bear paw prints she had seen in the soft Alaskan soil that had left their imprint on the girl. The Eskimos, with their drums and dog sled races, and their sad songs about their lives in Alaska, still rang in the child's ears. The tremors and the rocking of Mother Earth would be something which she knew that she would leave behind her in Alaska. There were things in Alaska that she could never, ever forget.

She realized that she really was leaving Alaska, and that she might never even get to come back for a visit. She knew that Texas was a long, long way from Alaska. It was a very sad time to have to say good-bye. She wasn't even sure if she would even like Texas, after living in a place as wonderful as Alaska was. The Army was flying them all back to the South, back to where it was warmer. Back to her other grandparents, Granny and Granddaddy that she had almost forgotten she even had. She felt that the fairies' dance was really over now. And with a heavy heart, she boarded the big army airplane, to fly away from Alaska.

When they were on the runway, waiting to take off in the big heavy bird of a plane, she waved and waved out of the window of the airplane. Georgina Jane O'Shaughnessy waved good-bye to her wonderful, kissin' cousins. She waved and waved to her funny aunt, who could take the plastic wrapper off her sofa, now that the girl and her family were leaving Alaska. And she waved good-bye to her sweet old Irish grandmother, Manga, who used to walk and walk and walk, in the cold, cold, Alaskan snow, just to make green biscuits for Georgina and for her sisters and for her brothers on St Patrick's Day. She waved good-bye to Alaska for the last time.

Now she really was saying her good-byes to them all. Her world would change forever after that day. No place could ever be a place as special as Alaska had been to the little girl who was leaving that day. Such a sad, sad day. Once she was up in the air, she looked down below her where everything looked so small. Everything looked like a miniature toy world down there on the ground in

Alaska. Manga had given Roger Eugenio and Peter Martin a fishing box full of matchbox cars for the trip. All of the cars down below her looked like those matchbox cars, not real ones, holding real people. It was curious how that happened. But there she was, flying in her first really big airplane. Did her daddy know how to fly a plane so big?

Up until then, Georgina had only flown with her daddy. But that was a secret. So, don't tell Mommy. But there she was. Up in the air. Up in the sky so blue. She had to squint because the sun was in her hazel eyes. She had to squint just to look down at that fabulous, slick glacier easing down the side of that mountain. Easing down the mountain and taking her little heart with it. It was like the world was coming to an end. Her world was coming to an end. Just then, Roraigh Arthur got sick at his tummy just as he did when they drove in the car. Roraigh Arthur got sick at his tummy and he vomited up a lapful of Katrina Josephina and Gretchen Gabriella's pink and green seventh birthday cake that Manga made. He vomited that cake all over his brand-new blue and white travelling sailor's suit. And that's when Mommy started to cry.

TO BE CONTINUED...PERHAPS.

About the Author

Shawn Irvin Manning was born in 1952 in an old military outpost, Fort Sill, Oklahoma, USA. She was the eldest of six (later seven) siblings. The novel, *When Fairies Danced* is a semi-autobiographical manuscript which charts her earliest years, but primarily from the ages of six to nine.

Manning obtained a Bachelor of Arts in Ceramics from the University of Dallas in Irving, Texas, which she worked towards for ten years during and after the births of four of her sons. She lived in Texas for twenty years before moving to Britain in 1989.

Her master's degree was in Visual Culture from what is now Bath Spa University. During this period in the 1990s she conducted interviews with popular ceramic artists which were published in various journals. Though she interviewed a number of international ceramicists, the principal focus of her research was 'The Female Body in Clay Form'. Her interest was in the dichotomy between high art and craft methodology. She gave lectures and visual presentations of this research in Bath, England and in Israel. She also covered conferences for the ceramic arts and curated a number of international exhibitions.

She has completed work for a Ph.D. in Creative Writing in Wales. After leaving West Wales, Manning taught English at Purdue University in Indiana, USA. She went to Tucson, Arizona, to spend the penultimate winter in the States and wrote her second novel.

This is her first novel. She is a published poet of approximately ten poems with Nobel House and in university papers.

Shawn Irvin Manning has five sons and a stepson. She has been married to Dr John Manning, a former professor of English and modern languages for twenty years. For eight and a half years as a couple, they took care of John's aging mother, Nancy, who suffered from dementia. Once retired, the three of them left the States in 2011 and moved to Costa Rica where Nancy died at the age of 91. They then lived in Cashel, County Tipperary, Ireland, for eight months before moving back to England.

Shawn has been an avid student of biblical studies for fifty years. Since leaving teaching at university, for eight years she has written letters to family and friends scattered around the world, which have been both journalistic in nature and demonstrate an interest in biblical eschatology.

She enjoys quilting and decorative painting. Shawn and John have two cats named Sweetie and Bobby Buttons. They are settled in England.